Elevation of the intended Free Masons Hall to be Erected in Bath.

Dear Sir

At a most numerous and respectable meeting held in this City on Monday last at the Greyhound Inn, to take into consideration the propriety of erecting a Masonic Hall, for the better accommodation, convenience and honour of the Craft in general, it was unanimously resolved that such a building was absolutely necessary for the purpose of reducing our present expenses and that the above Building should be erected by voluntary contribution. The sum required will not exceed two thousand pounds.

We confidently hope, that in applying to you as a well-wisher to our Honourable and Ancient Institution, we shall not be disappointed in receiving your assistance, addressed to Thomas Whitney, Apothecary, Cheap Street, Bath, who has kindly undertaken to receive all communications on the subject.

Very Fraternally yours
CHARLES GEARY
THOMAS WHITNEY
Wm UNDERWOOD WHITNEY
JOHN DIXON

Bath, July 7th, 1816

THE APOTHECARY'S HALL

The real story behind
The Bath Furniture Incident

by
Malcolm Toogood

Cepenpark Publishing Ltd
10 Sandpiper Gardens
Chippenham
SN14 6YH

CEPENPARK PUBLISHING LTD

First Published in Great Britain in 2018 by Cepenpark Publishing Ltd

A catalogue record of this book
is available from the British Library
ISBN 978 0 9564230 3 0

Printed in Great Britain by
CPI Antony Rowe
Units 1-4 Pegasus Way
Bowerhill Industrial Estate
Melksham, Wiltshire, SN12 6TR

Contents

Other Factual Books by this Author:

Porsche Catalogues (1991) - ISBN 978 1 85076307 0
Bath's Old Orchard Street Theatre (2010) - ISBN 978 095642300 9
Confluence 150 Years of Service 1863-2013 (2013) - ISBN 978 075521581 2

Fiction (as Phillip Malcolm)

The Mantis Pact (2012) - ISBN 978 095642302 3

Foreword

Previous attempts over many years to unravel this story were constricted by the historians of the time having access to just one part, or source, of material. This meant that certain facts were either taken out of context, or entirely omitted because the relevance was not obvious.

The information in this book has been gleaned over several years primarily by examining contemporary correspondence and minutes of meetings written at or near the time the events occurred. The wonders of modern technology have now made it possible to examine these various sources side-by-side and read them in conjunction with other material, revealing solutions to previous anomalies. In addition, the proliferation of on-line resources has enabled discovery of additional documentation and printed information that survived, but was previously obscured behind card indexes in unrelated public archives.

I would like to thank Trevor Quartermaine, the Curator of Bath Masonic Museum & Library, for all of his assistance in making documentation available, and to the Bath Masonic Hall Trust for their permission to use what I found. Thanks as well to Susan Snell and her staff at the Library of Freemasonry in Great Queen Street for their help with digging-out the various files that revealed so much of the background information about the various individuals and timelines. I also must thank Fritz Easthope and the Bristol Masonic Archive for their assistance with the old Antiquity Encampment records.

Particular thanks go to Paul Mallon for taking the time to travel with me to Devon, twice, to capture the images of the items that are at the centre of the story, plus to the Loyal Lodge of Barnstaple for granting permission for us to photograph the original furniture in their possession, and for their time and patience in assisting us with that task.

Obviously, not all of the evidence is still available after so long a period of time; indeed, some of the documents that do still exist are not in the locations they may have been expected to be, which means that certain archives may lack information that must have been part of them at some time. There is also at least one file of relevant documents residing in a dusty vault that I was not granted permission to examine. Which means there are still some small gaps in the historical accounts.

Where it has been necessary to deduce what is missing, I have confined such theories to areas where the evidence that does exist makes such assumptions less speculative, and have based them upon similar avenues of enquiry that actually led to further revelation and confirmation whilst the research was being conducted.

In order to convey the thrust of the historical information, I have included pertinent sections from the actual documents; *this content is shown in italic text, like this, throughout the book.* I have been particularly careful to reproduce these verbatim, which is why some of the spelling and grammar may appear incorrect to 21st-century eyes. Where emphasis, such as underlining or punctuation, has been added in correspondence, it has been reproduced by copying as closely as possible that emphasis; bold type has been used where the writer used larger writing or other stylised methodologies.

Throughout those texts there are numerous Masonic abbreviations and acronyms, which are explained in the chapters on Freemasonry in Part One. I have also used some of the more familiar abbreviations throughout my own text in order to make the story easier to read.

When I started this book, I had a completely different expectation of what I might find. In fact, the drafts of some chapters changed continually, and sometimes radically, during the project, causing the publication date to be delayed several times until those chapters became stabilised by the emergence of consistent corroboration.

Having read this book, the reader may choose to agree or disagree with my findings. If that final view is based upon actual evidence that has not come to my notice, I will be more than happy to view it and, if necessary, review my conclusions accordingly. But regardless, at the heart of this story is still the one man who, alone, history has portrayed as the main culprit for a monumental debacle suffered by an organisation that is itself, if nothing else, stability.

The question is, was he?

Malcolm Toogood
July 2018

AL5817

FREEMASONS' HALL

PART ONE
FOUNDATIONS

Introduction

Wander around any City in England and you will see grand buildings with illustrious histories, dating back hundreds of years. Some were built with a particular purpose in mind, others through the dreams of men of vision. All had their foundations laid with dedication and their doors opened amidst pomp and ceremony. Some are still being used for their original purpose by their only owners; for others the dream has long died and their usage changed many times. It is not often, however, that the latter occurs when the project is sponsored by one of the wealthiest titled landowners in the area and the beneficiaries are pillars of the establishment - literally.

This book tells the story of the machinations during the early nineteenth century surrounding the building of the first Freemasons' Hall in Bath, and of the events that led to the Fraternity in the city not only losing their home, but also its contents. Those contents included some of the finest regency Masonic furniture and artefacts that had been assembled within a provincial hall at that time, which is why this whole sorry affair is known locally as 'The Bath Furniture Incident'.

On the surface, history portrays the events surrounding the early years of that building, from its erection in 1817 to its sale in 1842, as synonymous with the rise and fall in the fortunes of a local wine merchant, Charles Geary. It was Geary who was reputed to have led the city's Freemasons into a project they could not afford, then obtained ownership of the building by dubious means before locking his fellow members out, thereby seizing all of the Lodge furniture and regalia, which he subsequently sold behind their backs.

I first encountered this story whilst writing the history of the building's successor, the original Bath Theatre Royal, which ultimately became the city's Masonic Hall in 1865, a status it has held ever since. I included a brief account of these events in a chapter covering the history of the Fraternity in the city prior to their acquisition of the old theatre. The sources of that information were the works of various local historians who have chronicled the events over nearly two hundred years since they evolved.

The historical facts used by those previous historians came from three prime sources: Robert Peach, a prolific writer on Bath in the late Victorian period and a local Freemason who would have been acquainted with people whose living-memory included the period covered; George Norman, founder of the Bath Masonic Museum and Library, who wrote a series of histories of the Bath Lodges in the 1920s; and Bruce Oliver, a Masonic historian from Barnstaple who wrote about the actual furniture involved.

Unfortunately, their studious work has suffered misinterpretation via subsequent regurgitation by many individuals, resulting in an account entering local Fraternal folklore that, perhaps, doesn't let the facts get in the way of a good story. So, before we consider whether this story is entirely true, or not, I must first relate it to you as received from the local Fraternity during my initial research in 2010:

From their creation during the eighteenth century up until the end of the Napoleonic Wars in the early nineteenth, Bath's Masonic Lodges had met in various city-centre hotels and inns. In 1816, none of the various hostelries in use were particularly suitable for meetings and there was a consensus that, if the four Lodges in the city pooled their resources, a more suitable building could be found that they could all share. A joint meeting was organised to discuss the possibility in greater detail, where it was unanimously agreed to build a new hall.

The proposed scheme was enthusiastically led by Charles Geary, Master of Royal Cumberland Lodge, the senior Lodge in Bath, and it was he who laid the Foundation Stone on the site, with full Masonic ceremony, the following year. Contributions were received from many local Freemasons, including Geary himself, but there was some disquiet about the amount of money being spent on the hall and its furnishings. This caused one of the Lodges, Royal Sussex, to withdraw from the scheme.

Nevertheless, by 1819 the hall was complete and it was dedicated, during a grand opening ceremony, by His Royal Highness Prince Augustus Frederick, the Duke of Sussex, Grand Master of the United Grand Lodge of England.

Afterwards, the three Lodges that remained part of the project used the hall regularly. The building had many fine attributes, but problems emerged that were attributed to the speed with which the project was advanced. Although most of the subscribers to the building were members of the Fraternity, the Lodges themselves held no ownership and occupied the building as tenants, the rental costs for which began to cause the individual Lodges financial difficulties.

In 1822, after just three years of use, matters came to a crisis. The Lodges and investors were persuaded by Geary into calling a Tontine, a form of Lottery whereby the ticket purchases repay a debt and the winner of the Lottery becomes the owner of the asset providing the collateral for that debt. As a result of his purchasing multiple entries, Geary emerged as the winner of the Lottery and, thereby, the sole proprietor of the building, making the Lodges his tenants.

The resultant rents, however, continued to be too high for the Lodges to afford, resulting in them building-up arrears. The following year, Geary gave an ultimatum to them that he would not allow any further debts to accrue and, as a result, two of the Lodges were unable to comply. With their finances already stretched by the high expenditure on the hall during the previous few years, they folded. The remaining tenant Lodge, Royal Cumberland, refused to pay their alleged arrears and were then locked-out of the building by Geary who, in so doing, locked-in all of their Lodge furniture, property and regalia.

Despite several appeals through the Provincial Grand Master, Geary was unmoved. As some of the property withheld by him included Warrants and other items imperative to the Lodge's existence, the matter was brought before the United Grand Lodge of England, who found Geary guilty of unmasonic conduct and threw him out of the Fraternity. This did nothing, however, to persuade him to relent over the furniture, still firmly locked within the building, which he then declared forfeit by the Lodge in lieu of the debt that they owed him.

Geary subsequently made some attempts to rent out rooms in the Hall building, but the income was sporadic, until an attempt was made by Royal Sussex Lodge to mediate and to persuade Geary to allow them to use the hall and its furniture. The reaction of the Provincial Grand Master was instant and final; he called a special meeting of the Lodge, which he attended, and advised them in no uncertain terms that any attempts to involve either Charles Geary or his building in their meetings would meet with severe action by the Province. Royal Sussex Lodge abandoned its plans immediately.

The stand-off continued for almost twenty years, until Geary agreed the sale of the building to a religious organisation. He then put the contents up for sale by auction as a single lot, but it failed to make the reserve price, mainly because the Bath Lodges boycotted the sale of what they considered to be their property. Geary then organised another lottery to dispose of the furniture, but once again he came up with the winning ticket himself. Finally, he organised a private sale of the furniture to a Lodge in Devon, without the knowledge of any of the Bath Lodges. Thus the entire contents of the Hall were disposed of for just one hundred guineas and lost to Bath Freemasons for ever.

For a Fraternity as dedicated to truth and virtue as Freemasonry, this is relatively sensational stuff, if wholly true. But there is more to these matters than meets the eye, and what was so intriguing about this story wasn't so much the manner in which a noble institution could become embroiled in such a catastrophe, but how someone who had attained and held high office in the Fraternity over many years, including Provincial rank, could acquire such notoriety for going from leading-light to pariah in the space of just five years.

Charles Geary held the chair of Royal Cumberland Lodge, the third-oldest Lodge in England outside of London, for more years than any other Master in its history, an achievement that suggests his being highly thought-of by his peers. The newspaper archive at the Bath Library revealed that he was also a successful businessman and, as a consequence, possessed considerable independent wealth, certainly to the extent that a few pounds of rent would hardly have caused him any major financial headache. He held several public posts in the city over the years, through which his actions, often involved with benevolence, caused his name to appear regularly in contemporary news columns, and always in a very positive light.

However, whatever misgivings I had regarding the story, this was a peripheral subject to the book that I was writing at the time, and with a print deadline rapidly approaching on that one, any further investigation had to wait.

Once the theatre book had been published, I began to look deeper into the circumstances surrounding the demise of this first hall. I decided to conduct some research for a potential talk on the subject, and made a visit to the Library and Museum of Freemasonry in London to view the annual returns of the two defunct Lodges in order to gain some idea as to how successful they had been prior to their becoming embroiled in an affair that would, ultimately, result in their destruction. I was also intrigued about what happened to their members after the Lodges had folded.

Buried in the files was some old correspondence, plus a document that provided a completely different view of Geary's involvement in the project - an independent report published in January 1824 regarding the failure of the hall project and compiled by two senior Bath Freemasons, Edmund English and Joseph Spry. It not only contained information regarding how the building had originally been financed, but also showed that Geary had initially been totally-opposed to the project. The report concluded with the comment that: *a great deal of misrepresentation has gone abroad on this subject.*

There is no copy of that document anywhere within the Bath Masonic Museum archives and, as no reference is made to it in any of the previous histories, it is doubtful that any researcher could have been aware of it, in which case it was quite possible that their accounts were based on incomplete information.

As I began to examine other contemporary documents, including correspondence and minute books in Bath, more names began to emerge as being involved in the project; one in particular, Thomas Whitney, began cropping-up regularly. I realised that I had encountered his name previously, in that same file of correspondence that had revealed the English & Spry report, but in a series of documents referring to a disciplinary matter that I had dismissed as irrelevant at the time. On revisiting London and re-reading them, however, they provided the link to a completely different aspect of the story that had barely been considered previously.

Once armed with that information, it was possible to review the historical information in a completely new light, which revealed sufficient new evidence to justify re-opening the case against Charles Geary as the sole cause of so much distress in Bath Freemasonry during the first half of the nineteenth century. I was able to search through the minutes of all of the various Lodges and Masonic Orders extant in Bath at the time, including those of the two defunct Lodges held in the UGLE archives, and compare the contemporary accounts side by side. This revealed timelines and parallel events that may not otherwise have been obvious.

What this also showed was that the more recent accounts had primarily-relied upon the original story written by Robert Peach, the only person who could physically have met some of the individuals involved in these events. Peach had written his version late in his life, some forty years distant from any contemporary accounts that he may have gleaned; as a result, when compared with the contemporary documents, various inaccuracies began to show, probably the most obvious of which was his reporting of one event as happening some fifteen years earlier than it had actually occurred.

Although none of the discrepancies were individually serious-enough to effect the story, taken together they were sufficient to doubt the veracity of Peach's accounts as the primary source to use on historical fact, particularly with regard to personal reputations that had potentially been gleaned from recollections, late in their lives, of other involved parties.

Using names of members obtained from the annual returns of the defunct Lodges, particularly those whose membership of the Fraternity in Bath ceased during the period being examined, further searches of local historical records, correspondence and national archives produced even more revelations.

As events began to emerge from the shadows of history, surrounding individuals who had never previously been considered as having any involvement came more to the fore. When their personal stories were subsequently probed in greater detail, some were revealed as having very murky backgrounds indeed.

Altogether, a picture was emerging that at the heart of this story was not, as previously suggested, just one apparently-greedy man, but several other characters all with widely-different agendas, ranging from political expediency to downright criminality.

The Early 19th Century

Context is the main drawback when looking back at events that occurred hundreds of years ago. It is not surprising that we find events in history difficult to understand when we look at them through eyes that have become accustomed to the relative comfort of the western world of the early twenty-first century, where there is an enlightened and prosperous society ready and willing to assist recovery from tragedy, should one befall us. But to unravel the mysteries of a series of events that occurred approaching two hundred years ago, it is necessary to somehow transport ourselves back to those times and build a picture of the backdrop to them.

With the early part of the events in this book playing-out primarily in the famous spa resort of Bath during the times portrayed by Jane Austen, it would be easy to read 'Persuasion' or 'Northanger Abbey' and imagine that we would be in the gentrified world of the Allens and the Elliots, taking the waters at the Pump Room in the morning, or indulging in the tittle-tattle of the dances at the Assembly Rooms surrounded by high-bred ladies in their finery and dashing cavalry officers in dress uniforms. Indeed, many of the visiting gentlemen indulging in those entertainments would likely have visited one of the Masonic Lodges in the city during their stay, being members of similar establishments in their home towns.

The truth was that by the time Jane Austen died so tragically young in 1817, before her most famous works had even been published, Bath was already transforming from the vibrant resort that was the winter watering-hole for the best of London society, to a comfortable retirement home for old military men and maiden aunts. In his journal of 1811, Louis Simond summed-up the city as follows:

Bath is a sort of great monastery, inhabited by single people particularly superannuated females. No trade, no manufactures, no occupations of any sort, except that of killing time, the most laborious of all. Half of the inhabitants do nothing, the other half supply them with nothings - a multitude of splendid shops, full of all wealth and luxury can desire, arranged with all the arts of seduction.

It may have still been fashionable to visit for a couple of weeks prior to the start of the season, but the main focus for wintering out of the capital was moving to the south coast, in particular to Brighton which was favoured by the Prince Regent. His patronage created the extraordinary Pavilion, the winter home for the Court that created a hub for courtiers such as Beau Brummell and Madame d'Arblay who transferred their allegiances from the Circus to the Steyne. So it is firstly worth examining exactly what Bath looked like in July 1816.

The old attractions of the centre, including the Abbey, Baths and Pump Room, were still in regular use, but were surrounded by a large amount of older property crammed-into limited space, that would not be demolished until late Victorian times. Beyond the old city walls much of the newer Wood family architecture - The Parades, Queen Square, The Circus, Royal Crescent - had inspired newer developments and shopping areas like Milsom Street and New Bond Street.

To the north, St James Square had emerged behind the Royal Crescent, from which Park Street and Cavendish Place threaded thin lines of houses up to Lansdown Crescent and Somerset Place, marking the furthest that the development had stretched up the northern slopes. The western border was effectively marked by Marlborough Buildings, although ribbon development was proceeding along the Bristol Road towards the village of Weston, then standing in isolation separated by around half a mile of open fields.

To the south and east, the River Avon defined the border of the city, although within that area there were still some undeveloped meadows, most significant among them the area we now know as the Southgate Shopping Centre. Although Southgate Street (or Horse Street as it was called then) had existed from the fourteenth century as the main road leading from the southern gate of the city to the Old Bridge that carried the road over the river towards Wells, there was no development between South Parade and the river, Henry Street only being completed in 1815. It would be 1840 before the Railway Station appeared encouraging the infill that obliterated the remaining fields to create the commercial heart of the Victorian city.

Beyond the river to the south, there was little development other than Holloway, a hotchpotch of dilapidated buildings from the late seventeenth and early eighteenth centuries. Holloway had formed the main road south, but was extremely steep, so in the later eighteenth century, the Wells and Exeter turnpike road had been constructed taking a meandering, but less graded, route that had bypassed Holloway, enabling that old area to become somewhat of a den of

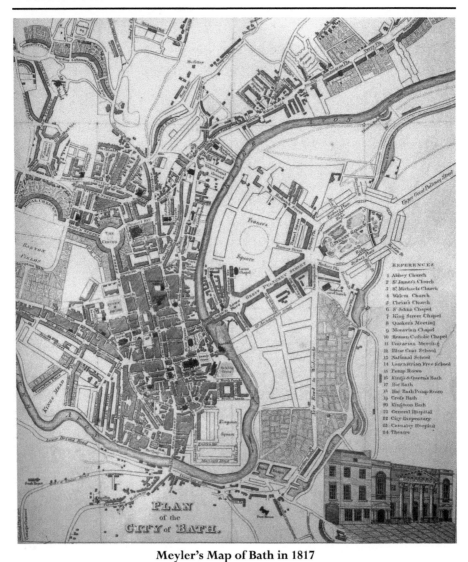

Meyler's Map of Bath in 1817
The areas shown in lighter line were only proposed developments at that time
Bath Masonic Hall Trust

iniquity. But being beyond the river, it was out-of-sight and out-of-mind with Claverton Street, now the busy heart of the Widcombe shopping area, leading other traffic away towards the several small industrial areas at the foot of Prior Park Road, which itself bore most of the traffic to and from the stone quarries on Combe Down. Much of what we now know as Widcombe and the Dolemeads was a mixture of fields and smallholdings bordering onto the stretch of the Kennet & Avon canal that had been opened in 1804.

The only other river crossing was at Pulteney Bridge, built in 1776 to open-up access to new developments on the Bathwick Estate along and behind Pulteney Street to Sydney Gardens. Little of this had been completed beyond Pulteney Street itself, so no through-routes existed. The other river crossings, now so familiar, at Cleveland Bridge, North Parade Bridge, Midland Bridge, Victoria Bridge, the Destructor and Windsor Bridge, were all constructed much later.

The main route to London remained as it had been since the fifteenth century, through the north gate at the top of the High Street, along Walcot Street and Walcot Parade to the London Road. Although some high-class developments had commenced further out at Kensington and Grosvenor Place, the area between those and the city centre was industrialised, containing some very run-down areas which housed the Penitentiary and Walcot Workhouse, the largest in the city, although only able to take a maximum of a hundred inhabitants. Because of this, the main carriage route avoided Walcot and took a more northern route into the centre along the more fashionable Paragon and George Street to Queen Square.

Other than horseback, stagecoaches were the main form of long-distance transport to and from the city, only the super-rich being able to maintain their own private carriages. Middle-class families would have a pony and trap, but the limits of comfort for that form of open carriage were no more than ten miles, restricting their use to local journeys only. It was possible to hire a post-chaise for longer journeys in private, but that was an expensive option. Public long-distance coach services were numerous, but were limited in terms of capacity. The average coach carried a maximum of twelve passengers, four inside and the remainder on external seats. So when a historian writes enthusiastically about the number of daily coach services between London and Bath having risen to six a day by 1815, that still translated to a maximum of just seventy people being able to make the journey each day by that method.

In terms of speed, the fastest coach services averaged just seven miles an hour, due not only to the condition of the roads, none of which were metalled, but also to the need to change the teams of horses every couple of hours. The term stagecoach referred to the need to break these long journeys down into stages, because the maximum distance a team of four horses could manage pulling such a heavy vehicle was just twelve miles. Therefore the journey from London to Bath would consist of nine stages, each terminating at a coaching inn where, whilst the horses were changed, the passengers took refreshment and, during the winter, the opportunity to warm themselves by the fire.

A trip from London to Bath would take around eighteen hours, even in a private carriage which was also subject to the same staging processes; the intervention of such perils as bad weather, broken wheels or highwaymen could extend that journey time considerably. Such journeys were, therefore, not undertaken lightly, so if someone was forced to travel to Bath on urgent business, the stagecoach was the most likely method they would have used; as a consequence, they were unlikely to be in the best of humour when they arrived.

It is, therefore, understandable why the post was widely used instead, as a letter would take the same time to travel as a person, and a reply could be received within a couple of days. There were, however, no typewriters or computers, so letters had to be hand-written and, if the subject was business, copies transcribed in the same manner for future reference. For circulars to numerous people, a printer would be used, the most efficient method being letterpress, where the type had to be manually set in a frame and each sheet printed individually - not an inexpensive undertaking.

Changing Horses A typical view at a Coaching Inn. *Courtesy The Postal Museum*

It was 1818 before there were any proposals for the introduction of Town Gas supplies in the city, although the second reading of the Bath Gas Bill in Parliament that year was heavily opposed by the Corporation and property owners. Hansard records: *The Mayor and corporation of Bath did not object to the principle of the measure, but it appeared to them that, as there was much difference of opinion with respect to the merits of the Gas Light, there was no necessity for the immediate adoption of the invention in Bath. As improvements were every day making in the preparation and management of the gas itself, it would be better to wait the result of those improvements than to take a hasty step of which they might afterwards repent.*

One clause of the bill exempted the property of one of the principal land owners in Bath, Earl Manvers, who declared: *If this bill for the partial lighting of Bath, were agreed to, the whole city might be injured, should it prove a nuisance rather than a benefit.*

Although the Bill was eventually passed, night-time illumination throughout the city remained almost exclusively by oil lamp or candle well into the 1820s; the introduction of any mains electricity supply would be well over seventy five years into the future.

Domestic plumbing was also nowhere near universal, the Water Supplies Act not coming into force until the middle of the nineteenth century. There were relatively few houses in Bath with piped water and supplies were primarily obtained from stand pipes in the back streets that used a pump to lift ground water, often from shallow wells. The disposal of the dead in city centre cemeteries added to the problems of water pollution, although the increasing use of coffins helped reduce the spread of disease. Where piped supplies were installed, the joints were unreliable meaning the flow was often intermittent, so users tended to leave taps on to catch the water when it came, adding to the losses from the system.

Gas-lit Bright Morning Star
This unit was fitted in Freemasons' Hall in 1822, and is one of the first specialised gas lights in existence
Bath Masonic Hall Trust

Sewers were equally problematic having been built to prevent flooding by draining-off surface water into the river. The few buildings with water-operated flush toilets drained them into cesspools, which often overflowed into the existing sewers, further polluting the local water supply. As the sewers were never intended to carry human waste, men were employed to 'flush' them using wooden boards, the resultant smell and risk of disease causing constant objections.

As the early years of the 19th century progressed, the business focus of Bath gradually moved from catering for short-term patronage from rich visitors enjoying the entertainments, to looking after the long-term needs of comfortable retirees with time to indulge their pastimes.

The two Assembly Rooms, the newer and larger Upper Rooms off the Circus and the older Lower Rooms on Terrace Walk, were competing for a shrinking market particularly at their gaming tables. Gaming was the real money-making part of these businesses, but became less popular as the austerity of the times reduced the disposable income of regular gamblers, confining them to the gentlemens' clubs of the capital. The form of the dances also changed, with traditional multiple-participation country-dance styles giving way to smaller quadrilles and intimate waltzes. Financial losses at both establishments were mounting when a major fire reduced the Lower Rooms to rubble in 1820, ultimately saving the Upper Rooms by removing its competition.

The theatre, highly popular during the second half of the eighteenth century, also began to suffer from the reduction in visitors. There were several periods when the Theatre Royal considered closing its doors, brought about by a rise in religious condemnation of the excesses of the Regency period. The austere message from the pulpits resulted in references to shirts and smocks being delivered in hushed tones from the stage and, according to one contemporary observer, *body linen was not so much as hinted at before a truly-refined audience.*

To fill the larger auditorium of the new Theatre Royal opened 1805, the nature of performances changed. Support pieces took on an almost music-hall style by blending musical performers with animal and even circus-style acts. Seat prices were reduced for the lesser areas, to encourage a wider clientele, but only succeeded in attracting more rowdy audiences, further alienating the traditional theatre-goer.

All of this, however, was secondary to the overall political and financial situation of the country as a whole.

War and Peace

In today's world, modern global communication systems relay images of conflicts in other parts of the world into our homes in real time, thus making it almost impossible for any escalation to occur without our being aware of such potential. It is, therefore, difficult to imagine what it was like to live in constant fear of invasion by a foreign power.

The last generation to experience such a fear in this country were those who endured World War Two when, for most of the six years that it lasted, enemy soldiers were poised across the English Channel ready to physically make that last twenty-mile hop to our shores. In addition, the enemy's air force was regularly raining mayhem down upon our towns and cities. Even then, information was regularly available, through the radio that most had in their homes, in daily newspapers and via access to recorded newsreels shown in local cinemas, the latter albeit days out of date and heavily-censored.

Thirty years earlier, the First World War was conducted almost exclusively away from these shores, bar the occasional naval action on east coast towns, or Zeppelin raid in the south east. News from the front was conveyed to the public in newspapers, by correspondents who telegraphed reports to their homeland newsrooms. Although, once again, heavily-censored, they were enhanced by eye-witness accounts brought back, whilst the conflict was still in progress, by soldiers lucky enough to survive to be able to do so. This provided combined reassurance that there was little chance of invasion, so public morale remained at a reasonably high level.

For virtually one hundred years prior to that, from 1815 to 1914, although there were numerous wars and overseas campaigns waged by the British Army, none posed any real threat to the sovereignty of these shores.

Before 1815, however, Britain was rarely out of danger of an invasion. Public media consisted of a relatively small number of newspapers that, for those able to read them, were expensive to purchase. Their content was gleaned from correspondents who were restricted to relaying their reports via messenger or postal services. So, when the content eventually arrived, it was often weeks out of date.

Soldiers went overseas for the duration of a war, relatively few of the fighting ranks coming back at all; when they did, the campaign had long finished. The public at large, therefore, had very little contemporary information available to them as to how high any threat of invasion was.

Up until 1789, all European countries were ruled by dynastic monarchies which, unless the succession ended by natural means, were generally only changed by external conflict or internal treason; the lot of the general population was little effected by such change, bringing a type of strange stability. But when the French populous decided to rid themselves of that top level of aristocratic government and create a republic instead, it spread immense panic rapidly through all levels of European society. However, the idealism of that revolution was soon dissolved by the adrenaline of power, after which it dissolved into a reign of terror, most of which was visited on its own people.

In 1797 a small landing party of French troops had come ashore in North Wales, reeking havoc for a few days before the locals captured them all. Despite their having been detached by foul weather from a larger force heading for an ill-founded attempt at invading the south of Ireland, the news of such an insurgence spread throughout Britain like wildfire. Within a year of those events, Napoleon Bonaparte had come to the fore, and once again, France had a ruler. He may not have been of the same stock, but he displayed not dissimilar tendencies to his aristocratic predecessors, seeking to re-establish the status of France by waging war on whoever chose to stand in his way.

As ever, Britain was not backward in coming forward, and was plunged into a war with its closest enemy, raising the spectre of invasion once more. Despite victories such as Nelson's at Trafalgar in 1805, and defeat for Napoleon in Russia in 1812, it would not be until Wellington finally overcame the French at Waterloo, that the threat would ultimately be lifted. When that finally happened, in 1815, peacetime was almost beyond adult memory, Britain having essentially lived in the shadow of European conflict for twenty-five years, and having been continually at war with one enemy or another for a further fifteen years previously. The economy was, therefore, based upon supporting those conflicts.

As often happens following such prolonged hostilities, after a brief period of celebration and elation, victory only brought depression in its wake. The national debt in 1815 was estimated at over eight hundred and thirty million pounds, despite the additional taxes raised by the exchequer throughout the conflict, primarily through the government's unpopular income tax. This had been introduced in 1799 to pay for the war effort, with rates starting at one per cent on annual incomes above sixty pounds, rising to a maximum rate of ten per cent on all income over two hundred pounds. The working classes barely earned more than a few shillings a week, so those levels meant that the majority of the burden fell upon the middle and upper classes, in particular property and land owners.

The ownership of buildings in the early nineteenth century was substantially different to today, most being leasehold. Land owners rarely sold any of their acreage unless they were desperately in debt, because the vast majority of their income was derived from leasing it out in parcels to those wishing to use it. Rurally, these were primarily farmers, but in cities the land was split into plots and leased to builders, who would speculate the cost of the bricks and mortar. Out of the rent received from the occupants, the builder would then pay the landlord for the continued use of the land.

As towns and cities expanded, occupiers progressed to owning their buildings, bringing a rise in the practice of speculative building. A landlord would lease a large parcel of land that a developer could split-up into plots, then erect individual buildings that he would sell to the first occupant, but only sub-let the plot of land to them. In this case, the builder made a one-off profit on the building, then derived a regular income from the difference between the accumulated rent from the plot leases and the total paid to the landowner for the entire parcel.

Buildings were classed as moveable property, in that they were expected to be removed from the land when the ground lease expired; if they weren't, then the landlord took possession of them as, by law, he owned everything remaining on his land when it reverted to him. Therefore it was important for a building owner to ensure that their investment bricks and mortar was protected by ensuring that the landlord was paid regularly, and on time.

Of course, through default many landowners also became building owners, and once they realised how this increased the regular income from town land, they began to become speculative builders themselves. Some borrowed heavily to do so, relying on a constancy of tenancy to cover the interest and capital repayments. But as competition increased, and demand slackened, when properties became vacant rents were reduced in pursuit of tenants that could still afford to pay.

In their attempts to reduce the financial burden on the country as a whole, primarily due to the high interest payments being made on the national debt, the Government attempted to continue their unpopular Income Tax beyond the end of the war, despite there being no legal basis for doing so. They tried to appease strong opposition from many property owners, led by the Corporation of London, by reducing the rate to five per cent, but this was still unacceptable to the majority of those liable for paying it. The result was a humiliating defeat for the Prime Minister, Lord Liverpool, when the opposition amassed sufficient additional votes from Government supporters to reject the proposals and force the repeal of the Act. This provided some respite to those land and property owners who were feeling the pressure of their indebtedness, but the effect would only be temporary.

Following the end of the war, with no further need for national expenditure on war production, the economy shrank rapidly, gross domestic product effectively halving within three years. This put a huge strain on the merchant classes who had become the main owners and renters of substantial town properties. Many lost their businesses and, although some were able to find employment through either their skills or their contacts, the reduction in their disposable income meant that they had to cut back on their expenditure. Consequently, many lost their homes; the less fortunate became classed as insolvent.

At that time, insolvency law was quite simple. If you were unable to pay your debts, your assets were seized and sold off to pay your creditors. If you had no assets, you were incarcerated in one of the many debtors prisons at the pleasure of those creditors. The distinction between the two punishments came at a particular financial point, or a definition of the activity that the person was engaged in. Those with assets of value were classed as bankrupts, the rest as insolvent debtors.

Traders, being businessmen who bought and sold goods or commodities, were always classed as bankrupts, but could not be declared as such by their creditors unless they were proved as indebted to a total amount above one hundred pounds. Everybody else, except farmers whose activities were considered essential to the benefit of the economy, fell into the grey area between these stark alternatives. This included tradesmen, those who sold their labour as opposed to goods, who were generally classed as insolvent debtors. At that time there was no legal way of reaching any arrangement with creditors to pay them off over an agreed period, unless the debtor had some other hold over their creditors that provided a means to force them into such a private arrangement, such as a high-enough position in society that would act as a deterrent to any trader-creditor with a large list of similarly well-heeled clients.

Once their assets had been seized, there was nothing to prevent a bankrupt from finding employment, as they still had their liberty. If the proceeds from the sale of assets was sufficient to ensure that their creditors were entirely-satisfied financially, or had jointly accepted a lower percentage of their debts as settlement, then a certificate of discharge could be obtained; failing that, a certificate would be issued after a period of five years had elapsed. In any of these circumstances, once the certificate was issued there was nothing to prevent the discharged bankrupt from immediately starting a new business.

Private individuals were always classed as insolvent debtors, and hence became prey to the clutches of the licensors of the debtors' prisons and the Court of Chancery, the system well-illustrated by Dickens in his novel *Little Dorrit*. Their position was more complex as, having lost their liberty in lieu of possessing little or no assets; they then had to find a way of discharging their debts from what they still retained, as well as covering the costs of their imprisonment. This invariably left them more indebted to their legal representatives than they had been to their original creditors.

However, once they had satisfied those debts, or their creditors had forgotten about them, they could give notice of applying for discharge. Unless a particular creditor held sufficient of a grudge to object, thus keeping them in debtors prison, they would be freed twenty-one days after the notice was issued.

Of course, freedom from prison did not necessarily equal freedom from penury, due to the dire circumstances then prevailing. Because finance was not the only problem effecting the general state of the country at that time.

Home Affairs

At the end of the Napoleonic Wars, the country was in Regency, due to the continued mental illness of King George III. The King had been sidelined by Parliament in favour of a Regent - the Prince of Wales, his eldest son and the future George IV.

The Prince's reaction to being created Regent was effectively to leave all decisions to Parliament. The government were, therefore, left entirely with the responsibility of coping with the national deficit, which they did by slashing public expenditure, forcing many businesses into bankruptcy and putting swathes of people out of work. Those soldiers that had survived the war physically-able were returning home into poverty. On top of that the entire harvest failed.

1816 became known as 'The Year without a Summer'. In London it snowed at Easter, there were snow drifts in Cumbria during July and ponds were frozen-over by September. Between May and September it rained nearly every day; those crops that weren't damaged by the cold rain, rotted away after harvesting due to the damp conditions. The lack of seasonal work for farm labourers merely added to the unemployment queues already swelled by the returning combatants.

The reasons for these unusual climatic conditions were twofold. Solar activity hit a periodic low, in addition to which there had been a major

Eruption of Mount Tambora
This contemporary painting shows the scale to the eruption, the effects of which are thought to have affected even the weather at the Battle of Waterloo. *Private Collection*

volcanic event in the East Indies the previous year when Mount Tambora erupted explosively. It was one of the most violent of such events in history, hurling nearly forty cubic miles of volcanic ash and debris nearly thirty miles into the upper atmosphere. This slowly spread across the globe further filtering the amount of sunlight reaching the surface of the planet.

Corn and grain prices trebled in weeks; those of oats multiplied sevenfold. Even so, they were still below the levels imposed by the Corn Laws, introduced the previous year to protect home production from cheap imported grain, preventing any importation of foreign grain until the import price rose beyond an artificially-inflated level. However, when that price level was breached due to worldwide shortages, there was none available to import. As a consequence, thousands died of malnutrition, associated diseases and infections; farmers were forced to slaughter their livestock to feed their families, further reducing dairy and meat production.

As well as unemployment, the returning troops had to cope with the usual family and emotional issues: relatives that had died, wives that had moved on to other relationships, children born after they left and so on. Those that had been able to put some of their meagre army pay aside soon found that it did not last them long. Many were classed as vagrants, leaving them open to arrest, temporary imprisonment or removal from the area they returned to.

The Luddites re-emerged, smashing production machinery, particularly weaving looms, further hampering any industry-led economic recovery. Much of this activity was organised by armed gangs who roamed the streets at night, enforcing their own curfews in order to open the ways for the destruction to occur. In July 1816, just one night of such activity resulted in the complete eradication of the lace industry in Loughborough.

The removal of Income Tax may have been popular among the property-owning classes but, in reality, all it did was limit the government's ability to finance any recovery. Further pressure was put upon the Exchequer when the overseas exchange value of the pound depreciated. Even in defeated France, a pound would only fetch the equivalent value of thirteen shillings, a devaluation of some thirty-five per cent. As a result, the cost of imports increased along with the monetary value of both interest and capital payments on overseas loans.

The Bank of England's response was to reduce the amount of paper money in circulation, but this also backfired when the result was an increase in the value of paper money against that of gold, the latter remaining the only currency for overseas trade.

The Prince Regent came under constant criticism for his excessive spending at a time of national penury. In 1815, the Royal household had overspent their eight hundred thousand pound annual budget by more than sixty percent and in Parliament some MPs were observing that the conditions in the country, with respect to support for the Regency, were not dissimilar to those that had existed in France prior to the Revolution of 1789. The Royal Family's response, in May 1816, was to organise a lavish wedding for Princess Charlotte to Prince Leopold of Saxe Coburg, involving a dowry of sixty thousand pounds and an annual allowance to the couple of a further fifty thousand.

From May 1816, riots began erupting across the country as the starving ransacked grain stores and warehouses in search of anything edible. These started in the rural areas of Norfolk and Suffolk, when workers assembled to set their own prices for basic foodstuffs, under the banner of *Bread or Blood*. Cambridgeshire was next, when a large assembly of fenmen in the small village of Littleport developed into a full-scale march on the City of Ely. This was eventually suppressed by

The Peterloo Massacre by Richard Carlile
This contemporary painting showing a riot in Manchester in 1819,
provides an idea of the events at meetings of the time. *Manchester Library Service*

the mobilisation of the Military, and at the subsequent trials, thirty four rioters were sentenced to death, although only five ultimately perished on the gallows, the others having their sentences commuted to long imprisonment or transportation.

Miners and foundrymen from Staffordshire marched on London, having been thrown out of work by the closure of many ironworks through the reduction in military production. Their banner slogans read: *Willing to Work, but none of us to Beg!* They reached the home counties before being persuaded to return by Government officials authorised to make them compensation and charitable payments. However, this did not prevent the spread of unrest to the capital, resulting in the Spa Fields riot in early December, followed by an attack on the Prince Regent's Coach as he was on his way to open Parliament in January 1817.

Nevertheless, the generosity of certain parts of the higher classes was still well to the fore, although much of the relief offered was either misguided or misplaced. A public meeting was organised in London by the Duke of Kent, brother of the Prince Regent and a leading Freemason: *to take into consideration the present distressed state of the lower classes and the most effectual means of extending relief to them.* He was supported by his brothers the Dukes of York and Cambridge, plus the Archbishop of Canterbury and the Bishop of London.

Unfortunately the meeting was usurped by politicians more intent on disruption than benevolence, and ultimately it descended into a public brawl. The Duke observed after the meeting that: *If they should be so happy as but to succeed in discovering new sources of employment, to supply the place of those channels which had been suddenly shut up, I should indeed despond if we did not soon restore the country to that same flourishing condition which had long made her the envy of the world.*

The meeting did result in private subscriptions exceeding one hundred thousand pounds which were used to set-up the distribution of soup and bread to avert starvation among three million labourers and their families across the country. But even this benevolence was not necessarily well-received; one fully-stocked soup-kitchen in Glasgow was destroyed by the crowd awaiting food purely through a perceived insult being received by one of their number. The disturbance grew into a two-day riot, during which hundreds of shops were ransacked before the unrest was finally quelled by the Army.

At that time, the Government accounted for an expenditure of just under six million pounds on poor relief. Although the system of Poor Laws allowed for labourers to wander around the country to find work when their current employment ended, the Law of Settlement contained a direct contradiction, in that workers were expected to find employment within the parish of their birth, any wandering away from their homes being deemed as vagrancy. When the disbanded army and navy units spilled their unwanted soldiers and seamen into this mix, many were viewed as rogues and vagabonds merely because they were moving around from town to town seeking employment.

In the capital, much of the money allocated for the relief of the poor was expended on jailing those deemed as vagrants, whose sentence lasted seven days, following which they were released and passed on to another jurisdiction. Middlesex employed several full-time functionaries to cart arrested vagrants across the county border, following which they would return at the earliest opportunity, thus ensuring constant lucrative employment for their shepherds. The reward for those who stayed within their home parish was to have their labour auctioned to the highest bidder by a parish overseer, who would retain the proceeds to support the labourer's family. As those returns were generally less than two shillings a week, once the overseer had taken his cut the residual standard of support was negligible, particularly when food prices rocketed.

Those who evaded such treatment crowded into neglected areas, such as George Yard in Whitechapel where two thousand people lived in just forty houses - out of sight, out of mind. But these conditions were not confined to the East End; immediately behind Portman Square, one of the most fashionable addresses in London, was Calmel Buildings where seven hundred Irish labourers and their families crowded into just twenty four houses. For those unable to elevate themselves to the delights of such hellholes, there was always The Workhouse.

It may be convenient to believe that such conditions of deprivation did not affect the genteel classes frequenting the Parades and Crescents of a provincial resort such as Bath, and that all residents of that fine city were of the nature found among the pages of a Jane Austen novel. The reality was nothing of the kind. Directly behind the house that the Austen family occupied between 1803 and 1805 in fashionable Green Park, and overlooked by its rear windows, was the area around Avon Street, the most notorious district of the city.

Avon Street Bath in the 19th Century. *Bath in Time*

Avon Street had been built seventy years earlier as up-market lodging houses, but by the end of the eighteenth century it had deteriorated to the point that one social chronicler of the day described it as follows: *Everything vile and offensive is congregated there, all the scum of Bath - its low prostitutes, its thieves, its beggars - are piled up in the dens rather than houses of which the streets consist. Its population is the most disproportioned to the accommodation of any I have ever heard; and to aggravate the mischief, the refuse is commonly thrown under the staircase; and water more scarce than in any quarter of the town.* In 1816, the year that 'Emma' was the latest of Jane Austen's works to be published, the Bath Herald was still reporting that: *in Avon Street at least three hundred persons obtain their livelihood by begging, thieving, or on the miserable wages of prostitution.*

But it wasn't just economic circumstances that took individuals into such areas. Unmarried mothers were considered prostitutes, but many found guilty of such a 'crime' were simply unfortunate female servants from upper-class households. In a report to the Governors of Bath Penitentiary in 1816, the author described an unfortunate girl who: *seduced but not depraved, her health destroyed but her mind not yet vitiated, finds herself by the offence of seduction, dismissed from her service and forever disabled from finding another.*

Such a fate was illustrated in rules of conduct given to servants containing warnings like: *Every street affords you instances of poor, unhappy creatures who were once innocent till seduced by the deceitful promises of their undoer; ungratefully thrown-off, they become incapable of earning their bread in an honest way.*

Yet it wasn't just the lesser areas where the criminal classes were prevalent. The streets in the centre were plagued by juvenile gangs, hawkers and beggars; the noise and disorder was wholly out of keeping with the city's reputation as a quiet resort, hence this contemporary satirical verse:

I always have heard that the provident Mayor
Had a terrific rod to make beggars beware
But I find to my cost they infest every street
First a boy with one eye, then a man without feet
Who cleverly stumps upon two patten rings
One bellows, one whispers, one snuffles, one sings
From Holloway's garrets and cellars they swarm
But I'll pause on this subject - I'm growing too warm!

This was written twenty years before the first police force was formed in the city, law and order being maintained by a series of Watchmen and Constables, all self-employed and, therefore, at times open to distorting the legal boundaries they were intended to police.

One such constable, named Taylor, was referred to by the judge in his address to the jury during a case in the Bath Courts in 1816: *I am informed that Mrs Taylor before she was married to Taylor, was well-known as a person of most immoral character - perhaps her influence may have corrupted her husband. I am likewise informed that another constable is allied to a woman who was not long since recognised as a prostitute. How far such an association is compatible with the proper and faithful performance of their duties I must leave to your better judgement.*

Prostitution in itself was not illegal, but 'keeping a disorderly house' (the coded term for running a brothel) was. There were few such cases brought, as the involvement of the middle-classes, whether as clients or as absentee landlords, meant that publicity was kept to a minimum. The anti-vice campaigns, often run by the same middle-classes, were deemed sufficient demonstration of the moral outrage such activities should receive until, from time to time, the cause was taken-up from the pulpit.

Such intervention would generally result in a round-up. One rector observed: *I was not a little astonished as I walked through Bath, to observe the streets so crowded with prostitutes, some of them apparently not above fourteen or fifteen years of age, plying their trade in places of public amusement and recreation - along The Parades, in the Park and at the Theatre Royal.*

The very next week, the Bath Herald reported that: *Constable Culliford, on patrol in St John's Court adjoining the Theatre at about ten o'clock, apprehended Louisa Hulbert and Mary Ann Elmes, single women well known as common prostitutes, wandering abroad and making great noise and disturbance, collecting a crowd about them and wantonly taking off the hats of the persons then and there passing, and both being intoxicated in liquor.*

Temperance was another issue that exercised the chattering classes continually. It was commonly seen as one of the main factors in the 'fall' of individuals to the hopeless squalor of their reduced circumstances, or of the inability of their offspring to restore themselves to society:

Neglect, starvation, ignorance, vice, filth and disease have surrounded them from infancy. They have been brought-up with scarcely any idea of modesty or personal reserve, and the language to which they have habitually listened has been of the foulest and most blasphemous description. Intoxicating drink has formed the only, or almost the only, pleasure of the class to which they belonged.

By the middle of 1816, Bath was filled with all manner of unemployed farm workers, demobilised soldiers, vagrants and low-lifes intent upon seeking the employment they needed or, if not, to prey upon the higher-class visitors who, it was perceived, could afford to be relieved of some of their wealth. In reality, most of those upper-class visitors were seeing their apparent wealth drained away by the rapidly-deteriorating economic situation. The city's Workhouses, Penitentiaries and Debtor's Prisons were already full to overflowing, as were the slum areas, and nobody had seen the sun for months.

This was the background into which the suggestion was made to erect a Freemasons' Hall in Bath.

What is Freemasonry?

This book is a historical account of what happened in Bath 200 years ago and the narrative centres around how a private Fraternal organisation dealt with what was essentially a building project, and its associated financial issues. Nevertheless, a lot of the procedures they adopted, and terminology they used to record the events, were steeped in the particular vocabulary of that Fraternity. Although this may still sound very familiar to modern-day members, the majority of readers will not themselves be Freemasons, and may even see the organisation as somewhat mysterious. It may, therefore, be helpful before I start the story to provide some information on the Fraternity.

Freemasonry is one of the world's oldest and largest non-religious, non-political, fraternal and charitable organisations. Its values are based on integrity, kindness, honesty and fairness. Members come from all walks of life and meet as equals, whatever their religion, race or position in society. Members learn moral lessons and self knowledge through participation in a progression of ceremonies, which are learnt by heart and performed within each Lodge. These follow ancient forms, and use stonemasons' customs and tools as allegorical guides. All of this translates into the three principles of the Fraternity - Brotherly Love, Relief and Truth.

Today in the UK, there are more than a quarter of a million Freemasons within the United Grand Lodge of England. Worldwide, that figure rises to six million, all with their own special reasons why they enjoy Freemasonry. For some, it is a way of making new acquaintances, some of which grow into lifetime friendships. For others it is about helping deserving causes and making a contribution to family and society.

When he (or she, because there are ladies' Lodges as well) enters the organisation, every Freemason embarks on their own journey of self-discovery. The Lodge provides a place of harmony and tranquillity, where members can push themselves to their limits or find a quiet haven in an increasingly complex world. They can progress, at their own pace and choice, through junior roles to senior positions within the Lodge, receiving the constant support of fellow members to help them achieve the potential within their own talents and to make a success of their own life. Each promotion brings greater understanding and responsibility, leading to increased self-esteem and confidence.

Freemasonry encompasses and embraces all of the fundamental principles of good citizenship, and instils in its members a moral and ethical approach to life, urging them to regard the interests of the family as paramount, but also teaches and practices concern for people, care for the less fortunate and help for those in need. From its earliest days, Freemasonry has been concerned with caring for those disadvantaged by circumstances beyond their control, and this work continues today through members playing an active role in their own communities.

There are no closed doors in Freemasonry and members are encouraged to speak openly about their participation. Anyone can visit and take a tour of the headquarters at Freemasons' Hall, in Great Queen Street, London, and Lodges throughout the UK regularly hold open days for anyone interested in discovering more about the organisation.

Now, all of that may come as a bit of a surprise to some readers. After all, aren't there numerous websites and publications that portray the Fraternity in a much less favourable light - that it is secretive, selfish or even downright sinister? So, is all of this openness just a modern way of avoiding reality, or was it ever so?

Firstly, Freemasonry is not a secret society, but it is a society with secrets - there is a difference. All Freemasons take an oath to protect those secrets, which are of a ceremonial nature. The Fraternity did get itself into a bit of a muddle following the second world war, during the early part of which the threat of a Nazi invasion made it important for the membership to be aware of that regime's persecution of Freemasons in both its own territory and other countries it occupied. But if you look at local newspapers prior to that, you will find regular accounts of meetings in local and Provincial Lodges, including the names of officers and speakers. In fact, as the reader will see, some of the information in this book has been gleaned from the archives of Bath's local newspapers.

The accusations of selfishness, for example in respect to businessmen favouring their Brothers in the Fraternity with regard to contracts awarded or employment scenarios, cannot be completely dismissed, because every large organisation has a small minority of the membership that may be tempted, on occasion, to deviate from the standard of behaviour expected of them. But the membership is self-policing, and there are many who may have joined under such a misapprehension, only to discover that it doesn't work that way, subsequently becoming ex-members rather rapidly. As for sinister, it is probably best to say that such speculation is found in the writings of the more marginal, and sometimes sensational, purveyors of conspiracy-theory, and is probably best left in those locations.

When you visit a Masonic Hall, there will be honours boards on the wall, listing the past Masters of the Lodges that meet there, some going back hundreds of years like the board for Royal Cumberland Lodge in Bath, shown here. In that list of names are some of the great and the good of the City - major business owners some covering several generations, civic leaders, some who served as Mayor of the City, plus doctors, lawyers, accountants, architects and the like. Some were also major benefactors for good causes in the City, some have even had streets named after them.

But you will also find those who had relatively-ordinary lives, working away quietly as shopkeepers, tradesmen, clerks, teachers, clergymen, travelling salesmen and labourers. Because there is no distinction between members in a Masonic Lodge, you could be seated

Royal Cumberland Lodge Honours Board
listing every Master back to 1732
Bath Masonic Hall Trust

30

between a Lord of the Manor on one side and a dustman on the other, and you would never know unless you found out in conversation. Plus those Past Masters, as they are termed, share one common quality - they were all considered just, upright and honest men when elected by their peers to take the highest honour a Lodge can bestow.

So, how does Freemasonry work? To become a Freemason, a candidate must first be at least 21 years of age and have a belief in a higher being or force. Contrary to many of the impressions assumed, they do not have to be known to, or recommended by, a member - you can, if you are interested, approach the Fraternity and express that interest, and they will speak to you about it. From those conversations, if the candidate fulfils the basic criteria and wishes to proceed, they must then be proposed and seconded by two existing members, fill out an application form and be interviewed twice by senior members of the Lodge, first informally in their own home and then formally at the Masonic Hall. If they are considered suitable at the end of that process, the proposal will then be put to a vote of all members of the Lodge and, if that vote proves clear of dissention, the candidate will be invited to their first meeting. That part of the process can take between six months and a year.

There are three degrees in what is known as Craft Freemasonry and those are all worked within a Masonic Lodge. At their first meeting, the candidate will be Initiated into the first degree as an Entered Apprentice. Some time later, once they have demonstrated an advancement in Masonic knowledge, they will go through their next ceremony, and be Passed to the second degree as a Fellowcraft. Finally, after another period of self-advancement, they will go through another ceremony to be Raised to the third degree of a Master Mason. That whole process can take up to a further two years.

Once a Master Mason, they can start progressing through the operative offices of the Lodge. There are seven of these, and each is served for one year, meaning that there is normally just one vacancy each year, with a queue of new Master Masons waiting for the opportunity to step onto the ladder, as it is termed. These offices are Tyler and Inner Guard, who protect the outside and inside of the Lodge entrance, the Junior and Senior Deacons, who assist a candidate during a ceremony, and the Junior and Senior Wardens who assist the Master.

The last of the progressive offices is Master of the Lodge, and is only conferred after election by all of the Lodge members. So it can be seen that this is not a quick process, and for good reason. Even in the fastest circumstances, it can take around ten years to progress from that first Initiation ceremony to the point that the Master Mason goes through the final Craft ceremony of Installation into the Chair of the Lodge.

This is a fair chunk of an adult's lifetime, and was especially so at a time when life expectancy was lower than it is today, as at the time of this story. So, patience is a virtue in Freemasonry, and not the only one expected of its members. It also means that the members will know an individual really well by the time they decide to devolve control of the Lodge to them, but even then it is only for one year.

This continual process should produce a new Master-elect for the Chair each year but, as progression is not compulsory, some members may decide it is not for them, because it does involve a lot of learning, particularly of what is known as ritual. This is actually the script of the ceremony being performed, because each is a form of playlet with a number of actors performing it. All of the words pertaining to the office held have to be rehearsed and recited from memory, along with the associated movements around the Lodge room.

In a Masonic year, a Lodge will perform one Installation and various of the Degree ceremonies, all completely different in content. So an officer will need to learn, and perform, their part in up to four separate scripts. The parts change completely with each office held, so new script parts need to be memorised each year. In addition, all Lodges hold regular committee meetings attended by senior and long-serving members where the administrative business is handled, annual calendars of the scheduled Lodge meetings are planned, etc. Most Lodges also have a rehearsal meeting in the few days prior to a Lodge meeting to allow all participants, other than the candidate, to rehearse together their parts in the upcoming ceremony.

Some Lodges also hold regular meetings called Lodges of Instruction, where aspects of the ceremonies are examined and explained in greater detail, enabling newer members to better understand what is actually being demonstrated. No member takes part in a rehearsal, or Lodge of Instruction, at a higher degree than they have attained, so the first time a member experiences a ceremony is when they are the candidate. This enhances the meaning of a ceremony to the candidate.

Sometimes the progression does not produce a suitable candidate for Master, which will mean that the Ruling Master, as he is termed, will remain for an extra year, or be replaced by a Past Master, a member who has held the Chair previously and therefore already has the experience to do so in a case of emergency. There are further offices in the Lodge that are generally held by a Past Master because of the experience needed to perform them, including Treasurer, Immediate Past Master (IPM), Chaplain, Secretary, Director of Ceremonies and Almoner. These posts are usually held for a number of years to provide continuity.

All offices of the Lodge, other than Treasurer and IPM, are essentially in the gift of the Ruling Master, although those choices are reviewed by a standing committee before being conferred at the Installation ceremony. The Treasurer is elected by the members and is solely responsible for maintaining the funds of the Lodge, collecting fees, paying bills, etc. Lodge accounts, independently-audited by two members selected for the purpose, must be presented to the membership once a year. These must show the contents of its various funds, for general use, charity, etc, and that these all remain in credit with all outstanding bills paid. A Lodge cannot borrow from anyone, not even its members, to cover running costs - if there is a shortfall, the members are expected to make it up equally between them.

The Immediate Past Master sits close to his successor in order to be able to assist and advise him. The Secretary conducts all correspondence on behalf of the Lodge, both within the Fraternity and beyond. It is his responsibility to ensure that all members are informed of every piece of correspondence that effects both them individually, and the Lodge in general. The Director of Ceremonies is exactly that, the person whose responsibility it is to ensure that every ceremony is conducted correctly and that all officers know their parts within it. The Almoner makes regular checks on the personal situation of every member and their immediate families, including the surviving partner of any deceased member. This duty is particularly important for those who are unable to attend Lodge, who the Almoner will visit regularly, and ensure that anything that member needs that the Lodge is able to assist with, for example medical situations, is dealt with expeditiously. The Almoner also provides a verbal report regarding Brethren absent through illness at each Lodge meeting, to assist other members to keep in touch.

In this country there are a number of additional degrees that are worked in organisations known collectively as Orders. These vary in age - some having existed continually since the start of Freemasonry, from 'Time Immemorial' as it is termed, some fading into obscurity and then revived, while others have only existed since the last century. Membership of all of these is voluntary, but will have an entry level requirement - for example, to join a Royal Arch Chapter applicants must have been a Master Mason for a proscribed period and be prepared to submit themselves to another ceremony, where they are Exalted as a Companion.

There are nine progressive officers within a Chapter, and again these are held for a year each. The final office, the Chair of the Chapter, is called the First Principal. There are only two ceremonies in a Chapter, Exaltation and Installation, but they are once again small playlets where the officer parts have to be learned and recited. If a Freemason decides to follow the progression in a Chapter, it can take around twelve years to achieve that Chair, although some of that will be concurrent with their Craft progression if they undertake both.

These two levels, the Craft Lodge and the Royal Arch Chapter, are the settings for the bulk of the Masonic part of this story. There was another Order tangentially-involved, a Knights Templar Encampment, which I do not intend to dwell upon other than to highlight that membership of this order depends first on the applicant being a Christian, and requires them to be a Master Mason of certain standing, a Companion for a proscribed period, and to be prepared to submit themselves to yet another ceremony.

Knights Templar are one of a limited number of Orders within Freemasonry that specify membership as being only for practicing Christians. All other parts of the Fraternity require a belief, but are not secular. That is why membership of a Lodge can include members of many denominations, who are able to meet together in harmony. Hence one of the two subjects on which discussion is not allowed during a Lodge evening is Religion, the other being Politics. That does not mean that Freemasons do not discuss those subjects, they are just as likely to be down the pub putting the world to rights as anybody. They just do not discuss them in Lodge, and I am sure readers can recall a dinner party when such restriction would have made for a more pleasant evening all round!

Whilst on the subject of dinner parties, there are two parts to a Masonic evening, whether in Lodge or an Order. The first is the ceremonial part, the second is a meal called the Festive Board where the members share food and companionship, plus a few toasts to the Crown, higher-ranking members, and so on. Some of the toasts are delivered accompanied by a short, and hopefully amusing, speech from the proposer, particularly the most important toast of the evening which is to visiting Brethren.

Visiting other Lodges is seen as one of the most important aspects of Freemasonry, although newer members of first or second degree are normally accompanied by a fellow-member of their own Lodge. This is because they would not have received their Certificate of membership of the Fraternity, which is only issued from Grand Lodge when they have achieved the degree of a Master Mason. This certificate is the equivalent of a Masonic passport, and enables a Master Mason to independently visit any other Lodge in the world where, if they are not already known to that Lodge, they will be expected to prove their membership. This is where some of the secrets come in, a process that is ceremonial but essentially no different from your need to prove your identity to a bank before they will discuss your account with you - and probably somewhat less tedious.

With regard to higher-ranking members, there are three Lodge levels within Freemasonry - the member's own Lodge, a Provincial Grand Lodge and the national headquarter Grand Lodge. All three operate in a similar manner, with a Master and officers, except that posts in the upper two are honorary with the officers drawn from the overall membership.

In this country, Grand Lodge is in London and administers all Lodges in England and Wales, plus some overseas Scotland and Ireland individually have their own Grand Lodges, although members visit freely across all three. Grand Lodge is headed by the Grand Master, at the time of writing the Duke of Kent, and meets ceremonially four times a year on quarter days, hence these meetings are known as 'Quarterly Communications.' All Ruling and Past Masters of Lodges are eligible to attend, if they so wish.

The intermediate level of Provincial Grand Lodge helps with local administration and assistance to local Lodges, in a territory normally along the lines of county boundaries at the time of foundation. It is headed by a Provincial Grand Master who is appointed from the local membership by Grand Lodge. The PGM, as the office is termed, usually serves for ten years. Bath has always been part of the Provincial Grand Lodge of Somerset.

A Past Master of a Lodge will normally achieve Provincial honours five years after completing their year in the Chair. This is the award of an officer rank within Provincial Grand Lodge, some of which are 'active' and held for one year, meaning that officer will visit and represent Provincial Grand Lodge at Lodge meetings throughout the Province, and sometimes beyond, during their year in office.

Once that year is complete, their rank becomes known as 'Past' - for example if a Bath member served as an active Junior Deacon, their subsequent honorary rank would be 'Past Junior Grand Deacon of the Provincial Grand Lodge of Somerset', which can be shortened to 'PPrJGD'. Those Lodge Past Masters who are not selected for 'active' posts within Province are immediately awarded an honorary 'Past' rank. All, whether active or honorary, retain their Provincial rank for the rest of their lives, and some who continue to advance their Masonic lives afterwards can receive a 'promotion' to a higher honorary rank in recognition of their contribution locally.

The same basic structure is repeated at Grand Lodge level, but what is known as 'Grand Rank' is only conferred upon selected Past Provincial Officers recommended for such honour by their Province for services rendered to the Fraternity.

All Lodges collect annual membership fees which together must at least cover the annual expenditure of the Lodge. This will include Grand and Provincial Lodge fees levied by those levels for each member, costs for the accommodation they use, repairs and replacement of equipment, and so on. A Lodge may borrow from the members and/or externally for major expenditure, such as building repairs if it owns the Hall it occupies. It can also derive additional income from such an asset, but in such circumstance it is expected to use any large excess to either reduce members' costs, or for charitable work. Which is why it is not unusual for Lodges sharing a building to vest ownership of that asset in a Trust, enabling the Lodge members to contribute normal accommodation fees, but allow the Trust to accumulate any excess in a sinking fund maintained to cover any future large expenditure, such as for major repairs.

Other than fees, members are expected to pay for their Festive Board meals, and make contributions to charitable causes sponsored by the Lodge, but only within the limits of their own personal resources. Charitable moneys are obtained through Lodge collections, raffles at the Festive Board, and direct donations from within its own membership and visitors. These moneys are administered by an officer called the Charity Steward, and can be used to benefit small local charities nominated by the membership, or one of the main Masonic charity funds.

Those central funds were amalgamated recently into one body called the Masonic Grand Charity, run by a board of Grand Lodge Officers. It supports a number of nursing homes owned by the Fraternity for aged Masons and their spouses, a hospital scheme that assists members and their families if they are in need of urgent medical care, and a school that accommodates the children of Masons who are unable to support them through ill-health or worse. There is a fourth fund, originally named the Grand Charity, which channels money to charities and good causes outside of the Fraternity, such as providing disaster relief in the event of a major catastrophe. That final branch alone has channelled more than £100 million to external causes in the last thirty years, all of that money coming from the membership.

To replenish these central funds, Provinces run Festivals in aid of one in particular, where they set themselves a target over a longer period, normally eight years, to raise from their membership. Somerset Province is running such a Festival up to the year 2020, with a target of £2.8 million pounds from its 4,000 members. At the time of writing, it is set to achieve this.

Other than the Provincial Festivals, which started in the late 19th century, none of what is contained in this chapter would have come as a surprise to the members of the various Bath Lodges meeting at the time that this story covers. Which brings me to a caution - having absorbed all of the above, some of what you are about to read will apparently fly in the face of it. That is because this story is an aberration, which is also what makes it so interesting. Not just because of what it is, but also because the Fraternity in general, at all levels, learned a great deal from it. Meaning that it is unlikely it would be allowed to happen again - or so one must hope.

Early Freemasonry

The origins of Freemasonry derive from various craft and trade guilds that evolved during medieval times, specifically those associated with stonemasons constructing the great cathedrals and castles of the time, and by the mid-seventeenth century, some had evolved into a gentleman's society. One of the earliest published mentions of the organisation was in the diary of Elias Ashmole, founder of the Ashmolean Museum in Oxford, detailing his first visit to a Lodge at his father-in-law's house in 1646.

Early records are sparse, mainly due to the uncertain political climate during the 1688 Revolution when many private Lodges destroyed their hand-written records for fear, among other things, of making unfortunate disclosures. The Grand Master in the latter years of the seventeenth century is reputed to have been Sir Christopher Wren, but due to his architectural activities, meetings were held irregularly.

The various Lodges that existed at that time remained primarily independent until, on 24th June 1717, four London Lodges came together at the Goose and Gridiron public house near to St Paul's Cathedral to create what would be the first Grand Lodge in the world. In 1723, The Premier Grand Lodge of England, as it was named, published *The Constitutions of Masonry*, essentially the organisation's first uniform rulebook; from this action additional Lodges in England, and Grand Lodges throughout the world, began to be deputised and subsequently warranted.

The first deputised Lodge to be formed outside of London had its inaugural meeting in 1724 at the Queen's Head in Cheap Street, Bath, under the guidance of the then Deputy Grand Master of the Fraternity, Dr John Desaguliers, philosopher, engineer and former assistant to Sir Isaac Newton. Among the founding members of the lodge were the Dukes of Bedford and St Albans, the latter being installed as Master of the Lodge, the Earl of Lichfield, Lord Hervey, Earl Craven, Viscount Cobham, Miloe Smith the Mayor of Bath, and Richard 'Beau' Nash, the latter dubbed 'The King of Bath' from his position as unofficial Master of Ceremonies in the city.

The earliest surviving minutes for a Bath Lodge are of the first meeting of a new Lodge on December 28th 1732, which indicate that it *met at Brother Robinson's, the Bear in Bath.* The new landlord of the Bear

The Bear Inn, Bath by RWM Wright
The building on the far right is the Queen's Head. *Bath Masonic Hall Trust*

Inn at that time was a Mr Robinson and the name of Johnson Robinson appears in the list of members, and he is also shown as being in the Chair of the Lodge in 1736. The original designation of the Lodge, as listed in the engraved list of 1733, was The Bear and Collar Lodge No.113. The Bear Inn was also in Cheap Street, next door to the Queen's Head on the opposite side of the entrance to Cock Lane, later renamed Union Passage. The Bear was the largest inn in the city, occupying most of the area that is now the pedestrianised part of Union Street.

At that time a Lodge meeting could take around two hours to complete, dependent on the amount and type of business to be conducted. After the formal activities of the evening were completed, most Lodge members would repair to a local hostelry for dinner together. It is therefore easy to understand the appeal of using rooms in public houses for meetings, the dinner afterwards being conducted in the same room without interrupting the proceedings.

Another reason was that it was not unusual for members to partake of certain substances no longer allowed during Lodge meetings. In his short history of Royal Cumberland Lodge written in 1873, Thomas Ashley relates of those early years of the Bear Inn Lodge: *It would be strange in these times to see charges for wine and tobacco in our minutes, though we might not object to the good old days when wine was two shillings a bottle.*

But these were always supplied in the Lodge Room to our Ancient Brethren, it taking several bottles to audit the Treasurer's Account, and when that was done, the balance struck and carried out, a postscript was added of 'one bottle more' and that deducted from the balance. The zeal with which this was pursued occasioned complaints of the late hours they kept, as well as running-up a long bill for candles, the consideration of which they postponed from time to time, and eventually with much difficulty discharged.

In the early 1750s, a group of Freemasons in London took issue with Premier Grand Lodge and formed a rival Antients Grand Lodge utilising their own version of the constitutions that they claimed were based upon more ancient principles, referring to the existing Premier Grand Lodge as 'The Moderns'. This schism in the organisation could have caused major problems, but these never arose as the two co-existed, essentially because each ignored the existence of the other. There is evidence of an Antients Lodge, numbered 100 in their engraved list, forming on 19th May 1762 at The Shakespeare's Head in Westgate Street, but the only records that exist show that it was short-lived.

Most pre-existing provincial Lodges remained part of Premier Grand Lodge, hence the Bear Inn Lodge in Bath were 'Moderns'. By the early 1760s, the Bear Inn Lodge had moved to the White Hart Inn, just fifty yards down Stall Street, opposite the entrance to the Abbey Churchyard. On 20th September 1762, a new Lodge formed, also at the Shakespeare's Head, named the Lodge of Perfect Friendship.

Although this Lodge received its warrant from Premier Grand Lodge, and therefore was a Moderns Lodge, there is evidence in the minutes of the Bear Inn Lodge that members were finding it inconvenient to visit the newer Lodge due to their being asked to take an *unprecedented oath prior to receiving admittance.* This may have been a reference to the practice of remaking, which was how many Lodges outside of London coped with accommodating stranger visitors who may have been members of Lodges warranted under the opposing constitution.

The Arms of Antients Grand Lodge
Bath Masonic Hall Trust

40

The schism was always far more defined in London, where it originated, whereas most provinces were more flexible in their attitudes, many Lodges actually using ceremonial that bridged the two constitutions. With Bath always full of visitors from the capital, remaking may have been the easiest way of avoiding the wrath of Grand Lodge should a Lodge unwittingly admit someone they shouldn't have. However, one would assume that the city's resident Freemasons would be fairly well-known to the other local Lodges.

So it may have been that, due to its location's earlier association with that Antients Lodge, the Lodge of Perfect Friendship became more inclined to that constitution from time to time. In fact when the inn's landlord relocated to the Greyhound Inn in the High Street in 1767, renaming it the Greyhound & Shakespeare, the Lodge relocated with him.

The Greyhound was also the home of the first Royal Arch Chapter to form in Bath, the York Chapter. The status of the Royal Arch was one of the primary disagreements between the Antient and Modern Grand Lodges, the former attaching far greater importance to it, so the emergence of so early a Chapter in Bath at the same public house as an existing Lodge could again suggest some Antients affinity within the Lodge of Perfect Friendship.

The next Lodge to form in Bath was the Lodge of Virtue on June 6th 1769. It originally met at the Saddlers Arms, which was next-door to the White Hart in Stall Street. By the mid-1770s it had moved to the Queens Head, thus renewing the association of Bath Freemasonry with its first home. It was a Lodge formed primarily for tradesmen in the city, maintaining that distinction throughout its life.

During the 18th century, as Freemasonry expanded, many Lodges were formed only to lose popularity and then dissolve within just a few years. Because of this, the Moderns regularly consolidated their lists of member Lodges, renumbering them to close the many gaps in the listings. By 1740, Queens Head Lodge had been one such casualty, and the Bear had become Number 101. However, although the numbering reliably aligns with the details recorded in the minutes of the Bear, some of the Grand Lodge lists were somewhat unreliable in their naming. This was due to Lodges named after their home hostelry not advising the secretary in London of their retention of the original name after subsequently moving venue. Hence the name 'Bear and Collar' on the early lists which never appears in the minutes, followed by more confusion in 1756 when, after moving to the White Hart Inn, it somehow became listed as the White Bear Lodge; there never was a public house in Bath called the White Bear. At the renumbering in 1770, the elder Lodge was listed as the White Hart Lodge, and Lodge of Perfect Friendship as the Greyhound and Shakespeare Lodge. By the next consolidation in 1781, the Bear Inn Lodge was actually back at its original home, Lodge of Perfect Friendship had moved to the White Hart, whilst Lodge of Virtue was located at the York House Hotel

In 1784, Thomas Dunckerley, a natural son of George II and the Provincial Grand Master for Somerset, warranted the creation of another new Lodge in Bath, numbered 458, issuing it with a new order of ceremony that he had been commissioned to produce by Premier Grand Lodge in London. Initial meetings were held in private rooms in Queen Square, but the following year the older Bear Inn Lodge amalgamated with this new Lodge and the combination was renamed The Royal Cumberland Lodge No.39, in honour of the Duke of Cumberland and Strathearn, then Grand Master in London. Royal Cumberland Lodge is one of the oldest in continuous operation in England, and still meets regularly at the current Bath Masonic Hall where, in 2007, it celebrated its 275th anniversary. To this day it still uses essentially the ceremonies presented to it by Thomas Dunckerley.

Dunckerley also encouraged several start-ups and revivals of Masonic Orders in the city around this time. A second Royal Arch Chapter was created in 1782, named the Chapter of Harmony. Early minutes, however, suggest that it may have pre-existed that date in some form, as all of the early members were existing Companions. It would eventually become the Royal Cumberland Chapter, although there is no clear date for when that name was adopted, the first mention of it in their minute book being in 1802.

The minutes of the Bear Inn Lodge show that it was conferring the degree of Scottish Master, the forerunner of the Mark degree, in special meetings as early as 1746. Bath was also the home of Antiquity Encampment of Knights Templar, the oldest such order in England, and hence bearing the number one. Although Antiquity Encampment's warrant was not issued until 1791, it bears the words 'Time Immemorial' on its banner, a distinction reserved for Lodges and Orders in existence before the creation of their governing body. Antiquity Encampment had also been part of the Camp of Baldwin formed in Bristol during the latter part of the eighteenth century. Anecdotal evidence suggests, however, that it may have existed much longer, possibly even predating Premier Grand Lodge.

The Provincial Grand Lodge of Somerset, formed in 1768, met regularly in Bath, primarily due to the first three Provincial Grand Masters all being based in or near the city. There are also sketchy historic records of what may have been a form of Royal Ark Mariners Lodge, started by Thomas Dunckerley. This comes primarily from a 1790 minute of Antiquity Encampment which states: *William Boyce took all the degrees of ye Red Cross, also Royal Ark Mariners, and many other sections and degrees, having first a dispensation, afterwards a warrant thereby to act.* However, if there were any other Masonic bodies other than Knights Templar and Royal Arch running in Bath at that time, it is doubtful that they lasted beyond the end of the eighteenth century.

The other interesting aspect of that minute is the reference to William Boyce, a long-standing member of Lodge of Virtue who, although he was taking higher degrees in 1790, was not exalted into Royal Arch until 1795, when he joined the Chapter of Harmony. He became a long-serving senior member of that Chapter and a key member of Royal Cumberland Lodge at an important time in its history.

The next renumbering came in 1792, and by the end of the eighteenth century there were three Lodges meeting in Bath - Royal Cumberland

**Banner of
Antiquity Encampment No.1**
Bath Masonic Hall Trust

Lodge No.36, Lodge of Perfect Friendship No.196 and Lodge of Virtue No.246. All were meeting independently in separate hostelries, but there appears to have been some consideration of them combining forces to share dedicated accommodation as early as 1776, when the members of Lodge of Virtue proposed the raising of a subscription of five guineas from each member of a Bath Lodge to achieve this. There is record of the discussion of this proposal in the minutes of the Bear Inn Lodge, but their members unanimously thought it was *not expedient to carry it into execution.*

As the first decade of the nineteenth century progressed, attendances dwindled due to the loss of eligible younger members to the war effort against Napoleon and France, but after 1812 things began to recover, one factor being the amalgamation of the two Grand Lodges in 1813 to form the United Grand Lodge of England with the Duke of Sussex as their first Grand Master.

In September 1812 a fourth Lodge was created in Bath at the Bladud's Head in Walcot Street. This was initially an Antients Lodge, a rather strange scenario in the circumstance that Bath had never seen the survival of such a Lodge for any great length of time, coupled with the imminent union of the Antients and Moderns that was well into the final stages of negotiation. The new Lodge was unnamed but received the low number of 49 under the Antients constitution, a number previously held by an erased Lodge meeting in Drury Lane, London. This was due to the necessity to recycle old Lodge warrants in order for Freemasonry to maintain exemption from the Unlawful Societies Act, introduced in 1799. At the union, this new Lodge received a low number and became Lodge No.69, still unnamed.

Although the actual union of the two Grand Lodges in London took place in December 1813, in practical terms it took several years to fully -integrate two organisations that were so disparate in their workings. The main aspect of this process was the design of a form of words and ceremony that would be acceptable to Brethren from both jurisdictions and, as it was these aspects that had caused the schism in the first place, Lodges continued to conduct business as previously until the new form was officially approved and issued. At the heart of this process was a small committee, hand-picked by the Duke of Sussex as the founder members of a new Lodge of Reconciliation constituted in 1813.

The first Master of that Lodge was Dr Samuel Hemming, the Headmaster of The Free School at Hampton from 1803 to 1828, and personal tutor to several of the Duke's brothers, including the future King William IV. The Lodge's primary responsibility was to compile the new ceremonials, that work taking three years; the form of working demonstrated by the Lodge of Reconciliation in May 1816 was formally adopted on 5th June 1816. To this day, the brethren of Old Hamptonian Lodge, Dr Hemming's mother Lodge, drink a toast to him at the conclusion of their evening as *the father of our ritual.*

Hemming then became a founder member of the Stability Lodge of Instruction, who were responsible for taking the new workings and demonstrating them to every Lodge in England. This process was not accomplished overnight, hence it may have been several more years before all English Masons were working the new ritual, christened 'Emulation'. As well as standardising the workings, the Duke had directed that the new ritual should be essentially secular to avoid any future disagreements

Dr Samuel Hemming
Bath Masonic Hall Trust

and attract a wider membership. With this process initially taking place in London, it is fair to assume that the process of instruction began by visiting Lodges in the capital, so it is doubtful that any of the Provinces received instruction until the following year at the earliest.

So in 1816 the Bath Lodges were still conducting their meetings, as they had done for many years, at various hostelries in the High Street. Royal Cumberland No.55 were at the Christopher Inn, with Charles Geary in the Master's chair, together with their associated Chapter with William Boyce as First Principal. Lodge No.69 met at the Greyhound Inn, just a few doors north of the Christopher, with John Dixon as Master; following a grand festival held in the city in March 1817, this Lodge was renamed Royal Sussex Lodge No.69. It shared premises with Lodge of Perfect Friendship No.243 whose Master was a local apothecary Thomas Whitney. It should be noted that this Lodge would also be renamed, in 1818, to The Royal York Lodge of Perfect Friendship, after which it was often referred to in minutes and correspondence simply as Royal York Lodge. Antiquity Encampment, which at this point was thought to have been under the control of John Dixon, is also believed to have been meeting at the Greyhound, although the most recently-minuted meeting had been at the Garrick's Head in 1814.

Bath High Street by Walter Williams
View from the Abbey end showing the Christopher Hotel on the near left, the White Lion
on the right immediately beyond the Guildhall and the Greyhound opposite it
Bath in Time

Lodge of Virtue No.311 were across the road at the White Lion; their Master was William Underwood Whitney, also a druggist and Thomas Whitney's younger brother. William had originally been a member of the Palladian Lodge in Hereford, the family's home town. He moved to Bath in 1815 to join his brother's business in Cheap Street, but not his brother's Lodge, instead becoming a joining member of Lodge of Virtue. Lodge returns of the time often list several members from the same family, so it was quite unusual for there to be two brothers of such concurrent seniority in different Lodges in the same city.

It was at this point that the next phase in the history of Bath Freemasonry was to evolve, a change that would within three years draw it to an eminence akin to its original foundation ninety years earlier, and then almost as quickly throw it into a whirlwind of controversy, from which parts of it would never recover.

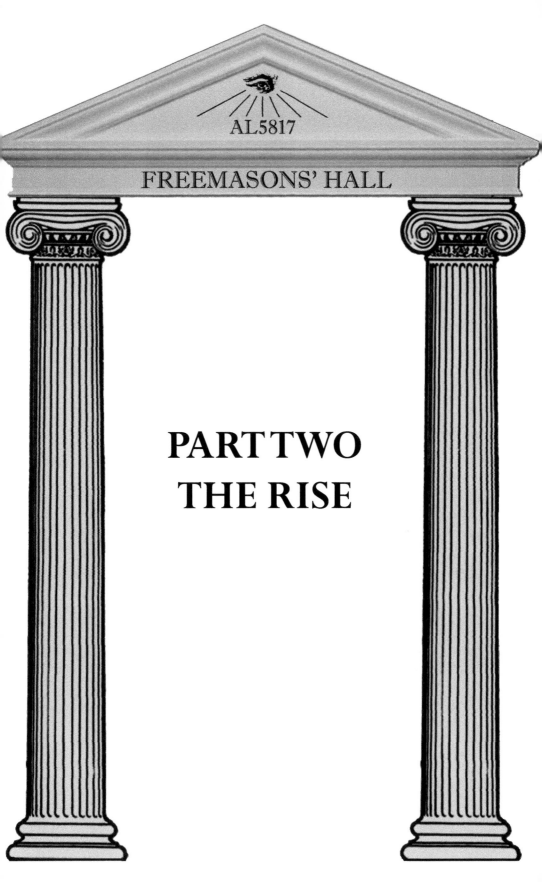

FREEMASONS' HALL

AL5817

PART TWO
THE RISE

The Main Players

There were six main protagonists in what would become a cause celebre, not only in the city of Bath, but through the offices of the Provincial Grand Lodge of Somerset to the very top of the United Grand Lodge of England. Three were leading members in Bath when Freemasons' Hall was proposed - Charles Geary, Thomas Whitney and Matthew Patton; two others, John Ashley and Captain Charles Maddison, would come into the picture a few years later. The sixth, and most senior, was a relatively-inexperienced Provincial Grand Master, Colonel Charles Kemeys Kemeys-Tynte.

Col. Kemeys-Tynte had only been initiated into Freemasonry in 1817, and was 42 years old when he was installed in 1820 as the fifth Provincial Grand Master for Somerset, a post he would hold for forty years. He was christened Charles Kemeys Johnson in 1778, the only son of John Johnson, a Lieutenant-Colonel in the First Regiment of Foot Guards, and his wife Jane. Lt. Col. Johnson was also a Groom of the Bedchamber to the Prince of Wales (later George IV) and his ancestral home was Burhill House at Hersham, Surrey.

His wife Jane's maiden name was Hassell; she was the niece of Sir Charles Kemeys, holder of the title to the Cefn Mably estate in Monmouthshire. The Kemeys baronetcy became extinct when that ancestor died unmarried in 1735, the estate passing through a female line that had married into the Tynte family, owners of Halswell House near Bridgwater, through which a separate baronetcy was acquired. When the last male descendent of that line also died childless in 1785, Jane Johnson was next in line; so her family, including their seven-year-old son Charles, all changed surname by Royal licence to Kemeys-Tynte and took-up residence at Halswell. When Jane died in 1824, all of the estates passed to her only son.

The Colonel was a reforming PGM, carrying on the work initiated by his predecessor, Arthur Chichester, in bringing some continuity to the Province. Bath is

Col. Charles Kemeys Kemeys-Tynte
Bath Masonic Hall Trust

48

geographically in the far north-east corner of the Province and even today, with modern transport networks in place, it can take a couple of hours to travel there from the more-remote southern parts. 200 years ago, those distances had to be traversed either on horseback or by horse-driven carriage; it would be the 1840s before Brunel's Great Western Railway provided a faster, and more comfortable, alternative.

Back then, as sometimes even now, Bath was viewed as somewhat of a Province within a Province. There had been discussions in 1818 among the Bath Lodges regarding submitting a petition to Grand Lodge for the City to be recognised as a separate district; minutes refer to this having the acquiescence of Arthur Chichester, although that was more likely wishful-thinking. Although the Lodges approved the move, there is no record of any presentation to Grand Lodge, suggesting that it remained a local discussion. If it was discussed at Provincial level, it would doubtless have received a resounding rejection from the collaboratively-minded Chichester.

Following his installation in 1820, Col. Kemeys-Tynte moved Provincial headquarters from Bath, where it had resided until that point, to the county town of Taunton; this was geographically more central, and just five miles to the south of his home at Halswell. Nevertheless, it was still a good day's travel from Bath, making regular attendance at Provincial meetings somewhat more difficult for the senior Bath officers, confirmed by regular mentions in Lodge minutes of their unavoidable absence on Provincial business.

The new PGM's early attempts at bringing Bath to heel, mainly on administrative matters, would earn him mild admonishment from Grand Lodge in London, due to some impetuousness on his part combined with his inexperience of the fine-workings of the organisation. However, he received high praise for how he dealt with a problem that flared up within weeks of his appointment, involving a dispute in Antiquity Encampment regarding its Warrant. Matthew Patton and John Ashley were at the centre of what was somewhat of a harbinger of the impending crisis surrounding Bath's new Freemasons' Hall, although the Colonel, like many others in the Province, were blissfully unaware of quite how serious a problem it would become. But it would not take long before events, combined with his rapid education in Masonic politics, would bring further and more successful opportunities to stamp his authority on his errant outpost.

Two of the three long-serving Bath members were initiated in the early years of the nineteenth century, Whitney in the Lodge of Perfect Friendship, Patton in Lodge of Virtue; Geary was already a Freemason when he moved to Bath where he joined Lodge of Virtue. All three worked closely together within Freemasonry and, along with William Boyce, were leading lights in Royal Cumberland's Royal Arch Chapter for well over twenty years. In 1804 Geary, along with other Lodge of Virtue members Boyce and Henry Dixon-Tylee, became joining members of Royal Cumberland Lodge after membership reached a low ebb; within months the three men occupied the major offices of that Lodge. Geary succeeded to the Chair the following year and held the position virtually uninterrupted for the next twelve years.

Fountain House today

Charles Geary was a dedicated Freemason, very rarely missed a meeting unless he was unavoidably away from the city, and regularly acted for absent senior officers after becoming Past Master. He held the rank of Past Provincial Senior Grand Warden, although no record survives of when he was in office in Somerset. Geary did, however, preside at the eventual installation of Arthur Chichester as PGM in 1817, in his capacity as the Master of the senior Lodge in the county.

He was a wine and brandy merchant with premises at Fountain House at the foot of Lansdown Road. He came to Bath after his marriage in 1797 to his first wife, Penelope Shew, the daughter of George Shew, a Dentist in Bath and also a member of Lodge of Virtue. Geary had been initiated on 23rd December 1793 into the St Andrew's Lodge No 321 meeting at the Robin Hood Tavern in Charles Street off St James' Square, just a few hundred yards from his London home in Mortimer Street. The marriage took place in Marylebone in London, and Geary retained interests in the capital, often being quoted as away on business there. He set-up his Bath wine business in 1799, the year after his wife commenced trading as a Mantua and Fancy Dress maker at the same address. Penelope died in 1805, and Geary remarried in 1807 to Mary Sharp at St Michael's Church at the foot of Broad Street.

His sister married Thomas Meyler, son of William Meyler, owner of the Bath Herald newspaper and Meyler's Library in the Abbey Churchyard. William Meyler was Master of Lodge of Perfect Friendship several times from 1791 and Deputy PGM for Somerset from 1803 to 1811 under Col. John Smith-Leigh MP. Thomas and Mary Meyler's eldest son was christened Charles Geary Meyler at Bath Abbey in 1805 and their library features later in the story.

Thomas Whitney had a similarly meteoric rise in Lodge of Perfect Friendship, entering the Chair in 1807, the year after he was initiated aged just twenty-four. Like Geary, he had an extensive, but occasionally punctuated, run in the position over the following ten years, and was appointed Provincial Senior Grand Warden by Arthur Chichester in 1817 and again by Col. Kemeys-Tynte in 1820. He was an apothecary with premises at No.1 Cheap Street, a prestigious location right at the corner of the junction with Union Street that ultimately became the home of Boots the Chemists from around the turn of the twentieth-century until the end of the 1960s.

Matthew Patton was a music seller, with premises in St Andrews Terrace where his wife Elizabeth taught harp and piano, and he occasionally taught violin. He took over the business from his father, also named Matthew, who was one of the founding members of that short-lived Antients Lodge formed at the Shakespeare's Head in the 1760s, although his name doesn't appear in any other Lodge in Bath.

Such a connection, however, might explain the younger Patton's preoccupation with Royal Arch Masonry, as he did not advance as an officer within Lodge of Virtue in more than fifteen years as a member there. Instead, as a Companion of the Royal Cumberland Chapter from 1803, he occupied some of their higher offices almost continually during that period, to become First Principal in March 1818. He appears to have been held in high esteem by his fellow Brethren, as he received several presentations from them during his career. Robert Peach, whose early Masonic career overlapped the last years of Patton's, described him in his series of articles on Freemasonry in Bath, published in the Bath Chronicle in 1893, as *a most amiable man, and if he lacked the intellectual power of many of his contemporaries, he was always animated by a true Masonic spirit, and a desire to do good.*

After Patton installed his successor, Baron Browne-Mill, as First Principal in 1819, the Companions voted that Patton be awarded with a commemorative jewel to mark his long and distinguished service. He was presented with that jewel on 16th September 1819, just a week prior to the Royal dedication of Freemasons' Hall. It had been commissioned from the famous Masonic silversmith Thomas Harper at a cost of thirteen guineas, well in excess of a thousand pounds at today's values. It was specially-designed and consisted of a star of Paris brilliants mounted in 18-carat gold. It went missing after Patton's death but resurfaced in 1924, when an Australian Freemason travelled halfway around the world to Bath to return it to the Royal Cumberland Chapter. It was subsequently

The Matthew Patton Jewel
Bath Masonic Hall Trust

donated to the Bath Masonic Museum in 1925, but was lost again after the Masonic Hall was badly damaged in the Bath Blitz of 1942.

The original presentation was especially significant to this story, in that it was made by Charles Geary who: *after a handsome address invested Companion Patton in the name of Royal Cumberland Chapter for his steady attachment as a member for 17 years.* It was also Geary who seconded the proposal for Matthew Patton to become a joining member of Royal Cumberland Lodge just months prior to that presentation, following which Patton became Master of that Lodge. He subsequently became Provincial Junior Grand Warden in 1820, and Provincial Senior Grand Warden in 1833, both appointments being made by Col. Kemeys-Tynte, whom Patton had installed as PGM at the Guildhall in Bath in 1820 in his capacity as Master of the senior Lodge in the Province.

John Ashley was a musician primarily engaged as principal bassoonist in the Theatre Royal Orchestra, although he also played regularly at various other events in the City. He also composed numerous songs and ballads that were published nationally. He succeeded Thomas Whitney as Master of Lodge of Perfect Friendship and held that post for five years, as well as being second in command to Patton in Antiquity Encampment.

Such facts make it more difficult to understand the seismic falling-out that subsequently occurred in the 1820s, not only within Freemasonry in Bath, but between these local gentlemen specifically. One factor may have been the rise in status in the city's Fraternity of another military man, Captain Charles Maddison, who had originally found his way into Royal Cumberland Lodge some years earlier.

He was born in India in 1770, the third son of Lt. Col. George Maddison of Stainton Hall, Lincolnshire. His first commission was as a Lieutenant in the 32nd Regiment of Foot in 1787. He then transferred to the cavalry, joining the 19th Light Dragoons in 1791 and served in India until 1797, when he retired. No reason was given for the retirement, taken at only twenty-seven years of age, but the year coincides with a move of the family home from Lincolnshire to The Priory at Dunstable, Bedfordshire, which could have been a factor. He held a purchased commission, which would have been difficult to resell as the regiment was too remote to be attractive to those wishing to purchase such a rank for social status alone.

He was initiated in 1809 into Tyrian Lodge in Derby, but then in 1810, by special dispensation of the then PGM for Somerset Col. Smith -Leigh, was passed, raised and became a member of Royal Cumberland Lodge. He had recently married Mary Harington, daughter of Reverend John Harington, a member of the long-established family from the Manor of Kelston near Bath. Maddison does not feature in Bath minutes again until 1820, when he joined the Lodge of Perfect Friendship. No mention was made on that occasion regarding any prior connection to Royal Cumberland Lodge, his previous Lodge being listed on the returns as Tyrian.

He was also distantly-related to Col. Kemeys-Tynte, who was his fifth cousin three times removed. Both were able to trace their line via a common ancestor, the second Duke of Cumberland, all the way back to 1338 and the Plantagenet King Edward III. In Regency times, such relationships were neither inconsequential, nor the subject of a surprise disclosure. There are documents in the Cefn Mably archives showing that Col. Kemeys-Tynte was drawing-up genealogical tables detailing the royal lineage as early as 1822, in connection with an eventual claim he would launch on the Baronetcy of Wharton.

How significant this close kinship would become does not emerge until much later in the story.

An Early Skirmish

With England having been at peace for nearly two years, by the middle of 1817 an optimism for the possibilities provided within a society freed of the fear of invasion was beginning to emerge, albeit tempered by the stringencies of an economy that was still short of liquidity. But just how unusual the atmosphere remained at the time that Bath's Freemasons set-out to build themselves a new home, is illustrated by a set of incidents that occurred during that year.

Bath was still an attractive resort for high society; the population remained highly-transient, with new faces regularly appearing, many with military commissions who were no longer needed by their regiments and therefore looking to take-up suitable positions in private society. Within every branch of the populous there were individuals keenly-aware of how rapidly social status could change; those in positions of high-standing were particular targets for anyone with an eye to the main chance.

Freemasonry was re-establishing itself after the union of the two Grand Lodges barely four years earlier, and was an attractive proposition for those seeking to establish society credentials. Lodge membership numbers stood-up well through the war years in the capital, but varied widely in the Provinces, making the chances of rapid advancement more viable where membership had become depleted.

Following the death in 1813 of the previous PGM, Col. John Smith-Leigh, the post had been vacant until it was filled in 1817 by Arthur Chichester Esq, who had been hand-picked by the Grand Master in London. He was not the first choice of the members locally, particularly in Bath, then headquarters for the Province, where the survival of the Fraternity in the later war years had been vested in a small number of long-standing and experienced members. Senior of those were Charles Geary, Master of Royal Cumberland Lodge, followed by Matthew Patton who had been prominent in Royal Arch in the city for more than fifteen years, then Thomas Whitney, Master of the second-oldest Lodge in the city. They were all members of previously-Moderns Lodges that had been governed by Premier Grand Lodge. The membership of the other Lodge in the city, by 1817 renamed Royal Sussex Lodge, had come from the Antients constitution.

Clashes of personality were lurking under the apparently serene surface of the Fraternity in the city and history portrays that the main source of the turmoil that ensued was the most senior of those Bath members, Charles Geary. Robert Peach described Geary in 1894 as *having a somewhat overbearing temper* and of *being covetous of office*. It is unlikely that Peach, Master of Royal Cumberland Lodge in 1852, ever met Geary, but he would have encountered Matthew Patton and Col. Kemeys-Tynte during their later years, which may have provided Peach with a direct link in contemporary history. However, the probable source of those impressions were incidents surrounding Geary's last year as Royal Cumberland's Master in 1817.

Peach suggests that Geary sought to hold onto the Chair, despite the desire of his members to have him replaced, by refusing to hold the annual election and, when further challenged, walking-out of the meeting leaving the members unable to proceed. As a result he was called before the Board of General Purposes in London, the committee that ruled on Masonic matters that could not be resolved at Provincial level. However, examination of the minutes of the subsequent Board hearing, plus associated correspondence, casts an entirely different light on the proceedings and gives some indication as to how the actions of some individuals within the Fraternity at the time were, perhaps, not as might have been expected. It also shows how history, when written based upon incomplete information, and perhaps a biased viewpoint, can be somewhat misleading.

Lodge convention has evolved considerably from those early years of United Grand Lodge. Today, an initiate also becomes a member of the Lodge initiating him; back then, there were two separate votes, one to approve the initiate and another for their application to join the Lodge. Those votes could be some period apart, as there was no onus on either the Lodge or the Mason to advance Lodge membership; indeed, Lodges in cities like Bath often had far more initiates than members, due to the transient nature of the population. Unusually today, Royal Cumberland Lodge still follows the older convention by asking an initiate whether he also wishes to become a subscribing member.

Between 1814 and 1816, meetings of Royal Cumberland Lodge had been sporadic and poorly-attended, due to a reduction in membership. At the end of May 1817 an emergency meeting of the Lodge was held at the Christopher Hotel. Geary was in London on business, so the only elected officers attending were the Junior Warden, Robert Payne, and Secretary John Physick, both long-standing members. Ostensibly this meeting had been called at the instigation of the Grand Secretary in London, and with the consent of Geary, to assist a cohort of Freemasons who intended moving to Bath from other Provinces.

The meeting was chaired by a visitor, Samuel Browne, a member of Lodge of Virtue in Bath; another visitor, William Redman from Lodge of Perfect Friendship, stood-in as Senior Warden. The remaining attendance were also visitors, named as Brothers Pitter, Rickards, Wyke and Bannatyne. Of those, only Thomas Pitter was local, being also a member of Lodge of Perfect Friendship. It was not unusual at those times for officers of one Bath Lodge to assist another by standing-in when attendance was low and, on the surface, this emergency meeting was only called to assemble the members and visitors prior to their proceeding to the Kingston Rooms for a Provincial Grand Lodge meeting where they would be introduced to the new PGM, Arthur Chichester. However, Browne conducted one other piece of business, the actual minute reading: *Brother Physick proposed Brothers Saml J Browne, Mark Watt, George Wyke, Rd Whalley Bridgeman, Fredk Bannatyne, John Maillard, Harvy Shaw to become members of this Lodge which was seconded by Brother Payne when they were unanimously elected.*

The proceedings were somewhat irregular as only three of those mentioned were present, plus the number of current Royal Cumberland members in attendance was insufficient to hold any election, the new 'members' essentially electing themselves and their associates. Rickards did not feature in the election, nor is he mentioned subsequently, so was probably simply visiting the city.

Five days later, another emergency meeting was called by Browne, who again took the Chair 'pro tem' with the other positions filled by new members; the only elected officer present was the Secretary Physick. At that meeting, three men were proposed and seconded to be candidates - Thorman, Hoey and Du Moulin. The former was approved at that meeting, the other two put forward to be balloted at the next. Three further new visitors were then elected members: Blossett, Frederick Maillard and Hogg; an existing member, Captain Barton, also reappeared.

It is not clear whether Thorman was initiated, but later evidence states he was transiting through Bath, and as the minutes record his paying of the necessary fees, it has to be assumed that there was an appropriate ceremony. Neither he nor the other two proposed initiates feature further in Royal Cumberland records. Geary returned for the regular meeting in June and, with all offices temporarily filled by new members, appointed Browne as Senior Warden. At the next regular meeting Robert Payne, the existing Junior Warden, stood down and John Maillard was appointed in his place.

On the surface this would all appear to be standard methodology to progress joining members into office within a Lodge that was in need of increased numbers, but the minutes reveal that Payne also resigned the Lodge entirely, which suggests a degree of unhappiness with proceedings. An analysis of the backgrounds of some of the new members throws an interesting light on the make-up of the cohort.

Four of the new members had good Masonic credentials: Bridgman was an Attorney and writer on the Law, *P.M. of the London Lodge, a member of the Princes Royal Lodge No.210 and past Grand Steward in the year 1791;* Stephen Allen Hogg Esq was from *The Lodge of Attention in Lynn, Norfolk,* and Major John Blossett from *Vectis Lodge of Peace and Concord No.578 in the Isle of Wight.* Lt. Frederick Bannatyne was a member of *Waterloo Military Lodge*, which was the Waterloo Lodge No 1682, formed by dispensation in 1816 for the 33rd Regiment of Foot, where a Bannatyne was listed among the commissioned officers at the time. The regiment was raised from West Yorkshire and fought at Waterloo commanded by the Duke of Wellington. All of the Lodges mentioned were extant at the time and would have been capable of providing confirmation of past Masonic histories of these gentlemen.

There were three others, Browne, Shaw and Barton, who appear to have already been members of Lodges in Bath. Captain John Barton had been initiated in Royal Cumberland Lodge on the same night that Charles Maddison was passed and raised in 1810. Although we do not know where Barton's Masonic career advanced in the meantime, he appears to have had little, if any, connection with Browne, so it is likely that he had, co-incidentally, returned to Bath and resumed attendance of his Mother Lodge.

However, Major Harvy James Shaw had only been initiated into Lodge of Perfect Friendship weeks earlier, after which he doesn't feature in their surviving returns. Samuel Browne joined Lodge of Virtue, also just weeks earlier, and only appeared on their return during 1817, where he is shown as having joined from the Royal York

Lodge of Union in Bristol and was proposed by Lodge of Perfect Friendship. There were no other details or dates filled-in, and those two sparse comments are in a different colour ink, suggesting that the Lodge had not been in possession of more than cursory information at the time of his joining.

Browne's precise previous Masonic history is non-existent; even the Bristol Lodge records do not show him. However, he may have originated from an Irish Lodge, the clue being the method of spelling his surname - Browne with an 'e' being very common among Irish gentry. There were a number of Irish Freemasons in Bristol at the time, many of whom had previously been members of Antients Lodges, but had moved to the Irish Constitution after the union and thus beyond the scope of membership in the United Grand Lodge of England. Because of this, there remained in Bristol a good deal of animosity and distrust between Antients and Moderns, and it took a number of years before ex-Antients in Bristol could bring themselves to attend Provincial meetings, due to arguments over the paying of dues to Grand Lodge.

At least three more of the cohort were members of Lodges in other constitutions, Wyke from Holland, Watt and John Maillard from Lodges constituted under the Grand Lodge of Scotland. Mark Watt was recorded as *an army Colonel from the Thistle Lodge in Edinburgh*. The reference to this Lodge is vague, as no Lodge has existed of that name in Edinburgh; the only Scots Lodge holding the name of Thistle in 1817 was in Dumfries, too considerable a distance away from Edinburgh to be classed as within that area. From further research, I found one Scots Mason named Mark Watt, who was a long-time resident of Edinburgh where he was a member of the Royal Society; he was regularly published in Scientific Journals, on subjects as varied as magnetism and spiders webs; in 1817 he would have been in his mid-fifties, but there is no record of his having been in the army. He died in 1843 at the age of 80 and is buried in Greyfriars Cemetery.

The only 'Colonel Mark Watt' that could be found was a Lieutenant-Colonel who was appointed Commandant of the Trafford & Hulme Regiment in 1812, a local Militia formed in Manchester, and responsible for home duties while the regular regiments were overseas fighting the French; this Colonel Watt died in London in 1836. It has to be said from reading later memorials, carrying Watt's name as prime signatory, that they appear more likely to be from the hand of a reactionary military man than a considered scholar.

John Maillard was stated as a member of *the Mount Olivit Lodge No.241 in St Christopher, West Indies*; his brother Frederick Augustus Maillard was a member of the *Sussex Lodge of Hospitality in Bristol*. John owned a plantation on St Christopher, where both brothers appear on court records as plaintiffs in cases on *'money matters'* during preceding years. However, at the time of his involvement in this affair, John was an absentee landlord, his estate being administered by another relative. John returned to the Caribbean in the early 1820s, serving as an Assistant Justice on the island for several years, dispensing some fairly summary sentences in the process. But his brother did not; Frederick died in 1827 and is buried at Langley Burrell, twelve miles from Bath.

John Maillard's Lodge on St Christopher, or St Kitts as it is now named, had become dormant in 1816 and the name quoted in the memorials, *Mount Olivit*, was wrong. Lodge 241, held under the Scottish Constitution on the island, was recorded as *The Mount of Olives Lodge*; Olivet is the Hebrew form of the name of the Mount and is not an unusual Lodge name, being used by several Lodges around the world. Although this point may appear trivial, when taken in context with the overly-pedantic nature of subsequent submissions by these gentlemen to Grand Lodge, it does appear strange that such a simple detail, known so well to one of their number, should be the subject of such a basic error.

Capt George Wyke was *Past Master of the Union Lodge No.3 of the National Grand Lodge, Holland*. This Lodge has been impossible to trace due to the major reorganisation of Freemasonry in that area that took place after 1815, when Belgium was annexed to The Netherlands after the end of the Napoleonic wars. Their previous governing body was called the National Grand Lodge of the United Provinces, but after 1815 it was replaced by a new Grand Orient of the Netherlands, with two regions of North and South. Wyke was a captain in the Grenadier Guards and also had associations with the Leeward Islands, his grandfather having been governor of Antigua, the next island in the chain to St Christopher, and from whom he also inherited a plantation.

If all of this begins to sound rather like a take-over by some dubious individuals, then correspondence held at Great Queen Street actually confirms this was probably the case. Browne had attended a Grand

Festival in Bath a couple of months earlier, then subsequently wrote to Grand Lodge on behalf of the cohort: *On looking over the list of Lodges I perceive the numbers 132 - 157 - 185, with many others vacant, and I think on a close examination it will be found that No.55 is vacant as there is no Lodge held in Bath of that number, there being only the Warrant & Furniture with no other officers or members that have met for the last 10 months or two years which I can offer as a fact having seen the minute book, the Master Mr Geary holding the warrant and Furniture. We are very anxious for a dispensation to begin another Lodge here, and I trust there will be no hesitation in granting it. If you cannot procure 55, I shall be grateful for your exertion to procure 132 or near that number.*

There was nothing unusual in these gentlemen desiring to join a Lodge in Bath, still the resort of choice for members of London society able to maintain two homes. What was unusual was the expressed desire for their new Lodge to have a low number in the engraved list. Indeed, rather than await for the suggestion as to which numbers were available, they actually named No.55 (Royal Cumberland) as their preference, mentioning a perception of it having minimal membership. That Browne was keen to be Master of this new Lodge is shown by his, somewhat fawning, reference to the Grand Secretary of his abilities: *I have succeeded as to be able to perform four parts of the duty of a Master as opening & closing the Lodge. I wish I was with you like Saul at the feet of Gamaliel to take lectures until I should be in some measure perfect.*

No hidden agenda had been apparent when the Grand Secretary organised a private meeting in London during April between Browne and Geary, with a view to accommodate the gentlemen and assist the revival of an old Lodge; it was that private meeting that brought-about Browne's chairing of the emergency meeting in May.

But in July 1817, Hogg proposed and Shaw seconded that an election for Master should take place, which had not been regularly possible for several years due to low attendances. Geary welcomed this, seeing it as a rubber-stamping exercise of his position as the incumbent for a final few months whilst he organised a regular progression for the new members into the regular election at the end of the year. Physick must have also read the situation similarly, as he issued the summons for the election at yet another emergency meeting on July 10th, upon which there were no indications of proposals for a replacement, the summons showing just the one candidate - Charles Geary.

On the night of the meeting, however, Browne's hidden agenda finally emerged. Only eight Brethren showed-up, six of whom were Browne and his cohort, and Geary found himself suddenly opposed in the election by Browne. Geary declared that, due to the new and late nomination, it would not be possible to go ahead with a properly-constituted election until details had been circulated to the membership; he then tried to adjourn to a later date.

However, Browne attempted to force the election, at which point Geary *took off his jewel, quit the chair and walked-out*. On the surface, this appears to be a petulant act; indeed that is exactly how Peach interpreted it. However, it was the only way that Geary could put a stop to proceedings that were already well out-of-hand - not only had Browne's nomination not been properly made or circulated, neither had he occupied the office of Warden in the Lodge for the minimum period of six-months required by the By-Laws. Further investigation revealed that Browne had never previously held senior office in any Lodge, let alone been a Past Master, as had previously been assumed when he was allowed to chair meetings.

How far removed this meeting was from convention is further demonstrated by Browne continuing with the election in Geary's absence, then having himself installed as the new Master, despite there being no Past Master of the Lodge available to perform the ceremony. Browne then wrote to Geary requesting his attendance at future meetings as the Immediate Past Master, but as this would have legitimised the election, Geary refused. Browne and his associates then lodged a petition to the Provincial Grand Master to have Geary removed from the Lodge membership. In it, Browne's cohort made a series of accusations stretching to eleven pages. The main points, decided at a meeting attended by the cohort, but neither the subject of summons or recorded in the Lodge minute book, were:

1. The conduct of Bro. Chas. Geary in singly opposing himself in his character of Master, to the united wishes of the other members of the Lodge, in protesting against the proceedings of a Lodge which he himself had called, in desiring to close that Lodge before the business expressed in the summons was concluded, in denying to the Brethren the privilege of the electing a master by ballot, by abdicating the Chair at the time of such election, & finally in refusing to convene another Lodge, upon the requisition of a competent number of the members, is unmasonic, irregular & highly to be reprehended.

2. The personal attacks made by Bro. Geary at the two last Lodge nights upon his S.W. Bro. S.J. Browne (who by reason of his - Bro. Geary's - incapacity to do the duties of a Master, has frequently officiated for him) are unworthy of the Character of a Mason & such as to merit our just censure.

The incessant and rambling nature of Masonic memorials and correspondence of the time can be somewhat persuasive of the veracity of what is being stated, and the language and wording was often cleverly framed to support that perception. Therefore, when read in isolation, it can all sound very plausible, a monologue that is not necessarily untruthful, merely adjusted to the bias of the writer. However, when examined in conjunction with other contemporary records, a lot of this lingual veneer is easily stripped away to reveal a somewhat different version of events.

Examples of this are the way in which the memorial stresses the apparent inability of the incumbent Master, Charles Geary, to conduct basic Lodge procedure, and the lack of Lodge meetings between 1813 and 1817. Minuted meetings of Royal Cumberland had been sporadic, due more to low attendances rather than any lack of desire to hold them, but this had occurred during a period of major national crisis and was occasioned by the number of younger members being away on military duties. At Grand Lodge level, those years were spent revising the form of ceremony, work not completed until 1816, following which the new procedures were rolled-out over a number of years.

As a result, members in Somerset may not have received their direct instruction on the new ceremony, whereas members in other Provinces could have. Therefore it should not be a surprise that, in early 1817, a Master of a Lodge in a city a hundred miles from the capital might not be able to open a Lodge in the latest manner, and would likely ask a visiting Mason from the capital to demonstrate that new method.

It was early September before Arthur Chichester placed the papers before the Board of General Purposes. Extracts from their judgement show that the Board were perfectly capable of seeing past the veneer: *The Board are of opinion that the election of Bro. S.J. Browne and the other Brethren specified in the Memorials as members of the Royal Cumberland Lodge was illegal and must be declared void. As to the election of Bro. Browne to be Master, the proceeding is altogether illegal. The Board think it proper to remark upon the unqualified manner in which Bro. Browne and his friends declare the Worshipful Master's incompetency, in which it is mentioned by*

Brethren just admitted within the walls of the Lodge, and against an old and zealous Mason, marks a great want of consideration and discretion. The Board, from what they have heard, are inclined to think that a better knowledge of Bro. Geary would have made the Brethren form a very different opinion of him.

In respect of the admission of members without notice being given in the Summons it possibly may be urged that the Brethren who were so admitted were ignorant of the Law; this plea cannot be made available to any of those Brethren as all Masons are supposed to know the Law; but Brother Browne has not the least opportunity of making such an excuse, because the Board are informed that while he was in London he was made acquainted with that Law by the Grand Secretary, and in fact the Law itself was pointed out to him.

So quite a mauling for Browne, particularly with regard to his ignorance of the rules, Geary's assertion of illegality of the election being upheld, and thus his re-establishment as Master. However, Geary also received a slap on the wrists for letting it all happen in the first place: *The Board cannot, however, but remark that the first act of irregularity was committed by the Worshipful Master in giving to Bro. Browne authority to represent the Lodge at the Provincial Meeting, and also to convene the Lodge; this act, although it appears to have been directed by a wish to further the interests of the Lodge and to oblige Bro. Browne, has in a great measure been the cause of the subsequent irregularities.*

The Board concluded by recommending: *With a view to the re-establishment of Harmony amongst the Parties, that the Brethren who have been improperly admitted members of the Royal Cumberland Lodge should be regularly reproposed and balloted for, and they trust that the result of such a measure would be to place them legally on the list of the Lodge.* In other words, now go away and do it all again - properly.

Geary's presiding over the laying of the foundation stone of Freemasons' Hall as the Master of the senior Lodge in the city, took place between the failed election in July and the Board hearing at the end of September, confirming that Browne had quickly been removed from the Chair by the PGM, accompanied by a restoration of the status quo. At the Lodge meeting in October, a letter was read from the Deputy Provincial Grand Master, Dr Henry Sully, advising that all of the new members were to be struck-out of the membership list; Geary remained in the Chair with Payne, who withdrew his resignation, and Physick appointed as his Wardens.

Barton, whose situation was simply collateral damage, was immediately re-elected at the same meeting. Over the next two months three of the delisted members, Wyke, Blossett and Shaw reapplied and were elected. In December 1817, the normal annual election took place and Robert Payne was elected Master, allowing Geary to finally leave the Chair; nevertheless he would be required to deputise regularly over the next two years due to Payne's intermittent attendance.

In January 1818, Browne, Hogg and Bridgeman all reapplied for membership, only to withdraw their applications three weeks later before a ballot could take place. Robert Payne, not prepared to countenance his own Mastership being threatened by the usurpers, had selected exclusively old hands as officers, meaning Browne and company would face a long wait before they could progress through those offices to succeed to the Chair. Browne's parting shot was to request the return of his joining fees, and this revealing minute rather succinctly sums-up their activities: *It was resolved that as the bills to a large amount were far beyond the whole of the fees received having been incurred by having expensive suppers (at the particular request of the Brethren who were then members) they are therefore not entitled to a return of their joining fee, and the Treasurer is requested to inform Bro. S Browne accordingly.*

Bannatyne and Hogg later joined Lodge of Perfect Friendship and were major subscribers to the first financing of the Hall. It is interesting that the new Hall was mentioned in that very first letter of Browne's in April 1817 to the Grand Secretary: *We have nearly £1000 subscribed in shares to the New Masonic Hall. I hope we shall begin it soon.* Whether this was an indication of his direct involvement in fundraising, or just a reference to insinuate that he was, it is impossible to know. Probably the best indication that it was the latter comes from the fact that nothing further was heard of Browne, Watt, Bridgeman or the Maillard brothers relative to Freemasonry in Bath.

Contrary to what has been written or insinuated subsequently, this was the only time that Geary was the subject of any disciplinary hearing at Provincial or Grand Lodge level. As far as Peach's assertion as to his having an overbearing temper or being covetous of office, it is easy to understand how that may have been apparent on a cursory look, but a full examination of the facts shows that to have been a somewhat unfair presumption and, as will be seen, not for the only time.

Freemasons' Hall

The building that would cause such a kerfuffle over so many years still stands in Bath's York Street, a road created in 1808 to provide a more usable carriage-link from The Parades to the Public Baths. It runs from Terrace Walk, where nowadays the open-topped tourist buses collect and deposit their many passengers throughout the year, past the edge of the Roman Baths to a junction with the city's main shopping spine, where it is now closed-off by bollards to form a cul-de-sac.

This was one of the very first purpose-built Masonic Halls in England. It was designed by the eminent architect William Wilkins, himself a Freemason, whose best-known work is the National Gallery in Trafalgar Square in London, a building that was once famously described by Prince Charles as *a much-loved and elegant friend*. Wilkins had worked in Bath previously, having remodelled the Lower Assembly Rooms on Terrace Walk, the facade of which bore a similarity to the final design for Freemasons' Hall. He was also responsible for numbers 11 to 15 York Street, directly opposite the hall, which were built for a Dr Richardson in 1819.

Freemasons' Hall today viewed from the Abbey tower

The building itself is somewhat shoehorned onto what was once the front garden of Ralph Allen's town house, a small building with a quite splendid Palladian frontage added by John Wood the Elder, but now almost completely obscured from view by the hall. The garden had once formed part of the city's bowling green, Wood describing the consequences of its conversion: *a third part of the Bowling Green having been granted for a garden to the House, Smock Racing and Pig Racing, playing at Foot-ball and running with the Feet in Bags in that Green, four of the Bath Diversions of those Days, thereby received their Final End.*

As can be seen, the originally-perceived design for the hall, depicted on the announcement of the project following the joint meeting on 7th July 1816, was for a two-storey building. However, although the Wilkins design that was eventually adopted gives the appearance from the street of a single storey, it incorporates a large basement beneath. This contained a kitchen, dressing areas, storerooms and a large room that ultimately became the lower lodge room. However, from the servery linking the kitchen to that area, it is safe to assume that this was originally meant to be the dining room.

The proposal document was signed by the Masters of all four Lodges,

Top: Ralph Allen's Town House
by Arthur Whitlock *By kind permission of the Artist*
Right: William Wilkins
Bust by E H Bailey *Fitzwilliam Museum*

The Original Design concept as displayed on the circular letter of 1816
Bath Masonic Hall Trust

showing that the project certainly started with the support of all Freemasons within the city. A committee was formed and Thomas Whitney was nominated as the person to receive correspondence; it appears that Whitney may also have been responsible for the original two-storey concept.

He was not long in broadcasting the intentions of the Bath Brethren far and wide: a postscript to a letter sent to Grand Secretary Edwards Harper, scribbled on the back of one of the printed circulars, reads: *On the other side you will see a representation of the intended new Hall we are about (if possible) to build. The brethren here are sanguine in their expectations of being able to accomplish it: I hope we shall not be disappointed. If the whole cannot be raised by contributions, it is intended to make up the difference by shares, at £10 each, paying the usual interest.*

The chosen plot of land was leased from the Kingston Estate and early on the morning of 4th August 1817, little more than a year after approval of the original proposal, the foundation stone was laid by Charles Geary, assisted by the Masters of the other three Lodges - John Browne of Royal Sussex plus the Whitney brothers. Geary closed the ceremony with this solemn prayer:

A Masonic Foundation Stone-Laying Ceremony
Bath Masonic Hall Trust

May the Grand Architect of the Universe sanction with his blessing our present pious undertaking and may the stone, here deposited, be the foundation of a noble edifice, and prove an ornament to this ancient city, and an honour to Freemasonry! From the precepts which may be hereafter taught within its walls, may virtue, morality, science and brotherly love, continue to be inculcated and flourish through many future generations to the embellishment of human nature, and the particular advantage of the chosen craft. May the Providence of Almighty God further and bless this, and every good work, and may his name not only be the foundation stone, but the rock of every earthly structure.

However, shortly after the stone was laid, Royal Sussex Lodge withdrew their support. No reason is apparent from their minutes, which are very sketchy for this period; in fact they make no mention at all of Freemasons' Hall until some ten years later. What does emerge from the minutes of all of the Lodges, however, is that Royal Sussex embroiled itself regularly in minor disputes with the other Lodges. These included complaints about their members being refused admission as visitors to other Bath Lodges, the non-return of property, and specific allegations about individuals; Thomas Whitney's name appears on one or two occasions in the latter category.

Whether it was one of those disputes that caused their withdrawal, or the decision was taken purely for financial reasons, we shall probably never know; however the background politics in the Fraternity, both locally and nationally, may give some clues.

Although the union of the two Grand Lodges had been confirmed in 1813, it took several years for the constitutions to be agreed in full. Even today, remoteness from the capital influences the speed at which change will take place and resistance to such change is only to be expected regardless of the subject or the organisation involved. In the Provinces, there would have been factions less-enthusiastic about adopting the new ceremonies, particularly in towns where there were Lodges existing in close proximity that had been meeting previously under different constitutions.

In Bath, the four Lodges fitted exactly this scenario: Royal Sussex was originally an Antients Lodge, the other three were Moderns although Lodge of Perfect Friendship may have operated in a manner sympathetic to both constitutions - in 1817 it was sharing the same lodge room at the Greyhound Inn as Royal Sussex. It should also be stressed that the new workings only applied to Craft Lodges - it wasn't until the 1830s that a similar process was conducted within Royal Arch, so their Chapters continued to work the older system, primarily founded on Antients' principles.

Bath was an important Masonic centre because of its social status and the number of regular visitors from the capital; local Antients Masons would have been in the minority, although their numbers would have been boosted by sympathetic visitors. The fact that they had founded a new Lodge just months prior to the union taking place may suggest that they already felt uncomfortable with the prospect of what must have been a well-signalled change. Being already reluctant to take part in the union, the inexorable progress of change, including the potential of a new shared home for all Lodges in the city, cannot have made them any less apprehensive about their future. Maybe the allowance of their application for renaming, granted by the Duke of Sussex in March 1817, was a political move by the Grand Master to reduce any feeling of alienation amongst their numbers. In such an atmosphere, the presentation to a previously Antients Lodge like Royal Sussex of an entirely new concept for their ceremonial would have produced a pivotal moment for the members, for once they moved forward on that basis, which they did, there was no going back.

One of the peculiarities of Royal Cumberland Lodge is that it still uses essentially the workings presented by Thomas Dunckerley in 1784. The Lodge never adopted the new ceremonial, and there is evidence in their correspondence during 1817 of their avoidance of receiving a visit from a representative of the new Lodge of Instruction. With Royal Sussex Lodge having made so difficult a decision on their part, it can only have rankled with their members that the senior Lodge in the city, and in the Province, decided not to follow suit.

The building was not dedicated on completion, due to the non-availability of the Duke of Sussex, who had been officially invited to perform the ceremony, and had graciously accepted earlier that year. A serious illness suffered by his mother, Queen Charlotte, would cause a delay of almost a year before the dedication ceremony could go ahead. So the Lodges made use of the lower room in the intervening period, after it was opened at the end of September 1818. That ceremony was conducted by Rev. John Portis, Chaplain of Lodge of Perfect Friendship, Royal Cumberland's new Master, Robert Payne presiding, assisted by Thomas Whitney. Royal Cumberland held its first meeting there on 9th October 1818, followed by the other two Lodges later the same month. Royal Cumberland Chapter joined them a month later, but Antiquity Encampment would not take up residence until July 1820, more than nine months after the dedication.

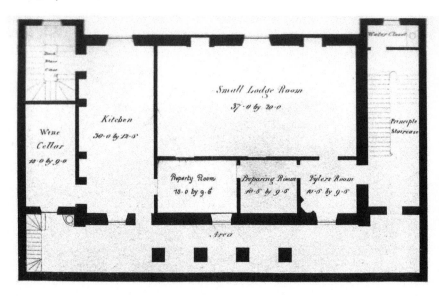

Freemasons' Hall Lower Floor Plan. *Bath Masonic Hall Trust*

The official invitation for the dedication had been issued to the Duke by Thomas Pitter, secretary of Lodge of Perfect Friendship, on behalf of the event stewards; this appeared to be against protocol, which dictates that the senior Lodge using a Hall is responsible for making such arrangements. However Pitter, a high-class lacemaker, had a connection to the Royal Family in that his patrons were Queen Charlotte and the Princess Elizabeth, the Duke's mother and sister respectively. Connections were all important in those days and Pitter had every opportunity to ask his Royal patrons for a favour, as he was heavily involved in the preparations for the Princess' wedding later that year to Prince Frederick of Austria, both ladies making an official Royal visit to Bath in late 1817.

According to a passage in Egan's 'Walks through Bath' published in 1819, features of the Hall included: *On the top of the building are three figures extremely well executed, figures of Masonry. On the left corner is Faith, in the centre Charity with an infant, and on the right Hope. On the architrave is the inscription - Freemasons' Hall AL 5817.* The statues have long since disappeared, but the evidence for their existence includes the original drawings and the special medal struck for the dedication in 1819.

The front windows are shown blanked-out on Wilkins' drawing. Several architectural historians have proffered, over the years, that they were opened-up when the building was later sold to the religious society. This was based on an assumption that, while the Lodges were using the building, the secrecy of the Fraternity would have dictated this. However, the contemporary aquatint which is used for the front cover of this book shows the front windows fully-glazed and the portico incorporating Masonic symbology on the pediment. The symbols and Masonic date were later replaced by the single date '1842' that appears there today, recarved by The Bethesda Chapel when they occupied the building after purchasing it at auction; this shows that the glazed windows were original and contemporary with Masonic use.

The aquatint was published in December 1818, one of a number of plates by the same artist incorporated in Egan's book, showing that the windows were glazed before the dedication ceremony. The only illustration that shows them blanked-off is that by Wilkins, which may have been an optional proposal for the facade design. Every other drawing shows the windows glazed, including the relief on the special medal struck for the dedication in 1819. Even the original two-storey proposal, visualised by a local Freemason, had glazed windows.

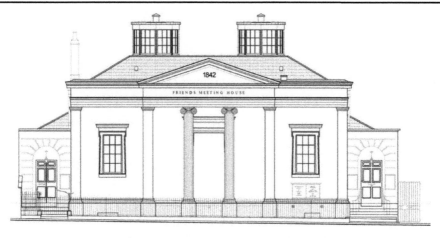

Above: Friends Meeting House showing the roof lights and open windows
Below: Wilkins' Proposed Elevation
showing the statues of the three graces and blanked-out windows
Bath Masonic Hall Trust

In contrast, there is no suggestion that the windows of the lower lodge room, where regular ceremonies were held, were ever blanked. Those windows would have been far easier to look through from the exterior via the small passageway at the rear of the building, used extensively as a public alleyway to Meyler's' Print Office, which stood directly behind Freemasons' Hall until destroyed by fire in 1826.

In fact, this modern assumption by non-Masons that windows must have been blanked due to the need for secrecy, is a view that may have caused mild amusement among Freemasons of the early nineteenth century, when an internal shutter would have served the same purpose, as was the case when utilising rented rooms of Inns and Hotels.

Dedication

The dedication of the building was conducted on Thursday 23rd September 1819 by the Duke of Sussex accompanied by senior officers of the United Grand Lodge of England and local Provinces. These included the Irish Grand Master, the Duke of Leinster, plus the PGMs for Gloucester, Warwick, Devon, Hampshire, Dorset, Rutland, Bristol and Somerset. Although the Duke of Kent, in his capacity as Scottish Grand Master, signified his intention to attend, he did not do so. Nevertheless this is an impressive turnout for a small provincial hall, all of whom took part in a procession through the city beforehand.

The Duke stayed in Bath for three days, the first occupied by the ceremonies surrounding the opening of the hall. There was a celebration concert and ball the following evening at the Kingston Rooms, just around the corner from the hall itself then, on the final day, Saturday, the Duke was presented with the freedom of the city by the Mayor and Corporation and given a guided tour of many of the local facilities. On the final evening, the Duke was again royally entertained with a municipal banquet at the Guildhall

The dedication ceremony and procession, as this extract from the report from the Bath Herald of 25th September 1819 shows, was quite an occasion: *The festival took place on Thursday when, the weather being extremely fine, the town was crowded with an assemblage of beauty and fashion that has not been equalled perhaps in the memory of the oldest inhabitant. There never was known so great an influx of strangers as thronged to witness this ceremony, conducted with that splendour which always characterises the processions of the honourable fraternity. The streets, at an early hour, assumed the appearance of the greatest bustle and expectation; at every window and house-top in the intended line of procession, groups of spectators of every degree, from the lady of title to the humblest domestic, were situated. The procession moved from the Guildhall, to the number of 900 brethren, decorated with different orders, emblems, ensigns and ornaments, many of them of the most elegant and costly description. They proceeded up Broad Street, and when the Royal Sussex Lodge arrived opposite the York House, the procession halted, and the brethren dividing, the Royal Grand Master passed through them to join his Grand Lodge, and walked uncovered down Milsom, Union, and Stall Streets, to the Masonic Hall in York Street, returning most graciously the salutations of the immense throng, consisting of nearly the whole population of the city and surrounding country, who delighted with the interesting appearance of the*

𝔄. 𝔏.
5819.

𝔄. 𝔇.
1819.

UNITED FRATERNITY OF
Free and Accepted Masons of England.

GRAND MEETING

FOR THE OPENING AND DEDICATION OF THE

𝕱𝖗𝖊𝖊𝖒𝖆𝖘𝖔𝖓𝖘' 𝕳𝖆𝖑𝖑,

IN THE CITY OF BATH.

To be honoured with the PRESENCE of
His Royal Highness FREDERICK AUGUSTUS

DUKE OF SUSSEX,

K. G. and M. W. G. M. of ENGLAND.

His Grace the DUKE of LEINSTER, K. P. and
M. W. G. M. of IRELAND.

His Grace the DUKE of BEAUFORT, K. G. R. W. P. G. M.
for GLOUCESTERSHIRE.

The Hon. WASHINGTON SHIRLEY, R. W. P. G. M.
for WARWICKSHIRE.

Sir CHARLES WARWICK BAMPFYLDE, Bart.
R. W. P. G. M. for DEVONSHIRE.

Sir WM. C. DE CRESPIGNY, Bart. M. P. and
R. W. P. G. M. for HAMPSHIRE.

WILLIAM WILLIAMS, esq. M. P. and R. W. P. G. M.
for DORSETSHIRE.

H. J. DA COSTA, esq. R. W. P. G. M. for RUTLAND.

W. H. GOLDWYER, esq. R. W. P. G. M. for BRISTOL.

ARTHUR CHICHESTER, esq. R. W. P. G. M. for
SOMERSETSHIRE.

*And many of the M.W. Officers of the Grand Lodge of
England, with the Officers of the several Provincial
Grand Lodges of Gloucestershire, Devonshire, Bristol,
Somerset, &c. &c.*

In addition to the above Illustrious and Noble Visiters,
His Royal Highness the DUKE of KENT, K. G. and
M. W. P. G. M. of SCOTLAND, has signified his intention of
being present, if possible.

Announcement published in the Bristol Mercury. *Bath Masonic Hall Trust*

19th Century Procession of Freemasons in Plymouth
This gives a flavour of the atmosphere at the dedication
by kind permission of B B Williams

sacred craft, gave way to them to pass unobstructed, and otherwise conducted themselves in the most orderly and admirable fashion. The ceremony was honoured with the presence of members of the Grand Lodges of England and Ireland, and of twenty-nine Provincial Grand Lodges. The line of immense length formed by these several bodies, advanced with imposing regularity, order, and solemnity; while the music, the banners, and the various emblems of the craft, heightened the effect of this magnificent sight, and added to the grandeur and animation of the scene. When the head of the procession arrived at the Hall, the Brethren divided to the right and left, for the Most Worshipful Grand Master, his Officers, the Provincial Grand Masters, &c. to pass up the centre, preceded by their banners. On the two following days, upwards of two thousand persons (chiefly ladies) paid one shilling for admission to view the Masonic paraphernalia which were displayed in due form in the hall. The public in general and the Fraternity of Masons in particular are chiefly indebted to the zeal and exertions of Mr T. Whitney, of this city, for the splendour of yesterday. It ought to be known that with him originated the first idea of erecting a Masonic Hall in Bath; in this he was ably supported by other Brothers, and it was accomplished by the spirit and liberality of Earl Manvers.

The Grand Tyler

A BAND OF MUSIC

Brethren, not Members of any Lodge, two and two
The above enumerated Lodges, according to their numbers, the
Juniors walking first

A BAND OF MUSIC

Members of the Provincial Grand Lodge of the County of Somerset, viz.

Provincial Grand Tiler
Provincial Grand Organist
Provincial Grand Sword-Bearer
Provincial Grand Superintendent of Works
Provincial Grand Director of Ceremonies
Provincial Grand Deacons
Provincial Grand Secretary
Provincial Grand Registrar, bearing the Seal of the
Provincial Grand Lodge
Provincial Grand Treasurer
Provincial Grand Chaplain
Provincial Junior Grand Warden
Provincial Senior Grand Warden

A BAND OF MUSIC

A Steward { Banner of the United Grand Lodge of England. } A Steward

Officers of the Grand Lodge of England,
The Grand Usher with his Staff
Two Grand Stewards
Grand Organist
Grand Superintendent of Works
Grand Director of Ceremonies
Grand Deacons
The Grand Secretary, bearing the Book of Constitutions
The Grand Registrar, bearing the Great Seal
The Grand Treasurer
The Grand Chaplain
Provincial Grand Masters, each preceeded by his Banner
Deputy Provincial* Grand Master for Somerset
The Pillar of the Junior Grand Warden
The Junior Grand Warden
The Pillar of the Senior Grand Warden
The Senior Grand Warden
The Right Worshipful the Deputy Grand Master

A Steward { *Visitor*, His Grace the DUKE of LEINSTER Grand Master of Ireland, preceeded by his Banner } A Steward

A Steward { The Banner of H. R. H. the Duke of Sussex, Grand Master } A Steward

Grand Sword Bearer

Two Stewards { The Most Worshipful Grand Master his Royal Highness The DUKE OF SUSSEX } Two Stewards

Two Grand Stewards

Two Stewards { The Standard of H. R. H. the Grand Patron } Two Stewards

Grand Stewards
Grand Tyler

[* *Vice* the P.G.M. absent through indisposition.]

The order of the procession gives an idea of the scale of it all. The route distance was over three-quarters of a mile which, even at a brisk walking pace, would take a good ten to fifteen minutes to traverse; at processional speed it would have taken two to three times that. With the numbers involved, the head of the parade would have arrived at the Hall well before the tail had set-off from the Guildhall. Any Brother could walk in the procession, but could not attend the dedication ceremony without a ticket. Provincial Officers were instructed: *to be in full Black Dress and to wear Cocked Hats which may be provided for the day by giving due notice of the number required. If not provided with a Grand Lodge apron you are requested to do so forthwith*

The size restrictions of the Hall itself, and of York Street, must have presented some problems. The dividing mentioned when the procession arrived at the Hall must have filled both sides of York Street along its entire length, as well as the side streets around it. The majority of the procession were not participating in the ceremony as *None but Masters, Past Masters, Wardens, and the several Provincial Grand Lodges were present at the Dedication.* So once the Duke had arrived the remainder returned directly to the Guildhall, as this description from Freemasons' Quarterly confirms: *After the ceremony of dedication His Royal Highness the Grand Master and the Brethren returned in procession*

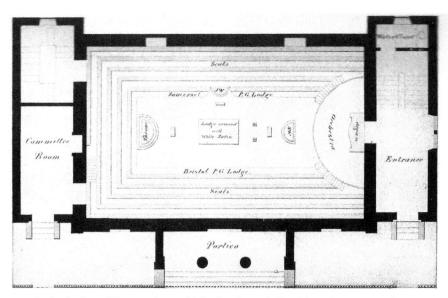

Left: Order of Procession published in the Bath Herald. *Bath Masonic Hall Trust*
Above: Plan of the layout of the Main Room for the Dedication
showing the ceremonial layout. *Bath Masonic Hall Trust*

through Church Street, Kingston Buildings, Abbey Churchyard, Wades Passage and High Street to the Guildhall, where the great body of the Brethren had previously assembled.

The interior plan shows five rows of seats on three sides. But the main room only measures fifty feet by thirty, and needed to accommodate several hundred, plus instrumentalists, banners and paraphernalia. Even at a pitch of twenty four inches (less than the tightest economy seating in a Jumbo Jet) that restricts the width of the working area to less than ten feet. There are three physical entrances into the room, at the North East and South East corners, and centrally in the west, but all three appear obstructed, including the obvious

The Duke of Sussex as Grand Master on the Throne of Solomon at Freemasons' Hall in London
The layout at the Bath Dedication Ceremony was similar to this
Bath Masonic Hall Trust

entry point in the west which seems to be blocked by the organ! In addition, the disposition and size of the furniture installed in the room needs to be taken into account.

The Master's chair in the east was placed atop a three-step platform surmounted by a canopy of red damask decorated with gold bullion swags and tags. Alongside were two bronzed coade stone guardian lions, each standing three feet high with a paw resting on a gilded ball. In front of the Master's Chair was the pedestal, flanked by two rococo pillars surmounted by celestial and terrestrial globes. In the west, the Senior Warden's chair stood on a lower platform with his pedestal in front. Between the pedestals was the enigmatically named 'Lodge covered in White Satin' and the two great pillars. These pillars are two feet square in planform which, if the drawing were to scale, makes the central Lodge artefact appear massive in size, further restricting the space between them and to either side to less than two feet each. In reality this could not have been the case, so this diagram, used in Masonic histories for a hundred years, cannot be entirely correct

A view of the empty original interior looking east helps to visualise things a little better. The space between the two doors would clearly accommodate the Master's chair arrangement; in fact the deep wainscoting would be a logical height for a three-step platform; it is therefore more likely that the Master's chair ensemble was set back against this wall. The more-recent photo of the western end shows the scale of that entrance. The squint built-in at the side of the entrance confirms that this was the main entrance door to what was originally intended to be the Lodge room. The height of the room would allow for the organ to have been installed on a raised platform above the door, a platform large enough to accommodate the instrumentalists as well.

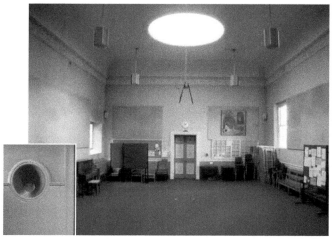

Above: Period engraving of the Main Room at Freemasons' Hall showing the entrances at the eastern end *Bath Masonic Hall Trust* **Left: Recent view of the Main Room** showing the single entrance at the western end. The inset shows the squint by the door *McLaughlin Ross llp*

79

If seating was provided, it would probably have been two or three rows either side of the Grand Master for his higher officers. As so many of high rank attended the dedication ceremony, it makes more sense for most to have stood for the duration, otherwise it would have been impossible to carry-out the perambulations which included *processing the Lodge in White Satin borne by four Tylers.*

After the ceremony, a Grand Lodge was held at the Guildhall attended by all Brethren who took part in the procession; this was

Period engraving of the Main Room at Freemasons' Hall in London
showing a large assembly standing on stepped platforms, which gives an indication that the benches shown in the plan may have been raised platforms instead. *Bath Masonic Hall Trust*

followed, at six o'clock that evening, by a dinner attended by over five hundred Brethren that continued into the early hours of Friday morning. Both were held in the banqueting hall at the Guildhall, the only location capable of holding such an attendance in the city. The dinner was a particularly successful occasion, and somewhat of a triumph for Thomas Whitney.

The Bath Herald reported comprehensively on the events during the day, but only contained a brief overview of the dinner, possibly due to there being a print deadline to meet. However, in the Bristol Mercury, published two days later, the coverage filled many columns, and included a more complete account of the part of the evening after the main guests retired: *Immediately on His Grace and the Duke of Leinster quitting the room, Brother T. Whitney was literally carried to the Chair by the rest of the Brethren, and seated amidst the acclamations of all present; who could not but recollect that it was to Brother Whitney's unremitting perseverance and strenuous exertions that the éclat of this day was owing. Brother Whitney declared his efforts, great as they might have been, were more than compensated by the brilliant result; and in the handsomest manner acknowledged the aids he had met with in the kind assistance of the Craft in general. Brother Whitney quitted the Chair at half-past twelve; but some of the brethren, under the Presidency of Brother T. Calley, prolonged their pleasures till nearly four.*

Several mementoes of the ceremony were purchasable by attendees, including an official commemorative Masonic jewel that had gone on sale the week prior so that it could be worn by Brethren attending. The jewels were produced by Robert Payne, Master of Royal Cumberland Lodge and a local silversmith who subsequently received regular Royal Patronage. There is no available record of prices or how many were issued; a silver one is on display in the Bath Masonic Museum, and another of silver-gilt set with diamonds and amethysts in the UGLE Museum in London. The latter was presented to Bro. W.C. Hayes, Grand Director of Ceremonies, demonstrating that special versions were presented to Grand Officers.

The prestige that the ceremony brought to the city was undeniable, as was Thomas Whitney's major involvement in the success, a fact borne-out by his appointment the following year to Provincial Grand Senior Warden for the second time.

Commemorative Jewel for the Dedication of Freemasons' Hall
showing the design on both sides. *Bath Masonic Hall Trust*

As the building had been in use by the three Lodges and Chapter for nearly a year prior to this marvellous occasion, normal proceedings continued afterwards much as previously. There is nothing untoward in Lodge minutes regarding the running of the building that may have forewarned of any storm to come. There are indications, however, of some of the fault lines beginning to form beneath the surface, which may have been created by the need for closer co-operation between the Lodges themselves. Having existed for so long in separate locations, and therefore independent of each other, they may have found the need to compromise in their usage of both premises and equipment more difficult than may have been envisaged. Or could these have been the first indications of friction between individual members who previously may have met only as infrequent visitors? Being Freemasons, the latter should never have been any influence on proceedings, but the times they were a-changing.

One factor that came into play was the sheer success of the enterprise. The publicity that the Fraternity received locally from the grand spectacle of the dedication, coupled with the upsurge of general confidence following the end of the protracted hostilities with France, encouraged applications for membership. The normal way of handling these would have been to allow waiting lists to lengthen, but minutes of at least one of the Lodges show that the influx was being accommodated at the expense of stability.

Lodge of Virtue, with William Underwood Whitney back in charge, trebled its membership in just three years; in response, their Secretary wrote to the Grand Secretary in London: *I am requested by several members of the Lodge to ask your opinion wither or not it would be possible for us to obtain a warrant for another Masonic Lodge in this city by Petitioning the Grand Lodge for the same, as our Lodge has become so very numerous that Harmony does not prevail in the manner in which it ought, and the zeal for Masonry seems as great as ever in Bath. If you should think it probable we shall succeed, we shall feel much obliged in your giving me the outlines how we shall proceed and likewise having your support.*

A reply came from the Grand Secretary within days: *With request to my opinion whether or not it would be likely for you to obtain a Warrant for another Lodge in Bath, it is a matter not at all competent for anyone to judge of without first seeing the Petition which must be recommended by your Provincial Grand Master in conformity with instructions contained in the Book of Constitutions. One thing I venture to predict, that you are not likely to succeed upon the statement you make, that Harmony does not prevail because, if the new Lodge is to be composed of inharmonious members, there can be little prospect of real advantage to the Craft in general. It is gratifying to learn that your Lodge increases in number. I sincerely hope it keeps pace in respectability.*

Although there had been rapid promotions in previous years due to low membership numbers, progression through Lodge offices should take several years to enable the individuals not only to gain the experience necessary before taking charge, but also to allow the members to be able to make the necessary judgement of the character involved. However, a Lodge is democratic, and the vote of a new member carries the same weight as that of a member of many years' standing.

The problems that rapid influx to a small Lodge introduces, as Geary experienced in Royal Cumberland in 1817, is that the new can rapidly achieve a position where they can outvote the old, a situation that this following letter from Lodge of Virtue to the Grand Secretary in 1821 suggests had, by then, begun to evolve: *I am directed by the W.M. of Lodge of Virtue to request that you will have the goodness to inform him as early as possible, whether a Brother is eligible to fill the Chair as Master of the Lodge, without acting as Warden twelve months, as it only says in the Book of Constitutions, that a member shall be a Warden before he can fill the situation. Our Election night takes place on the ensuing Thursday and there is two Brothers who have served the office of Senior Warden, each twelve months, and two have served the office of Junior Warden no more than two or three months. The latter imagine they are as fit to fill the Chair as those who acted as Wardens for the twelve months.*

They were not the only Lodge to be demonstrating similar trends. In 1818 alone, the recently renamed Royal York Lodge of Perfect Friendship's membership rose from twenty-five to sixty-four; by the end of 1819 it stood at ninety-two, and during 1820 a further seventeen new members arrived, although they were balanced by an equal number of resignations during that year. The amended name of the Lodge was from the acquiescence by the Duke of York to have his name appended, no doubt due to applications made by their Past Master, Thomas Whitney.

His Royal Highness would soon have cause to regret that decision.

The Financial Committee

Thus far, the only detailed references to the financing of the building have come from the original circular of 1816, and the comment in Thomas Whitney's note to the Grand Secretary. So what exactly were the pecuniary arrangements for this building?

The land on which the Hall was erected was leased from the Kingston Estate, owned by Earl Manvers. The lease was for a period of ninety-nine years, with an annual ground-rent payable for the use of the land, but no copy survives to give the names of the organisation or individuals who were the lessees. The building was erected by a local builder, Walter Harris, who was paid for his work and materials, the ownership of the completed building resting with a syndicate, of which the subscribers were also shareholders. No documentation survives from 1817 to show exactly who those original shareholders were, their individual level of investment, or what arrangements existed for their receipt of any dividend.

The Second Earl Manvers
by Henry Pickersgill. *National Portrait Gallery*

The only indication of the total size of the subscription is the original statement that *the sum required will not exceed two thousand pounds*, but there is no mention of whether that amount was to cover the bricks and mortar alone, or to include the fixtures, fittings and furniture. Neither is there any record of whether the entire sum had been raised by the time the Hall was first put into use in October 1818. The only indication as to the progress of fundraising is in the letter from Samuel Browne to the Grand Secretary in April 1817, in which he mentioned there being nearly a thousand pounds subscribed at that point, although there is no way of confirming that assertion.

Lodge Minutes during 1818 show that a Trustee was appointed from each of the three Bath Lodges taking part, a post related to the formation of the Bath Conjoint Masonic Fund, a Trust intended *to be applied in liquidation of any contingent expense and debts that may arise or be incurred beyond the annual income to be derived from the Hall.* The Trustees elected were Charles Geary for Royal Cumberland, Dr Browne-Mill for Royal York and Mr Withers from Lodge of Virtue. There is no form of deed or trust document surviving within the archives in Bath, nor any accounts for the fund, which was a separate body from the Lodges.

However, purely by chance, the minute book of the Financial Committee did survive, primarily because it contained very few minutes and, at a later date, a frugal Lodge secretary decided not to waste the paper, so used the rest of it as a notebook. It eventually found its way into Bath Masonic Museum archives and from this, together with contents of contemporary notes and correspondence from other sources, it is possible to put together a picture of the conduct of the day-to-day finances for the running of the Hall.

The Financial Committee was first convened on 15th October 1818, a week after the opening of the lower lodge room. Three representatives were seconded from each Lodge: Brothers Barton, Payne and Physick from Royal Cumberland; Brothers Ashley, Thomas Whitney and Redman from Royal York and from Lodge of Virtue, Brothers Jones, Gough and Ferrett; Robert Payne was elected Treasurer and William Redman the Secretary. A set of proposed fees were agreed at that first meeting, including each Lodge member to initially pay five shillings, then subsequently three shillings and sixpence out of quarterages. Quarterages were the annual fees paid by each Mason to his Lodge, out of which the Lodge covered its expenditure; they were termed thus as they were paid quarterly, not annually as is the case today. Additionally, the Lodges were to pay one guinea for every initiation, five shillings for every joining member and five shillings for every passing and raising of Brethren not initiated in a Bath Lodge. The same fees were payable by the Royal Arch Chapter.

Another meeting was convened a week later to formulate the charges to be levied for external lettings of rooms in the building indicating that, from the outset, there was a recognition that external income would be necessary to balance the books. At that second meeting, Thomas Whitney was elected chairman of the committee. Over the next few months, the committee met regularly, tinkering with the fee structure and adjusting Chapter fees, allowing for Chapter members to pay lower total contributions if they also belonged to a Bath Lodge.

On March 3rd 1819 a general meeting of all Lodges was convened at the Hall. Although not shown as such, this must have been the first Annual General Meeting for the Trust, as Dr. Browne-Mill took the chair. The main business was to agree the various charges for Hall usage, but there was also one change to the committee officers with the replacement of Redman as Secretary by Thomas Pitter. All Resolutions proposed by the Financial Committee were carried, except that Lodge members were exempted from paying Chapter fees, and Royal Cumberland Lodge agreed to pay double the level of the others. External lettings were to be charged as follows: *For letting Freemasons' Hall not less than one guinea be required for the use of the Hall on general occasions, and not less than Two Guineas for any Public Meeting, Dinner, &c; Five Shillings for each meeting for Bankruptcies, Sales of Estates, &c for the Morning and an additional Five Shillings for the Evening.* Once the business was completed, it was minuted that: *The Secretary should proceed to collect the Moneys from each Master of the Lodge.*

Each Mason in Bath thereby became a member of the Hall in addition to his Lodge, hence the 'joining fee' of five shillings collected directly by the committee, whereas quarterages were paid from the Lodges. Royal Cumberland's quarterages were considerably higher than those of the other Lodges, hence their agreeing to double their fees to the Hall. This higher membership cost may be one reason why their numbers were generally lower than the other Bath Lodges.

It is relatively easy to approximate the level of revenue this would have produced, based upon the membership numbers shown in annual returns for the Lodges at the time. The 'joining fee' would have yielded a one-off collection of thirty-five pounds, and the quarterages one hundred pounds per annum. As Bath was a popular place to commence a Masonic career that subsequently continued elsewhere, initiations were numerous; based on average intake, initiation fees would have boosted the income by twenty to thirty guineas per annum.

Annual income of the order of one hundred and thirty pounds should have been sufficient to cover all general expenditure, including rent. There should have been little problem in collecting the income, as the Lodges were better-off with this arrangement; individual room rents previously paid by them on a meeting-by-meeting basis to various innkeepers were nearly double what they had committed to pay for use of the Hall. Assuming that the capital expenditure for the Hall, together with its lavish fixtures and fittings, had been fully-met, this arrangement makes perfect financial sense. Having established the pecuniary basis going forward, the Financial Committee then met three times in rapid succession to put cash collection into action.

On March 17th, it was proposed that *a circular be sent to each subscriber requesting one Instalment be immediately paid amounting to One Pound five shillings per share.* This suggests that either no subscriptions had been fully paid, or that an additional call was being made on the subscribers; it also blurs the lines of responsibility, because the Financial Committee, part of the Trust, were being delegated to look after subscribers' interests. At the same meeting it was further proposed that: *the Secretary be authorised to receive the sums now due upon the quarter.* On April 7th, Secretary Thomas Pitter was: *requested to produce from the Lodges the sums now due for makings to the Financial Committee.*

After that, during the remainder of the twelve months following the AGM, only two committee meetings were held where business was conducted, on June 24th 1819 and March 27th 1820. This suggests a somewhat cavalier attitude on the part of those, such as the Treasurer and Secretary, whose prime duty it was to keep a sharp eye on the financial situation. The minutes of the March meeting are short and sweet: *In consequence of the absence of the Secretary who has failed in furnishing the Committee with the account of monies due and received by him from the different Lodges, the Committee have not been enabled to close their accounts prior to the present day.*

Three days later, on March 30th 1820, the second AGM was held. Before proceedings began the committee specifically requested that the senior Trustee, Charles Geary, take the chair. There was some disquiet with the committee's performance over the previous year, although to be fair to Whitney, he had called at least five additional meetings that were minuted as non-quorate due to there being only one other attendee. At the AGM, Geary first called upon Whitney to make his chairman's report which, according to the minutes, the meeting found to be a *very encouraging statement of the future prosperity of the undertaking.*

This is surprising, as it was probably cobbled-together quickly - just three days earlier there had been no accounts available at all. This is further illustrated by none of the amounts being shown in the minute book; in fact spaces had been left to fill them in at a later date, most of which never were. What exactly Whitney reported is not minuted if, indeed, he was able to report anything at all.

At the ensuing election of committee members only two, Barton and Redman, held-on to their positions; the new members were Patton and Turner from Royal Cumberland, Portis and Hogg from Royal York and from Lodge of Virtue Tarratt, Ardlie and Tylee. Following that change Thomas Whitney, the prime mover in the project, no longer held any position relative to the management of the building. He then proposed that, in future, the Trustees be considered as members of the committee, an indication that he recognised the necessity to assemble quorate meetings in the future. This was carried unanimously.

Pages from the Financial Committee Minute Book
showing the gaps left for later addition of the monetary amounts
Bath Masonic Hall Trust

However, Whitney's grasp, and that of some of the membership, of the developing overall scenario is best illustrated by his then proposing a vote of thanks to Captain Barton for *indefatigable & essential services rendered by him to the Committee, previous to, and after the Dedication of the Hall,* and that a Jewel to the value of five guineas be presented to Barton. The newly-elected Matthew Patton then proposed an amendment doubling the value of the award to ten guineas; both proposals were carried unanimously. To his eternal credit, Barton refused to accept the award insisting that the debt on the Hall must be first liquidated. This was agreed by the members, with the appended *hope that the Committee will soon be able to accomplish Bro. Whitney's, motion* - as opposed to Capt Barton's more realistic request. This was the first overt mention of any debt in relation to Freemasons' Hall.

At the first meeting of the new committee, after selection of officials, the following observation was made: *On the minutes of the general meeting on Thursday evening last being read they were found incomplete the receipts & disbursements of the last year not being inserted it was proposed by Bro Turner & seconded by Bro Hogg that a meeting be called on Tuesday evening next & that Bro. T Whitney & Bro Payne be solicited to attend with the particulars necessary to explain & complete the same.* The next minute also requested: *that the minute books of the three Lodges & Chapter be produced on Tuesday next & opened for the Committee to correct & perfect the list of arrears due from each Lodge to the Financial Fund.* This shows that the outgoing Secretary, Pitter, had still not furnished any accounts for the previous twelve-months; it also suggests that the Lodges were not providing the committee with statements of their indebtedness, neither had the committee established a working methodology for collecting the fees. In the end only three amounts were entered, and even those display evidence of alteration.

It is obvious that a veil was being drawn over events at that second AGM, with certain facts coming to light that the Fraternity in general did not wish to become common-knowledge. There had been no minuted meeting of the Financial Committee between June 1819 and March 1820, a long time for their eye to be taken off of the ball. A pre-occupation with preparations for the dedication ceremony at the end of September 1819 might explain the lack of meetings during the first part of that period, but subsequent to that there had been developments elsewhere involving one of the key members of the committee.

In January 1820, Royal York Lodge met to ascertain the status of their secretary, Thomas Pitter, who had not been seen in the Lodge since the previous June; in his absence they decided to examine the accounts in preparation for submitting their annual returns. It was only then they discovered that Pitter had: *never paid a farthing to the Lodge beyond his Joining Fee.* Digging deeper, they discovered a gaping hole in their funds, with a missing amount of some £118-6s in cash.

Subsequent Lodge minutes then record: *Having received a letter from the defaulter, stating the probability of his immediately leaving Bath and having no other security than his individual bond to offer, it has been decided to take immediate steps to secure his person in the hope that by his arrest, his relatives in London (who are of great respectability) might be induced to come forward and extricate him from so disgraceful a transaction. Colonel Browne gave his necessary affidavit to the Mayor's Court as to the debt due to the Lodge, so as to prevent the escape and to secure the defaulter. The Committee are, however, informed by their Solicitor that there is strong reason to suppose the defaulter has escaped.* Col. Browne was the Lodge's newly-elected Treasurer; he was not related to the previously-mentioned Samuel Browne.

It was Thomas Pitter, as secretary to the steward's committee, who had written the official invitation in 1818 to the Duke of Sussex to conduct the dedication of the Hall. Pitter's lace and jewellery business, in Bath's New Bond Street had, at that time, appeared flourishing;

PITTER's
GOLD and SILVER LACE Repository, Bath,
THOMAS PITTER, Pall-Mall, Gold and Silver Laceman to their MAJESTIES and the PRINCESS ELIZABETH, begs leave to inform the Nobility and the Publick in general, that he has opened a REPOSITORY, No. 15 GREEN STREET, where he submits to their inspection an Assortment of new and elegant articles for every description of Fashionable Dress.

Gold and Silver Tambour Threads and Twists made on a principle different from any other person; which have gained him universal approbation among the first circles of fashion.

T.P. Informs the Ladies that the CIRCASSIAN NECKLACE and BRUNSWICK MINIATURE CHAIN, which he is the inventor of, cannot be procured but at his repository.

N.B. Every article will be sold at the same prices as in London.

Advertisement from The Bath Chronicle, November 6th 1800

however his history was somewhat murkier. In 1792 he joined his father to become the fourth generation in the family business of Hill, Thomas Pitter & Son of the Strand in London, high-class lacemen and swordmakers. Within five years the business had collapsed and both father and son were declared bankrupt. This may have been due to the change in fashion away from very expensive lace in times that were made austere by the effects of the French revolution and the resulting turmoil in European politics. But for a business established for over fifty years in a prime location in the capital, such a rapid fall would suggest other factors at work.

The father, Thomas Hill-Pitter, managed to acquire a certificate of release from bankruptcy fairly swiftly by separating his affairs from those of his son. Thomas Pitter himself, however, had to wait several years before he could obtain release, which he had presumably achieved when he first arrived in Bath towards the end of 1800, setting-up his gold and silver lace repository in Green Street and advertising Royal patronage. However, he did not last more than a few months in the city, next re-emerging in the capital in 1802 with a different lace business in Jermyn Street. This was after the full five years of his bankruptcy had expired, but the new venture lasted barely a year before he was once again declared bankrupt. Lightning tends not to strike twice without reason.

He then became an itinerant seller, with advertisements appearing in Ipswich in 1803 and Derby in 1804. In 1805 he returned to Bath running Pitter's Fancy Shop in Hetling Court, just around the corner from the baths. Five years later he had moved a short distance to the more fashionable Bath Street where he was once again declaring himself as *Laceman to Queen Charlotte and Princess Elizabeth*.

By 1810, as well as the continued twin problems of being somewhat out of fashion and highly-expensive, the hand-making of lace was being marginalised by the new mechanised techniques pioneered in Devon, hence the emergence of the Luddites in opposition to this change. His business was somewhat-insulated from this by his status and the high-class, but ageing, clientele in Bath, allowing him to upgrade once again to the highly-fashionable location of Bath's New Bond Street. However, the marriage of his younger Royal patron in 1818 resulted in her leaving England to live in Austria; this was followed almost immediately by the long illness of her mother. The combined effects may have been the final straw for his Bath business.

Whereas his previous bankruptcies had occurred through there being no alternate source of finance, this time he held several positions of responsibility within organisations that had ready availability of funds. The extent to which he used those funds to alleviate his difficulties did not come to light immediately, but once matters were fully-investigated it emerged that it wasn't just Royal York Lodge that had a hole in their accounts. Having failed to apprehend Pitter, who fled the city during March 1820, it rapidly became apparent from enquiries that his relatives would not be coming to the aid of the Lodge as hoped; maybe they weren't as respectable as first thought - more likely they had revealed his less-than-impressive financial history.

Royal York Lodge reported him to Grand Lodge where, it appears from a reference to him made in 1817, he held office in the Grand Stewards' Lodge. There were two reasons for this action: the first to alert Grand Lodge to his actions, thus limiting his ability to wheedle his way into any other Lodge; the second in the hope that they may receive some high-level assistance in their quest for a settlement. The Board of General Purposes made contact with Pitter relatively quickly, sending the Lodge a proposition from Pitter's solicitor to repay the money by instalments, in return for the Lodge taking no further action against him. The reason given for Pitter's new-found liquidity was that he had recently come into an inheritance after the death of a close relative. There is no official record of such an occurrence - his closest relative, another Laceman named John Pitter whose name appeared on the lease of the premises in New Bond Street, did not die until 1829.

The Lodge replied that they would agree in principle to the offer, provided it was accompanied by a valid third-party guarantee that Pitter would honour the arrangement. Further correspondence made it obvious, however, that Pitter would be unable to find anyone willing to vouch for him, so the Lodge refused to enter into an agreement based solely on the word of an embezzler. It was almost a year before any further action occurred, when the correspondence took a strange turn after Pitter submitted a memorial to the Board of General Purposes to be remunerated for services provided during his tenure as secretary of the Lodge and of the Hall Financial Committee.

At one point, the Board wrote to Royal York Lodge expressing their disappointment that the Lodge did not find itself able to come to an accommodation based upon Pitter's claims. In an understandably indignant reply, the Lodge pointed out that they were *bound to deny that his conduct while Secretary to them entitles him to a just claim on the Lodge for remuneration, nor can they admit that he has ever been treated with cruelty by them as stated in his Memorial. We think the truth of this will be readily seen by recapitulating a few of his valuable services as an accountant and Secretary to the Lodge.* They then outlined a number of instances where Pitter had taken funds in his control for his own purposes, concluding: *He invariably denied having received any part of this total of £396-4s-0d.* This was a substantial sum of money in 1820, equivalent in disposable value to almost fifty-thousand pounds today. However, in terms of Royal York Lodge's part of it, totalling £132, that value was much higher, being essentially their entire cash assets.

Little more on this subject appears in the Royal York minutes afterwards, suggesting that nothing could be done about the losses. Pitter's activities, however, extended far beyond the Lodge, and there is little doubt that the Hall Financial Committee had been a major victim, causing a negative effect on the Hall's cashflow. One reference in Royal York's letter reads: *He received as Collector at a Salary to the Financial Committee, from shareholders for the Hall about £180, out of which he purloined £113-4s-0d by clandestinely substituting a printed receipt of his own for the Printed receipt of the Bankers who act as Treasurers.*

This shows that Pitter had access not only to the Financial Committee's funds, but also those of the subscribers to the Hall. It is impossible to know exactly how much he had spirited away, but the final figure for receipts collected by the Hall Financial Committee during the eighteen months from October 1818 to March 1820, an estimate clearly inserted in the minutes much later than it was purported to have been announced, was £821-13s-5d. This is a good six hundred pounds more than the approved Lodge and membership fees would have produced at the levels agreed.

So where could that excess have come from? Advertisements in the local newspapers give details of external lettings of the upper room after the dedication ceremony. These included, in April 1820: *Mr. Lloyd begs leave respectfully to announce his intention of giving an Evening Course of Astronomical Lectures illustrated by the Dioastrodoxon or the Grand Transparent Orrery on Monday, Wednesday and Friday, the 1st 3d, and 5th of May.* Whether such short-term events could have generated that level of income in the six months prior to the 1820 AGM is highly-doubtful.

The only other source of large revenues during the period would have been subscriptions from shareholders, but with overall expenditure during the period exceeding receipts by £7-14s-7d, a loss had been recorded in the very first year of operation. Even if that loss was ameliorated by utilising subscription moneys, nobody appears to have recognised what this heralded for the future. Regardless, it is clear from the minutes that the new committee had no idea of either what income they were due or, worse still, what outgoings they owed to their suppliers. By the end of May 1820 they had established that there was little cash in the coffers because they minuted that *an application be made to the three Lodges to advance the following sums, viz: the RC £25 & their Chapter £5 the RYL of PF & the L of V £20 towards the payment of sundry claims due against the Financial Committee.*

They received the requested amounts from Royal Cumberland Lodge and Lodge of Virtue, but no record is shown of any receipts from the Chapter or Royal York Lodge. The parlous state of the latter's finances must have precluded them from assisting and the Financial Committee minutes of July 14th indicate that: *RY of PF be requested to furnish their amounts up to June 24th without delay, the Financial Committee being unable to procure without it.* Recognition of Royal York's actual dilemma must have quickly dawned, because five days later it was minuted: *that the Committee do adjourn in order to enable the RY Lodge to furnish another correct statement up to midsummer.*

Matthew Patton was already busy on the Financial Committee, remaining a member for the next two years, during which time he was responsible for proposing a large number of the resolutions adopted. It was he that proposed Charles Geary to become chairman in 1820; Geary also took on the treasurer's job for the first few months afterwards, another indication of the committee needing an experienced and steady business hand on the tiller during a difficult period. At that time, Patton was Master of Royal Cumberland Lodge and First Principal of their Chapter, the latter also struggling to come to terms with their contributions to the Financial Committee, as the minutes of July 19th record: *the Treasurer of the RC Chapter be requested to furnish a correct statement of their account up to midsummer & that the Secretary be authorised to write to him for that purpose.*

As if the financial position wasn't difficult enough, problems began to emerge with the building itself. The July 28th minutes record: *that Bro Turner be deputed to wait on Mr Harris the builder of the Masonic Hall to explain to him professionally what the legal decisions are relative to builders when a neglect of duty or unworkmanlike method has been adopted, to inform Mr Harris that as the dry rot is in different parts of the building & occasioned by the want of proper precaution in not ventilating the floor & the committee considered him responsible.* It was nearly six months before the results of that action were available, the minutes of December 27th recording: *The following arrangement was entered into, namely that the whole of the repairs should be made good and charges one half part thereof to be paid by Mr Harris, and the other half part thereof by the Proprietors. Brother Turner submitted that though he received his authority from the Financial Committee, yet that they in fact were not competent to interfere with any matters relating to the building itself, because the members composing the Financial Committee represented in their official capacity the three Lodges in Bath, and not the Proprietors of the Building, and therefore if the Financial Committee applied a farthing of the Trust Money committed to their care to any use connected with the Building itself, they ought to have a security given to them by the Proprietors of the Building for a reimbursement thereof.*

Thus Turner focuses the lines of responsibility that had been blurred previously, providing the first clear indication that the Lodges were not the proprietors of the building; neither were the Financial Committee, who represented the Trust Fund. The repairs were accomplished without the need for the Financial Committee to commit any of their funds to the work, not that they had the cash to do so in any case, because at the next committee meeting in January 1821, it was recorded: *the following sums due from each Lodge were approved: The Royal Cumberland £56-5-0, the Royal York £163-11-11 & the Lodge of Virtue £89-12-0, from Sept 29 1818 up to Dec 25 1820.* This amounted to a total of more than three hundred pounds owing to the Hall Financial Committee in just over two years of operation, not including Royal Cumberland Chapter.

No account books survive for Royal York Lodge or Lodge of Virtue to show what payments had been made by them, and there is no indication as to what part of the Royal York debt had been accounted as paid by Pitter on their behalf, but not remitted, although it must be assumed that most would fall under that category. The account books of Royal Cumberland Lodge show that very few payments had been made by them up to January 1821, and none whatsoever before June 1820. The first payment, recorded on June 26th 1820, was for £20 in response to the appeal at the end of May; a further £10-3s was paid in November and £4-11s-6d in January 1821, making a total of £34-14s-6d.

Royal Cumberland Lodge was neither a cash-rich nor profligate Lodge. Their total income during 1818 was just £35-8s-6d, out of which they paid expenses of £32-15s, almost exclusively on charges from the Christopher Inn for rooms and meals prior to their moving to the Hall. At the end of 1818, their audited balance was just £5-19s-5d. By contrast, from 1819 the membership increased rapidly, and by the beginning of 1821, annual income had tripled, with a balance in hand in excess of sixty pounds. It is not difficult to recognise, however, that the unusually-high balance was primarily due to their not having discharged their account with the Hall Financial Committee, accounting for all but four pounds of that balance.

Yet, when the account was presented to them, it remained unpaid; in fact no further remittance was recorded as made by Royal Cumberland Lodge during the rest of 1821. All of which begs the question: why did they not discharge the debt when they had the funds to do so? The Lodge could not claim to have been unaware of the discrepancy; Geary was their appointed Trustee throughout, Payne and Barton, who were on the Financial Committee from its inception in 1818 to March 1820, were also their Master and Treasurer respectively up to the end of 1819, and Patton served on the committee from March 1820, when he was Master. This collective amnesia remains completely baffling.

But a more fundamental question has to be: if the Financial Committee was not receiving any funds from the Lodges, where was the money coming from to sustain their cashflow? It wasn't coming from external income because at the December 1820 meeting: *Capt Barton proposed that the large Room be immediately prepared to enable the Committee to let it and it was also proposed that Benches for the use of the Hall and other requisites be forthwith procured either by purchase or hire together with one or two Chandeliers for the purpose of lighting the room.*

Neither did they appear constrained in their expenditure, because in August 1820: *An estimate was given by Mr Stothert to fit up the necessary Tubing Lights & Gas Meter, the whole not exceeding Twenty Six Pounds.* The Committee therefore accepted the offer of Mr Stothert who was forthwith ordered to proceed. This despite the apparent reluctance of Earl Manvers, as recorded in Parliamentary records, to have any such installation on his land. In December it was also recorded that: *John Pallin a Carpenter who had been employed in making alterations in the Lodge Room be required to tender his account relating to the same.*

The only advertised external letting during that period shows that a Mr Flemmington, a Ventriloquist, provided: *his popular entertainment of "A Trip to Paris" for one night only on February 13th - Admission Four Shillings.* In April another Ventriloquist, styling himself as 'Senior Christopher Lee Sugg', appears to have jumped the gun and advertised his performance before he had received permission for the usage of the Hall. According to the entertainer, this had been caused by a communication-breakdown between Patton, Geary, John Ashley and William Whitney. The latter two were the other Lodge Masters at the time, but as neither held any position on the Committee, it is difficult to understand where they figure in the affair. There is no indication as to whether the entertainment took place, but what it does show is a distinct lack of management continuity at the time.

By May 1821, the situation had become serious enough to decide: *that a compleat statement be made out containing the various debts due on the Masonic Hall and laid before the shareholders & that Brothers Turner & Manners be requested to superintend it.* What emerged could not have been palatable, because in June it was decided: *it was more advisable to depute Bros Turner & Redman to apply to certain members of the three Lodges to raise the sums required to enable the Financial Committee to discharge the various claims upon the Masonic Hall in preference to calling the shareholders together.*

One wonders who those perceived benefactors may have been; they can't have been Geary, Patton or Thomas Whitney, because they were three of the four Committee members forming the quorum of the meeting, Whitney having returned to the committee when Rev. Portis withdrew. That the overtures were unsuccessful can be discerned from the next meeting, on August 13th, when the committee contained five new names, including the Master of Lodge of Virtue, Brother Ferrett. Two matters stand out from those minutes: yet another demand for payment to the financially-beleaguered Royal York Lodge, and a proposal that was accepted from Brother Spry of Royal York Lodge, seconded by Brother Payne of Royal Cumberland Lodge, for a Fellow Crafts Meeting to be convened the following week.

The Fellow Crafts Summons was not, in itself, unusual as it is the standard method by which members are called together to discuss some business requiring an urgent solution. What is significant about this one is that it was issued during the summer period, when Bath Lodges did not meet, and was sent to every member of the three Lodges at the Hall. It is not difficult to imagine what caused such a request, but when the meeting was convened it had to be immediately postponed for another week *for want of certain papers in the possession of Brother Spry.* There is no official record of what transpired at the subsequent meeting, but there is an account of it that I will come back to later.

Normal usage of the Hall by the tenant Lodges was also proving difficult in 1821, as can be judged from an advertisement placed in the Bath Chronicle over the Christmas period regarding the annual St John's Festival Dinner: *It was the intention of the Stewards to have held the Dinner at the Freemasons' Hall, but the want of accommodation for the comfort of a large party has induced them to alter their original plan, and to dine at the York House.* The only external lettings at the time were for two Astronomical Lectures by a Mr Rogers just prior to Christmas 1821, and a public meeting in early January.

There were no further minutes of the Financial Committee until March 4th 1822, when they record that: *the newly appointed Committee met, viz: Bro. Patton, Turner, Hay (RCL), T Whitney, Maddison, Manners (RYL), Tarratt, Webber, Beauchamp (LoV).* Charles Geary remained in the Chair, but three members did not attend - Turner, Hay and Manners. An audit was conducted of the accounts for the previous year, from which it was shown that all three Lodge debts had increased: Royal Cumberland to £77-16s, Royal York to £226-11s-11d and Lodge of Virtue to £114-12s. In addition, two Chapter debts were shown for the first time, a second Chapter having been started attached to Royal York Lodge during 1821. The Chapter accounts were: *the Royal Cumberland Chapter from Oct 1818 to Dec 1821 £41-12s-6d, and the Royal York Chapter from its commencement up to Dec 25th 1821 was as per acct delivered £28-7s.* This took the total tenant debt to nearly five hundred pounds.

The Hall finances were totally out of control, but there are no further entries in the Financial Committee minute book. Instead, another Fellow Crafts Meeting was held on 28th June 1822, where proposals were presented by Brother Spry that brought the matter into public focus.

Tontine

The first outward indication of the gathering storm was the issue, in late June 1822, of a tontine to raise a total of four thousand pounds. This had been the subject of the second Fellow Crafts Summons resulting in the meeting of 28th June 1822, which was not minuted. The tontine had been originally proposed by Dr Spry at the previous Fellow Crafts meeting in August 1821, but failed to gain any support. Nearly a year later, with the financial position worsening, a situation arose that triggered the intervention of Earl Manvers.

Now illegal, a tontine was effectively a public lottery where the deeds to a building were the prize, the proceeds from the ticket sales being used to provide the full purchase price to the owner as soon as the subscription was filled. The methodology for this particular kind of wager allowed each ticket purchaser to nominate the life of someone known to them, and the winner would be the owner of the ticket that named the last of the nominees remaining alive. There is an original copy of the tontine document in the Bath Masonic Museum archives, and the contents are provided in full in Appendix 1. It reveals that, in this particular raffle, the lower age limit for nominees was set at sixty years, in order to accelerate the cause of the successful ticketholder.

From an account of the 1821 meeting, it emerges that the fundraising was intended to clear a total debt of £3780 accumulated since the project commenced in 1817. It is, therefore, worth examining quite how such a huge sum came to be expended, nearly double the original budget of £2000.

The Lodges had run up debts to the Hall Financial Committee of over five hundred pounds covering general running costs. Even if some had the intention to pay those off, it is doubtful they had the ability at this juncture. If the Hall was to be passed into new ownership, which in effect is what would occur once the tontine

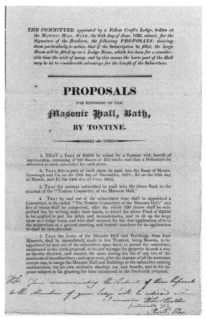

Tontine Document front page
Bath Masonic Hall Trust

was completed, then the original shareholders would need their investment returned, quoted as being around one thousand pounds, although the meeting records it as little more than four hundred.

So where had all of the cash come from, not only to sustain the running of the building for four years, but also to cover this shortfall in the original financing? Nothing is shown in Lodge or committee minutes, but the picture becomes clearer through an independent report produced by two members of Royal York Lodge of Perfect Friendship, Edmund English and Joseph Spry, which was printed and circulated to their members in January 1824.

One of the authors, Dr Spry, was instrumental in launching the tontine, so would have had insight into what had been occurring over the previous few years; English, an auctioneer in Bath, also had a good grasp of one of the causes of the debacle, because among the revelations in Royal York's 1820 letter to Grand Lodge is that Pitter had: *collected upwards of £90 for a member of the Royal York Lodge (Bro. English) who employed him confidentially, and he kept the whole of it except £10 lately paid.*

This report, the full contents of which are in Appendix 1, has nestled in a file of Bath correspondence at the Museum of Freemasonry at Grand Lodge for many years. It fundamentally alters the perception of Geary's role in the debacle and also reveals that he had originally opposed the entire enterprise, not thinking it likely to succeed. He was later persuaded to change his mind and become a Trustee, a decision he must ultimately have viewed with deep regret. It also raises the veil covering the initial funding of the project, for it was the second Earl Manvers who became the main financier, although it is doubtful that was ever his intention.

Based on the original plan to raise the cost of the building by private subscription his father, the first Earl Manvers, had agreed in 1816 to lease the land to the Lodges for a ground rent of £14-10s per annum; he died just weeks after they had voted to go ahead with the project. Although his ancestral seat was in Nottinghamshire, he had inherited the Kingston Estates, including several acres of prime land in the centre of Bath, essentially consisting of the Abbey grounds granted by Henry VIII at their dissolution in 1535. This inheritance came via his mother, sister of the last Duke of Kingston, when that Duke died childless in 1780. It is this connection that also explains the involvement in the project of William Wilkins, who was architect to the Kingston Estate.

The highly-conservative first Earl would never have allowed such a project on his land if improperly-financed by the lessees, but his son was somewhat more enthusiastic to maximise return on assets When the subscriptions from Lodge members proved sluggish, he agreed that the Kingston Estate would advance a thousand pounds to allow building work to continue while remaining subscriptions were collected. This explains how the original budget was covered - a combination of private subscriptions and the Earl's loan. Had the budget been achievable, and subscriptions raised in a reasonable time, then the project would have started on a sound financial basis.

But it didn't and, worse still, once it emerged that the loan could not be repaid quickly, no decision was taken as to how it was to be serviced. As this was a form of short-term bridging-finance, the interest rate was higher than would have been obtained by mortgaging the project. Although the loan enabled the building to be completed and put into use, it would eventually emerge that neither the subscribers, the Financial Committee or any of the Lodges or Orders had paid a penny of interest to the Earl during the entire period since its advancement in 1817. English and Spry estimated this interest alone amounted to £480. Neither had any ground rent been paid during the same period, so the total owed to the Earl rose to £1550, including the original capital advanced. That is what brought the knock on the door from the Earl's bailiff bringing matters to a head in 1822.

The debt, however, did not fall on the Financial Committee or the Lodges, but on the original subscribers . It is they who were looking for a way of not only getting rid of what had become a millstone around their necks, but also to minimise their losses in doing so. Reading the contents of the tontine, two things stand out: firstly clause 14, forcing the winner to *immediately grant a lease of the whole to the Masters of the Three Lodges for the time being,* meaning that this tontine was essentially offering a form of sale and leaseback agreement. However, this was a form of lottery with a prize that possessed a monetary value. The vast majority of winners of tontines immediately sold their new possession to realise the cash locked into it, a fairly easy thing to do as the prize normally came with vacant possession. However, this one came with sitting tenants and, worse still, tenants with a poor payment record. While this may have proved attractive to a professional investor, it is doubtful it would have appealed to a private individual, which could be a major reason why it was undersubscribed.

The second is clause 15, allowing the winner to *take possession of the Masonic Hall and Buildings, but not of the jewels, paraphernalia, and furniture of the Lodges and Chapters, which shall be deemed and declared to be the property of the Lodges and Chapters respectively.* Although this appears to give a separate ownership status to these items, the wording is curious as they would only be *declared to be the property of the Lodges and Chapters* at the conclusion of the lottery, which suggests that they were not owned by them at the time of the declaration of the tontine.

It also emerged from the report that additional responsibility for the debt fell on two individuals who had stood personal surety to the Earl on both the Lease and Loan documentation - Charles Geary and Thomas Whitney. It is no surprise that the Earl's lawyers would have required some form of additional guarantee from gentlemen who could prove their financial independence. It is doubtful these two had envisaged such an outcome when they took on that burden, but would have had no doubt their Brothers would come to their aid if it did

Even so, the sum owed to the Earl was less than half the total needed to be raised by tontine; so where had that additional debt arisen from? According to the Rate Books in the Bath City Archives, nobody paid a penny in local taxes on the building between 1817 and 1823. There must also have been trade debtors who stood exposed as suppliers to the Financial Committee, their bills being held awaiting settlement of the Lodge rental invoices. The proprietors themselves were expecting rent to be paid by the tenants, via the Financial Committee, the level of which may be gauged from the tontine where the ultimate new owner would lease them the building *at a net annual rent of £100, the Lodges doing all repairs, and paying all rates, taxes, and outgoings whatsoever.*

If the rent expected to be paid to the original proprietors had been set on a similar level, even if that and the local taxes were added to the level of Lodge indebtedness to the Financial Committee, it still leaves more than a thousand pounds unaccounted for. What this had been spent on cannot be known without any accounts to hand, but some at least must be due to the fraudulent activities of Thomas Pitter.

Nevertheless, one cannot but marvel at the level of optimism displayed in 1822 by all involved, because if it wasn't sufficient to be indebted to a level that would ruin the majority of the membership, they also wished to raise an additional: *£1,000 towards the expense of elevating the Hall.* The preamble to the tontine refers to: *the large Room* *will be fitted up as a Lodge Room, which has been for a considerable time the wish of many, and by this means the lower part of the Hall may be let to considerable advantage for the benefit of the Subscribers.* A thousand pounds is a considerable sum for just fitting-out one room, so as the term *elevating the Hall* is used, this must have been another grand plan to add the extra storey to bring the building more in-line with the original proposal. No drawings exist to show what exactly was intended, but it was recorded that the Committee: *had the ready consent of Earl Manvers to any improvements that might be made at the Masonic Hall.*

What made this so fanciful a notion, bearing in mind the overall predicament of the enterprise, is the further presumption: *that £780 would be allowed by the proprietors to stand over till it could be conveniently paid, subject to interest until it was liquidated.* The law governing tontines did not allow any encumbrance to remain on an asset once fully-subscribed, so had the process been successful, the stand-over would not have been legal. Regardless, the organisation had patently failed to raise more than five hundred pounds by subscription in five years, so an expectation that it could suddenly find the means of raising half as much again in less than a year by a similar method, appears barmy!

The tontine document also explodes another historical myth, because not only did the tontine fail due to the required subscriptions falling far short those needed to make it valid (only 52 of the 200 shares being subscribed), far from Charles Geary loading the dice in his favour it records that he purchased just two shares for himself. Earl Manvers, the actual landowner, bought more than the apparently avaricious Geary, and the fact that the Earl subscribed to the tontine shows that he must have stayed his demands on the proprietors in anticipation of its success. Thomas Whitney also purchased two shares, but the glaring omission from the list of subscribers was one of the leading members of the Financial Committee at the time, Matthew Patton.

The tontine effectively bought the Financial Committee a year in which to not only promote it and ensure a full subscription, but also to collect-in enough of the outstanding fees from the Lodges to at least clear some of the indebtedness and give a further chance of success if it fell short of target. That they did none of this is shown by the distinct lack of committee meetings between July 1822 and March 1823. Once again it appears that they just sat back and awaited the inevitable success of the scheme. The Lodges continued to use the Hall, but as far as payments are concerned, the Royal Cumberland Lodge account book shows a meagre ten pounds paid during that time; however, this wasn't due to their sitting on funds - their audited balance at June 1823 stood at less than five pounds. Minutes of the final Financial Committee meeting on March 10th 1823 record one receipt - Charles Maddison paying just under twenty pounds towards the Royal York account.

It must have been obvious by the time the second tontine instalment became due on March 25th 1823, that contributions had fallen far short of expectations. The only record that exists bearing that date is the document of assignment transferring ownership of the Hall to Charles Geary, and permitting him to take-over the lease for the land. Far from the later intimation that Geary had 'rigged the raffle' to his benefit, the tontine had failed, and with it had gone the last chance for the Fraternity to escape the huge indebtedness that had accrued.

English and Spry record the true events: *Brothers Geary and Whitney having become security for the original £1000 loan, neither principal or interest of which had been paid from the period of its advancement, Earl Manvers came to the resolution of legally proceeding against the above Brethren, the fear of which induced Brother Geary to take the premises on his own shoulders, most probably with the ultimate loss of more than £1000.* That thousand pound loss is the difference between the debt from the account books and the declared debt to be cleared by the tontine process. It is thus revealed that it was Charles Geary who had been bankrolling the enterprise.

This development must have come as a great relief to Thomas Whitney who, although also a successful businessman, clearly did not have the substantial personal resources available to Geary. When the bailiff's knock had first come in 1822, he must have contemplated potential personal ruin. It would therefore be fair to assume that he would have held no malicious feelings towards the Masonic Brother that had so generously relieved his financial embarrassment. How he would feel about those that had caused it, however, was a different matter.

Neither could this have been an easy time for Geary, already in the shadow of the death of his young second wife, Mary, at the end of 1821, followed closely by that of his elder brother, John, just weeks later in January 1822. Left without their constant support, and with his own business to run, it is not surprising that his Lodge attendance, previously so regular, became sporadic as developments surrounding ownership of the Hall unfolded. By the time he took full possession, his Lodge and Chapter attendances were virtually non-existent.

Although English and Spry avoided speculating as to how the situation had developed, in a very fair and even-handed account they did specifically note that in their examination of the hall accounts: *every sixpence has been appropriated to the payment of various debts, salaries, furniture and ornaments of the Lodges.* They made it clear that they had no idea how their own Lodge was going to settle its share of any outstanding debt, but believed that Geary had acted in good faith in relieving the entire Bath Fraternity of an embarrassing situation, concluding with the statement: *As a great deal of misrepresentation has gone abroad on this subject, the undersigned Brothers suggest the propriety of printing the above statement, that every member may be furnished with a copy, and that the Provincial Grand Master be requested to convene a meeting of the three Lodges, that this matter may be finally settled and that Peace brotherly Love and Harmony may again be restored within the precincts of the various Lodges in Bath.* I suspect from that wording that the report was printed so that it could be circulated amongst the members of the other Lodges as well. If it was, one can only speculate as to why this direct appeal unfortunately fell on deaf ears, both in Bath and wider afield.

In the light of some of the revelations thus far, it is probably no great surprise that the project failed. The finances were more founded upon dreams than reality, and there were factions already forming within the membership, fed by personal differences that were not obvious until later ignited into dissension. Added to this tinder box was the short reign of the new PGM, a country gentleman reformer with little sympathy for the society nature of Bath, and personally selected by the Grand Master in London to replace another reformer, who had been initially popular in Bath, but was then hounded out of post.

Col. Kemeys-Tynte's apparent lack of response to the appeal in the English & Spry report may indicate that he had decided not to have his fingers burned again in Bath, and that his political nous had evolved sufficiently to recognise the need to keep a reasonable distance between such matters and his office. Or maybe he simply concluded that it was just as well that Freemasons' Hall was in the ownership of a Bath gentleman with both the adequate resources to maintain it, and the Masonic experience to provide the necessary stability for a Bath Fraternity not averse to making waves.

Whether that was the view of all of the members locally would soon become apparent, as the ripples created by the Hall debacle began to spread across the entire Masonic community.

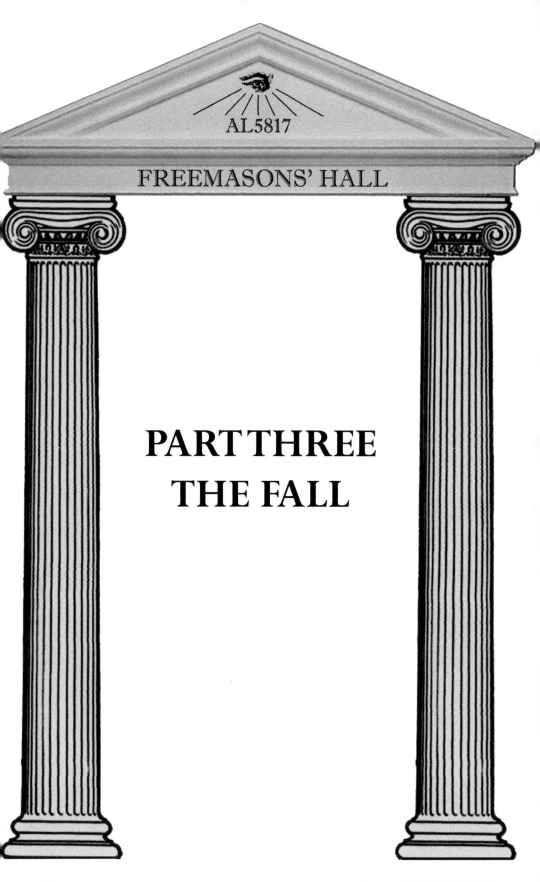

FREEMASONS' HALL

AL5817

PART THREE
THE FALL

Assignment

At the point the tontine was set-up, the total debt accrued by the various participants had reached £3780. By applying official government inflation over the intervening near-200 years this would equate to a sum in excess of £310,000 today.

The state of the finances of the individual Lodges and Orders at that time showed that it was doubtful that they could even assemble the odd eighty pounds of that debt between them - the entire financial position was dire. One would hope the tontine figure included sufficient funds to cover the expenditure between launch and completion, in which case the debt at the time the tontine collapsed was, presumably, no higher than calculated.

The emergency meeting of the Hall Financial Committee that was called in March 1823 was attended by six members: Capt. Maddison (as Master) and Manners representing Royal York Lodge of Perfect Friendship, Tarratt (as Master), Govey and Hayes Jr representing Lodge of Virtue, plus Charles Geary as Trustee and Chairman. It is pertinent that the heads of at least two of the tenant bodies were in attendance, but that Matthew Patton, as the head of three others, was not. Neither were there any representatives of Royal Cumberland Lodge or Chapter there, because Geary was no longer attending either regularly, so they could not have expected feedback from him. This is such a glaring absence from a vital meeting, that it suggests some form of boycott. If so, it has to be asked - to what end?

At that meeting Geary announced his offer to resolve the situation by personally relieving the organisation of all outstanding debt. In return, he would take over all of the assets, which would have included ownership of the building and the right to collect any outstanding rents owed by tenants. There can have been little resistance, because the legal papers were drawn up within three weeks and on March 25th 1823 the remaining shareholders signed away all of their rights, the pertinent clauses in the release document being:

Charles Geary of the City of Bath Wine Merchant hath proposed to the several persons parties hereto That if all the Subscribers to the said building will execute such Release and Discharge as hereinafter contained and permit him the said Charles Geary to obtain a lease of the said Building from Earl Manvers (the ground landlord thereof) to and for the absolute use and benefit of him the said

Charles Geary He the said Charles Geary will obtain such lease and pay off all the debts and incumbrances affecting the said building Save and except the sums of money subscribed by the Subscribers towards the erection of the said Building.

And further Know Ye That we the said parties hereto and each and every of us Do hereby assign release and quit claim unto the said Charles Geary his executors administrators and assigns All Estate right Title Interest Claim and Demand whatsoever both at Law and in Equity or otherwise howsoever of us and each and every of us of into or out of the said Building and premises called the Masonic Hall and all their right members and appurtenances To the end intent and purpose That the said Charles Geary may obtain a Lease of the same Building and premises to and for his own absolute and exclusive use and benefit.

The full contents of the document are provided in Appendix 1. One of the most striking differences to the tontine contents is the lack of any clauses in this one covering separate ownership of the contents of the building, or compelling Geary to lease anything back to the Lodges.

There were a total of forty signatories who between them surrendered five-pound shares to the total value of £505-19s-0d. Nineteen, including Thomas Whitney, Baron Brown-Mill, Reverend Portis and George Manners, wrote-off double-figure investments of up to fifty pounds each, the remainder small sums; among the smallest was Matthew Patton, who lost £2-10s, essentially half a share. In all of the attempted schemes to finance or save the hall, that was the only sum of money Patton is registered as having personally given towards the project; it was also less than half of the additional sum Patton himself had proposed two years earlier simply for a gift to someone who had served but a year on the committee.

Over the next two weeks, Geary had the 94-year balance of Earl Manvers' lease signed over to his personal liability, in return for which he repaid the Earl's entire loan capital, the unpaid interest on the loan, plus six-years' unpaid ground-rent, in total more than fifteen-hundred pounds. He then advised the Lodges and Chapters that he wished to enter into early negotiations with them, firstly to assess their balances of accumulated unpaid rent from the previous five years, and secondly to enter into legal agreements for their tenancies going forward.

But it was not just the Hall Financial Committee that were having to face-up to increasingly-embarrassing financial problems. Royal York Lodge were the worst effected, through the previous fraudulent activity of Thomas Pitter; and it was Thomas Whitney who had handled much of the fallout from that as Secretary to the Lodge. There are no records available for the Royal York Chapter created in 1821, but Thomas Whitney had been prominent in obtaining the Charter for that Order. His brother William had recently vacated the chair of Lodge of Virtue in favour of Thomas Tarratt, who was also encountering problems surrounding the actions of another previous Master, and Hall Financial Committee member, Elias Ferrett.

With the exception of Royal Sussex Lodge, who remained detached from the entire Hall scenario and appear to have survived fairly well without it, the other Lodges and their allied Orders essentially fitted into two distinct camps, one containing Royal York Lodge of Perfect Friendship, its newly-attached Chapter plus Lodge of Virtue, all under the general influence of the Whitney brothers, the other comprising Royal Cumberland Lodge, its attached Chapter and Antiquity Encampment of Knights Templar, all headed by Matthew Patton.

Antiquity Encampment did not to move to the Hall until 1820, previous to which they shared the Greyhound Inn with Royal Sussex Lodge and its own new Royal Arch Chapter, formed in 1818. John Dixon, the Eminent Commander from 1811 to 1813, had been the prime mover in reviving the Encampment in 1811, following a period when the Warrant had remained dormant. He had also been the first Master of Royal Sussex Lodge, originally founded as an Antients Lodge in 1812 by long-standing Atholl Masons, so the Encampment's revival may well have been achieved under the same auspices.

There are large gaps in the minutes of Antiquity Encampment, but the period of time they used the Hall is covered, revealing a fairly turbulent course of events over the two years preceding their taking-up residence at the Hall, during which time Patton essentially usurped control from Dixon. These events will doubtless produce echoes in the mind of the reader as the story progresses but as, like other parts of the story, they are fairly convoluted, I have covered them separately in Appendix 4, in order that the main story can proceed.

Matthew Patton had left the Hall Financial Committee when the tontine was called. His opposition to that process is clearly-shown by the omission of his name from the list of subscribers, and although his views are not apparent in any of the minutes from the tontine period, they emerge in later correspondence to the PGM and Grand Lodge, when he ascribes the Fraternity's problems in Bath as being due to: *the very disorganised and distracted state into which the Conduct of those individuals more immediately concerned in the Speculations of the Bath Masonic Hall had left the comparatively few subscribing Brothers and Companions.*

There is some evidence within Lodge minutes that, throughout his Masonic career, Patton's overall grasp of business and financial matters were perhaps not his greatest ability. There are a couple of early entries where Patton is reminded of his need to clear his account covering wine consumed at meetings, which he appears to have overlooked for several months; he did, however, settle these promptly when reminded, suggesting that he may have been more absent-minded than financially-embarrassed. However, a much clearer indication of the other-worldliness he possessed with regard to financial matters is provided by the minute and treasurer's books for Royal Cumberland Chapter, the order he effectively controlled for over twenty-five years.

On February 22nd 1822, the Chapter minutes proudly announce the following: *The Most Excellent Companion Patton reported that he had waited upon Companion Redman, Treasurer, respecting the finances of this Chapter and also for the purpose of assisting in auditing the accounts of the same for the last three years. The accounts were minutely examined together with all vouchers, found to be perfectly correct and duly signed. Companion Redman (being present) expressed the pleasure he felt in announcing to the Chapter generally the very flourishing state of its funds, having proposed to be discharged all arrears due to the* [Hall] *Financial Committee together with other open demands a balance appears in favour of the Royal Cumberland Chapter - in cash, quarterages and fees due - of upwards of* **One Hundred Pounds.** The last three words are written larger in the minutes to add emphasis.

Examination of the Treasurer's book, however, indicates that reality was vastly different; the audit entry for February 20th, countersigned by Patton, states that the balance was actually £24-0s-2d, less than a quarter of that declared in open Chapter two days later. As that was an emergency meeting, scheduled just weeks before the fateful meeting of the Hall Financial Committee that resulted in the launch of the tontine, it suggests some form of political manoeuvring.

The Chapter Treasurer's books show that in the thirty-five years it had existed, it rarely held balances much in excess of twelve pounds; neither did it make or hold any long-term investments. So Redman's claim, and Patton's confirmation, should have been met with some degree of incredulity, if only from those that had held the Treasurer's post previously. Prior to the Chapter moving to Freemasons' Hall in 1818 from the White Lion, where the Landlord's bill averaged just under £1 per meeting, it had settled all outstanding bills promptly and regularly, so it had no cashflow problems that could have caused it embarrassment going forward, particularly as moving to the Hall provided reduced fees overall. In terms of what had actually been paid to the Hall Financial Committee, there are just three entries in the Chapter account book between October 1818 and February 1822:

August 13th 1819 - *Paid the Financial Committee of this Hall for contributions from the Chapter on 20 exaltations and 2 joining from the first meeting in the Hall on 10th November 1818 to this - £22-1s-0d*

January 9th 1821 - *Paid Companion Geary on account of fees due to the Financial Fund up to the 1st Jan 1821 (being £15-3s-0d) - £11-5s-0d*

February 11th 1822 - *Paid Companion Geary on account of money due from this Chapter to the Financial Committee - £4-14s-6d*

The total of just over £38 covered a period of occupation exceeding four years at an average of under ten pounds a year.

It wasn't just the Chapter that was suffering from financial delusion at the time. On April 4th 1823, little more than a week after the assignment had been completed, Royal Cumberland Lodge minuted: *it appears that in the proportion of such receipts the Lodge in account with the Finance Committee accruing to the generally accepted plan stands indebted in the sum of £67-9s-0d to Xmas last. On the other hand, the Lodge by various Cash payments stands Cr with the Committee in the sum of £69-17s-6d leaving a balance in favour of this Lodge of   . The said acct having been minutely examined by the WM & Treasurer.* The space is not an error in this book, it is yet another gap in a minute book left for the later recording of an amount that had not been calculated before the meeting took place. In addition, the *WM and Treasurer* quoted as having *minutely examined* the accounts were one and the same person - Matthew Patton.

What the Chapter remittances illustrate is that it was no longer paying for its accommodation regularly, as it had done when resident at the White Lion, and that it had been in arrears almost throughout its Hall tenancy. Although very few records of the Financial Committee have survived the passage of time, they do include two statements of indebtedness, the one on March 4th 1822 stating: *Royal Cumberland Chapter, £41-12s-6d.* This shows that just weeks after the last of those three recorded payments from the Chapter, it still owed more than forty pounds; worse still, from that date it paid not a penny more to the Hall, despite occupying it for a further eighteen months.

At the same Chapter emergency meeting where the claim of a three-figure balance was made, it was also minuted: *Companion* [William] *Whitney in a handsome address gave notice of his intention at a future meeting, and in conjunction with several other members, to propose that a handsome consideration be voted to the Most Excellent Companion Patton for his very great attention and constant laborious duties he has for so many years devoted to the Welfare, Improvement and Instruction of the Royal Cumberland Chapter, to which Companion Redman* [the Treasurer] *united in bearing testimony to the Long and Valuable Service of the Most Excellent Companion and declared his intention to giving support to such consideration at a more numerous meeting, which the present flourishing state of the Chapter Funds would admit of.*

At the next meeting on 4th March 1822, Redman proposed: *that a Piece of Plate of the value of Twenty Guineas be presented to Companion Patton which proposition was immediately seconded by Companion Bury, and the sense of the Chapter being looking the same way was carried unanimously, the choice of such piece of plate to be left to Companion Patton as might be most agreeable to his wishes.* To put this in context, twenty guineas was the equivalent of a year's wages for a skilled labourer in 1822; it is significant that William Whitney neither proposed nor seconded the motion he had previously put forward. The gift was purchased on May 9th, after which the Chapter's cash balance was just £6-5s-2d; the plate was presented on July 23rd.

This was not the only presentation that Patton received in that year; there was the strange sequence of events surrounding his being awarded another piece of plate by Royal Cumberland Lodge, also in recognition of his services to them. On his leaving the chair of the Lodge early in 1822, the minutes record: *A committee was appointed to ascertain the state of the funds of the Lodge in order to allow the Lodge an opportunity of presenting to Bro. Patton, a handsome piece of Plate, and that an urgent appeal be made to every Member who stands indebted to pay up their arrears without delay.* The following month, having received the full report of the sub-committee: *it was agreed to adopt the further suggestion that Twenty-five Guineas should be allocated for the presentation to Bro. Patton and that an additional Five Guineas should be obtained by voluntary subscription.*

The sub-committee also reported that: *the accounts of the ex-treasurer, Bro. Stroud, were audited and found correct, and the sum of £27-6s-2d was handed over to the new treasurer, Bro. Tarratt.* This would suggest that the membership had voted to utilise all but £1-1s-2d of their total available funds towards the presentation, at a time when the building they were occupying was on the point of total financial collapse.

A general meeting of all Lodges was assembled on April 18th 1822 to consider the overall financial situation at the Hall. The very next evening, April 19th, the piece of plate was presented to Patton by the new Master of Royal Cumberland Lodge, John Morris. The inscription read: *Royal Cumberland Lodge, No.55, in grateful testimony of zealous and indefatigable exertions to promote the Honour and Interest of this Lodge as a standing mark of merited worth and as a token of fraternal esteem THIS PIECE OF PLATE was unanimously presented to Bro. M. Patton, PWM by this Lodge on the 19th day of April, 1822, and of the era of Masonry 5822. Masons on the square of duty, Fill the social Goblet up; Drink, for Wisdom, Strength and Beauty, All unite to pledge the Cup.*

Just how surreal this was in the circumstances prevailing is revealed when, just two months later, a circular was received from Provincial Grand Lodge requesting donations towards a similar testimonial presentation to the previous Deputy PGM, Dr Henry Sully of Wiveliscombe. A proposition was made to contribute five guineas, but when it became apparent that insufficient funds were available to meet that, Charles Geary proposed the sum be two pounds instead. Even that proposal was lost, and eventually it was agreed to send a letter stating that: *in consequence of the embarrassed state of the Lodge funds, owing to the Building of the Masonic Hall, and other circumstances, it was not possible for the Lodge to contribute towards the purchasing of the piece of Plate to be presented to Bro. Sully, although at the same time this Lodge duly acknowledges the services rendered by Bro. Sully as DPGM.* It is already too apparent what those 'other circumstances' were.

Dr Sully was surgeon to the Duke of Cumberland, who was later to become King Ernest Augustus I of Hanover. He was a very popular DPGM, and was unanimously nominated by all of the Lodges in the Province to succeed as PGM after Lt. Col. Smith-Leigh's death in 1813, but was eventually passed-over for the post when the Duke of Sussex selected Arthur Chichester in 1817; Chichester, recognising that wide support, immediately appointed Sully his deputy. When Chichester was forced to resign three years later, the Lodges again looked to Sully as successor, but he made it clear that he no longer wished to be considered.

Provincial minutes show that Thomas Whitney was particularly active in the collection of subscriptions for Sully's testimonial, and his local knowledge would have meant that he was well aware of the distinct contrast to the recent generous award by Royal Cumberland Lodge to a member of barely three years' duration. The following month, Royal Cumberland Lodge minutes record that: *In reference to the resolution relative to Bro. Sully, Bro. Geary again urged the necessity of the Lodge contributing towards the purchase of a piece of Plate for Bro. Sully, when the WM put the question, and it was agreed by a majority of the members that Two Pounds should be given from this Lodge.* A majority, rather than unanimous, vote in support of a repeated recommendation from a long-standing and senior member speaks for itself.

On top of his previous performance at the Trust AGM regarding the proposed doubling of the amount to be spent on Barton's jewel, Patton's acceptances of presentations to a value way above the gifting organisations' current financial capabilities indicates a somewhat laissez-faire approach to financial matters that should have brought his ability to independently audit anything into some question. That image was not improved by his appointment as Chapter Treasurer in 1823, at around the time that the tontine failed. To be fair, he inherited a fairly dire position, with a balance of just £1-18s-11d, although he must have had more than just an inkling that this would be the case. It must, however, be noted that when he finally relinquished the post nearly three years later, the books were showing a deficit of £15-14s, the only time that the Chapter has been in the red in its entire history!

Immediately after his taking control of the finances, the account books show two pages of credits and debits in his handwriting, all dated for the previous year, meaning that the books were not up to date when he took over. Redman, who had proudly claimed just twelve months earlier that the Chapter held a three-figure credit and no debt, albeit with Patton's rousing confirmation, had only attended three of the fifteen meetings held since his re-election in 1822. So was this another case of misappropriation by an Officer, or just Patton's simple inability to see inaccuracies in books that he claimed to have audited? Ultimately matters had reached a point where it was obvious that they needed to react quickly, and the fact that nobody opposed Patton's election as Treasurer of the Chapter suggests that the membership were fully-aware of what a fool he had made of himself in his support of Redman, thereby awarding him the task of sorting it all out..

There is an interesting letter in the files at UGLE sent to the Grand Scribes by Matthew Patton on 27th June 1823. It begins: *I am quite ashamed that the dues of Royal Cumberland Chapter 55 should have remained so long unsettled. The truth is the duties of every office have for the last four years in a great measure devolved upon myself and my avocations interfering I have not till this period been enabled to compleat the discharge of every demand against the Chapter.* It was accompanied by a remittance of eleven pounds to bring the Chapter's account up to date, and reference to a return he had sent three days earlier which: *contains all who have been exalted or have joined the RCC within the Masonic Hall since 1818.*

That other return had been accompanied by a further payment of £15-7s-6d to cover the registration fees for those new members, suggesting that no return of new members had been made by the Chapter from the time they moved to Freemasons' Hall. That return, very helpfully, provides is a list of those new members, a total of forty-five having been exalted between October 1818 and March 1823; this shows that the fees due from Royal Cumberland Chapter to the Financial Committee for this aspect alone would have totalled £47-5s-0d, far more than had ever been remitted in total by the Chapter to the Hall to cover not only this aspect, but also members' fees, quarterages, etc.

In a postscript to his letter, Patton adds: *The returns of the RC Lodge 55 I made you some week or ten days since - the cash for which I shall collect and send without delay - having the weight of similar duties upon in both connections but shall not intrude long upon your indulgence.* This demonstrates that the financial administration of both Patton's Lodge and Chapter had been dire, during a period when he was in the Chair of both; his only excuse for it was that he had been covering all of the posts responsible for this!

Yet this was also a man who, whilst presiding over such continued indebtedness to the governing body, and others, had accepted personal gifts from the two organisations to the combined value of more than fifty guineas. Although this could not be classed as embezzlement, because he did not initiate the presentations, a twenty-first-century court of law would take an extremely dim view of such acceptance of valuable gifts by a senior officer who, by dint of his office, would need to be aware of the prevailing financial circumstances.

Before moving on, it is worth recapping on exactly what positions Patton held which, as a consequence, gave him access to related financial information over the three-year period leading-up to the signing-over of the Hall to Geary at the end of March 1823:

He was an original subscriber to the Hall, so would have received all shareholders' communications and been able to attend all shareholders' meetings.

He was a member of the Financial Committee from March 1820 to July 1822, during which time he only missed one meeting; he was instrumental in setting the charges for the Hall, would have heard all financial discussions and received copies of all accounts, etc.

He was Master of Royal Cumberland Lodge for two years from December 1819, giving him full knowledge of all correspondence and accounts for the Lodge at a time concurrent with his membership of the Finance Committee; in other words, he would have been privy to all discussions on financial matters at both ends of the relationship between the Lodge and the Financial Committee.

He was First Principal of Royal Cumberland Chapter for five years from March 1820, so the same comments apply as with the Lodge;

Likewise, Antiquity Encampment where he was Eminent Commander from 1819 to 1823.

In addition to all of that, he was a regular visitor to Lodge of Virtue, where he stood-in at times when they lacked a qualified Past Master to assist; he was also Provincial Junior Grand Warden in 1820. He visited Royal York Lodge rarely, but the last record of his doing so was on October 26th 1820, when the financial situation within that Lodge regarding Thomas Pitter was discussed at length. There is no record, however, of his having ever visited Royal Sussex Lodge up to that time.

Nevertheless, there cannot have been a Freemason in Bath more aware of what was transpiring within the Fraternity in the city between 1820 and 1823, than Matthew Patton. He held a quite unique situation enabling him, if he wished, to act as a galvanising influence during those difficult times for the Fraternity in the city. Yet all he seems to have done is accept valuable gifts that his Lodge and Chapter could scarcely afford to give, utilising funds that should have been earmarked for supporting the building that they occupied. One cannot help but draw a parallel with Nero at the time of Rome burning.

The question was, would this particular senior Freemason now help his fellow members to extinguish the flames engulfing their home, or instead fan them from the sidelines?

The Cracks Appear

As all of the financial cracks began to show at the beginning of 1823, Thomas Whitney comes to the fore in the story. There was no doubt that his involvement was central to the creation of Freemasons' Hall; that matters had been allowed to develop to such a state must have rankled with him, and not just those involving his personal financial future.

Masonic historians Robert Peach and George Norman intimate that he could be a prickly character at times, although there is little evidence in records prior to 1823 to support this assumption. During the period from 1816 to 1821 Whitney's conduct appears exemplary. His dedication to any cause with which he was involved was undoubted, but there is evidence that he expected others to maintain the same level of commitment and, if they didn't, he could remain a thorn in the side of anyone he considered deserved the reward of constant reminders.

Being centrally involved with the unravelling of the activities of Thomas Pitter, his predecessor as Royal York Lodge Secretary, Whitney would also have been aware of how far those wider activities had also affected the Financial Committee. As a regular attendee of committee meetings, he will have known the extent of the indebtedness of each Lodge and Order, and of their individual attitudes to the resolution of that indebtedness.

The revelations of Pitter's fraudulent activity had brought Royal York Lodge to a painful recognition not only of their lack of funds, but also of the lack of recent returns to Grand Lodge in London. Whitney entered into correspondence to assess the depth of the problem, which turned into somewhat of a running-sore from 1821 following the disclosure by the Grand Secretaries of an apparent lack of any record in London of Whitney himself being registered as a member of the Lodge, or of his subsequent payment of fees, going back to when he had joined in 1807. This all seems rather strange, as the surviving returns for the Lodge clearly show that his fees were regularly remitted prior to the involvement of Pitter, after which all returns became dubious and rare. However, Whitney offered his opinions regularly in correspondence such as: *you much astonish me by saying I have never registered. There is evidently some serious neglect in the past, of someone in your office.* Such comments cannot have endeared him to those receiving them.

Across at Royal Cumberland Chapter, minutes in early 1823 showed that a number of outstanding financial commitments had been found, including the apparent non-receipt of the proceeds from the sale of an old pedestal. The minute reads: *Most Excellent Companion Patton reported that the sum of £2-10s-0d having been received by Companion T Whitney for the old pedestal belonging to this chapter, disposed of to the Worthing Chapter by the request of Companion T Whitney in 1821 - and it appearing that by some error the said sum of £2-10s-0d had been paid by Companion T Whitney into the [Hall] Financial Committee contrary to any order from this Chapter. It was therefore agreed that the consideration of the same be left to the three Principals of the Chapter as the due appropriation of the said sum of £2-10s-0d in discharge of any amounts that may appear against this Chapter.*

This is the first occurrence of any confusion over the ownership of a piece of furniture within the Hall building, the status of which will be discussed in more detail later. It also shows that the Chapter was aware that it owed a sum to the Financial Committee, and wished to confirm whether the sale of something they considered to be their property had been credited against their account. At the time of this minute, Thomas Whitney was no longer a member of Royal Cumberland Chapter; he had resigned in March 1821 to allow his brother William to take-up an office of the Chapter. It is worth noting that, at the time of his resignation, the minutes state: *The Chapter in accepting the resignation proposed that a letter be sent to Comp Thos Whitney, expressive of the regret they felt in the loss of so valuable a member, which was unanimously agreed to.*

Thomas and William worked together in the family's Apothecary business and, as a consequence, only one could attend a Masonic meeting due to the other being needed to tend the business in their absence. This explains why they were members of different Lodges and, following his resignation from Royal Cumberland Chapter, Thomas joined the new Royal York Chapter instead; therefore, if he needed to attend his old Chapter after 1821, he would have done so as a visitor. He was minuted as a visitor from Royal York Chapter at the January 1823 meeting of Royal Cumberland Chapter where this matter was first raised, but there is nothing in those minutes to indicate that Thomas Whitney, or anybody else, made any comments with regard to the matter, suggesting that the query was not over why the money had been given to the Financial Committee, but simply whether it had been correctly credited to the Chapter's account.

Three months later, on April 29th, Thomas Whitney arrived once again as a visitor to Royal Cumberland Chapter and requested admission; his brother not being in attendance that night shows that this must have been by prior arrangement. This was the first meeting of the Chapter following the assignment of the Hall to Charles Geary, and the minutes record: *Companion Thos Whitney this evening requested to visit this Chapter, but the Most Excellent Companion Patton having some private communication to make, the sense of the Chapter was taken, when the Chapter unanimously declined the visit of Companion Whitney for this evening.*

Nearly two hundred years ago, visiting was a far more formal process than it is today, the visitor remaining outside of the room until the Lodge or Chapter was ready to receive him. Consequently, rejecting a bone fide visitor was considered quite a slap in the face, and such rejections were often the source of extended correspondence between Lodges, occasionally leading to disciplinary hearings at a higher level. Patton could easily have imparted a communication and then let Whitney in, but what exactly it was of such importance to warrant sending a high-ranking ex-member away is not revealed in the minutes, which record very little business being transacted that evening. Other than some correspondence, the only announcement Patton made to the Chapter was that it had achieved: *the discharge of all present demands against the same, with the exception of the Grand Chapter fees, which would be discharged at the earliest convenience.*

This was not the case, however, because probably the largest outstanding debt, to the Financial Committee, had definitely not been discharged. Maybe Patton realised that this financial announcement would be immediately challenged by Whitney; regardless it cannot be overlooked that, because of their business arrangement, neither of the Whitney brothers attended that meeting. If Thomas Whitney's visit was in order to resolve the issue over the sale of the pedestal, that can only have added to the perceived slight dealt him by his old Chapter. He would not be given the opportunity by Royal Cumberland Chapter to visit them again for a further three months.

In the meantime, in June 1823, Thomas Whitney was involved in a minor skirmish with Provincial Grand Lodge. According to the minutes of the meeting held in Wiveliscombe, Whitney had presented a bill for £7-14s-6d on behalf of his Lodge for a banner ordered by the Province six years earlier; although no specific details are included in the minutes as to what sort of banner it was, or why it had been ordered through Lodge of Perfect Friendship, the timing of the purchase would align with the date when there was a major Provincial meeting in Bath, presided over by the PGM for Dorset, for which: *the PGL of Bristol agreed to lend various articles of which the PGL Somerset were in want*. For obvious reasons, such articles would not have extended to a Somerset banner.

The 1823 claim was peremptorily rejected for lack of proof or support that it was entitled to be discharged by the Province, who also concluded that it was *highly improper to have been made*. At the same Provincial meeting Dr Sully was presented with the memorial piece of plate mentioned previously. So at that one Provincial meeting, Whitney experienced the successful culmination of an appeal that he had both proposed and widely promoted, followed by having his other business dismissed as *highly improper*. The request for payment of this old bill had clearly evolved from the need to find funds to balance the Royal York Lodge's books, although whether Whitney had acted with the full knowledge of his Lodge is not obvious. However, he had been the Acting Provincial Secretary when the banner was purchased, and Master of the Lodge of Perfect Friendship at the same time; so was this assumption of impropriety taken as a personal slur?

Within weeks of this provincial meeting, Whitney received a personal summons from Royal Cumberland Chapter together with a demand against him for the alleged missing £2-10s. The first page or so of the Royal Cumberland Chapter minutes of July 22nd 1823 contain a laborious preamble on the need for calling the Emergency Meeting, but a simple précis would be that Whitney had, allegedly, been instructed to sell their pedestal by Patton and to pay the proceeds directly to the Treasurer, Redman, but had neglected to do so. When later approached on the matter, Whitney had referred Patton to Geary, whom Patton claimed had subsequently referred him back to Whitney. As it was considered that Whitney had failed in his duty to the Chapter, they wished to examine the facts with him and, if found to be correct, then they wanted their cash there and then. I will let the minutes take it from there:

The decision of the Principals of the Royal Cumberland Chapter was this evening respectfully communicated by the First Principal [Patton] *to Companion Thomas Whitney in open Chapter, upon which Comp. Thos. Whitney came for the purpose of explaining his reasons, and shewing good sufficient cause for the non payment into the Chapter Treasury of the said monies £2-10s-0d received by him in Trust and due to this Most Excellent Chapter, in the course of which explanation, and without the slightest apparent provocation, Comp. Thos Whitney's conduct became most Unmasonic and Outrageous, by personal abuse of the First Principal, and although called to order several times from the Chair, for such his gross misconduct, he still persisted, using the most Violent, Insolent and degrading language and Epithets possible, Clenching, Raising and Wielding his fist at the First Principal, with threatenings, contrary to either Law or Masonry, concluding his abuse by several times calling the Most Excellent First Principal 'Scoundrel and Liar', Desiring the First Principal in a most authoritative and Vociferous manner to acquaint the Principals of the Royal Cumberland Chapter that he never would pay the money. For this dreadful and unparalleled Outrage committed in Open Chapter, against the Peace, the Character, Harmony and Dignity of the same, so contrary to every principle of the Order, disgraceful to himself as a Man and highly derogatory to the Character of a Mason. The First Principal considered it his painful duty to Order Comp. Thos. Whitney immediately to withdraw from the Chapter, and directed the Janitor to conduct him from thence for gross Contumacy, Injustice and Insults, the Chapter receiving Comp. Thos. Whitney's conduct with abhorrence, detestation and regret, resolved upon referring the same to the Consideration, and adjudication of the Supreme Grand Chapter of England via the Provincial Grand Superintendent as early as possible.*

That this appears somewhat of an overreaction by Whitney to a simple request, would clearly be an understatement; but it begs the question - what on earth pushed such an experienced Mason over the edge like that? One other item of business was minuted, something easily missed in the shadow of reading about such an unprecedented event within a Chapter meeting; nevertheless it is very relevant: *The Office of Treasurer having become Vacant by the resignation of Comp. Redman, it was proposed by the 1st Principal that Comp. Morris be elected Treasurer for the ensuing year, seconded by Comp Marsh and agreed to.* Following this turbulent meeting, and presumably to bridge the gap between the outgoing and incoming Treasurers, Patton took immediate control of the account books, which revealed the dire position mentioned previously. Only Patton's writing appears in those account books for the next three years, as Morris did not take-up the appointment.

The minute suggests Redman's resignation was contemporary with this meeting. Whether tendered prior to it, or while it was in progress is not clear, but it does beg the question as to whether his action was in consequence of the business on the agenda. As mentioned previously,

Redman had rarely attended Chapter meetings since his triumphant re-election the previous year, and this resignation came just months after he had been replaced as Secretary of the Hall Financial Committee.

Such lack of attendance could have been due to illness, absence from the city, or any number of legitimate reasons. So was Redman's resignation just co-incidental, or did he, as a long-serving fellow member of Royal York Lodge, have more of an insight of the causes behind Whitney having been placed in the position he had found himself that evening? Nowhere in the Chapter minutes is there any reference to the sale of the Pedestal, prior to the apparent 'discovery' by Patton of the deficiency in payment two years after the claimed event. Therefore there is no minuted instruction for those funds to be collected, or paid, by anyone to anyone.

Regarding the pedestal itself, there is one aspect that was missed by everybody involved, probably because the event occurred before the time that any of the individuals became members of the Chapter. I refer here to a Chapter minute twenty years earlier, dated 22nd February 1802, co-incidentally the first date at which the title Royal Cumberland Chapter, rather than Chapter of Harmony, appears in the records. It refers to an agreement between the Chapter and Royal Cumberland Lodge wherein the Lodge loaned the Chapter a complete set of furniture for its use, including a pedestal, under the following conditions: *we do hereby promise on the faith of Masonry for ourselves and our successors to deliver up the same when demanded to the same Thomas West, or to the Master of the said Lodge for the time being.* There is no other pedestal recorded as having been acquired by the Chapter in the intervening twenty years. Although Patton declared he had instructed Whitney what to do with the funds, it transpires that he had no authority to dispose of an item that was not even the Chapter's property in the first place, wherever the proceeds ended-up.

Nevertheless Whitney's behaviour was inexcusable, and Patton moved immediately to bring him to book. He wrote to Col. Kemeys-Tynte as the Provincial Grand Superintendent, begging the Colonel's intervention on the matter. The following reply was received: *This evening's post has brought me your two letters containing charges against T Whitney's conduct which I was not at all surprised at, when first I heard of it from a prior communication. I am sorry to say, however, that it is out of my power to assist you on this occasion, as I hold no rank whatever in the Province as a Royal Arch Mason.*

There are several interesting aspects of that short note: the PGM was already aware of the matter *from a prior communication,* suggesting someone else from Bath had informed him about it; he also was *not surprised* by the behaviour, so he may have personally experienced something similar, maybe over the banner issue. But the most interesting was the revelation that there was no Provincial Grand Superintendant presiding over Royal Arch Masonry in Somerset at that point in time.

This only appears to have spurred Patton on, however, and by 31st July he had produced another letter of three and half pages of foolscap, addressed to the Grand Scribes in London, and even more florid than its local predecessor. It contained three charges against Whitney, the first that he had withheld payment of the proceeds of the pedestal sale, the second regarding his behaviour at the Chapter meeting. This was surely sufficient, as the minutes alone read poorly enough; just submitting those would be sufficient to place Whitney in a thoroughly bad light. But Patton felt they needed embellishment, not simply by the establishment of his own credentials and efficacy in the preamble, but also in charge three: *That (he) Mr Thomas Whitney has disseminated a most calumnious and palpable falsehood against the First Principal of the Royal Cumberland Chapter viz "That the First Principal had gone round Bath and had poisoned the minds of all the Brethren against coming forward to subscribe to the Masonic Hall Tontine" with a wilful intention of creating a schism in the Royal Cumberland Lodge and Chapter injurious to the best interests and contrary to every principle of Freemasonry.*

There are subtle differences between the content of charge number two and the actual minutes, which Patton would have had at his disposal when drafting the charges, discrepancies that a modern defence attorney would have little difficulty in utilising to dismantle Patton's case. According to the minutes, Whitney was communicated the decision of the Principals before being asked to provide his explanation, then in the course of providing that explanation, lost all reason, accused Patton of being a liar, was called to order and, when he failed to calm down, was conducted from the room. In Patton's charge, it is claimed that Whitney provided his explanation as the first act of the drama, became immediately offensive and abusive of Patton whilst doing so, was called to order, failed to do so, and then was communicated the decision of the Principals; following that he began using epithets before concluding by calling Patton a liar, after which he was conducted from the room.

What's the difference? Well in the former, the contemporary account written by a third-party immediately after the event, he came to provide an explanation and something set him off; even the minute-taker displayed doubt as to what that might have been. In the latter, the accusation laid before the investigating body, Whitney came spoiling for a ruckus and immediately caused one. As it was Patton who formulated the charges, the only obvious reason he could have for altering the context would be to deflect the focus of the tribunal away from there being provocation. So, why would Patton feel it necessary to change the sequence of events when submitting his charges? More to the point, why add a third charge that was less-provable than Whitney's well-witnessed disgraceful behaviour?

There was no further reference to the matter for three months until October 29th, when the Chapter minute book records that advice had been received from Grand Chapter that Col. Kemeys-Tynte had been appointed as Provincial Grand Superintendent for Royal Arch in Somerset. This enabled the Colonel to call a Provincial Grand Chapter hearing on 7th November to investigate the charges against Whitney. The hearing, in Bridgwater, was attended by Patton, Whatley and Marsh, the three Principals on the night of the July meeting, and by Whitney supported by Charles Geary. The decisions were:

On the first charge: *it clearly appearing that Mr Geary had no authority whatever for receiving and detaining the said sum of £2-10s not being the Treasurer of the Royal Cumberland Chapter & it appearing Mr Thos Whitney had received positive orders to pay the said sum to the Chapter Treasurer Comp Redman, by the First Principal, the first charge was therefore fully proved.* Whitney was ordered to pay the £2-10s to Royal Cumberland Chapter.

The second charge was also found proven. Despite a weak attempt by Whitney to justify the unjustifiable, he was: *Ordered to make before the Council then assembled a full and Ample Apology to the Royal Cumberland Chapter, for his Unmasonic Conduct and Language on 22nd July last. This being done, before the Provincial Grand Superintendant & to the satisfaction of all present, the parties severally subscribed their names that no further proceedings be Instituted on the subject and the Object of the Royal Cumberland Chapter as regarded the Dignity and Interest of the same being thus satisfied.*

The meeting then turned to the third charge, and the following was recorded: *The proving of the first and second charges, thus closing the particular business of the Royal Cumberland Chapter against Mr Thos Whitney, the First Principal of the Royal Cumberland Chapter under advice of the Provincial Grand Superintendant waived the third charge - for Slander & Defamation.*

It is a shame that these minutes, obtained from the Royal Cumberland Chapter minute book as no Provincial record survives, do not give any indication of what exactly caused Col. Kemeys-Tynte to advise Patton to drop the third charge. Neither do they record what Geary's contribution to the proceedings was, although they do indicate, through the use of underlining and exclamation marks, the discomfort felt by at least one Chapter representative present that a fellow-companion should appear against them in support of the accused.

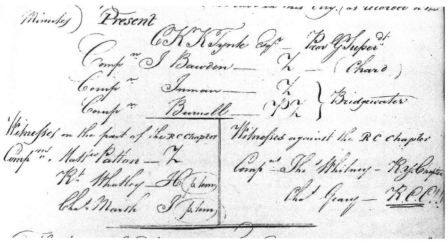

Excerpt from RCC Minutes for the Bridgwater Hearing
showing the exclamation marks. *Bath Masonic Hall Trust*

This was somewhat of a let-off for Thomas Whitney; his acceptance is shown in the Chapter account books, in Patton's own hand, by the £2-10s being duly paid to them by Whitney immediately following the Provincial hearing. Which makes it somewhat puzzling as to why their minutes of 30th January 1824, nearly three months later, record that: *It was proposed and unanimously agreed to that a letter be addressed by the Scribe to Mr Tho. Whitney in demanding the said sum viz: £2-10s due to this Chapter.*

In the minutes of the same meeting it was also recorded that *it was proposed and unanimously agreed that a Letter be sent to Comp. W. Whitney and other Comps. in arrears requesting a settlement of the same.* It is not unusual to find such a resolution in any Masonic minute book, but it is unusual to see one member singled-out for specific mention out of a number in arrears which, from examining the account books, were attributable to more than a dozen members at the time. This could suggest that someone in the Chapter had an axe to grind with the Whitneys, and was intent on continuing to do so.

At the following meeting, the minutes record that: *The Most Ex Z* [Patton] *reported in furtherance of the resolutions of the last Chapter night that he had ordered the 1st Scribe to address a letter to Mr. Thos. Whitney requiring the payment of £2-10s due for the Chapter Pedestal, which had been paid.* This is a rather ambiguous minute as it could be read, out of context, that the payment was made subsequent to the letter. However, it can also be read that the payment had previously been made, and the letter sent in error, which was the truth of the matter. Presumably Thomas Whitney's response had stated this in no uncertain terms.

So what does this storm-in-a-teacup tell us about the undercurrents within Bath Freemasonry at the time? There is no doubting Whitney's behaviour was way beyond the pale in the circumstances, that cannot be called into question. But what made him behave that way? There is a clue left to us by the minute writer that evening, early on within the phrase: *in the course of which explanation, and without the slightest* **apparent** *provocation.*

That is not an adjective used to confirm there had been no provocation whatsoever. So was the writer expressing disbelief of an act so totally against the character of a fellow Mason who had held higher Provincial Office than anyone in the Chapter that night, and someone he had known for many years? Or was he indicating that something had occurred, either within Chapter that night, or previously outside? Regardless, he personally felt it necessary to insert that one word to record his disquiet, however slight, for posterity.

Furthermore, what caused Patton to assert that a schism was being created? Nowhere in the research into writing this book have I found any other reference to that specific accusation against him, of undermining the tontine, mentioned in his own charge three, and certainly not before he issued his charges on 31st July 1823 - not in Whitney's correspondence, not in minute books and not in any previous histories.

Yet it would provide a telling explanation of a pivotal part of the affair, the failure of the tontine, if some implication appeared in what had transpired, and sure-enough there are some inconsistencies between the lists of subscribers to the two major financing schemes, the original subscription and the tontine.

Having an essentially failed-investment on their hands, some might interpret anyone taking part in the second scheme as throwing good money after bad. However, success of the tontine would have guaranteed a full return of their investment, and maybe more; on the other hand, failure of the tontine would only result in the total loss of that original investment.

There are 32 names on the copy of the Tontine in the Bath Archives. Of those, four were not members of the Fraternity, including Earl Manvers the landlord, and Walter Harris the builder. The majority, 21 in number, were members of Royal York Lodge, two were members of Lodge of Virtue, three from Royal Sussex Lodge and one from a Lodge outside of Bath. Only two subscribers were members of Royal Cumberland Lodge, Charles Geary and Robert Payne, the latter being Master of Royal Cumberland when the Hall was built and dedicated.

If these names are compared to the list of 40 subscribers to the Hall itself that accompanied the surrender document, 24 of those were from Royal York, three from Royal Sussex, five from Royal Cumberland and three from Lodge of Virtue. There are an additional five names that have not been found on any Bath returns, including Walter Harris the builder. This shows that, in both cases, the main support for what passed as a methodology for financing the Hall had come from the Royal York Lodge of Perfect Friendship - Thomas Whitney's Lodge.

Running a comparison, there were just thirteen names that appeared in both lists; of those one was Harris the builder, one was from Royal Sussex and two (Payne and Geary) were from Royal Cumberland Lodge; the remainder were all from Royal York Lodge, including Whitney. There was little support from Royal Cumberland Lodge in either case, but of their two original subscribers who did not enter the tontine, one was Patton himself; the other was John Morris, Master of the Lodge at the time that the tontine was called, and the person subsequently elected as Treasurer of Royal Cumberland Chapter, but who declined to take that office.

What is slightly curious, however, is that although there was additional support from Royal York for the tontine, there was also an apparent reluctance of fifteen of the original 24 subscribers from that Lodge to enter into the rescue plan; so was there any common denominator between those names?   A quick survey of the account books reveals that twelve of those fifteen names were also members of Royal Cumberland Chapter.   Some of those names were of long-standing, others influential current and past officers. Although this is by no means any proof of skulduggery, in the circumstances it is somewhat more than mere co-incidence.

It had been almost two and a half years since Thomas Whitney had resigned from Royal Cumberland Chapter, and he appears to have visited his old Chapter on only one other occasion after he had taken that decision.   Could it possibly have been that, as Whitney looked around the Chapter whilst making his explanation, he suddenly realised just how many Hall Subscribers who were members of his own Lodge, and also members of that Chapter, had failed to support the tontine.

More to the point, could the accusation levelled by Patton in that third charge to the Grand Scribes have referred to the actual content of Whitney's outburst in the Chapter meeting - an intimation that First Principal Patton had influenced members' decisions? In which case, could the minute-taker have chosen not to relate the content, because he realised that there may have been an element of truth in it? And finally, as he was also in attendance at the Provincial hearing, could that minute-taker have privately indicated his disquiet to Col. Kemeys-Tynte, causing the Colonel to make his recommendation to Patton of withdrawal of the third charge?

Such speculation is, of course, academic because Whitney had placed himself in serious hot water by his own loss of composure; provocation, however derived, was no defence in the circumstances. The question was, would his apology suffice in bringing an end to the matter, or would there be further consequences?

Ground Zero

By the end of April 1823, Geary had removed all of the encumbrances on the Hall by repaying the debt and having the lease signed over to his personal liability; he then commenced the process of creating legal agreements with the Masonic tenants for their usage, presumably of the basement level where the Lodge room was situated. Surely, having been relieved of their embarrassment, the rest of the members would rally-round and help formulate a sound financial basis for the building going forward? Alas, no.

Whatever transpired among all of the parties in the six months between the signing-over of the building to Geary and the next major act of the drama in October 1823, correspondence shows that Geary was consistent in his requests to meet with the Lodges to negotiate the matter to a conclusion. However, they all failed to respond positively, even to entering into legal rental agreements commencing from his acquisition date, something any landlord should fairly expect. Regardless, the Lodges and Orders continued to use the building as if nothing had happened. The new landlord must have been brought to the same conclusion as his predecessor - that he was unlikely to receive any rent from the sitting tenants.

History shows that, on October 17th 1823, Geary took peremptory action and locked the doors of the building against all tenants; by doing so, it is also claimed, he took hold of their goods and chattels as surety until they concluded negotiations. Whether this conduct was unmasonic, as would later be claimed, is not for discussion here; the question is, was it legal? There is also a second question: was it just the inaction of the tenants that brought this about, or did something else happen? Something that has been previously overlooked.

George Norman asserts at this point in the story that: *With the assignment of the property to Bro. Charles Geary as sole proprietor, a change came over the scene, for having obtained possession of the property in March 1823, he determined to bring matters to a crisis during the ensuing summer. What his motives were must be gathered from the story as told in the minutes of the Royal Cumberland Lodge.* He then goes on to include excerpts from those minutes and correspondence, none of which relate to the period between March and early October 1823, which would encompass the entire extent of what we, somewhat optimistically at times, refer to in this country as 'summer'.

Bruce Oliver's account includes a very short reference to this time, which also suggests that Geary set about seeking redress as soon as he took over the building: *Thus, on the 25th March 1823, Bro. Charles Geary became sole proprietor. Unfortunately, by the autumn, disagreement had arisen, Bro. Geary refusing the use of the Rooms until the various Lodges had:"entered into some satisfactory and proper arrangement of Rent to be named for their use of the Lower Lodge Room etc., during the last five years. It is my determination not to suffer any Furniture or properties whatsoever to be removed from the premises."*

The actual text, taken directly from Geary's handwritten letter dated 20th October, and therefore after the Hall had been closed, reads: *until a deputed Committee be formed from the Lodges & Chapters meeting at the Masonic Hall for the purpose of entering into some satisfactory and proper arrangement of Rent to be named, & for their use of the Lower Lodge Room &c during the last five years, it is my determination not to suffer any Furniture or properties whatsoever to be removed from the premises. I am ready to meet at any proper time such an authorized Committee.*

Out of context, the text of a letter can be interpreted whichever way the reader desires, but in context all I see in this letter is Geary saying: 'Look guys, if you will form a committee that I can sit down with to thrash this out once and for all, then I'll let you back in.' For whatever reason, that is not how it was interpreted by history. More importantly, of course, that's not how it was received by Royal Cumberland Lodge, and specifically their Master at the time - Matthew Patton.

But before moving on to those reactions, it is worth examining the legalities of the perceived seizure of goods. Previously, it has been assumed that the whole of the contents of the building were the property of the Lodges and Orders meeting there, and that in ultimately disposing of them some twenty years later Geary performed an illegal act. However, closer examination of the Assignment reveals that Geary had acquired from the subscribers and the Hall Trust: *the said Building and premises called the Masonic Hall and all their right members and appurtenances.* The definition of the word appurtenance is 'something added to another, more important thing; equipment, such as clothing, tools, or instruments, used for a specific purpose or task; a right, privilege, or property that is considered incident to the principal property.'

The original subscribers to the building had paid for its erection, albeit with the assistance of a large loan, the discharge of which they were liable for. Those subscribers were private individuals; they may also have been Freemasons, they may also have been members of the Lodges who became the tenants, but their membership did not connect or assign their ownership of shares in any way to their Lodges. Fixtures and fittings that were purchased by, or under the auspices of, those subscribing shareholders were therefore part of the shareholders' assets. This may beg the question as to why the Lodges themselves chose not to be subscribers; had they done so, then they would have had a legal claim to the syndicate's assets. But previous examination of individual Lodge finances explains that adequately - they simply did not have the levels of cash needed to do so.

Following their occupation of the building in 1818, the tenants (that is the Lodges and Orders) formed a Trust to manage their occupancy. The terms of the underlease (assuming there was one) between the subscribers and the Trust are not known, but under the finance laws of the time, any debts accumulated by the Trust and due to the their landlord, would have been securable against Trust assets. Payments made by the Lodges, scant though they were, were made to cover their running costs, which the Financial Committee were expected to disburse as necessary. That they did so, to the extent that the restricted cashflow allowed, is shown by the statement by English and Spry in their 1824 report.

Some of the debts run up by the Trust involved the acquisition of fixtures and fittings which became the property of the Trust. The same legal status would have been accorded to anything donated to the Trust for joint usage by any of the Lodges during the period from the creation of the Trust, in 1818, to its ultimate demise in 1823. Although, once any dispute was resolved, a Lodge might ultimately be able to reclaim any property it could clearly demonstrate sole ownership of, it would not be possible to lay any claim to residual property of joint ownership until all the debt had been discharged.

Therefore by paying-off the entire debt and in return acquiring, entirely legally, not only the property of the subscribers, but also **all** of the joint assets held by the Trust, Geary would have become the owner of everything within the building, other than specifically-identifiable property of a third party tenant, such as one of the Lodges. In other words, Geary was not depriving anyone of their assets, but securing **his** acquired assets against potential removal under a misguided claim. The question is, therefore, not was he acting legally, but did the members actually realise that the majority of the furniture and equipment in the Hall building was not owned by their Lodges or Orders, but had been provided for their use by the Trust, through the Financial Committee, within the terms of a tenancy agreement?

That Geary's action was legal, therefore, is indisputable and fell far short of the court proceedings threatened in 1822 against himself and Whitney by the previous landlord, which had only been averted by Geary's action to take control of the building. Had the Financial Committee still existed after the assignment in March 1823, Geary would have been able to negotiate with it. As he was continually requesting that one be formed, it follows that it had disbanded. Putting it succinctly, not only had the original subscribers, including Patton, evaded being personally-liable for a substantial debt of the order of eight-times the value of each of their shares, the members of the Financial Committee had also walked away from a similar liability in the defunct Trust.

The first to record Geary's action, unsurprisingly, was Royal Cumberland Lodge; the minutes for their first regular meeting of the season, convened on 17th October 1823 by Worshipful Master, Matthew Patton and attended, among others, by their Junior Warden Brother Hay, read as follows: *The W.M. directed that the minute as regard the removal of the Lodge be read as laid down by the Grand Lodge regulations. The W.M. then informed the Brethren that he had directed Brother Pinker to call on Bro. P.M. Geary for the keys of Masonic Hall, when Bro. Geary said "The Hall was closed against all Lodges until an arrangement was made with him." In consequence of Bro. Geary's refusal to give up the keys of Masonic Hall or open the same the following letter was addressed to him.*

The tone of this minute should be noted, as it contains no reference to the removal being temporary; indeed the first sentence referring to Grand Lodge Regulations is applicable when a Lodge permanently removes its meeting place. The letter the minute referred to reads as follows: *The Royal Cumberland Lodge having removed to the White Lion in consequence of the measures you have thought proper to adopt, you are requested forthwith to deliver up the Furniture and properties belonging to the R.C.L. and any claim there may be against the Lodge you will send the same to the Treasurer. The Secretary with the Tylers will call upon you on Wednesday morning next at 10 o'clock to receive the said properties.*

133

The demand for release of furniture confirms the permanency of the removal, and there is also a flavour of there being no great surprise in the minutes. That Royal Cumberland were able to convene at the White Lion, the busiest coaching inn in the city, in the very room they had used prior to their removal to York Street five years earlier, on a busy Friday night and within hours of first discovering that they were locked-out of the Hall, does suggest either some prearrangement, or a deal of good fortune. It should also be noted that there is no mention of the Lodge warrant in the demand.

Eleven days later, on October 28th, there was a groundhog-day-style report in the minutes of Royal Cumberland Chapter recording what they claimed to be their first encounter with the situation: *The Janitors of the Chapter on waiting upon the First Principal for Orders as usual on the morning of the day above stated, were desired to prepare the Chapter Room &c, upon which they waited upon Mr Geary, a Companion of this Chapter, for the key of the Chapter Room, when they received for answer "that the Masonic Hall was closed against all Lodges as well as Chapters, until arrangements were made with him (Mr Geary) and Orders were given to the resident Tylers for the retention of all Warrants & other Properties on the premises." This being viewed by the three Principals of the R.C. Chapter as an Outrage, contrary to every principle of the Order committed by Comp. Geary & the meeting of the Chapter was necessarily suspended until a report of the same be forwarded to the Prov G. Superintendant praying redress, the Royal Cumberland Chapter, having overpaid its account with the Masonic Hall Financial Committee, were now Creditors in the sum of Three Pounds one shilling and sixpence to June 24th last.* This was signed by the three Principals of the Chapter.

Read in isolation many years later, this minute sounds as if the Chapter walked-into an unexpected scenario. However, the context changes entirely if read in conjunction with the parent Lodge minutes from days earlier, and when the names of the officers are revealed. Furthermore, there was no separate accommodation for the Chapter - what is referred to as *the Chapter Room* was the same lower room used by the Lodge.

Therefore Patton, as First Principal, ordered the Janitors to prepare the room fully knowing that it would be locked against them - all three of the Chapter signatories, Patton, Hay and Seine, were aware of recent correspondence between Geary and their parent Lodge, because they had attended regular and emergency Lodge meetings during the intervening ten days, where this was discussed. What is also somewhat incongruous is the final statement of the perceived condition of the Chapter's account with the Hall, showing a very precise amount which presumably their treasurer, also Patton, had suddenly been able to pluck from their account books at a moment's notice. Having already examined that aspect, it is obvious that the quoted figure was fictional.

The main contrast to the minutes of the Lodge is that the Chapter's Warrant, sometimes referred to as its Charter, was not available to them, and no location was given for the meeting, being shown in the minutes as *Late of Freemasons Hall.* The real reason that the Chapter meeting had to be suspended, as opposed to the Lodge meetings going ahead, was that the Chapter's Charter was not in their possession, whereas the Lodge's Warrant obviously was.

Returning to the correspondence initiated by Royal Cumberland Lodge the previous week, the reply was received from Geary on October 21st and discussed at an emergency meeting of the Lodge convened at the White Lion on 24th October, attended by Patton (as Master), plus Marsh, Hay and Seine, with visitors from Royal York in Maddison (Master), Ashley (IPM), Wilson and Muttlebury (Wardens), but not by any representative from Lodge of Virtue. It was decided to request by letter that Geary: *will furnish them with answers to the following queries: First - What right and title have you for excluding the Lodges from the Masonic Hall? Second - What right for detaining the Furniture and Properties belonging to the Lodges?* then solicit the opinions of the other Lodges.

Geary's response reads: *In reply to your Letter received Sunday proposing to me two questions, I have to answer them as follows: 1st - Because as Proprietor of Masonic Hall I have a right so to do, and 2nd - Because I think myself legally justified in preventing the Furniture, &c from being a second time removed, until the Rent in arrear is discharged.* It was received by the Lodge on Tuesday morning the 28th, the day of the Chapter meeting, and around the time at which Patton instructed the Janitors to obtain the key to the Chapter Room. It was not discussed, however, until the next regular Lodge night on Friday 31st, attended by the same four Royal York officers.

The underlining is in the original letter, and is significant because it suggests that an attempt, at least, had been made to remove something from Freemasons' Hall after Geary had taken it over. Unfortunately, there is nothing in any archives to confirm what was removed, or when the incident occurred. However, this information might explain the past tense of the phrase used by Geary in his letter of 20th October - *in* *which you inform me the Royal Cumberland Lodge **has** removed from the Masonic Hall.* There appears to be some subtext here, because at least two members of Royal Cumberland Lodge thought the removal temporary as they: *proposed and seconded that an exact account of the expenditure be kept during the time this Lodge is held out of Masonic Hall.* Could it be that Geary had thwarted some recent clandestine attempt by somebody to remove their Lodge or Order without the knowledge of the other members, possibly in order to escape any surviving liability? If that was the case, it is one possible explanation for Geary's decision to close the Hall altogether.

At the 31st October meeting, a follow-up letter from Geary was also read-out, in which he named the three Lodges and two Chapters as joint debtors to him for their previous five years of usage; it is interesting to note that Antiquity Encampment is not mentioned as a debtor, despite the evidence of their being tenants at the time. So it can only be deduced that they had maintained their account up to date throughout.

In the absence of the forming of a committee to make any arrangements to settle the matter, Geary provided two options:

Being told I have not named the Sum due to me for the Rent of the Masonic Hall, I now send you the most moderate that can well be stated, being the sum that has been approved by several of your own Body for the use of the Lower Lodge Room, &c from October, 1818, to October 1823, 5 years at £60 per ann £300 not including the Large Room, the profits of which have been appropriated to the use of the Lodges and Chapters, by which means I am a considerable loser - my outgoings during that time having been in Ground Rent alone £84-16s-0d.

OR

If any Brother or Brethren will purchase the Building by taking it at what it has cost me, I will in that case abandon my just claim to the arrears of Rent before mentioned, and if neither of the above offers are accepted, I shall continue (as I find I can do so legally) the doors of the Lodge Room closed against any meeting whatsoever.

Had his initial action not been a considered one, the latter comment shows that Geary had taken formal legal advice, which had confirmed that he was within his rights under the law, as it existed at that time. The first offer confirms the level of indebtedness he had cleared in terms of ground rent alone owed to the Earl, as well as revealing that the Financial Committee had utilised income from external rental of the upper room for uses other than to settle such outgoings, although it doesn't explain what those uses were. But it does demonstrate that Geary did not intend to profit from the past, twelve pounds per year for each Lodge or Order being the equivalent payment for just eighteen members' quarterages, well below the actual memberships during that period and taking no account of charges for initiations, etc.

It is also worth quoting here what English & Spry observed in their later report: *It appears that the demand made by Brother Geary on the various Lodges, is £300, at £60 the year for five years. Whether or no this is a legal demand is not the question, Is it a just one? Though Brothers English and Spry are not aware how this demand is to be paid, upon looking over the whole circumstances, seeing the debt Brother Geary has entailed upon himself, and the relief he has afforded his Masonic Brethren, they consider the sum very moderate.* Geary's second offer was also generous albeit, in the prevailing financial circumstances of the local Fraternity and its members, unlikely to be taken up.

After the ensuing discussion, in which the Royal York Lodge officers also took part, the Royal Cumberland Lodge members resolved that: *the Master and Officers be empowered to take such measures for the purpose of obtaining from Bro. Chas Geary the properties belonging to the Royal Cumberland Lodge as they may think advisable, but suspend any hostile measure until the decision of the Royal York Lodge be obtained on the subject, and that a copy of the resolution be sent to the Royal York Lodge.* No reply was ever received from Royal York as it was about to be embroiled in problems of its own, of which more later.

Royal Cumberland Chapter then, apparently, met on 7th November and sent a memorial to Col. Kemeys-Tynte on the matter: *in consequence of the unmasonic conduct of a Mr Geary a Companion of this Chapter, in abruptly closing the door of the Bath Masonic Hall without the least notice or authority whatever we are prevented holding our regular Chapter meetings. Mr Geary having also seized the Warrant and Furniture of the said Chapter to the great injury of the same and the almost total obstruction of its regular business. We humbly request your Official interference towards the recovery thereof.*

The date of the Chapter's memorial is the same day as the Provincial hearing in Bridgwater, attended by Patton, to resolve the issue of Thomas Whitney's behaviour at their July meeting. The minutes also confirm that Patton attended the November 7th Chapter meeting in Bath, and that he was also a signatory of the memorial. But he could not have been in two places at once, which would suggest that he convened some form of meeting with his Officers prior to leaving for Bridgwater, then took the memorial with him for hand-delivery to Col. Kemeys-Tynte

Patton, in his capacity as Master of Royal Cumberland Lodge, subsequently received a letter from Col. Kemeys-Tynte dated the following day, 8th November, confirming permission for the Lodge to change their registered venue to the White Lion *Provided the Removal of the Lodge to that House meets with approbation of a majority of the members.* He also clarified his position on the other matters: *As to the Furniture and other Property of the Lodge I have no official power to assist you in the recovery of it - but in regard to the Warrant of the Royal Cumberland Chapter I have written by this Post to Companion Geary desiring him to send it to me. This, of course, will be also a sufficient answer (for the present) to the Statement I received yesterday from you signed by the Three Principals of that Chapter.* This confirms that the November 7th memorial from the Chapter was received by Col. Kemeys-Tynte on that same date, the day of the Provincial Chapter hearing. That rapid delivery time could not have been achieved by post.

It is also worth noting that Patton had elected, within days of allegedly discovering the lock-out, to by-pass his Secretary and send a personal letter to the PGM to ask for authority to permanently remove the Lodge to the White Lion, instead of asking for a dispensation to meet there temporarily whilst they attempted to resolve the problems surrounding Freemasons' Hall. Consequently, the content of Patton's letter was not recorded in the Lodge minutes, only the reply to it.

The proviso in the reply from Col. Kemeys-Tynte shows that he may have had his own doubts as to whether Patton was acting in full consort with either his Lodge or Chapter; he may even have had a suspicion that another agenda was in operation, something that would have become apparent during the hearing at Bridgwater. With both parties to this latest dispute (Patton and Geary) in attendance, it would be difficult to imagine that the Colonel did not take the opportunity of having, at the very least, a private word with both. Perhaps that was the reason for Geary subsequently sending an unsolicited further offer to the Lodge on 17th November: *As a first step towards a reconciliation of the present differences relative to the Masonic Hall, I have to request you will make a return and pay the Fees due from the Royal Cumberland Lodge to the Financial Committee up to Midsummer last, with as little delay as possible . I am in possession of the return up to xmas last. The Royal York Lodge have already paid the sum due from them on this account.*

This letter was read-out at the following Royal Cumberland Lodge meeting on 20th November, but no action recorded; however, the agendised consideration to the Lodge's future accommodation was deferred, following which the long-serving Treasurer Tarratt resigned his membership of the Lodge. He was replaced in the post by Patton who, in doing so, completed his monopoly of executive and financial powers within both Lodge and Chapter. This can no longer happen, as the rules of the Fraternity were later amended to prevent any Lodge Officer from holding more than one regular post.

Royal Cumberland Chapter minutes then record that two letters were received addressed to Patton from Col. Kemeys-Tynte. The first, dated November 26th, granted sanction to hold future meetings of the Chapter at the White Lion; the second dated 6th December read: *According to my promise - I wish to inform you that the Charter of the Royal Cumberland Chapter was yesterday put into my possession in Trust for the Chapter.* Again, the wording is interesting, because it would appear that Geary must have passed the Charter to the Colonel, but requested that it be retained by him until the disputes were resolved, otherwise why would the Colonel not have returned it to the Chapter immediately?

But where was Royal Cumberland Lodge's warrant? There is no mention of that either in the Colonel's letter or the Lodge minutes, which surely suggests that the Lodge must already have held it at The White Lion, otherwise they could not have conducted their meetings there. In which case, it can only have been removed from the Hall prior to the lock-out.

In December 1823, Patton was replaced by Hay as Master of Royal Cumberland Lodge, after which the entire matter disappears from their minute book for some time. This may suggest that the new Master did not have the same commitment to this cause demonstrated by his predecessor, or that the Lodge had simply accepted the legality of the situation and returned to normal business.

The other Lodges, however, were not in so comfortable a position.

Virtue holds the Key

W hilst reviewing all that was occurring within Royal Cumberland and Royal York Lodges and their associated Chapters, it is easy to forget that there was another Lodge occupying the Hall who could not avoid being embroiled in the turmoil.

Lodge of Virtue do not feature much in the historical accounts because most of their records were lost over the years and, more importantly, they simply went about their business with a quiet normality that, to be fair, would be very much the 'norm' as far as Masonic Lodges are concerned. They were always considered to be a tradesmens' Lodge, with their membership drawn from businessmen, shopkeepers, builders, publicans, etc, and from what records do survive, their proceedings were conducted in a businesslike manner. That doesn't mean that they were immune from controversy, however.

Earlier in this book, I touched on the problems that rapid expansion of membership was causing within Lodge of Virtue, in terms of selecting a Master in 1821. They also had problems with retaining Treasurers for more than a few meetings at a time, all of which stem from around 1819 when Elias Ferrett resigned the post. A challenge was subsequently made to his accounts by his replacement, Brother Collett, which suggested that there was a discrepancy of some sixty pounds. Ferrett managed to account for all but four guineas but, in doing so, appears to have relied upon support from one section of the membership, who subsequently called upon Collett to apologise for laying false charges. Collett refused to do so and immediately resigned.

Examples of missing funds, accusations and hubris surrounding the proceedings of all of the Bath Lodges are all-too-familiar by this time and, needless to say, there is no record of the other four guineas being subsequently accounted for at a time when Ferrett was also a member of the Financial Committee. The minutes do record, however, a series of skirmishes showing a factionalising within the Lodge, particularly surrounding Ferrett and his supporters.

Excerpts from a letter sent by Senior Warden Thomas Tarratt during 1822 highlight problems with returns and payments to Grand Lodge due to the actions of Elias Ferrett, who by that time had attained the Master's chair: *It will be necessary to enter into the circumstances incurred by the resignation of two candidates for the Mastership of the Lodge in 1821, which by leaving Bro. Ferrett the only candidate, the Chair fell to him, not by the choice of the Lodge. During his situation in that office, the Lodge has greatly suffered in its Interest by his perfect incapability of sustaining with credit, the due observance of our ancient Institution. Thirteen Pounds was collected from the last Lady Day and it was distinctly understood by the Lodge, that he would remit the amount. That Ferrett has failed to discharge his duty, the communication the Lodge has been favoured with from you, amply proves; to explain the reasons I am not enabled to do.*

Tarratt goes on to explain how their newly-elected Master, William Underwood Whitney, could not be installed due to Ferrett's refusal to do so; the younger Whitney brother was entering the Chair of the Lodge for the fifth, and final, time. Consequently, the Lodge had requested Matthew Patton, a regular visitor, to conduct the Installation at a meeting that was boycotted by Ferrett and his faction. The letter continues: *Regular and repeated summonses were delivered to every member, and particularly to Past Master Ferrett, and the Treasurer requesting them to appear with the Cash accounts and transfer them to the present Officers, when they then and now, positively refused to give any information. It is necessary to say that Past Master Ferrett has secretly removed the Warrant and Book of*

The Damage on the Master's Pedestal
where it was jemmied by the members of Lodge
of Virtue, is still evident on the unit to this day
Photo: Paul Mallon

Constitutions, and still holds possession of the cash collected as stated, on Lady Day. Bro. Ferrett retains nearly the whole of the properties of the Lodge with the exception of the Minute Book and Jewels which the Lodge was fortunate enough to secure. That last part refers to Ferrett having also taken away the key to the pedestal, where the jewels were stored. The members overcame that problem by jemmying the lock!

The Lodge appealed to Col. Kemeys-Tynte for assistance and, almost contemporary with Tarratt's, another letter had been sent from the Colonel to the Grand Secretary: *I have had considerable trouble at various times in endeavouring to bring about a reconciliation in the Lodge of Virtue at Bath, which has a long time been in the greatest confusion from party Dissensions, and I am sorry to say that the misconduct of many of the Brethren of that Lodge is become so irreconcilable, that I fear it will be necessary for me Officially to suspend that Lodge from its Masonic Functions. I shall, however, give them one more chance of recovering the Respectability as well as the Masonic Harmony of the Lodge (Both of which are at present entirely destroyed).*

The reply from the Grand Secretary came a few days later, the first part of which perhaps reveals the PGM's naivety at that time with regard to procedure, having been in post barely a year: *Allow me to say that not having stated the particular case, nor the circumstances which have transpired, it would be difficult to frame any Form of Suspension applicable to the occasion.* A second letter accompanied it: *By this day's post I have received a Letter from Lodge of Virtue, excusing the Lodge for having neglected so long to pay the Contributions due to the Grand Lodge. The late Master, E. Ferrett, who it seems has received money from the Lodge for the purpose and never remitted it, although in April last he transmitted the Lodge returns, amounting to £26-14s-6d for three years, stating that a sum of £10-6s had been remitted (without mentioning a date, or channel of communication); he says, " I have not sent the balance, nor shall I until I have received an acknowledgment of what has been already sent." My answer of April 18th, disavowing the receipt of any such remittance, and asking an explanation has not to this hour been replied to. I will take leave to suggest that there is an old Past Master in the Lodge whose Masonic experience ought to have taught him that before matters had taken the extraordinary turn they have, it was his province to have prevented these unmasonic proceedings, I mean Mr. William Whitney.*

There is no confirmation of when or how the missing fees were paid to Grand Lodge, although Ferrett did answer a summons from the Colonel, and they met during October. No record exists of that meeting, and Ferrett did not attend the Lodge thereafter.

From the contents of another letter from Secretary Tarratt at the beginning of November, his influence remained through some disquiet over the previous installation of William Whitney: *Is it **absolutely necessary** under every **circumstance**, that the Immediate Past Master **must alone** install the Worshipful Master Elect? Some unreasonable objection exists in the opinion of the late Past Master, who will not explain that reason, but who removes the Warrant, Constitutions, etc, for the sole purpose (and without the* *consent of the Lodge) to prevent the Lodge from assembling and discharging its duties, to the great injury of the Lodge in particular, and the Craft in general.*

In response, an emergency meeting was held on 20th November when Col. Kemeys-Tynte travelled to Bath to install William Underwood Whitney as Master, assisted by Matthew Patton. The Colonel then suggested and put to the vote that the whole of the Minutes and Transactions of the Lodge for the previous six months should be revised. The Lodge, however, declined to do this and the Colonel had no option but to concede to them remaining as they were, although he left the Lodge members with his fervent hope that no further complaints would be laid before him, following which the Lodge, and William Underwood Whitney, were left to sort the rest out for themselves. However, the lessons from the PGM's first encounter with Lodge irregularities in Bath were well-learned.

Despite the membership having rapidly diminished during Ferrett's jurisdiction, and then further after his departure as his supporters melted away, the minutes for the next year indicate that Lodge settled to conducting business as usual, although the confusion surrounding the returns that should have been compiled by Ferrett would continue to haunt them. In June 1823 Secretary Tarratt was installed as Master and must have been looking forward to further restoring the Lodge to its former status when he presided over the first meeting of the new season at Freemasons' Hall. Little did he know that another maelstrom was about to engulf all of the Lodges that were resident there.

When solving any mystery, the vital clue is often a very simple fact that has been overlooked purely because it was exactly that - simple. Previously, the historical records were very vague on exactly when Geary chose to close the doors, and this had been attributed to the Masonic Lodges in Bath having never met during the Summer months, barring emergencies. On viewing the first problems with the lockout occurring during October, it was easy to assume that this had happened as the Lodges started to assemble again after the summer break, and that Geary could have locked the doors at any time during those intervening months, most likely on the September quarter day which was the six-month anniversary of his taking possession of the property.

But whilst perusing the one surviving Lodge of Virtue minute book, covering the period from 1818 to 1831, there it was - this glaringly-obvious clue that had been previously missed. Their first meeting of the season, on Tuesday October 7th 1823, had been held, as usual, at Freemasons' Hall, which cannot have been closed to the Lodges at that date. Royal Cumberland Lodge's first scheduled meeting was ten days later on Friday 17th, the very meeting they had to hastily rearrange to the White Lion, which meant that Geary can only have taken his decision to close the Hall during that ten day period.

Regardless, Lodge of Virtue was also locked-out and it is interesting that this Lodge, still quite numerous in membership and therefore possessing greater resources with which to seek-out a new home, took considerably longer than the few hours it had taken Royal Cumberland. Lodge of Virtue were unable to assemble for their normal meeting at the beginning of November, and more than two further weeks elapsed before they were finally able to hold an emergency meeting at the Saracen's Head Inn in Walcot Street on November 21st. This may have been due to their needing to recover their Warrant from the Hall, but they seem to have achieved that with little trouble, and certainly without recourse to Province for assistance in doing so.

That the delay was more likely due to the sparseness of availability of suitable accommodation within the city, is shown by the peripatetic arrangements in the weeks following. They met at The Greyhound in the High Street on the 24th, and then The Freemasons Arms in Abbey Green, where the rental arrears for the Hall were discussed on 18th December. They finally settled at the Castle & Ball Inn in Northgate Street on January 7th 1824, when the minutes read: *In consequence of a difference existing between Bro. Geary Past Master Royal Cumberland Lodge (proprietor of the Bath Masonic Hall) and the three Lodges, Bro. Noble proposed that the Lodge of Virtue No.311 to meet for the present (until they be happily accommodated) at the Castle & Ball Inn, Bath which was seconded by the Worshipful Master and unanimously agreed to by the Brethren present.* This short minute shows, in contrast to any of the Masonic bodies in Bath associated with Matthew Patton, that Lodge of Virtue clearly recognised Geary as the bone fide proprietor of the Hall.

From viewing the documentation available, Lodge of Virtue maintained good relations with Charles Geary throughout this difficult period, and were able to resolve their situation quite rapidly. It is also apparent that the lockout that occurred ten days after their meeting at the Hall on October 7th had nothing to do with any actions taken by Lodge of Virtue or its officers. So what could possibly have happened during that ten day period to cause such a reaction from him?

Suspension

One fascinating aspect of historical research is that, regardless of how much information is suppressed, sooner or later clues to it re-emerge from a different source. Which is essentially how I stumbled upon the final piece of the jigsaw, a much-earlier circular letter that had somehow found its way into a pile of returns in the UGLE Library archives relating to a different Lodge. This essentially provides one side's explanation of a situation, but its mere existence begs the question as to why it was not mentioned in the various judgements and reports that were distributed subsequently and, more importantly, why some of the contents were never officially refuted.

The letter was sent by Thomas Whitney to his fellow Royal York Lodge members, and is dated 9th October 1823, although there are additional postscripts dated two days later. This predates the appearance by Whitney at the disciplinary hearing of the Provincial Grand Chapter on November 7th 1823, dealt with earlier in this book; in fact, at the time the circular was written, the Provincial hearing in Bridgwater was not even under consideration - there having been no Provincial Grand Superintendent in post on 6th October, and Grand Chapter having apparently disregarded Patton's charges.

It is a long letter, full of indignance, printed for circulation to more than seventy people and contains this important paragraph: *On Monday Inst,* [6th October 1823] *instead of the usual Summons of the Lodge, the Tyler left with me a letter from the Worshipful Master. It commenced with "Sir," and proceeded to state, that in consequence of very gross misconduct on my part, when a Visitor to the Cumberland Chapter, for which, "no provocation can plead an excuse" and "feeling deeply" for the reputation of the Craft, and the credit of his own Lodge, it became his paramount and painful duty, to* **suspend** *me from my Masonic privileges as a Member of the York Lodge, until "the decision of the Grand Chapter shall be promulgated." -Signed Charles Maddison WM. A Copy of which suspension, he tells me, he forwarded to the Provincial Grand Master.*

Whitney then grandiosely condemned Maddison, further adding that he had appealed to the Provincial Grand Master, and would take the matter higher if necessary. Then the focus of the letter changed completely, with Whitney launching an outright attack on his previous accuser: *Mr Matthew Patton I consider as the origin of the un-Masonic persecution* which I have experienced during the past 18 months. *My success in obtaining for my Lodge in spite of no common opposition, the Chapter now attached to it, has never been forgiven by that individual, who often endeavoured by every art and stratagem to wheedle me from my purpose; because he knew, if successful, it could not promote the interest of his own, but must as he said, deprive him of many Members. The prosperity of the York Lodge, incredible as it may appear, has found in him its deadliest enemy! Envy and malice have been manifested by him on several petty occasions, and more attempts than one made, to create a jealousy and distrust in his Lodge, **against** that of my own; which shall be proved by a **Member** of the Cumberland Lodge if required. To his intrigues and machinations may be traced with the greatest facility, much of the disquietude and much of the disorder that has so lamentably disturbed the harmony of the York Lodge, and the interest of the Establishment in general.* Whitney stated that he was prepared to make a full statement of: *the unmanly and scandalous insults I have received from him* [Patton], *under **protection** of his official situation.* Finally, he indicated his unawareness of the content of the serious charges brought against him, but was prepared to defend his position when he knew them.

There follow three postscripts, the first two dated 10th October. The first of those gave the content of a further letter Whitney had received from Maddison on that day: *Sir, - I have this moment received intimation from the Grand Secretary that a "Craft Lodge" is not competent to notice offences committed in a Royal Arch Chapter, consequently you are restored to the privileges of your Lodge. C. Maddison WM, RYL No 243."* The second detailed a further rapid development: *A few hours **afterwards**, I also received a Note from the Provincial Grand Master, now in Bath, stating that his "interference" was no longer "necessary".* The third postscript, dated 11th October, confirms Whitney's assertion that he had no previous awareness of the charges issued by Royal Cumberland Chapter to Grand Chapter: *Mr. Matthew Patton has this day, for the first time, put me in possession of a Copy of his "Serious Charges". Since I have read them I have again entreated the Provincial Grand Superintendant to grant immediate inquiry. I have no other chance of Justice. An instance of a more depraved and deliberate determination to misrepresent and deceive, I can scarcely conceive it possible to produce!!*

I have only quoted the pertinent passages, leaving aside a lot of the emotional embroidery, but Whitney was absolutely correct regarding the illegality of his suspension. That Maddison had 'jumped the gun' is also clear from his quick withdrawal of that sanction. However, what devalues this circular is the blinkered nature of some of the commentary. Whitney had behaved incredibly badly at the Chapter meeting as the minutes record; although there is no evidence as to why he did that, he can hardly be justified in terming those minutes *a depraved and deliberate determination to misrepresent and deceive.*

Nevertheless, the personal attack upon Patton and his motives, within Whitney's public response to his Lodge 'suspension', contains no reference to the tontine process and was circulated months after Patton's charges were originally sent to Grand Chapter. It therefore precludes this circular letter from being interpreted as any reason for Patton's third charge stating that Whitney had *disseminated a most calumnious and palpable falsehood against the 1st Principal of the Royal Cumberland Chapter.* The circular's contents were never used by Patton as proof of that third charge, either during the Provincial hearing or in any subsequent process. If Whitney's assertions could stand-up under closer scrutiny, that would have been another valid reason why Patton was persuaded by Col. Kemeys-Tynte to withdraw that third charge.

But what persuaded Maddison to take such unilateral action? He presumably had no backing from his Lodge, their having not met since the summer break. As demonstrated by the swift reaction by Col. Kemeys-Tynte, who urgently travelled in person to Bath to rapidly-undo what Maddison had set in motion, neither did he have authority from the Province. This is confirmed by the postscripts, which show that Maddison had, without the knowledge of the Colonel, written directly to the Grand Secretary who had also rapidly told him that he was acting unconstitutionally.

The sentiment in the circular shows that matters were already out of hand, and a solution to the running sore between Patton and Whitney was becoming a matter of urgency, now publically-revealed as simmering away since well before Whitney's outburst in the Chapter meeting. It provided the trigger for the announcement of the appointment by Grand Chapter of the Colonel to fill the vacant Provincial Grand Superintendant situation, confirmed by a letter from Col. Kemeys-Tynte to Edwards Harper, the Grand Scribe, on October 16th seeking advice on how to form a Grand Chapter to hear the case, where he says that he had: *strongly recommended him* [Whitney] *to make some amicable arrangement with the other party* [Patton]. *This however I now find to be quite out of the question.*

None of this explains the long delay before Whitney was made aware of the charges against him, or why that revelation came through unauthorised action of the Master of his Lodge. Surely such outrageous behaviour as Whitney's at the Chapter meeting in July would have been broadcast verbally within the Fraternity locally within days, especially as it occurred within a Chapter drawing membership from all of the local Lodges. If not, and Maddison had only recently become aware of it, the only inference that can be drawn is that someone must have prompted him into action, someone who was fully aware of the charges; someone frustrated by the apparent inertia of Grand Chapter. Even so, for such external influence to have any effect, Maddison would need to have been receptive to it. So was there any indication of previous friction within Royal York Lodge, particularly between Maddison and Whitney, that may have caused Maddison to be looking for an excuse to act?

Other than Thomas Whitney being refused access to Royal Cumberland Chapter in April, and the admonishment he received from Province in May over his request for payment for the banner, there is nothing that could be interpreted as frictional during that time, except in a curious letter that Maddison wrote to the Grand Secretaries on 10th June 1823, for which I could find no prompt either in actual correspondence or events: *I am sorry you were under a misconception relative to the want of harmony in the Royal York Lodge; nothing I believe can be more perfect. Our Lodges have been beautiful and numerously attended, there is nothing to operate against us except the horrible state to which the Lodge finances have been brought. It is true there was one disturbed spirit among us, and only one, but that is, I hope, subdued.* It is easy to presume this *disturbed spirit* was Thomas Whitney, and that he was causing problems that are unminuted.

There is further reference to this in Maddison's evidence to a later disciplinary hearing at Grand Lodge in 1824, where he observed *that all the disgrace which has been brought upon the Craft in the Province of Somerset originated in the unworthy cause of finance and pecuniary difficulties arising principally if not entirely from the measures pursued by Brother Whitney.* Leaving aside his failure to recognise the effect of Pitter's activities, of which he would have been well-aware as a member of Royal York Lodge at the time they were exposed, this was not the only time that Maddison is recorded as referring to the *cause of finance* being *unworthy*. This was a 19th century attitude prevailing among those of inherited wealth, and it is not difficult to understand how this would be an awkward concept for someone of a lower class who had built-up any personal wealth purely through their own hard graft. It is also worth recalling that Maddison joined the Financial Committee just weeks before the tontine was called, when their *finance and pecuniary difficulties* were already obvious; he is only minuted as attending two of its meetings, the second of which was to agree the assignment to Geary in order to bail them out.

However, his June 1823 letter also confirms that the financial situation in Royal York Lodge was still troublesome, Pitter's activities having left them, among other things, well in arrears with their contributions to Grand Lodge, and lacking in copies of the necessary paperwork. Correcting most of the administrative discrepancies had fallen on Thomas Whitney's shoulders as the Secretary of the Lodge at the time. The day after Maddison was installed as Master in January 1823, he wrote to Grand Lodge with regard to what he perceived as an overpayment of Grand Lodge fees. His approach was unsuccessful, but the letter confirms that the Lodge were still actively looking for ways of recovering lost funds.

On 27th February 1823, just a month after Maddison's installation, it was minuted that Royal York Lodge were considering removing from Freemasons' Hall. Two weeks after, the decision was deferred *until the future accommodation of the Lodge could be determined*. A month later the minutes record *that in consequence of a communication from Bro Geary the further consideration as to whether Royal York Lodge should quit Freemasons Hall is postponed indefinitely*. By the timing, that communication can only have been Geary's confirmation that he had taken-over all of the liabilities of the Hall, and that the accommodation was safe from being seized by the previous Landlord.

If the discussion regarding removal floundered on the Lodge not being able to afford fees higher than those charged at the Hall, the sudden withdrawal of access to the Hall in October would have been a major setback. The meetings held in November and December 1823 were at an unstated venue, probably the White Lion Inn. We know little of what transpired, because entries in the final Royal York Lodge minute book abruptly cease on 26th June 1823. This is quite frustrating, as minutes for those meetings would lift the veil on some important occurrences.

However, instead of revealing those secrets, the final minute book provided another simple clue. Sat on the desk in front of me at Great Queen Street were the minute books for both of the defunct Lodges, and as I closed the final Royal York book, I saw that the binding, size and gold-blocking were all identical to that of the final Lodge of Virtue minute book sat next to it. I also realised that the Royal Cumberland Lodge and Chapter minute books I had been trawling through previously in Bath were also identically-bound. A quick check of the first entries confirmed that both books on the desk commenced at the Lodges' first meetings in Freemasons' Hall in 1818; a subsequent check of the other books on my return to Bath revealed the same start point. Therefore all of the Lodges and Orders had started new, identically-bound, Minute Books on commencing occupation of Freemasons' Hall.

So what is the significance of that, you may ask? Well, it means that the books were designed to be held together in the same location in the building, and that being the case, the reason why Royal York's book stopped so abruptly can only have been because it had remained locked in the Hall after Geary closed the doors. That had happened prior to October 17th, when Royal Cumberland Lodge were locked-out, meaning Royal York Lodge could not have held any meeting at the Hall in October prior to Royal Cumberland's, and revealing that Royal Cumberland Lodge and Chapter minute books were not in the Hall when it was closed, because they continue uninterrupted to record the events already related, another confirmation of Geary's assertion regarding items being removed from the Hall.

More importantly, this confirms that there could have been no official prediscussion within open Lodge of Maddison's decision to suspend Thomas Whitney, as communicated to him on 6th October. Maddison and his Wardens had also attended the meetings of Royal Cumberland Lodge at the White Lion following the closure of the Hall. On October 24th, they had been present, and presumably acquiesced, when the decision was taken to send the letter to Geary demanding to know under what right he had acted. They were also present a week later when the reply was read-out and the decision taken to adopt hostile measures, but not until the decision had been ratified by Royal York. This means that Maddison and his Wardens were acting without any authority of their Lodge, which had not met since June, the scheduled Royal York Lodge night in October 1823 would have been Thursday 30th, between the two Royal Cumberland meetings.

That Maddison was still in the position of having to obtain the permission of his Lodge to proceed with the action decided on the 31st October shows that there could not have been a Royal York Lodge meeting the previous evening at any location, otherwise the matter would have been discussed and he would have had some form of mandate to proceed under.

The only clues regarding those later Royal York meetings come from some correspondence and later Board of General Purposes documentation, the combination of which shows that meetings were convened on 7th November, 27th November and 23rd December. The meeting of 27th November was a turbulent affair, because on 9th December, Col. Kemeys-Tynte wrote to the Grand Secretaries: *The Brethren at Bath are in great Confusion amongst other circumstances that have occurred, the W. Master* [Maddison] *& Both the Wardens of the Rl. York Lodge have struck work having resigned their Offices without having appointed any successors. The Warrant of the Lodge is now in my possession, after a good deal of trouble to obtain it from Bror. Geary, & at their desire.* The letter concluded: *I fear I must go there personally next week for the purpose of endeavouring to settle these disputes though as they chiefly originate in money matters (over which I can have no control) I can hardly look forward to a favourable result.* There is no correspondence giving dispensation to the Lodge for the November meetings, both held without the Lodge being in possession of its warrant. The meeting on the 27th resulted in a request being sent to the PGM for his assistance in securing its return.

The causes of the disturbances will be dealt with in a later chapter, along with their repercussions, but regardless of that difficulty, the December meeting was held constitutionally because, following his reluctant visit to Bath during which he returned the warrant, Col. Kemeys-Tynte was able to write again to London on 17th December in a more positive frame of mind: *I am happy to inform you that the misunderstanding between the Rl York Lodge and other persons at Bath seems to be taking a more favourable turn & I trust that through the mediation of Dr Muttlebury & some others of the more sensible & right minded Brethren, we shall eventually bring the business round to a Proper & Reasonable Conclusion.*

The festive season always tends to encourage positive thoughts for the future, but these are often wiped-out in the cold hard light of a new year. It would be but a matter of weeks before the Colonel would realise how optimistic that letter had been.

Timeline

From all of this additional information, it is finally possible to establish a timeline on the sequence of events during those fateful weeks towards the end of 1823.

With the commencement of the Masonic season, Secretaries and Tylers were beginning to distribute summonses for the first meetings. Charles Geary, the new proprietor of the Hall and thereby the employer of the resident Tylers, was readying himself for a renewed effort to bring the matters of legal tenancies to a conclusion. However, he already knew he had a problem with both Royal Cumberland Lodge and Chapter, due to the strong influence of Matthew Patton in both, a man who seemed not to understand why Geary had been forced into taking-over the building in the first place, and who viewed Geary as nothing more than a speculator preying off the Fraternity in the City.

On the other hand, Geary knew that he had some degree of support from Royal York Lodge and Chapter, where more than half of the members had been subscribers to the previous finance schemes, and where the main driver in the project, Thomas Whitney, still held considerable influence. However, that Lodge had been severely weakened financially by the illegal activities of its past Secretary, Thomas Pitter, a person who had left his mark on more than one institution in the City, including the Hall itself.

The other tenant, Lodge of Virtue, had opened negotiations not only on the tenancy agreement, but also on how they could discharge their outstanding debt from the previous years, despite their own financially-embarrassed state due to their Past Master Elias Ferrett's actions.

In chronological order, this is what happened next:

Monday 6th October - Thomas Whitney is suspended from Royal York Lodge of Perfect Friendship by the Worshipful Master, Charles Maddison. The reason given for the suspension is Whitney's behaviour in an unconnected Royal Arch Chapter some ten weeks earlier. Whitney appeals to the PGM, Col. Kemeys-Tynte, by letter.

Tuesday 7th October - Lodge of Virtue meet at Freemasons Hall on their normal Lodge night.

Wednesday 8th October - Col. Kemeys-Tynte receives Whitney's letter and decides to travel to Bath.

Thursday 9th October - Whitney drafts a letter for general circulation regarding his suspension, also stating that he is not in possession of the charges laid against him in July by Matthew Patton, regarding the events at Royal Cumberland Chapter.

Friday 10th October - Whitney receives a letter from Maddison withdrawing the Lodge suspension, plus a letter from Col. Kemeys-Tynte advising that he had travelled to Bath to intervene on Whitney's behalf. On the same day, whilst at Bath, the Colonel receives a letter from the Grand Scribes advising his appointment as Provincial Grand Superintendent of Royal Arch for Somerset and enclosing a copy of the charges issued by Patton.

Saturday 11th October - Whitney receives, for the first time, a copy of the actual charges that Patton had preferred against him. He adds postscripts to his circular letter.

Monday 13th October - Whitney issues his circular letter.

Thursday 16th October - Col. Kemeys-Tynte writes to Edwards Harper, Grand Scribe, asking for guidance as to how to convene a Provincial Royal Arch hearing in the matter of Patton's charges.

Friday 17th October - Geary officially closes the doors of the Hall. Royal Cumberland Lodge convene at the White Lion Inn, from where they write to Geary demanding their rights.

Monday 20th October - Geary replies to Royal Cumberland Lodge saying he has no intention of relenting until formal arrangements for the tenancies are in place.

Friday 24th October - Geary's letter is discussed at a special meeting of Royal Cumberland Lodge attended by officers of Royal York Lodge.

Sunday 26th October - Geary receives a letter from Royal Cumberland Lodge demanding the authority for his action

Tuesday 28th October - Geary sends letter to Royal Cumberland Lodge advising them that the authority lies in his situation as landlord for the building. Matthew Patton contrives Royal Cumberland Chapter's lock-out.

Wednesday 29th October - All Somerset Royal Arch Chapters receive official notification from London that Col. Kemeys-Tynte has been appointed their new Provincial Grand Superintendant. Royal Cumberland Chapter receive letter from Col. Kemeys-Tynte giving notice of the Provincial Hearing on 7th November.

Thursday 30th October - Geary makes unsolicited offer of settlement, either by the payment of arrears or by the Brethren purchasing the property from him.

Friday 31st October - Royal Cumberland Lodge meet, again with the Royal York Officers in attendance, to consider their position.

Friday 7th November - Provincial Grand Chapter is convened in Bridgwater to hear the charges against Thomas Whitney, with all of the main protagonists in attendance, bar for Maddison who remained in Bath. Meetings of Royal Cumberland Chapter and Royal York Lodge also take place on this day, the former minuted as chaired by Patton, the latter by Maddison, concurrent with Whitney, Geary and Patton either being in, or travelling to or from, Bridgwater.

Monday 17th November - Geary sends his conciliatory offer to Royal Cumberland Lodge, in which he states that Royal York Lodge have cleared their arrears.

Thursday 20th November - Royal Cumberland Lodge defer consideration of future accommodation.

Friday 21st November - Lodge of Virtue meet at the Saracens Head Inn in Walcot Street

Monday 24th November - Lodge of Virtue meet at the Greyhound Inn in the High Street

Wednesday 26th November - Col. Kemeys-Tynte grants sanction to Royal Cumberland Chapter to hold meetings at the White Lion Inn.

Thursday 27th November - scheduled meeting of Royal York Lodge that results in the resignation of Maddison and his officers.

Saturday 6th December - Col. Kemeys-Tynte advises Royal Cumberland Chapter that he has their Charter in his possession, but does not make any arrangements to return it to them.

Tuesday 9th December - Col. Kemeys-Tynte writes to the Grand Secretaries asking for guidance on how to overcome the resignation of all senior officers in Royal York Lodge. He refers to an attached letter enquiring whether a Past Master can summon a Lodge for the appointment of officers, and suggests he may have the power to do so.

Wednesday 17th December - Col. Kemeys-Tynte writes again to the Grand Secretaries thanking them for their assistance and advising that *the misunderstanding between Royal York Lodge and other persons at Bath seems to be taking a more favourable turn, and that the mediation of Dr*

*Muttlebury and some others of the more sensible and right-minded Brethren, we
shall eventually bring the business round to a proper & reasonable conclusion.*

Thursday 18th December - Lodge of Virtue meet at the
Freemasons Arms in Abbey Green to discuss arrears.

Tuesday 23rd December - Royal York Lodge meet to select a new
Master.

Thus, as 1823 drew to its close, Freemasons' Hall was closed to all
Lodges and Orders in Bath. All of the furniture and equipment that
they used was locked inside, with a few exceptions:

Royal Cumberland Lodge's Warrant and Minute Book have escaped,
along with the Royal Cumberland Chapter Minute Book, which are
all in the possession of their organisations;

Royal Cumberland Chapter's Charter has been released by Charles
Geary and is in the hands of Col. Kemeys-Tynte for safe-keeping;

Royal York Lodge of Perfect Friendship's Warrant has been released
by Charles Geary and returned to them via Col. Kemeys-Tynte;

Lodge of Virtue's Warrant and Minute Book have been returned to
them directly by Charles Geary.

It is unlikely that it will ever be possible to decipher precisely what
forced Geary's decision to close the Hall. All these events were part of
a larger domino effect, where the pieces started tumbling three years
earlier, with the discovery of Thomas Pitter's absconding with the bulk
of the cash assets of both his Lodge and the Hall Financial Committee,
then subsequently with the formation of Royal York Chapter, the
original trigger for Matthew Patton's antagonism towards Thomas
Whitney.

The failure of the Lodges to negotiate new tenancy agreements over a
period of more than six months was central to creating the background
conditions whereby something would have to give, sooner or later.
Matthew Patton was clearly unhappy about the initiation of the tontine,
and identified Geary as the main reason for that.

Whitney's suspension by Maddison could have been a factor, but not
because Geary reacted to it. Exactly what prompted Maddison to take
unilateral action against Whitney at that point in time will also never be
known, but as he is not shown as an attendee of the Chapter meeting
back in July where Whitney embarrassed himself, he can only have
heard of the incident from a third-party. Afterwards, the attempts by
Col. Kemeys-Tynte and the Grand Secretaries in London to regain

some equilibrium were always running just that crucial bit of time behind the game.

It is impossible to know exactly at what point Geary knew of the issues in Whitney's letter, but it is fair to assume that Matthew Patton would have become quickly aware of the part of the content that referred to him. This could have hardened Patton's attitude to the situation, particularly if he read the Colonel's swift reaction as an indication that Whitney was likely to escape unpunished for his behaviour. If he was disgruntled by the Grand Chapter's lack of action on the matter, and the lack of any local senior representation in Royal Arch, Whitney's circular letter would not have eased his mood, so he could have seen a removal of his Lodge and Chapter from the Hall as the only method of protest remaining to him on both counts. In the circumstances, it is doubtful that he would have thought through exactly what that could lead to, especially if the attempt to do this was first conducted clandestinely. If this did happen, as claimed by Geary, it can only have occurred during the week of 13th to 17th October, otherwise Geary would have reacted to it earlier.

The decisions reached in Bridgwater, and the actions ordered by Col. Kemeys-Tynte, should have formed the foundations for reconciliation; in fact, with the benefit of hindsight, they were the last chance of preventing matters from spiralling completely out of control. With it being a Friday, the long carriage journey back to Bath followed by the weekend to ponder on matters may have produced an atmosphere wherein proper negotiations could have taken place. However, this is the point where another action by Maddison exacerbated the situation, his calling of a Royal York Lodge meeting while the main protagonists were all out of town.

Friday was not the normal meeting night for Royal York Lodge, so it would have been an emergency meeting convened at a substitute venue. As there are no surviving minutes for Royal York Lodge for the period after the Hall was closed, there is no record of what was discussed, or of where that substitute venue was, but it was probably the White Lion, where Royal Cumberland had established themselves.

The meeting may have been called to discuss the proposals from Royal Cumberland Lodge with regard to taking action against Geary; it may have been about Thomas Whitney's abortive suspension. Even stretching this to being purely a co-incidence, Thomas Whitney's humour could not have been improved by it, particularly as he had suffered no loss of his Masonic privileges through the Provincial Chapter hearing. Could this action have been read as another example of Maddison jumping the gun?

Although their personalities and backgrounds were so different, Patton, Geary and Thomas Whitney must have found common ground at some time in their careers in order to be able to work so closely together in Royal Cumberland Chapter for many years - although there is no indication that any of them were ever close personal friends.

They were all successful retail businessmen of independent means, so they should all have possessed the necessary flexibility and worldly experience to be able to manage the minor setbacks and temporary frustrations of life. Their created wealth, however, was relative. Geary possessed easily the most lucrative business, with a high-class clientele, Whitney's was one of necessity and the most prominent of its type in the City. Neither were of a nature to be overly-effected by fads or trends, whilst Patton's was susceptible to sudden changes in style, fashion or economic conditions.

Colonel Kemeys-Tynte and Captain Maddison were both, first and foremost, landowners and military officers, two forms of status that were not renowned at that time for being particularly tolerant of dissension, however justified. Both were men of inherited wealth, but the Colonel was an only son in a line of baronetage possessing several estates, whereas Maddison was a third son of a gentrified military family. As the senior in every aspect, the Colonel had the necessary authority to bring all of this under control, but he was relatively-inexperienced in Masonic politics.

There are several obvious contrasts between the two groups: the difference in social perception of 'new' and 'old' money; the expectation of military men in terms of reaction to their issuance of instructions, as opposed to retailers who are more predictive in their judgement of how customers may behave. Nevertheless, other than the military background and the Colonel being his distant relative, quite why Charles Maddison decided to become so deeply embroiled in this matter is not entirely clear.

All of these factors would come into greater focus as the story moves forward from cause to effect.

AL5817

FREEMASONS' HALL

PART FOUR
THE
FURNITURE

The Bath Furniture

O ver the intervening 200 years, the focus of this story has moved from the building itself to its contents, this sorry affair becoming known within the Fraternity as 'The Bath Furniture Incident'. This is primarily because successive historians have concentrated more on what happened twenty years on from the point in history that we have now arrived at. So, before moving on to what happened next, this may be a good time to examine exactly what was locked inside the Hall.

As will be explained later, all of the contents were acquired in 1843 by the Loyal Lodge of Barnstaple No.251, and some of the more important of those contents are still in use in their Lodge room in Barnstaple. Their current building, Trafalgar Lawns, was built in around 1810, so it is an ideal setting for this furniture, most of which is actually contemporary with it. What was acquired by Loyal Lodge is listed in a document entitled *Catalogue of the Magnificent Furniture Costly Jewels &c lately attached to the Freemasons' Hall, Bath* which was included in a letter circulated by Charles Geary in October 1842, advertising the method of disposal.

The original copy of this circular received by Loyal Lodge is on display in their Lodge Room. It states that *the Sum of £645-15s-0d. has been expended in the production of this Superb Collection*, another indication of the causes of the financial problems suffered at the Hall. To give some perspective to this figure, simple inflation would make it equivalent to well in excess of £60,000 today. However, it is highly-doubtful that it would be possible to acquire even some of the items today for that sort of figure.

When we visited Barnstaple to take the photographs in this section, they very kindly allowed us to set up the Lodge Room as closely as we could to what we had deduced the upper room at York Street would have looked like to anyone entering on the day of the dedication, and the photo opposite was the result.

Since acquisition of the furniture, Loyal Lodge have had three homes. From 1843 to 1868, they used the main Assembly Rooms in the centre of the town, their having to move there from the previous cramped accommodation primarily because of the purchase of the furniture. In 1868 they moved to premises they acquired in Queen Anne Street, where they remained until 1967 when they moved to Trafalgar Lawns.

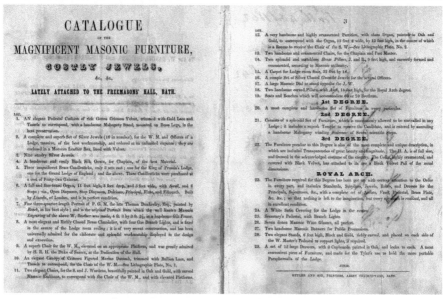

The catalogue of 29 items of Bath Furniture
acquired by Loyal Lodge No.251 in 1843. *Bath Masonic Hall Trust*

It is obvious when comparing the contents of the Lodge Room at Trafalgar Lawns today to the inventory, that some of the items purchased in 1843 are no longer in use. For example, there was a damask canopy over the Master's Chair, and the tracing board had a cover, neither of which have survived. Some of the missing items have been disposed of over the intervening years, either through their no longer being of ceremonial use, or simply through succumbing to the passage of time, and these are covered in more detail in Appendix 2.

Seventy-five years ago a member of Loyal Lodge, Bruce Oliver, conducted substantial research on the furniture, his conclusions being published in 1944. That research was conducted at the Lodge's previous home in Queen Anne Street, and gives us a useful snapshot of what remained at that point in time. As can be seen by comparing the picture of the current Lodge Room on the previous page with that taken by Bruce Oliver in 1944 shown opposite, there are items in the current room that were not in use at Queen Anne Street in 1944, and vice versa.

It can also be seen that Trafalgar Lawns is smaller in size than Queen Anne Street was. However, the 1944 picture shows a room not dissimilar in size and layout to York Street, so the reader can see why I deduced that it was unlikely that those present at the dedication in 1819 were seated on benches, more likely they stood on stepped platforms around the room.

There are also two items that are obviously missing from both pictures. I previously mentioned a short passage from Pierce Egan's *Walks through Bath* published in 1819, regarding the statues on the pediment of the Bath Masonic Hall building. That book also contained a description of the interior, which included the following:

The interior of the building is very complete and convenient in all its various parts; and well worthy of being visited. The great room or hall is 50 by 30 feet. It has two fireplaces with fluted pillars against the wall. Opposite the entrance to the room stands the Master's Chair, upon an elevation with an ascent of three steps of black and white marble, supported by two lions the left and right foot of each are on balls to correspond.

The lions were not listed in the catalogue, so clearly did not even make it to Barnstaple, neither are they among the small number of incidental items now in Bath Masonic Museum. But before introducing too many mysteries, let's take a look at what still survives today, and where it may have originated, using information derived from Bruce Oliver's 1944 article, 1842 catalogue descriptions, contents of various Bath Lodge minute books and, where applicable, my own research.

The furniture in the Lodge Room at Queen Anne Street, Barnstaple in 1944
Bath Masonic Hall Trust

The Master's Chair is described in the catalogue as *A superb Chair for the W.M., elevated on an appropriate Platform.* It has a crimson seat and padded arms, black velvet back with the central Sun, or Blazing Star, in orange silk. The woodwork is painted black with the compo ornament picked out in gold and crowned with the All-seeing Eye set in a Triangle depicted in the Tympanum, formed by scrolls of Acanthus Leaves rising to support the Badge of the Prince of Wales.

Left:
The original Master's Chair in Barnstaple
Below:
The Replica Chair in Bath

All Photos in this chapter: Paul Mallon

From clawed feet the legs rise in spiral fluting to Lions' Masks placed just below the front rail of the seat, which has a central panel featuring the three Great Lights. Above the masks are panels occupied by small figures and above them, seated on balls, rise the scroll arms housed into the fluted columns supporting the back, on which are a golden Sun, Moon, Seven Stars, a pair of Compasses and a Level. There are two further symbols, both abandoned when the two Grand Lodges amalgamated in 1813: a Beehive commending the employment of time by practical industry and the Phoenix, here resting on flames and Acacia leaves.

A replica of this Master's Chair is in daily use in the current Bath Masonic Hall, having been presented to them in 1930 by W. Bro Leonard Fuller, Provincial Senior Grand Warden for Somerset. The replica was made by the Bath furniture makers Mallet & Son.

Determining the provenance of this chair, and indeed any other items of this furniture, is somewhat problematical, because Lodge minutes on the subject are sparse - only Royal Cumberland's being complete, and references to acquisitions, etc, are only mentioned if an approval vote for the expense was involved. As for capital purchases by the Finance Committee, no detailed records survive.

Bruce Oliver dated the chair design to the 1790s, and thought it was originally the Master's Chair from Lodge of Virtue, because it is contemporary with the columns that stand either side. However, Lodge of Virtue was a tradesmens' Lodge, so it is doubtful they would have desired, or been prepared to purchase, so expensive a chair.

The Prince of Wales feathers should set the design between 1790 and 1812, when Prince George was Grand Master of the Moderns, prior to his becoming Regent. In which case it could have been acquired by

Royal Cumberland in their early years after amalgamation with the Bear Inn Lodge when they were thriving, and prior to the period they struggled for numbers due to so many of their younger members being away for long periods fighting the French. Indeed this was the reason why, in 1803, some Lodge of Virtue members, including Charles Geary, became joining members of Royal Cumberland in an attempt to ensure its continuance.

There is another aspect that has not been previously considered, and that is shared usage of facilities. There were periods when two Lodges shared the same room above an Inn, and in those days they met fortnightly. These chairs are neither small nor easily portable, meaning that it is doubtful the furniture of one Lodge would all be moved around and replaced by that of another every time they met, so in these cases they would also have shared the equipment of one Lodge.

In 1797, Royal Cumberland moved from the Bear Inn and joined Lodge of Virtue at The White Lion, where the latter had been in residence for nearly ten years. Two years later, both moved to The Bird Cage Inn until 1801, when Lodge of Virtue moved to the Gloucester Inn and Royal Cumberland to The Christopher. It took several years after this move for Royal Cumberland to build its membership to the point that it could support itself, let alone buy any expensive furniture.

There was an earlier short period, from 1781 to 1786 when Lodge of Perfect Friendship moved in with The Bear Inn Lodge at the White Hart in Stall Street. When the older Lodge amalgamated with the newly-formed Royal Cumberland Lodge in 1786, the combined Lodge moved back to their original home at the Bear Inn, leaving Lodge of Perfect Friendship in possession of the Lodge Room at the White Hart until 1803. So there is a possibility that some furniture changed hands in 1786, especially if the combined Lodge obtained new equipment at that point.

However, that would be too early for the Master's Chair now in Barnstaple so, if not originating from Royal Cumberland, it is more likely it was specifically-acquired by the committee for the Royal dedication of the Hall Project, probably second-hand. After all, if you have invited the Grand Master to dedicate your new Hall, then you would need something suitable to accommodate him. Indeed, the catalogue specifically states in the description that this chair *was greatly admired by H.R.H. the Duke of Sussex, at the Dedication of the Hall.*

The Senior Warden's chair is 18th century with Adam influences, and has square moulded legs carved with the compasses. The rail across the front of the seat is carved with acanthus leaf scrolls either side of a central panel displaying the Volume of the Sacred Law with the square and compasses. The back is wood, grained and painted with a sunken central circular panel with the Warden 's Level painted in the centre, surrounded by the ourubos symbol of Wisdom and Eternity entwined with ivy. The back supports are fluted columns crowned with Corinthian capitals and balls. The semi-circular pediment is later than the body of the Chair, as also is the florid, rococo top ornament, in the panel of which is again painted the Senior Warden's Emblem.

Bruce Oliver identified this as a modified Master's Chair, originally from the Bear Inn Lodge, their 1768 minutes stating that Brother Davis *was paid six guineas for a new Master's Chair,* and the design of the chair would match that dating. They amalgamated with the new Royal

Cumberland Lodge in 1786, and two years later a further minute recorded that *an addition be made to the Master's Chair with the Master's Emblem, under the inspection of Brother Birchall,* which would explain the extra ornamentation.

He also believed that, as the Senior Warden's emblems are painted-on, that particular modification was made after the chair came to Barnstaple. That is unlikely, because the catalogue description shows that this chair arrived as that of a Senior Warden, meaning those particular changes were made much earlier in Bath, more likely, at the Hall to match the grander style of the chair acquired for the dedication.

The Junior Warden's Chair does not match the other two at all and, it has to be said, looks rather ungainly in their company. In fact, all but the tallest Junior Warden would find it difficult to surmount this chair without the use of the stepped platform beneath it. It is late Sheraton dating from the early 19th century, and the overlength of the legs suggest that this was also originally a Master's Chair.

The plumb rule and book are a later addition, the only other emblems being the Square and Compasses inlaid in the top blocks of the legs. The turned legs are reeded, the arms finish with scrolls and house into fluted columns finished with gilt Corinthian caps and balls supporting the oval back. The red leather seems to have been the original covering, although the seat has been renewed at some point.

Bruce Oliver suggested that this may have been the Master's Chair from Lodge of Perfect Friendship, as they were the most successful Lodge in Bath at the time that this chair was made. However, there are no obvious references in surviving Minute Books to back this up.

The catalogue description for both Wardens' Chairs actually reads *Two elegant Chairs, for the S. and J. Wardens, beautifully painted in Oak and Gold, With carved Masonic Emblems, to correspond with the Chair of the W.M.* which, unless the cataloguer was being particularly tongue-in-cheek would seem to rule out this monster of a chair as being the one for the Junior Warden that came from Bath.

There are two further chairs that may give a clue, which currently provide seating either side of the Master for the IPM and senior Grand or Provincial Officer.

They are also of late Sheraton Style, and could be those described in the catalogue as *Two handsome and Ornamented Chairs, for the Chaplain and Past Master*. They may also be what was described in an 1810 Royal Cumberland minute observing an expenditure of *Two Pounds for two Elbow Chairs*. If that is the case, were they purchased to match the Master's Chair in use at that time, obtained when they moved to the Christopher some years earlier and now the Junior Warden's here?

However, there are also two minutes from Loyal Lodge mentioned by Bruce Oliver that may hold the answer. The first dates from 1821 and mentions a *chair made for the Worshipful Master by Bro George Hearson (Cabinet Maker) at a cost of £8-18s-11d*, to which in 1829 *two Corinthian capitals and gilded & spherical balls were added*.

So, there is an outside possibility that the Junior Warden's chair may not be from Bath at all, but is the Master's Chair in use by Loyal Lodge when the new furniture arrived. Maybe some unexpected fate befell the one from Bath, and this one was pressed into service instead, but as no minutes seem to exist on the matter, this will just have to remain in the realm of speculation.

If the two chairs on the previous page are not those listed in the catalogue as *Two handsome and Ornamented Chairs, for the Chaplain and Past Master*, then that item may relate to these two, currently used as the chairs for the Deacons, because they bear the appropriate insignia:

Bruce Oliver described these as *mahogany chairs of Hepplewhite character, dating about 1785, beautifully shaped and carved with Anthemion ornament*. However, they are more likely of oak and of earlier Gothic-style, maybe even dating back to the early days of the Bear Inn Lodge. The Masonic symbols in the panels above the upholstered backs, are original and painted, with the emblem of the I.P.M. depicted as the Gallows type which would seem to confirm this earlier dating.

Moving on from chairs, there are no descriptions in the catalogue that specifically mention the other items at the principal officer stations, except for an entry that states: *1st DEGREE - A most complete and handsome set of Furniture in every particular.*

Commencing with the pedestals, that for the Master is particularly decorative. Made of mahogany, with the south side opening as a door disclosing a nest of drawers, each complete with a drop handle. The exterior is painted and marbled, each face decorated with painted symbols. On the front is the Circle, Blazing Star and letter "G", around which are sprays of acacia, and corn. In the four angles are the Square, Level, Plumb Rule, and Past Master's Jewel. On the north side are two pens in saltire, for the Secretary, and on the south two keys in saltire representing the Treasurer.

This undoubtedly came from Lodge of Virtue, as there is clear evidence of the door being jemmied at some stage in its history, which would correspond with the incident mentioned earlier when their Past Master Elias Ferrett refused to give up the key.

The Wardens' pedestals are of a much more simple design, as can be seen from this picture of the Senior Warden's station. They are, however, of the same painted and marbled finish as that of the Worshipful Master, and so would also have originated in Lodge of Virtue. They both retain their marble tops, but that feature has been lost from the Master's Pedestal, it having been fitted with a mahogany replacement at some time.

On the wall opposite the Junior Warden's station is the object described in the catalogue as *A large Masonic Dial to stand opposite the J.W.* This is a painted clock showing 'High Twelve'.

Finally in this section we have what is described as a *Secretary's Pedestal, with Branch Lights.* This is, again, ornately painted and in a style that matches some aspects of other furniture that would have been procured for the Hall. There are no 'branch lights' fitted to it, which is unsurprising as those lights would have been candelabra when this was first used, later replaced with gas lights.

Returning to the Master's station, this is flanked by two 5-foot-high Rococo Pillars surmounted with Cary's Globes.

The wooden pedestals are square in plan, shaped and heavily ornamented in compo of French-Chippendale character. The ground work is painted a pale salmon colour, with the ornament gilt. They are late 18th century, and Bruce Oliver considered them to have come from Lodge of Virtue. There is nothing I have found that would give cause to doubt that.

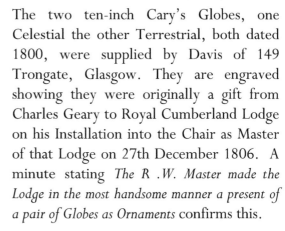

The two ten-inch Cary's Globes, one Celestial the other Terrestrial, both dated 1800, were supplied by Davis of 149 Trongate, Glasgow. They are engraved showing they were originally a gift from Charles Geary to Royal Cumberland Lodge on his Installation into the Chair as Master of that Lodge on 27th December 1806. A minute stating *The R .W. Master made the Lodge in the most handsome manner a present of a pair of Globes as Ornaments* confirms this.

Next to each pedestal are *Three magnificent Brass Candlesticks, only 3 sets cast; one for the King of Prussia's Lodge, one for the Grand Lodge of England and the above. These Candlesticks were purchased at a cost of 42 Guineas.*

There is little to add to that catalogue description, other than they are made of ormolu, essentially gilded-bronze, with allegorical silver plates inlaid and feature elegant and delicate workmanship throughout. They vary in height to maintain the classical symmetry of the Roman Orders of Architecture they represent - Ionic, Doric and Corinthian. Each is complete in its architectural details of entablature, Capital, Shaft, Base, and Pedestal resting. They are contemporary with the date of the Hall, so were clearly purchased by the Financial Committee specifically for the Hall project, at a price equivalent to 7% of the total value of the contents.

At the western end of the Lodge Room are *Two splendid and matchless Brass Pillars, J and B, 9 feet high, and correctly formed and ornamented, according to Masonic authority.*

Bruce Oliver described these as *Striking in appearance, these two Columns are fine examples of the work of those who follow the Craft of Tubal Cain. The shafts proper are not tapered, but cylindrical, they are three & one-sixth diameters in height from the base mouldings to the necking of the Capital which is two diameters in height and Corinthian in character, but Lotus flowers and leaves in wrought brass replace the conventional volutes and acanthus leaves. Above the capital is a brass bowl overlaid with a chain "network" from which are suspended brass balls symbolising Pomegranates.*

There is little to be added to that, other than they are probably the finest examples of Masonic pillars you will see in any Lodge Room, including at Grand Lodge.

Bruce Oliver dated these to around the end of the 18th century, although it is difficult to understand that degree of accuracy bearing in mind that they are made according to Masonic design, and therefore not subject to fashion. He also expressed reservations regarding their setting in the York Street Hall because, if the brass plinths incorporated made them self-standing their height is only 5 ft 9in, which might make them somewhat insignificant in their traditional position without the additional wooden plinths, which he thought may have been added in Barnstaple.

I think that reservation is unfounded for two reasons: first, the catalogue description of their being *9 feet high* clearly shows that the wooden plinths came with them from York Street. Secondly, in the early 19th century pillars were generally smaller, because most Masonic Lodges still met in rooms in inns and hotels, where the ceilings were lower.

As to where they originate from, I somehow doubt they belonged to one of the Bath Lodges, for much the same reasons previously mentioned - the sheer expense of acquiring them. Which would make them yet another expensive acquisition by the Finance Committee, although there is no way of knowing if they were second-hand or specially commissioned by them.

Loyal Lodge possess a fine set of 19th century large tracing boards, similar to those still used by Royal Cumberland in Bath. However, Bruce Oliver believed these had not come from Bath, as the designs date from 1823, a date when the Bath Hall finances were already in freefall. He highlighted a Loyal Lodge minute from 1836 when the Lodge was presented with three such boards and this, together with none being listed in the 1842 catalogue, confirms them as not part of the Bath Furniture. There is, however, another board of older design that is part of a table in one of the robing rooms at Barnstaple.

It contains symbols that disappeared after the creation of United Grand Lodge in 1813, but are still retained in Royal Cumberland workings presented to them in 1786 by Thomas Dunckerley. Bruce Oliver observed that the design on the table legs and body was similar to that on the contemporary organ from Bath, leaving no doubt that this is Royal Cumberland's original tracing board, that had come from Bath in 1842. But is there more to it?

The use of three tracing boards to represent the symbolism employed, one for each degree, evolved after the adoption of Emulation ritual in 1816. Before that, various procedures and artefacts were used, commencing in the early 18th century with the symbolism being drawn on the Lodge floor with chalk before the meeting, and erased after.

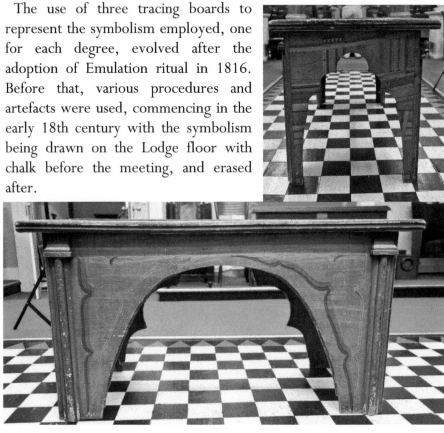

This developed into the use of embroidered floor cloths that could be folded and stored away, and then to a board with combined symbolism painted onto it that would stand permanently in the centre of the room, covered when not in use. These objects were originally called 'Trasel' or 'Trestle' Boards, because they would normally stand on a trestle in the centre of the room; this eventually evolved in Emulation ritual to 'Tracing Board'. During that evolution, there was a period during the latter part of the 18th century when they were termed 'The Lodge'.

Preston's 1772 book, *Illustrations of Masonry*, contains an explanation of a space in the centre of the Temple being called the 'Lodge'. In his 1781 edition, in describing the Ceremony of Consecration, he uses the phrase *The lodge which is placed in the centre is covered with white satin.* There is another clue in the 1842 catalogue where an item is described as *A White Satin Covering for the Lodge in the centre.* And, sure enough, when I looked in the Bear Inn minutes, in 1771 there is an instruction to Nicholas Tucker, a former Senior Warden, to *paint a Lodge.*

So not only is this table, almost abandoned to oblivion in a side room, the very artefact that was termed in the report of the 1819 dedication of Bath as *the Lodge veiled in White Satin* which was paraded around the Lodge Room during the consecration ceremony, it is probably the rarest of all the artefacts brought from Bath in 1842.

Another item on display, in the dining room at Barnstaple, is described in the catalogue as a *Fine three-quarter-length Portrait of P. G. M. the late Thomas Dunckerley, Esq., painted by Beach, in his best style; and is the original Portrait from which the well known Masonic Engraving of the above W. Brother was made, 4 ft. 3 by 3 ft 3½, in a handsome Gilt Frame.*

This portrait was presented to Royal Cumberland Lodge in 1786 by the artist Thomas Beach himself, although he was not a member of the Lodge at that time. Because of the dating, it was clearly to commemorate the merging of this new Lodge with the old Bear Inn Lodge, and to honour Dunckerley's assistance in promoting this.

A pupil of Sir Joshua Reynolds, by 1786 Beach was already a portrait artist of some significance with his own studio in Westgate in Bath where he regularly painted the great and the good either resident in, or visiting, the City including several portraits of the famous actress Sarah Siddons. In fact, his 1782 portrait of the actress shows her seated in the

very same green chair in which Dunckerley is shown in this portrait. So this was a gift of some consequence for the Lodge who nevertheless minuted their insistence on paying the five guineas for the frame.

Beach was, however, initiated the following year and admitted a member of the Lodge, at which time all of his fees were waived. The portrait hung in their Lodge Room wherever they were resident, and was moved to Freemason's Hall when it opened in 1818.

Which brings us to the final items in this section, and probably the most impressive, although they are never on display except at a Lodge Meeting. They were described in 1842 as: *A complete and superb Set of Silver Jewels, for the W. M. and Officers of a Lodge, massive, of the best workmanship, and ordered at an unlimited expence; they are enclosed in a Morocco Leather Box, lined with Velvet.*

Although it may not sound like it, this is an understatement. Because this set of Officer's Collar Jewels were all made by the man now accepted as the finest silversmith ever to make Masonic jewels - Thomas Harper.

Harper was born in 1744 and, it would appear, spent the early part of his working life in South Carolina, before returning to set-up his first workshop in London in 1783. He became a leading light in the Antients Grand Lodge, rising to the position of Deputy Grand Master at the time of the Union in 1813. After the Union, he served on the Board of General Purposes until his death in 1832.

But it was for his exquisite Masonic jewels that he is most remembered, and these examples of his workmanship, all bearing his hallmarks from 1817 and 1818, show examples of all three types that he is best known for - pierced jewels, cast jewels and plate jewels, some of which are adorned with Paris Brilliants - the highest quality imitation diamonds.

The hallmarks show that these must have been purchased new by the Hall Committee, and the statement *ordered at unlimited expense* is no exaggeration, as a single Harper Jewel would have cost between five and ten guineas at that time. It is not difficult, therefore, to see that this set could easily have accounted for a quarter of their total expenditure on furniture and equipment.

So there you have it, or at least part of it, because this chapter probably accounts for about half of the list of items brought to Barnstaple. If you want to know more about the rest, and what happened to it, then that information, or as much as I can glean, is given in Appendix 2 at the back of this book.

But before we move on to the aftermath of the Hall closure, what of those mysterious sentinel lions mentioned earlier?

Descriptions of the Hall said they were made from painted Coade Stone, an early form of reconstituted stone that could be easily moulded into complex shapes making it ideal for large statues and sculptural facades. They never made it to Barnstaple because they have been hidden in plain sight since 1830 when they were mounted atop the Queen's Gate for the opening of the new Victoria Park in the City, by the then 11-year-old Princess Victoria, after whom it was named.

The Queen's Gate in 1845. *Bath in Time*

Of course, we modern Bathonians didn't know that - to us they were just another pair of old stone statues like many others around the City. But following the award of a Lottery Grant in 2006, they became part of a general restoration project. When they were removed, it was discovered that there had been an inscription on the base of one that, for some unknown reason, had been covered-over at some time. When the later covering was carefully removed the inscription revealed said: *Presented by C Geary Esq.* - which makes complete sense as he was a major supporter of the Park project.

Further examination produced fragments of the original bronze paint and gilding allowing them to be restored to their original condition - but also to confirm their provenance.

They are now back on top of the gateposts.

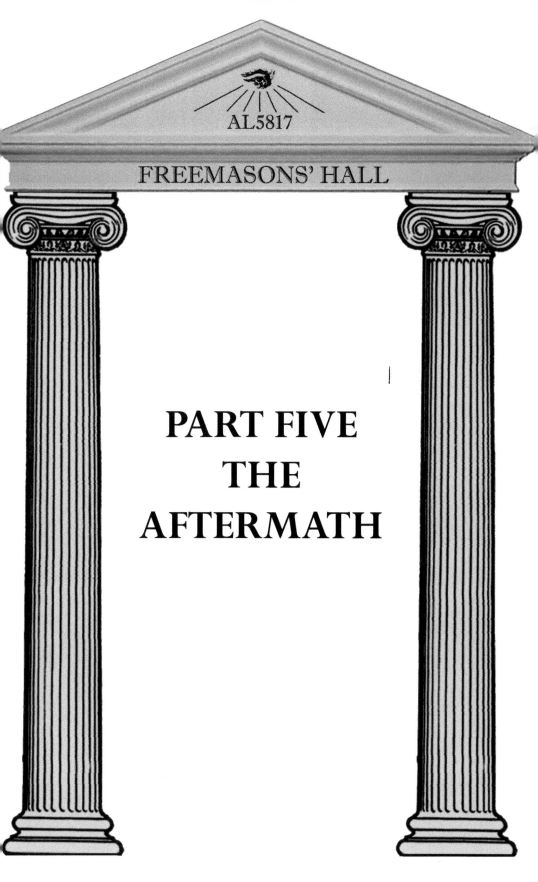

AL5817

FREEMASONS' HALL

PART FIVE
THE
AFTERMATH

The Aftermath

A s the New Year Bells sounded-in 1824, there was little chance that Freemasons' Hall could ever fulfil its name again, unless there was a swift turnaround in the deep animosities that had developed between the parties. It would have taken a strong politician to overcome them, but if such an individual did exist, they certainly showed no intention of tackling this particular hornet's nest.

Charles Geary stood steadfastly behind his legal right as the owner, and landlord, to negotiate a lease with the Lodges and Orders, through meeting a deputed committee representing them. Realistically, if he allowed tenants to simply reoccupy a building for which they had shown no intention of paying rent, either before or since he had acquired it, then he had no methodology for obtaining any future return on his investment.

Matthew Patton had removed the organisations he held sway over, Royal Cumberland Lodge No.41, Royal Cumberland Chapter No. 41, and Antiquity Encampment of Knights Templar No.1, and was stubbornly maintaining that Geary held no rights at all in the matter. There is no obvious indication that Antiquity was still meeting regularly at this point, their surviving minutes coming to an abrupt halt around this time and Masonic historians in later years stating consistently that they became dormant at around this time until revived in 1855. So I do not intend to include that Order any further in the main story, but have included more details about their history between 1811 and 1823 in Appendix 4.

Lodge of Virtue were probably the closest to coming to an accommodation with Geary, despite their finances remaining fragile due to a dwindling membership.

But Royal York Lodge of Perfect Friendship were in disarray, with no officers and little in the way of funds. Their attached Chapter must have been in a similar state, because most of the Companions were also members, or by now ex-members, of the Lodge. No records survive of Royal York Chapter, or of the date it closed, so I will make a similar assumption to that concerning Antiquity, and make no further commentary about it.

The other Lodge in Bath, Royal Sussex, together with its own attached Chapter, remained unaffected by all of this due to their withdrawal from the original project and subsequently having no connection with Freemason's Hall at all. However, it will be necessary to include them from here onwards, as they do become featured as the story progresses. There would also be a new Lodge formed in Bath in the not-too-distant future, and so that will also feature as we go forward.

So January 1824 is as good a point as any to establish exactly where all of these organisations physically resided because, in the aftermath of the lock-out, each Lodge found itself essentially back to square one with respect to accommodation. Much as they had been prior to 1816, they became spread around the various hostelries in the City that had suitable rooms to rent:

Royal Cumberland Lodge No.41 were at the White Lion on the High Street, along with their associated Chapter.

Lodge of Virtue No.311 had established themselves at the Castle & Ball Hotel in New Bond Street.

Royal Sussex Lodge No.69 were still at the Greyhound in the High Street, along with their associated Chapter.

Royal York Lodge of Perfect Friendship No.243 were homeless, but surviving correspondence suggests they were using the Greyhound for their emergency meetings held in order to re-establish themselves.

This section will examine how the Lodges and individuals coped with the next turbulent months, and how their histories developed over the next few years, starting with the one in the deepest trouble, Royal York Lodge of Perfect Friendship.

Friendship No More

After Geary closed the Hall, matters within Royal York Lodge began to unravel rapidly. The convoluted events surrounding the actual failure of the Lodge, played out over the next twelve months both in Bath and London, could fill a small volume in themselves. Consequently, to prevent it detracting from the main narrative, this section is just a summary of them, the full details being contained in Appendix 3 at the back of this book. Also, for ease of reading this section, all references to Royal York Lodge of Perfect Friendship No.243 will be simplified to 'the Lodge' and those to Royal York Chapter No.243 to 'the Chapter'. Any other Lodges or Orders will be referred to by their full name.

It is also first necessary to clear-up a common misconception about the age of their Chapter. There is evidence of a Royal Arch order existing in Bath in the early 1760s entitled the York Chapter, but it had disappeared decades before the Hall scheme was even under consideration. The Royal Arch was not part of the original union of the two Grand Lodges in 1813, and this was not resolved until 1817 when all extant Chapters were required to declare an attachment to an existing Lodge. However, granting of permission from the Duke of York to rename the Lodge did not occur until 1818, so a 'York Lodge' did not exist in 1817 for any 'York Chapter' to make such declaration.

A year later, Grand Chapter received an application from this Lodge to create a new Chapter attached to it, but this was refused; however, this clearly shows that there was no Chapter attached to the Lodge at that time. Grand Chapter ultimately changed its mind two years later, when Thomas Whitney finally obtained their permission to start a new Chapter; but it did not come into being until 1820. Nevertheless, some Masonic researchers have mistakenly aligned them, because references to that original York Chapter showed it meeting at the same hostelry as this Lodge back in the 1760s.

Before moving on to what happened from the start of 1824, let's briefly recap on what occurred in the last three months of 1823. On November 27th 1823 the Master, Charles Maddison, and both of his Wardens resigned the Lodge - for clarity, not just their offices but entirely from the organisation - sending the Lodge into a tailspin. By the time of that meeting, matters had moved on considerably. Col. Kemeys-Tynte had refused to become involved in the wrangle over the property in the Hall; he had also resolved the issues surrounding Whitney's behaviour at Royal Cumberland Chapter, with the obtaining of a full apology from Whitney before Provincial Grand Chapter.

There are no minutes of the fateful Lodge meeting available to show whether Maddison and his lieutenants simply resigned, or were forced from office. However, there is a clue in later correspondence from Whitney to Grand Lodge, where he mentions: *At a Lodge held on the 27th of November last, the S.W. of the York Lodge produced a Letter from the late W.M. Bro. Maddison, dated November 15th, 1823, wherein was announced his resignation of the Chair, and his desire that his name be erased from the list of Members.*

This shows that the Senior Warden was in attendance, otherwise he couldn't have *produced the letter*. There is also the date of the letter, which shows that Maddison had tendered his resignation nearly two weeks prior to this meeting. However, no indication is given of whether that information had been circulated prior to the meeting, or was delivered as a bombshell on the night. It is not unusual for a member to resign by letter, but very rare for a Ruling Master to do so. So unless Maddison had to leave Bath suddenly and permanently, in which case that fact would have emerged in later evidence, this action does show some disregard for his elevated office, and for his Lodge.

These timings might suggest that the damage was done not on 27th November, but nearly three weeks earlier when Maddison called the emergency meeting on the same day that Whitney was at the hearing in Bridgwater. That would have been just a week after the reference in Royal Cumberland minutes on 31st October to *suspend any hostile measure until the decision of the Royal York Lodge be obtained on the subject.*

As this implies that the Lodge officers in attendance as visitors to Royal Cumberland on 31st October were not prepared to take such a precipitative decision until they had consulted with their own members, maybe that consultation was brought before the emergency meeting on 7th November. In which case, in the eyes of some members, the unavoidable absence of Whitney at Bridgwater may not have reflected well on Maddison's choice of date, particularly as the Lodge could not have been aware of the results of the hearing in Bridgwater on that same day - news could only travel as fast as a post coach in those days.

If members had also viewed Maddison's unilateral action at the beginning of October against a long-standing Past Master as contributory to the closure of the Hall, then his position would have been severely difficult. In that case, his attendance at meetings with other Lodges to discuss action against Charles Geary could have been seen as exacerbating the situation. But if his attempt to persuade the members to join with Royal Cumberland in taking action before any results from the Whitney hearing were known, his position may have become untenable - particularly as when the results did arrive from Bridgwater, they were not what Maddison might have hoped for.

Nothing in that scenario suggests it could lead to resignations by other officers, and with the regular election of a new Master being due within weeks, even if the members were unhappy with Maddison and neither of the two other senior officers were acceptable to succeed to the Chair, the membership of the Lodge should have been sufficiently strong in numbers to allow an experienced candidate to fill the void for sufficient time to resolve any issues. But was it?

It was recorded in Grand Lodge minutes during 1824 that Maddison gave evidence that this Lodge was *reduced in little more than one year from upwards of 100 members some of whom were of the highest respectability to only 5 efficient members.* As will be seen later in this chapter, that lower number was recorded less than three months after this fateful meeting, which would suggest to a casual observer that the higher number was in place when Maddison took over at the start of 1823, and that the precipitous fall in numbers was caused by the problems that brought his resignation.

However, examining the returns reveals a different picture. At the end of 1819, just after the dedication of the Hall, Lodge membership stood at 92. A year later it had risen to 99, but at the end of 1821 had dropped back to 89. Then, during 1822, it virtually halved down to 53 and by the time of this meeting had fallen further to 37. So a major reduction had occurred during the previous year under the Past Master, John Ashley, who had been in the Chair since 1818, and it then fell further under Captain Maddison.

Hence official records show this Lodge never had *upwards of 100 members* and the reduction had occurred over a longer period than *little more than one year*; so what could have been the cause? The most obvious would be members joining a different Lodge for one reason or another. So I conducted a search of the national membership registers, and discovered that, of the 52 who left in 1822/23, two went overseas, fourteen joined other Bath Lodges, although not all immediately, but the vast majority simply left the Fraternity altogether - they never joined another Lodge anywhere. This is consistent with the general waning of interest in Freemasonry during the mid-1820s, after the massively-successful years following the end of the Napoleonic Wars - only 14 of the 89 members listed in 1821 had been in the Lodge for more than four years. Maddison himself had been there barely three.

Alternatively, as more than half of the 52 names who left were classed in Lodge records as gentlemen, military officers or with professional occupations, this may have been as a result of a perception of a loss of status for the Lodge, possibly a fallout from Pitter's fraudulent activity, both in the Lodge and at the Hall. However, examining the remaining 37 members showed a similar spread of these occupations, so the Lodge still held members *of the highest respectability,* they had not all deserted it as may have been the intended implication.

During this search process I accidentally stumbled across a piece of information that is very pertinent. It transpires that both Captain Maddison and Reverend Portis, the Lodge (and Provincial) Chaplain, became joining members of the Lodge of Perpetual Friendship No.219 in Bridgwater on 1st November 1823, where they were followed on 6th December 1823 by Immediate Past Master John Ashley.

At a cursory glance, this may not appear significant, because if there were wholesale resignations at this time it would be expected that some long-standing Members would wish to join another Lodge as soon as possible. However, even if the prevailing scenario rendered another Bath Lodge unacceptable, there were many Lodges far closer to home than Bridgwater, a good six-hour carriage ride away even in the better summer months. Add to this conundrum that the Lodge they chose to join was Colonel Kemeys-Tynte's Lodge, and this begins to look more contrived, especially with what transpired the following year at Grand Lodge. But add to all of that the joining date in Maddison's case of 1st November being a week prior to his calling of the meeting when Whitney was away, two weeks prior to his submitting his resignation letter, and nearly a month ahead of that letter being presented to the members, and the plot most-definitely thickens.

Whatever occurred on November 27th, the immediate resignation of both Wardens as well suggests something irreconcilable on the night. This was most likely regarding views on the situation at the Hall held by polarised factions within the membership. However, because the contents of Maddison's resignation letter are not available, there could just as well have been something incendiary in that - his views on the conduct of the Lodge, or maybe even the revelation that he had already joined another Lodge. Interestingly, according to later evidence submitted to Grand Lodge with regard to who would take-over in the Chair following the presentation of the letter, Whitney had been requested by several members at the meeting to *allow his name to be proposed, but this he instantly and decidedly refused.*

However, it was not terminal, as after Col. Kemeys-Tynte returned the Lodge's Warrant to them in December, he wrote to London his hope that *through the mediation of Dr Muttlebury & some others of the more sensible & right minded Brethren, we shall eventually bring the business round to a Proper & Reasonable Conclusion.* It is interesting that the Colonel saw a potential solution with Maddison no longer a member of the Lodge.

Dr James Muttlebury had been Junior Warden. Having rescinded his resignation, he was given dispensation by Col. Kemeys-Tynte to convene the Lodge so that a new Master could be elected early in January 1824. Muttlebury had been inspector-general of hospitals in the British Army for over twenty years before retiring to Bath, when he also became a member of the Lodge, and must have been seen by the Colonel as a safe pair of hands capable of finding a candidate acceptable to all members, however marginally.

How many members attended the meeting on January 5th 1824, or who they were, is not known, although they must all have had the best interests of the Lodge in mind in their attempts to find a replacement Master. The first to be approached was Ashley, unsurprisingly as he was the Immediate Past Master, but Grand Lodge minutes show that he *positively refused the Chair in consequence of the discord and confusion existing in the Lodge and occasioned by the proceedings of the late W.M.* The reference to *the late W.M* here would be Maddison. That Muttlebury himself was approached next will be recognised, by anybody who has served on a troublesome committee, as a standard ploy in the circumstances - if someone has been persuaded to take the chair pro tem, it sometimes only needs a small nudge to persuade them to take the job permanently; Muttlebury had obviously seen that one coming!

Muttlebury then proposed that Baron Browne-Mill take the Chair. This choice was unsurprising, as he was a long-standing Past Master, an independent gentleman with a substantial inherited fortune, highly-respected and uncontroversial. His election must have left the members believing that there was every possibility that the Lodge could be recovered under his leadership. Therefore his subsequent change of mind, after considering the matter for just a few days, makes little sense except for it being co-incident with English & Spry publishing their report regarding the change of ownership at the Hall.

Browne-Mill had been the first Trustee of the Hall for this Lodge and, as such, had chaired early Financial Committee meetings, working closely with his co-Trustee Geary. But he had been away from Bath for long periods during the intervening years, due to his owning property in the West Indies so, when he read the report, he may have realised that matters were not as cut-and-dried as may have been related to him.

Thus, at the next meeting on 12th January, instead of overseeing the publicised installation of Dr Browne-Mill as the next Master, Muttlebury found himself back to square one. Next to be approached was Rear-Admiral Joseph Bullen, a long-time resident of Bath, but not the more famous Admiral Charles Bullen, fellow hero of Trafalgar alongside Nelson, with whom he is often confused. Joseph Bullen did serve with Nelson twenty years earlier on the ill-fated Mosquito Coast raid that resulted in a very unwell Nelson visiting Bath for the first time, where he was nursed back to health by no other than Dr Spry's father. When Bullen declined, the offer went to Charles Manners, but he also declined; Manners would later be a signatory on charges against Geary submitted by Royal Cumberland Lodge.

As a result of all of this, another meeting was called for 29th January. However, Muttlebury failed to attend that meeting so Whitney *took the Chair and named to the Brethren the disappointment and regret relative to Brother Browne Mill, and then proposed Brother Redman as WM for the ensuing year. He was accordingly elected.* This was the same William Redman who had resigned from Royal Cumberland Chapter the previous year after the pedestal saga had reared its head. Within a few days he became the second to do a delayed u-turn, and the sixth overall to decline what had become a poisoned-chalice. But not before summonses were issued for a meeting to conduct his Installation on February 12th.

As he had already withdrawn, that meeting became yet another attempt at finding a suitable candidate from a rapidly-diminishing field. One such potential candidate was Thomas Whitney. It is recorded that Muttlebury visited Whitney on the morning of February 12th to advise that *a Professional engagement would prevent him being present.* As a retired medical doctor, it is possible that such an occurrence may have occurred, but it sounds more like a rather lame attempt by Muttlebury, as the person delegated to hold the chair pro tem, to have the meeting postponed until he could consult the PGM. Alternatively, he may simply have given-up after so many failed attempts, deciding that he would not be a party to any further developments.

In this, Muttlebury's second successive absence, Whitney again took the Chair. Whitney's version of events related *it was not until this period of proceedings (that is when every Member of the Lodge eligible to the Chair had given his decided negative) that I would permit my name to be proposed in open Lodge as WM.* This may have been an attempt to bring the whole matter to a suitable conclusion, but it can only be described as a dumb move in the circumstances - the first of many. There were just seven members in attendance for the election that evening, from which Whitney emerged as Master-elect. However, no Installation took place, that would have required a further summoned meeting.

It did not take long for this final election to also unravel and on 20th February, Col. Kemeys-Tynte directed Past Master John Ashley *to defer the Installation of any Brother as WM until his name has been regularly laid before the Members of the Lodge, and afterwards confirmed at a subsequent meeting.* So, it would appear that Muttlebury was no longer involved as Master pro-tem, otherwise the Colonel would have written to him. Without an elected or appointed Master, responsibility deferred to John Ashley as the incumbent Immediate Past Master - although we mustn't forget that Ashley had also, apparently, resigned and was now a member of the Colonel's Lodge in Bridgwater.

Ashley's response was that the Lodge had proceeded in their usual custom and that he was unconscious of any irregularity *as far as Bro. Whitney had informed him.* This confirms Ashley was not in attendance but, even so, with his experience he should have recognised that it was not regular for a Master to be proposed without his name being printed on the summons and then elected on the same night, which is essentially what the Colonel was telling him. What Whitney had to say on the subject was of no relevance, although he also knew they had not conducted the business in accordance with the rules, because he effectively said so in later evidence given to Grand Lodge.

Col. Kemeys-Tynte replied on February 24th: *I am sorry to say that the statement made in your letter to me of the 22nd inst is not upon such authority as I can consider satisfactory, I therefore feel it my duty to inform you that the proceedings of the Royal York Lodge must remain suspended until you send me more satisfactory answers to my questions, and those answers such as you can vouch for the truth of yourself.*

The Colonel then asked four questions, the first three aimed at determining the timing of events, but the last more specific: *As there appear to have been only seven Brethren present (Tylers included) at the late supposed election of a Master, are they all regular Masonic members of the Lodge, paying their contributions to the Lodge, as well as to the Grand Lodge and Provincial Grand Lodge, or were any of them in the capacity of serving Brethren?* Although this may appear simply an administrative question, it does request some rather focussed information.

I have had reservations about this question since I first read it; not in the general circumstance of the Lodge struggling to assemble sufficient numbers, in which case the Colonel would need to ensure the meeting was quorate, but in the very specific aspect regarding *serving Brethren*, which could only have been prompted from the need to confirm information received independently of the Lodge.

Ashley responded by return, the first three answers confirming the timings of announcements and meetings, although he added that *the day was altered from Monday to Wednesday for the convenience of the PM (Ashley) that being the only day he is disengaged.* Which is strange as February 12th 1824 was a Thursday, the normal Lodge night, and he did not attend. His fourth answer was: *The Brethren present were Bros. Whitney, Shew, Sharland, G. Loder, Jarratt and the usual Tylers, Pinker and Rolf. The three former pay accustomary fees, as subscribing members, Jarratt and Loder pay to the Grand Lodge and Provincial Grand Lodge, but not Quarterages.*

Col. Kemeys-Tynte visited Ashley in Bath on 12th March to confirm that he could not lift the Lodge's suspension due to the election irregularities, but in so doing he only highlighted the timing issues, leaving the door open for the Lodge to have one last chance to get its act together, reissue summonses correctly and recover from an otherwise-untenable position.

It was not to be given that chance because, in the meantime, Thomas Whitney had decided to go over the head of the Colonel and appeal directly to the Board of General Purposes at Grand Lodge. This was ostensibly on behalf of the members of the Lodge, in his view numbering thirty-seven. Although this was the number shown on the most-recent return, it was probably, by then, somewhat optimistic. However, it is doubtful whether any members remaining loyal to the Lodge were aware, or supportive, of such an appeal. In the document, dated 19th March 1824, Whitney outlined the reasons why he believed the PGM had unjustly suspended the Lodge, some of which were barely -concealed personal allegations. The essence of the appeal, however, revolved around the status of Loder and Jarratt.

The Board met the following month to deliberate on the appeal, taking evidence in person from the Colonel himself, plus Maddison and Ashley. That Whitney chose not to attend did the Lodge no service. In the end the Board concluded their report succinctly: *It appears to this Board that the appeal of Brother Thomas Whitney is frivolous, vexatious, and disrespectful to the Provincial Grand Master.* This decision was ratified by the Grand Master, then the entire appeal and judgement, dated April 24th 1824, were printed on four pages of close-type foolscap paper for circulation to all Lodges in the Province of Somerset. The details were ordered to be copied into their Minute Books, a laborious task for the secretaries as, in long-hand, they extended to many pages.

The Colonel then instructed Ashley, as Past Master, to convene the members of the Lodge to meet him. The May 1824 minutes of Lodge of Virtue show that other Bath Lodges were also invited: *A letter was read from Br. Ashley WPM of the Royal York Lodge No.243 requesting the members of the Lodge of Virtue to meet the Provl Gd Master Bro. CKK Tynte at the White Lion on Saturday the 29th inst at 11 o'clock in the morning, the PGM having an official communication to make.*

It is not clear if this was a full Provincial meeting, or for Bath Brethren alone, but a subsequent letter from the Colonel to Grand Secretary William White outlines what happened: *I read Thos Whitney's appeal against me to the Board of General Purposes & afterwards had the report of the Board read (by Bro. Portis the P.G. Chaplain) which gave general satisfaction. Thomas Whitney being present I told him publickly that even then, if he would make such an apology as I thought he ought to HRH the Grand Master that I would hold out the Hand of Fellowship. He desired me to dictate one, which I declined, observing that it ought to come from himself. Since that time I have endeavoured by various means to persuade him to do so, but without avail.*

At the September quarterly assembly of Grand Lodge, it was ordered: *That the last Past Master of the Lodge 243, at Bath (there not being either a Master or Wardens) be summoned to attend the Quarterly Communication in December, to show cause why the said Lodge should not be erased from the List of Lodges and its Warrant declared forfeited for its many irregularities and unconstitutional proceedings, particularly for initiating into Masonry Messrs George Loder and Stephen Jarratt for small and unworthy considerations, and that in the meantime the suspension of the Lodge be continued, giving power however for the Members of the Lodge to meet for the purpose of considering and preparing their defence, the Past Master being made responsible that no other business be transacted at any such meeting.*

That was effectively the end. In his history, George Norman related that no Past Master attended for that final opportunity for the Lodge to be rescued, a duty he assigned to Thomas Whitney, and it was thus removed from the official lists. However, Grand Lodge minutes for 1st December 1824 show otherwise:

The W Bro John Ashley the last Master of the Lodge No. 243 at Bath attended pursuant to his summons. He stated that upon receiving the Order of the last Grand Lodge he communicated its contents to the existing Members of the Lodge viz Brothers Redman, Shew, Spry and Long, and appointed a time for their assembling to take the subject into consideration, that the day he had appointed proving inconvenient, he desired the Brethren to fix one which would suit them, and at the same time requested Brother Redman a Past Master in case he knew any Members - besides those he had specified to apprize them of the Meeting or else to furnish him, Brother Ashley, with their names. That not having heard anything further from the Parties, he summoned another meeting for the October but there being only two in attendance who had not any proposition or suggestion to make no business was done nor did he hear anything further upon the subject from any of the Brethren until a short time prior to his coming to London when one of the Brethren delivered to him a paper signed by the said Brothers Redman, Shew, Spry and Long and purported to be certain Resolutions passed at the Meeting held on the said   of October. Brother Ashley, however, stated that no such paper was offered to the meeting nor in fact were any resolutions proposed, neither had he been consulted upon the contents of that Paper or requested to sign it. He added that so far from approving its contents he must conscientiously declare the irregularities of the Lodge had been so numerous and their proceedings had excited so much disgust amongst the

Members of the Craft in Bath that there did not exist the slightest chance of the Lodge being revived either with Credit to its Members. The paper being read, it was moved: That the Royal York Lodge of Perfect Friendship No.243 at Bath be erased from the list of Lodges and its Warrant declared forfeited. It was moved as an Amendment that the further consideration of the Question be deferred until the next Quarterly Communication which amendment being negatived the Question was put on the Original Motion and passed in the affirmative there being only four hands held up against it.

So that was that for a Lodge that had probably been the most consistently-successful in the City over more than sixty years, and it is difficult to ignore the irony in the officially-recorded reason for the erasure of Royal York Lodge of Perfect Friendship being *in consequence of having fallen into internal discord.*

It is also difficult to ignore several other aspects: another gap in minutes for later insertion of a date that should have been available in the submissions; some reservation on the part of certain attendees that the decision required longer consideration; and the final coups-de-grace being delivered by the very Past Master who had been responsible for most of the irregularities he referred to, without receiving any personal admonishment for his involvement. Neither did his successor Captain Maddison, who presided for ten months over the rapid disintegration of the Lodge, exacerbated by his walking away from the wreckage.

So, what exactly was this great irregularity that had taken place that made the position of the Lodge irrecoverable?   We know that an election took place in February 1824, and that Whitney emerged as Master-elect, that was not in dispute; it was whether that election was valid that would ultimately decide the fate of the Lodge.   But surely that validity simply revolved around the timings and/or non-issue of relevant summonses for election and Installation of a new Master, and whether sufficient members remained to hold such an election?

Instead, the actual reason being used to delete the Lodge was the membership status of two individuals, Stephen Jarratt and George Loder.   The question of their membership arose from the statement of John Ashley to the Colonel that *Jarratt and Loder pay to the Grand Lodge and Provincial Grand Lodge, but not Quarterages,* thus suggesting their status as what was termed by the Colonel as *serving Brethren.* In his appeal, Whitney asserted that *as they pay their annual contributions with the other Members to the Funds of the Grand Lodge, and Provincial Grand*

Lodge, this has ever been considered by the Lodge, a sufficient title to vote when necessary; and this is the question to be determined:- Whether these Brethren registered Masons, and paying the above quarterages, had or had not a right to vote on the night of my Election?

The Board's conclusion on 26th April 1824 was *that it appears by the evidence of Brother J Ashley, given before the Board that they were introduced and initiated by Brother Whitney, in the year 1818 as Musical Brethren, without payment of the customary initiation Fees, that no dispensation was produced in the Lodge, to authorise such a Proceeding and these Brethren paid nothing more than the registering Fee. Under these circumstances that these Brothers are not legal Members of the Lodge, and could not be entitled to vote on any occasion.*

So the initial charge of their not paying the correct annual fees somehow morphed into their not having legally joined the Lodge five years earlier. Which is strange, as Lodge returns list Loder and Jarratt as having been proposed on May 14th 1818, initiated May 28th 1818, passed June 30th 1818 and raised 31st July 1818. They are shown listed as members right up to the final return of the Lodge, as well as having paid all of their dues up to date of the final return in the records of Grand Lodge at the time of these issues arising - all of this documentation being available to the Board at their deliberations. As will be seen by reading the full account of those 1824 hearings detailed in Appendix 3, most of the evidence that assisted that conclusion was supplied by John Ashley, and it contained numerous inconsistencies.

But in terms of the overall story, this becomes somewhat academic, as do the matters of timing of summonses, etc, most of which would have been relatively easy to overcome by reissuing them correctly and proceeding with a new election. Except that, by that time, there apparently were few members still wishing to belong to the Lodge and, more importantly, no other Past Master remaining to conduct the installation of the new Master, whoever that may have been.

The substance of historical accounts has been that the Lodge failed simply because of the financial strains placed upon it by the costs of the Hall. Finance cannot be ruled-out as a factor due to the fraudulent activities of Thomas Pitter, but there were other misconceptions, such as Whitney being named as the official who failed to attend Grand Lodge to give proof that the Lodge should not be dissolved. This may, in part, have been misconstrued from the activities of Thomas Whitney between the April hearing and the Grand Lodge meetings in December 1824. Having had his appeal rejected by the Board of General Purposes in April, he managed to bring the matter before the September meeting of Grand Lodge, where one part of that decision was overturned - the part found against him personally that his March 19th appeal had been *frivolous, vexatious and disrespectful to the Provincial Grand Master*. This did not, however, effect the bulk of the decisions against the Lodge which were all upheld.

Whitney, however, continued to create unrest, resulting in a further series of Board hearings in November and December 1824 on charges brought against him personally by Colonel Kemeys-Tynte and Captain Maddison. All were found to be proven, the Board recommending *the Justice and propriety of expelling the said Thomas Whitney from our Order*. On the weight of the evidence, this was the overwhelmingly correct conclusion, but did not prevent Whitney manufacturing yet another appearance before Grand Lodge on December 22nd 1824, where he was *suspended from all Masonic Functions and Privileges for the space of 12 months and do then attend the Grand Lodge to be admonished.*

Those hearings are also covered in greater detail in Appendix 3, but it is interesting that there was sufficient doubt in Grand Lodge to enable his punishment to be considerably reduced. Perhaps Grand Lodge recognised various discrepancies throughout the evidence on both sides and decided that, should they apply the higher penalty, it would only lead to further appeals and disruptions, and it was best to put this all to bed in the most expedient way available. As with everything else in this story, the end of the Royal York Lodge of Perfect Friendship was nowhere near as simple as it may have appeared to a casual researcher.

This also completes the picture of the individual who, according to Fraternal history, had enthusiastically promoted the new Hall from the first meeting in 1816, produced sketches for its design, underwritten its financing, organised the dedication ceremony conducted by the Grand Master, served on the Finance Committee, had been involved with the tontine and had subsequently become embroiled in disagreements with the PGM, ultimately resulting in his being removed from the Fraternity - albeit by suspension rather than expulsion.

But the name of that individual was not Charles Geary, as historians have insisted, but Thomas Whitney - and is why this book is entitled *The Apothecary's Hall*.

Dogged Pursuit

We will now look at the how matters unfolded in the oldest Bath Lodge, Royal Cumberland, and its associated Royal Arch Chapter. For ease of reading this section, all references to Royal Cumberland Lodge No.41 will be simplified to 'the Lodge' and those to Royal Cumberland Chapter No.41 to 'the Chapter'. Any other Lodges or Orders will be referred to by their full name.

At the end of 1823, George Hay replaced Patton as Master and, from the lack of any reference in minutes for most of 1824, the Lodge appeared to have temporarily abandoned interest in the Hall. Patton's personal pursuit did not cease, however, because in January 1824 it was taken-up by the Chapter, of which he was still First Principal and where Lodge secretary Coward held the equivalent post of Scribe. Chapter minutes of 30th January 1824 read as follows: *It was proposed and unanimously agreed that a letter be addressed by the Scribe to Companion Geary (a member of this Chapter) demanding a restitution of the Furniture and Properties Illegally seized by him in the Bath Masonic Hall belonging to this Most Excellent Chapter, together with a balance of cash in Comp. Geary's hands (as Treasurer of the Financial Committee) due to this Chapter.*

Once again there is a detachment from financial reality in this proposal, because the Financial Committee had not existed for nearly a year, neither had a treasurer held any funds. The letter itself reveals that the sum demanded was the £3-1s-6d asserted three months earlier as being owed to the Chapter. In fact, Geary's demand for sixty pounds in full settlement of the five-year debt owed by the Chapter was probably well short of what they were truly liable for. Regardless of that, a demand for a refund of three pounds from a man who had personally paid-out more than a thousand-times that amount to relieve the pecuniary embarrassment of those officers, amongst others, was almost laughable, even without the pompous threat at the end of the letter that: *such means will be adopted for the recovery, as the Chapter in its judgement may deem expedient.*

At the following meeting of the Chapter, it was recorded that *a verbal answer was received by the Janitors that "no part would be given up."* Janitors are the Chapter equivalent of Tylers and, at that time, both posts were held by the same permanent employees at the Hall whose wages were paid, in the absence of any management committee, by Geary. The Chapter then resolved that: *in order to set the question at rest & as a means*

201

of meeting the professed wishes of Mr Geary, that a respectful Memorial be drawn up and forwarded to Supreme Grand Chapter via the Provincial Grand Superintendant for this Province praying that an enquiry be instituted into the outrage thus committed and to grant such redress as may best conduce to the Interests and Harmony of Masonry, in general and of this Most Excellent Chapter in particular.

The resultant memorial, in true Patton style, rambled through the patronising, effusive and long-winded to three pages of foolscap paper; the highlights were:

> *The Chapter lay before the Supreme G Chapter certain charges against Mr C Geary, In having in the month of October last forcibly closed their regular chapter room & denying access thereto on a stated Chapter meeting - without giving any notice thereof & without legal claim or authority whatever to do, as also for seizing, retaining and still withholding the properties of the said Royal Cumberland Chapter, in defiance of a requisition from the Chapter to deliver them up*

> *The Chapter has faithfully and fully discharged each and every account (to the delegated authorities), the Chapter therefore disclaims all further knowledge, agreement, concern or connection with the Building whatever, or with the gentlemen connected with the building, and therefore knows of no demand that may be unjustly urged or due upon such account - the Chapter has ever been most punctual as well in the discharge of every legal demand upon its funds and therefore looks with anxiety to that protection & support from the Supreme Grand Chapter in the Provincial Grand Superintendant - which it has ever been known to grant in resisting oppression - for a restitution of its furniture as well as for a small balance of cash (in Geary's hands as receiver) over and above the Chapter account due viz £3-1s-6d*

> *the Chapter knowing nothing of Mr Geary or his assumed character as Landlord of the Premises - is most anxious for a meeting on the subject generally, but in the very disorganised and distracted state into which the Conduct of those Individuals more immediately concerned in the Speculations of the Bath Masonic Hall had left the comparatively few subscribing Bros & Compns no one can be found who would venture to preside at such a meeting*

> *the Chapter has no wish to visit the very improper Conduct of Mr Geary (a member) by any mark's displeasure - provided he restores the properties and makes a full and ample apology for such misconduct*

Having the advantage of viewing correspondence and minutes over the years preceding all of that, the reader is probably in a better position to judge the probity of those contents than the Grand Scribes may have been. There are one or two interesting aspects, such as the reference to *the gentlemen connected with the building*; note the plural, a further misperception by Patton, as Geary was the sole proprietor. Not that Patton recognised that status, as illustrated by the assertion of *knowing nothing of Mr Geary or his assumed character as Landlord of the Premises*. The additional plural in the reference to *those Individuals more immediately concerned in the Speculations of the Bath Masonic Hall* confirms that Patton viewed more than one person to be responsible for the prevailing situation, a grouping that must, at the very least, have included Thomas Whitney, although the Provincial disciplinary hearing having been concluded, that individual remained beyond the reach of Patton's direct authority.

Grand Chapter itself never became involved, because the only correspondence the Chapter received in reply, from any quarter, was the advice from Col. Kemeys-Tynte that he had appointed John Bawden as Deputy Provincial Grand Superintendant. Charles Geary attended the next recorded Chapter meeting in June 1824, the first time that he had attended for nearly two years, an action that demonstrates some strength of character. It being the first meeting since the memorial was written and dispatched, the duty of reading it aloud to acquaint the Companions of the contents fell to Patton, as First Principal. Following that, the minutes record: *Companion Geary (being present) requested to know if any answer had been received by this Chapter to the beforementioned Appeal against his conduct (dated April last) - being answered in the negative.*

No further mention of the matter appears in subsequent minutes of the Chapter; presumably Col. Kemeys-Tynte saw through the barely-veiled personal attacks contained in the original memorial and decided to spike it. It is doubtful that the Chapter would have received any different encouragement from Bawden, and the two senior Officers of the Province must have hoped that the intervening three months, when the Lodges in Bath were closed, would act as a calming influence.

However, at the very first regular meeting of the Lodge at the start of the next Masonic season, on 7th October 1824, Patton proposed a similar Memorial to be drafted and sent by the Lodge this time, and not to Province but to the Board of General Purposes. It is pertinent that this was also the first Lodge meeting after the September 1st quarterly meeting of Grand Lodge, where Geary had presented his affidavit containing information that resulted in the decision of the Board against Thomas Whitney being overturned. As an attendee at that quarterly meeting, Patton would have witnessed developments first hand, including the contents of the affidavit.

This time Patton accused Geary of unmasonic conduct, seconded by the serving Master, George Hay, and approved unanimously. Their Appeal, somewhat shorter but no less erroneous, included two charges:

1st For having in the month of October, 1823, forcibly and without any legal right whatever closed the doors of their Lodge Room in the Bath Masonic Hall upon a regular Lodge night without giving the least notice thereof to the Lodge and denying all access thereto with a wilful intention of obstructing the regular business of the Lodge - calculated either to break up the same, or to create such differences among its Members generally as could not fail in proving highly injurious to the Honor, the Dignity, and best Interests of the Lodge - the same being contrary to every principle of Freemasonry.

2nd, For Illegally Seizing, detaining and still withholding the valuable Furniture and other Properties of the Lodge (upwards of One Hundred Guineas in Value) in defiance of every demand from the Lodge to deliver up the same, under a pretended claim of Rent due, as he styles himself, to him as "Landlord" The Lodge having discharged every Legal claim to the delegated authorities at the Masonic Hall for its occasional use, is ready to prove when called upon that instead of being indebted to Mr Geary the Lodge, according to its Books holds Mr. Geary its debtor in nearly the sum of Twenty Pounds - that Mr Geary was not at that period, nor was he ever known, or acknowledged directly as identified as "the Landlord" of the Masonic Hall - the same being built by shares and subscribed for by many Brethren whose claims as Shareholders remain the same to this day. This was signed by Hay, Patton and seven current and past officers, including the Organist, an honorary post that is not normally involved in Lodge business.

The inability of Patton to obtain redress via his Chapter must have rankled with him throughout the summer months, and far from his vitriol showing any signs of being abated by the break, here were the same charges, this time presented from his Lodge, more stridently and with even more outrageous assertions attached. Leaving aside the references to conduct, of which Patton himself was becoming far more culpable than Geary, the assertion that the original subscribers, who included Patton, still retained a claim to the Hall is nothing short of self -delusion. That Geary could be perceived, in the circumstances, as taking *an Assumption and Exercise of Power, Unparalleled in the Annals of Freemasonry,* is beyond all comprehension.

The minutes of the following meeting record an answer received from the Grand Secretary that was usually succinct, in stark contrast to Patton's consistently wordy memorials: *A letter was read from the Grand Secretary acquainting the Lodge that the Provincial Grand Master was the proper authority in the Province to Investigate "all Masonic Complaints" as laid down by the Book of Constitutions - the Provincial Grand Master having been forwarded a Copy of the Appeal November 3rd Inst - the question remains with him for his Investigation and decision.*

It is understandable that Grand Lodge would be reluctant to become embroiled in this issue, as it already had another matter on its hands involving Bath, which was somewhat more serious. That matter, as seen in other chapters, was also occupying the time of both the Provincial Grand Master and his new Deputy, and it is doubtful that either would have wished to deal with yet more problems at Bath, particularly those not of a wholly-Masonic manner. It cannot have been far from their minds that these continual memorials and appeals were emanating from one prime source, and were beginning to look like a personal vendetta. Maybe Matthew Patton genuinely did not understand what he was signing, along with the other original subscribers, in March 1823; after all, we mustn't forget Peach's observation that *he lacked the intellectual power of many of his contemporaries.*

However, the senior officials possessed a reasonable grasp of the issues surrounding the Hall, and could not have overlooked the political pitfalls of the scenario that Geary had, effectively, put quietly to bed. The damage such a high-profile financial failure may have caused to the Fraternity's reputation cannot have been lost on them, particularly when there was an involvement with the building, however peripheral, of national figures including the Grand Master himself. The Duke of Sussex was also Col. Kemeys-Tynte's close personal friend, and as the solution Geary had engineered had resolved the core problem at a stroke, the Colonel was hardly likely to allow it to be undermined by a lone member whose grasp of the issues was so desperately flawed.

Just how flawed was revealed by the suggestion in this latest appeal that Geary would have been personally in debt to the Lodge to the tune of twenty pounds. Geary had previously been Master of the Lodge for many years, and at no point during that time appeared in any list of defaulters. He was a businessman of some considerable means, and had no financial reason to avoid his responsibilities. In fact, the Treasurer's books show that he not only paid his quarterages regularly and on the very day they became due, but was one of the very few members to pay them annually in advance.

By-Laws of all Lodges indicate the time that any member is allowed to stay in default before being recommended to Grand Lodge for suspension; this is generally twelve months. Furthermore, quarterages and dues at that time were in multiples of shillings rather than pounds, and those members minuted as recommended by their Lodge for suspension during the 1820s rarely had accumulated debts amounting to more than five pounds. So for Geary to be personally indebted to an amount of twenty pounds carried the suggestion that he had not been paying his dues for virtually the full extent of his Masonic career!

Regarding the Memorial, there is no record of any correspondence arriving from Province during the remaining part of 1824 or the early part of 1825; in fact one gains the impression that the matter had, effectively, been quietly ignored. However, Patton was not about to let matters fall, and he found yet another reason to have disagreement with Geary at a Provincial meeting held in Bath in February 1825. This was the meeting when the result of Whitney's final hearing at Grand Lodge, together with his suspension, were announced

Following that meeting Patton wrote a letter to his Lodge: *containing charges against the Conduct of Bro. Geary (PM) of this Lodge for "Slander, defamation and Falsehood - more particularly for asserting at the late Provincial Meeting in this city that Bro. Patton was the cause of all the Masonic disturbance that had taken place in this city".* In response it was *Ordered that a Fellowcrafts Lodge be summoned for Thursday next to hear the same and Bro. Geary be summoned to attend for the purpose.*

There is no mention of any such remark in the Provincial minutes for that meeting, although there are two specific mentions of Geary, the first in connection with a motion that was proposed: *that a vote of thanks be given to Charles K K Tynte Esq, MP, Provincial Grand Master, for his dignified and truly Masonic conduct in the chair.* The result of the vote was recorded as: *Resolved unanimously (with the exception of Bro Geary of Bath).* The secretary also recorded that: *the previous Meeting's minutes were read and with the exception of Bro Geary confirmed unanimously.* This is extraordinary, as the specific identity of minority voters whether for, against or abstaining, is never recorded in Masonic minutes. What makes this particular minute-taking even more dubious, and petty, is that Geary did not attend the previous Provincial meeting, neither were the Lodge shown as represented by any attendee. So, as only those present at a Masonic meeting are allowed to vote on the accuracy of the minutes, Geary had no option but to abstain on the second matter.

At the resulting Lodge Fellowcrafts meeting, it was minuted that Geary refused to attend, although no reason was recorded; Geary had not attended his Lodge for more than two years, so it was hardly likely that he would be in a position, or frame of mind, to do so at such short notice. Another meeting was arranged that Geary was also unable to attend, minuted as his *being in London*. At the regular meeting on March 17th, attended by nine members including Geary, the minutes record: *there being so few members present, it was unanimously agreed to summon a Fellowcrafts Lodge for Thursday next, in order to ensure a full meeting of the Brethren, when the Investigation is intended to be disposed of.*

The week's delay produced just four additional attendees. The meeting was advised by Geary that he did not intend to answer any aspects of the charges brought against him. Regardless, Patton recited all of his evidence which included a letter, claimed as unsolicited, from Charles Maddison: *Understanding that Brother Geary accuses our worthy Brother Patton of having made communications to me relative to Masonry in this city and even the private affairs of the late Royal York Lodge, which have produced the disgrace brought upon the Craft, I beg most unequivocally to deny that he ever made any communication to me of such tendency, nor has my conduct either as Worshipful Master of the late Royal York Lodge or in my other official situations, or in any respect been influenced by any circumstances or conversation which ever occurred between Brother Patton and myself.*

It is worth noting that Geary's alleged accusation, essentially a repeat of that made by Thomas Whitney in his circular letter eighteen months earlier, had simply identified Patton as the source of the problems; no indication was made of his influencing Maddison's actions. So, once again, Maddison's attempt at gilding-the-lily only revealed the potential of his deeper involvement in the demise of the Hall.

It was then resolved that the charges were fully proved and Geary was suspended from the Lodge. The following note was added: *That it is also the Unanimous Opinion of this Lodge that the Conduct of Bro. Patton PM during the several years he has been a member of the Lodge, has been Uniformly governed by the strictest observance of every Masonic duty and Interest towards the welfare of this Lodge - and that the general conduct of Bro. Geary towards Bro. Patton has been highly vexatious, defamatory, and Unmasonic.* As shown in the previous chapter, the word vexatious had already featured elsewhere in this story.

This was somewhat of a pyrrhic victory for Patton and, by his inaction, one has to wonder if Geary had simply given-up on this Lodge. Examination of the account books show that Geary was never in arrears up to the final quarter day in December 1822, always settling his account promptly. However, no payment was received from him after the first quarter day in March 1823; this co-incides exactly with his acquisition of the Hall, and with his non-attendance following Patton's return to the chair at that same time.

Although the conclusion will remain that Geary failed to defend himself because he knew he was guilty as charged, he could have achieved the same result by simply failing to attend. Why would he bother to turn up, twice, unless he wanted to make the point that, regardless of how much he justified himself, he would always face more accusations from his 'bette noire' until he was worn down by it all. To my mind, he had made his own choice as to when he would accept that inevitable defeat. If he believed that would be the end of the matter, however, he was sadly mistaken.

In April 1825 Geary was: *written to for his account and demand against the Lodge.* On June 24th: *Bro. Patton (PM) proposed that a Letter be sent to the Deputy PGM requesting an early decision of the Memorial of this Lodge for the recovery of its Furniture against Bro. Geary - Seconded by the Worshipful Master* [Hay] *and Unanimously approved of.* That letter was not sent to Bawden until August, when it was addressed jointly from the Lodge and Chapter: *The Royal Cumberland Lodge & Chapter having some time since placed Memorials in the hands of the PGM for Investigation, containing certain Charges against the Unmasonic Conduct of Bro. C Geary, a member of the above Lodge and Chapter for the illegal seizure and detention of its Furniture, Regalia &c &c The Lodge has unanimously resolved upon addressing you Officially on the subject to Investigate such inquiry into the said Charges as may best conduce the Honor & Happiness of Masonry in general & this Lodge in particular.*

The reply from John Bawden came quickly and decisively: *I have received your letter requiring me to institute an enquiry into the conduct of Mr C*

Geary for the seizure and detention of the Furniture, Regalia, etc belonging to the Royal Cumberland Lodge and Chapter. I have already given my opinion on this subject, and I now repeat it, that I consider this proceeding of Mr Geary to have arisen from causes of a private nature, unconnected with Freemasonry, and that I have no authority whatever to interfere and certainly no power to compel a Restitution of the goods detained.

Nearly two years after the doors were first locked on Freemasons' Hall, that was surely the end of the matter as far as both Lodge and Chapter were concerned. Although history has portrayed that Geary was thrown out of the Fraternity for his actions, and in truth Patton had tried everything he could to achieve that goal, in the end Patton had to settle for Geary being suspended from his Lodge alone. Was it not now time to move on? Unfortunately not.

During 1826, letters were sent to a number of Lodge members asking them to bring their accounts up to date; these included Geary, despite his being suspended. In December, Patton was once again installed into the Chair of the Lodge. At his installation meeting, in the very first matter of business conducted after the ceremony: *it was resolved unanimously that Bro. Geary having been repeatedly written to for Quarterages due from four to four and a half years, and refusing to pay them, be returned to Grand Lodge and Provincial Grand Lodge as a defaulter.*

The account books show that, at the point that Geary was suspended from the Lodge on March 24th 1825, his arrears totalled £4-1s-6d, all accumulated between March 1823 and that date, during which period he had not attended. His suspension in 1825 was not for a defined period, but *at the pleasure of the Lodge*, which meant indefinitely until such time that the Lodge decided to remove it; clearly that would never happen whilst Patton had any influence on the matter. Nevertheless, suspension concludes any financial obligations, so Geary could not accumulate any further debts from that point, a fact reflected in the account books by both his name and 'debt' being removed from the accounts-receivable section after the next quarter day in June 1825. Therefore, a year later, when the Lodge made the defaulter return, there was no official account of that default in their records.

The letter accompanying the return to Grand Lodge was entirely predictable: *The return of two Brothers as defaulters the Lodge has painfully but unanimously resolved upon from the long and continued contempt in particular experienced from Bro. Geary who (as reported to Grand Lodge) stands suspended during the pleasure of the Lodge for former improper conduct to which may now with propriety be added a fraudulent attempt to deprive the Lodge of its funds and properties under a fallacious deceptive pretence of a "set off" against an assumed claim which he well knows the Lodge has nothing to do with - the Lodge having repeatedly rejected the attempted imposition as dishonourable & contrary to every principle of Masonry. By a unanimous resolution, the Lodge respectfully submits a claim to have these sums refunded or allowed which have been paid by the Lodge to the Grand Lodge viz for 4½ years Bro. Geary and for four years Bro. Tylee or must the Lodge petition the Board of Finance or other on the subject?* It was signed by William Day in his capacity as Immediate Past Master.

The other so-called defaulter, Henry Dixon-Tylee, joined from Lodge of Virtue on the same day as Geary in 1804. As a professional organist, he had provided his services to all of the Bath Lodges for more than twenty-five years, but by 1826 he had become seriously ill and, being unable to work, fallen on hard times financially. It was Geary, not the Lodge, who had personally written to Grand Lodge on Tylee's behalf the previous year to ask for some charitable relief for him, as he would do again in support of Tylee's widow after the death of her husband in 1827. Although I could find no reference to any action in the minutes, Tylee's entry in the account book is annotated as suspended *for non-payment of quarterages* on 25th March 1826, along with another member called Mulligan, who owed an identical amount of £6-18s-0d. The latter, however, was never returned as a defaulter.

It is worth examining the condition of other members' accounts at the December 1826 quarter day, the point at which Geary and Tylee were returned as defaulters. Incredibly, of the twenty-five members listed seventeen were in arrears, six to amounts in excess of the £4-1s-6d attributed to Geary. The obvious question is why were these gentlemen not also returned as defaulters?

They included Cooper and Bamfylde, who owed £4-6s-6d each, having not paid since June 1824. Both were army officers, so may have been away from Bath for the period; George Bamfylde was also the son of the DPGM for Devon, so there may have been political repercussions to any action in his case.

The other four, Hay, Coward, Marsh and Manners, were all regularly -attending current or past officers, as well as being signatories, along with Patton, to the earlier charges against Geary. All of their arrears commenced prior to that action, at which time Hay was the Master of the Lodge, Coward the secretary of both Lodge and Chapter, Marsh the long-standing minute-taker, and Manners the Organist. Hay would eventually settle his account in 1829, by which time it stood at £7-8s-6d. Henry Coward cleared his arrears of £7-1s-6d, stretching back four years, a few months later, but was allowed to run-up further debts thereafter. Charles Marsh's arrears were eventually settled at Christmas 1828 when they stood at £11-14s. Charles Manners had not paid a penny since June 1820, accumulating £16-4s-6d by 1830 when a note was appended in the account book: *not having paid these quarterages, this name is not carried forward.* He was never reported as a defaulter. The Treasurer who made this note was William Day.

There is no record as to what transpired in relation to the default letter submitted, nor any further mention in Lodge minutes of this or any other matter involving Charles Geary. Geary is recorded, however, as joining Enoch Lodge No.11 on 30th December 1822, which met near his London home of Lees Mews, just off Grosvenor Square. This date coincides with the quarter date at which he last made any payment to his Bath Lodge, and also the point that he stopped attending. It can only be assumed, therefore, that he had already decided to leave, and joined a London Lodge to enable him to remain in Freemasonry, but away from the machinations in Bath

There is, however, no record of his having submitted his resignation to the Lodge, but the fact that Geary is not recorded at Grand Lodge as a defaulter would suggest that they took the view that he was, by the time the arrears commenced, no longer a member here. Had he been officially recorded as having resigned by March 1823, none of the subsequent accusations levelled at him, all instigated by Patton, could have been made by the Lodge. So one can only speculate why his resignation does not appear to exist in Lodge records.

In December 1827, Patton *was handsomely thanked for his unceasing exertions so long manifested the cause and welfare of the Lodge.* On June 6th, 1828, he was presented with yet another elegantly-chased piece of plate: *In offering his best thanks to the Brethren of the Lodge, Bro Patton assured them of the grateful sense he should ever feel for so distinguishing a mark of their kind approbation of his Conduct.* There is no mention this time of the inscription on his award, but one has to hope that it made no reference to the three basic principles of the Fraternity: Brotherly Love, Relief and Truth.

Lost Virtue

Just nine months after paying-out thousands of pounds to acquire Freemasons' Hall and the assets associated with it, and with sitting tenants removed permanently and refusing to settle any of the debt they had accumulated, the new landlord had no apparent way of returning any of his investment. Previous history related that, following the ructions of 1823, the building remained empty for the next twenty years before it was eventually sold, and with the apparent animosity existing between the Bath members and Charles Geary, it is easy to assume that there was no Masonic activity there during that period.

But was that really the case? To complete the picture we also need to look at the third Lodge that had previously occupied the Hall, and for ease of reading this section, all references to Lodge of Virtue No.311 will be simplified to 'the Lodge' and any other Lodges or Orders will be referred to by their full name.

At the beginning of 1824, the Lodge was meeting at the Castle & Ball Hotel in New Bond Street. Within the year, on October 24th 1824, they returned to Freemasons' Hall where they remained for the next six years. This is contrary to the historical accounts, all of which insisted that there were no Masonic meetings at the Hall after Geary locked the doors, and also that this Lodge folded shortly after Royal York Lodge. It also confirms that they had settled any legal issues with Geary, showing that he was not resolved against the Lodges occupying the Hall come-what-may, as again had been the insinuation.

Not that the condition of the Lodge was that buoyant following their return, but with Tarratt returned to the Chair for a second year running, and some fifteen members attending his installation, the position was not as dire as previously believed. However, by the following year attendances had dwindled, and in the absence of alternative candidates, Tarratt agreed to continue pro-tem until an election could be held; this happened in December when Hayes became Master, and during 1826 there were new initiates for the first time in several years, as well as three joining members, all from the then-defunct Royal York Lodge; these were William Redman, the ex-Treasurer of Royal Cumberland Chapter, and the last member to refuse the Mastership of Royal York Lodge in 1824, Robert Shew, Geary's brother-in-law from his first marriage, and Abel Sharland.

Redman succeeded to the Mastership at the beginning of 1827. Eight months later, the name of Matthew Patton suddenly appeared within correspondence relating to the Lodge. For some reason he had become hot under the collar regarding irregularities he perceived within this Lodge, and on September 13th 1827 wrote a somewhat shambolic letter as Master of Royal Cumberland Lodge to the Grand Secretary Edwards Harper, referring to a proposed joining member from this Lodge, a Mr Keeling: *Bro. Keeling is a highly respectable young man was made during the last year in 311, paid the fees demanded viz £4-0s-0d but could never obtain his certificate. This I have just learned from him & I understand others are similarly situated. The Lodge I found must, having no Installed Master & but two or three nominal members remaining - The point of receiving members 311 so circumstanced I apprehend must be submitted to the Provincial Grand Master as other applications from other non-certificated Brothers from 311 have been made to us and must resolve itself into an exposure of the many irregularities of that Lodge. I merely name this business as Master of 55 I shall feel it a duty in acting according to the constitution to investigate and submit to the proper authority cases similar to the present or many worthy Brothers who would do honor to the Craft must be excluded to their Masonic Privileges of the fraternity. The Brethren I believe intend addressing you officially on the subject of their Certificates and it is highly proper something should be done to remedy the evil, Bro. Tarratt late Master of 311 having left Bath entirely since his late Bankruptcy & now resides in London.*

Most of the content of this letter was quite outrageous, as the Minute Book clearly shows that this Lodge had an installed Master, certainly more than just a nominal membership and were meeting regularly. The return for the previous year shows not only Keeling, but two other new members, Weston and Wood, all of whom had been correctly returned to Grand Lodge and had their certificate fees of 17 shillings each remitted in full. So if there was any reason for a delay in issuance of the certificates, it was not due to any irregularity in the Lodge, but more likely the age-old problem of generating them quickly enough in London. What makes the letter appear even more absurd is the fact that Keeling was Secretary of this Lodge at the time and was himself in direct correspondence with the Grand Secretaries on the matter.

The intimation that the financial status of the previous Master had anything to do with this situation was also nefarious. Thomas Tarratt had indeed suffered the bankruptcy of his Haberdashery business in Milsom Street, but that had only occurred a couple of months prior to

Patton's letter. Examination of the official records show that he was discharged from that situation by the end of the following year, with all debts settled. Furthermore, not only was he not the current Master, he was not even the Immediate Past Master, as he had left the chair at the end of 1825, eighteen months prior to the failure of his business.

It must be assumed that the existence of this letter never came to the knowledge of the Lodge, as there is no reference to it in their minutes. Presumably the Grand Secretaries set Patton right, as there is also no further reference to the matter in Royal Cumberland Lodge Minutes. So was this just the latest round in Patton's continued personal vendetta against those associated with the Hall? In which case, what was the *'evil'* he referred to?

The Master of the Lodge at that time was William Redman who was, according to correspondence at that time, also First Principal of the Royal York Chapter, although other evidence shows that Chapter as not meeting since 1823. In the meeting of the Lodge on October 19th 1827, Redman proposed that the Lodge apply to have Royal York Chapter attached to it. It is already apparent how protective Patton was of the status of Royal Cumberland Chapter in Bath, so maybe he had advance information that this was about to happen, and decided to try to stop it. If that was his motive, he needn't have worried, because the reply from Grand Chapter put a halt to any such change, stating that application for attachment could only be made by petition signed by *a competent number of Companions still belonging to the Chapter*, suggesting that they already knew there were insufficient, if indeed any, to do so.

More likely, however, Patton had caught wind of the next development in the Lodge, minuted on 30th October 1827: *Bro Shew proposed Bro T Whitney Apothecary of this City as a joining member seconded by Bro Keeling.* Thomas Whitney's twelve-month suspension had been completed at the beginning of 1826, and the vote was unanimously in favour. The following month Thomas Whitney attended for the first time, taking the membership to eleven.

Co-incident with this, the Lodge Secretary Keeling embarked on correspondence with Grand Lodge on an application to have the name of the Lodge changed to the Royal York Lodge of Virtue: *The sanction of His late Royal Highness the Duke of York having been once obtained for a Lodge in Bath to take his name (the letter written by himself containing his approbation is still hung up in our Lodge Room) we, on that presumption, took the liberty of addressing HRH the Duke of Sussex MW Grand Master, to give his sanction to our reviving it in commemoration of that illustrious individual, trusting that by a steady perseverance in correctly following the laws of the Constitution, we shall in part, alleviate the stigma caused by the erasure of that name from the list of Lodges and likewise, enlarge the number of our members and also, we feel assured, that the revival of that name will be more pleasing than otherwise to the Fraternity in Bath in general as there is no Lodge in the Province of Somerset that takes the name of the Royal York.*

The reply was unequivocal: *The MW Grand Master only granting the use of the titles of the Royal Family if the holder of it permits it, and there being now no Duke of York, permission cannot be granted. It is also worthy of remark that the Royal York Lodge formerly held in Bath, has for misconduct and violation of the laws been by Grand Lodge erased from the list of Lodges, consequently it would naturally be inferred that there could be no desire amongst any of the Fraternity in the City of Bath to revive even the name of such a Lodge having been so disgraced.*

The following month, Thomas Whitney was proposed and elected as the next Master of the Lodge. This time there would be no clash of commitments with his brother William, as the latter had resigned his Lodge membership back in 1824. Initially, I had concluded that this may have been due to all of the problems surrounding his elder brother, but then I found a reference to William appearing at the Old Bailey in London on 22nd June 1824 as an Insolvent Debtor. He was quoted as *assistant to Thomas Whitney, Apothecary and Druggist, and living in Holloway, Bath, formerly Prospect Place.*

The address sequence shows quite a comedown, as Prospect Place was a reasonable address on the outskirts of the City, but Holloway was one of the less-salubrious areas near the centre. As the debt must have been of a personal nature, it has to be assumed that William ended-up in Debtor's Prison, as he did not return to Bath until the late 1830s, at which point he set-up in premises on the London Road separate from his brother. William will appear again later in another part of the story.

From 1828, Charles Geary appeared occasionally in the Lodge of Virtue minutes as a visitor, although this is not surprising as he had been a member thirty years earlier. At Christmas 1828, a vote of thanks was recorded: *In consequence of Bro C Geary having in his usual most Masonic and kind manner, granted the use of the Lodge room to the members of this Lodge, free of expense.* In return for this, the Lodge voted to pay him 2s.6d a night for gas and light.

Thomas Whitney continued in the chair for a second year in 1829, during which the Lodge issued a memorial to the Fund of Benevolence on behalf of Past Master Hayes, who had fallen on hard times. The first reply from the Grand Secretaries, on 26th November, addressed to Whitney as Master, was a refusal due to Hayes, apparently, not having made contributions since 1823, and concluding: *This being the second irregularity of the kind which has occurred with your Lodge, it is submitted whether it would not be more proper in the Lodge to refer to their books & furnish a recommendation more consonant with the facts, and therefore avert the serious consequences of its being brought under consideration of the Board of General Purposes!*

This spiky reply from Edwards Harper barely concealed his obvious contempt for Whitney, but was it in itself *consonant with the facts?* Robert Shew, then Secretary, obviously didn't think so, and his response simply asked for copies of Grand Lodge returns: *that we may be able to trace the error.* Harper replied quickly: *I beg leave to observe that the duties of the person employed in this office does not enable us to render such copies, which by the Constitution, it is required should be kept by each Lodge in their own books, besides if you were furnished with copies and even the returns themselves, nothing could be deducible therefrom beyond what has already been communicated, that the name of Bro. Hayes has altogether been omitted to be returned since 1823. Should you still be of the opinion that copies are essential to clear up this point, it would be proper to send someone to do this duty.*

If Harper thought that would be the end of the matter, he obviously didn't recognise that, to someone who seemed to have made almost a sport in recent years of getting under the skin of Grand Lodge, this type of answer was merely a red rag before a bull. The response was signed by Shew, but clearly drafted with the aid of Whitney: *As our present Worshipful Master and myself are called upon to explain the errors, if any, of a member of our Lodge who has left Bath, we are still of the opinion that copies of the Lodge returns are essential to clear up this point. We have not the slightest wish to offer an opinion on the positive duties of the persons employed in your office but the Constitutions inform us that you are required to do generally all such things as heretofore <u>have</u> been done or <u>ought</u> to be done by a Grand Secretary, and as your office is the only depository for all the returns, Petitions Memorials, etc., from the several Lodges, one cannot conceive it contrary to your duty, or at any rate, that of your Clerk or Assistant to furnish the copies we* *require. However, as you refuse to comply with our request (except on condition which amounts to a prohibition) we have now to request you will transmit to the Master of the Lodge, as the least trouble to yourselves, the <u>original returns</u> and the Master hereby undertakes to return them in safety to your office within one week after he has received them.*

The Christmas break then intervened, and the next meeting in late January was attended by Hayes and also by a visitor, Dr Muttlebury, by then a member of a new Lodge in Bath. One wonders quite why Muttlebury should be there, other than as an observer to check-out the reaction to Harper's latest reply, a letter that had presumably been previewed elsewhere: *On a reference to the Papers as within the register book of your Lodge, it appears that the name of Bro. Hayes has been duly entered from the returns, and the quarterage posted against his name, and the <u>mistake has arisen from an erroneous extract</u> made on the Petition! - consequently the correspondence on the subject should <u>not</u> have taken place, and for which I assure you <u>I am truly sorry for!</u> The Petition will now come regularly before the ensuing Board of Benevolence with every assistance I can render it. Sincerely <u>apologising</u> to you for <u>the trouble</u> this occasioned.* A further letter was later received confirming that ten pounds had been granted to Bro. Hayes. So a lesson learned that even high-ranking officers can make mistakes if they let their emotions control their actions.

At that same meeting Shew and Whitney swapped offices with Shew becoming the final Master of the Lodge. He held the Chair throughout 1830 and the Lodge even attracted another joining member, who having joined never attended again. But the year was primarily marked by a set of correspondence between Whitney, as Secretary, and the Provincial Treasurer, Bro Stradling, over the supply of audited accounts for the Provincial Lodge Fund. The Lodge's view was that they were entitled to these each year under the Constitution, but none having been received since 1820, they were requesting copies of at least the most recent ones. It became apparent that Province was not going to play ball; they bounced Whitney's letters between officials, first filibustering and then simply ignoring them. In the end, the members concluded that they were never going to obtain the copies requested and the correspondence was suspended. It is doubtful that this episode had any significance as to the financial status of the Fund; more likely it was an unwritten statement by Province that they had no intention of getting involved with Thomas Whitney again.

At the end of the year, Shew decided he would not serve again as Master. With nobody else prepared to stand for election, Shew, Whitney and Sharland all gave notice they would resign the Lodge at the next meeting, at which meeting it was proposed that Shew continue for another twelve months as a titular Master to allow the remaining four members to find sufficient new recruits to continue. Essentially the Lodge went into hibernation, the minutes of the final meeting on 30th December 1830 ending: *The Lodge closed in due form and perfect harmony until this day twelve month. N.B. As it is not likely the Lodge would resume its duties until the expiration of the above period , the installation of the Worshipful Master was considered unnecessary.*

The final act took place in September 1831, when Robert Shew wrote to Grand Lodge, presumably in response to a request for the submission of an annual return: *In consequence of the Provincial Grand Treasurer Bro. Stradling having declined to send for the information of the members of the late Lodge of Virtue, a copy of the receipts and disbursements of the Provincial Fund, which by the By Laws of Grand Lodge as well as that of the Provincial Grand Lodge they are entitled to once in every year, the Brethren came to a resolution on Dec 8th 1830 to withdraw their names as members of the Lodge and as I have no means of reimbursing myself for any money advanced by me on behalf of the late Lodge of Virtue, I must decline receiving any more letters unless free of postage.*

Again a sad end for a Lodge that had also existed for more than sixty years, but once again these later records show that, far from it being another immediate victim of the Hall debacle, it had continued to meet for a number of years, albeit sporadically at times. What's more, it had done so in the very building that was supposed to have been its downfall.

Honour Returns

There is one Lodge that has not been mentioned thus far, simply because it didn't exist when all of the problems arose at the hall. It was formed in 1825 as a The Lodge of Honour, and the main driving force behind it was Charles Maddison. For ease of reading this section, all references to Lodge of Honour No.798 will be simplified to 'the Lodge'. Other Lodges or Orders will be referred to by their full name.

After the demise of Royal York Lodge in 1824, there were a large number of ex-members in Bath who needed a Lodge to join. The fact that few sought to join the three remaining Lodges may be indicative of those ex-members' view of their relative position in society, with Lodge of Virtue, always considered as a tradesman's Lodge, attracting just three Royal York members in 1824 and Royal Sussex Lodge, still seen as somewhat separatist in line with its Antients pedigree, attracting none. If so, Royal Cumberland Lodge should have benefitted as the Lodge with the oldest pedigree. That only four Royal York members joined them is quite significant, particularly as their attached Chapter retained a number of ex-Royal York members among its numbers.

The reason for this, apparent, lack interest in the other Lodges is easily found in the unconcealed enthusiasm by some of those ex-members to form a new Lodge in the City that would be distinguished by that familiar desire of it being of a somewhat more exclusive character. On 24th January 1825, within weeks of the final erasure of Royal York Lodge, these ex-members held a meeting at the York House Hotel and resolved that:

A Memorial be transmitted to the RW PGM in order to its being presented to the MW Grand Master, soliciting his Royal Highness to grant to the above-named Brethren his Warrant for forming a new Lodge in the City of Bath. That his Royal Highness be respectfully requested to denominate it The Tynte Lodge, as a merited compliment to the present RW Provincial Grand Master of Somerset, in testimony of the sincere respect, esteem, and truly fraternal regard in which he is held by the petitioning Brethren. That as soon as His Royal Highness shall have granted the Warrant, or the RW Provincial Grand Master shall have granted his dispensation for forming the new Lodge, the said Brethren be convened for the purpose of organising and regulating the same.

The primary signatories were Sir Walter James, Past Provincial Grand Master for Kent, Admiral Bullen and Captain Charles Maddison.

The PGM's reply came swiftly from Halswell: *In granting a Dispensation to Yourself and the very worthy and excellent Brethren, who wish to establish a new Lodge in the City of Bath, it gives me the greatest pleasure to find the genuine Principles and true interests of Free Masonry, supported by so numerous, so respectable and so honourable a set of Gentlemen, and I beg to assure you and them that the pleasure I feel in forwarding their wishes on this occasion is only exceeded by the deep sense I entertain of the flattering manner in which the Application has been made to me and the great honour they have done me, in wishing to associate my name with their own, in the cause of Honour, Independence and Free Masonry.*

A further meeting was then convened to finalise the contents of the official petition to the Duke of Sussex, which decided to name the Lodge "The Tynte Lodge of Honour and Independence", to meet at the York House Hotel, co-incidentally where the Duke had stayed during his visit in 1819. The 17 signatories included eleven ex-members of Royal York Lodge, among them the last Master, Charles Maddison, and several with Provincial rank including the serving Somerset Provincial Secretary. Their first Master was to be Sir Walter James and his Wardens Admiral Bullen and John Soden, all also past members of Royal York Lodge. Having ticked all the right boxes, or so they thought, they sat back awaiting their Warrant.

The reply from the Grand Secretary, William White, was sent directly to Col. Kemeys-Tynte as PGM, granting the petition but with some modifications: *His Royal Highness was graciously pleased to accede to the prayer of the Petition and signed an Order for the Warrant being made out. In making this communication, I am however commanded by His Royal Highness to say that as Grand Master, it would not be advisable at present to attach your name as part of the denomination of the Lodge, lest it might be interpreted as demonstration of a party feeling, or as a desire to make a triumph in regard to the decision of the Grand Lodge upon the unmasonic proceedings at Bath, which have recently occupied so great a portion of time in the Grand Lodge and which have unfortunately occasioned so much trouble. His Royal Highness rests assured that, from your knowledge of his feelings, you will ascribe this decision to his anxiety for the peace and welfare of the Craft, and that when the Petitioners have maturely weighed all the circumstances of the case, they will be equally satisfied of the propriety of the Measure. When the lapse of a little time shall have allowed the present existing excitement to subside, His Royal Highness will feel great pleasure in giving directions for the Lodge to bear your name in conformity with the wish of the applicants.*

As regards the addition of the word "Independence," His Royal Highness commands me to say he feels he cannot with propriety admit it, inasmuch as when His Royal Highness was Deputy Grand Master, the Marquis of Hastings, then acting Grand Master, publicly declared in Grand Lodge, his objection against a Lodge assuming such a title, and in which objection the Grand Lodge fully concurred. Under these circumstances, therefore, the Warrant of the Lodge will be made out for the present under the denomination of the "Lodge of Honour." The Lodge retains that name to this day.

However, the petitioners had been confident enough that they would receive the full name applied for, as they went ahead and ordered some items of Lodge equipment, including a full set of large Harris Tracing Boards. Two of these survive in Bath Masonic Museum (the third was lost after a bombing raid in 1942, when it was used to board-up a window in the current Bath Masonic Hall - face side out!) On the rear of the survivors is emblazoned the name of the new Lodge, obviously painted before the Grand Secretary's letter had arrived.

The Lodge was given the number 798, and the listed founder members also included Col. Kemeys-Tynte himself, George Hay, the incumbent Master of Royal Cumberland Lodge at that time, and Frederick Bannatyne, one of the gentlemen who had been involved eight years earlier with the attempted takeover of Royal Cumberland Lodge. He was the only one of those individuals to actually achieve membership in Bath of what was perceived to be *a Lodge consisting of Gentlemen of rank and respectability*. Many more considered as such would be listed among the joining members, including nine with hereditary titles, ten senior army officers, four doctors and five clergymen.

In all 17 of the 37 final members of Royal York Lodge, plus seven who had resigned during 1822/3, joined Lodge of Honour in its first two years of existence, and at the end of 1827 the new Lodge's membership stood at a very healthy 61.

One of Lodge of Honour's Tracing Boards
showing the name painted on the rear
Bath Masonic Hall Trust

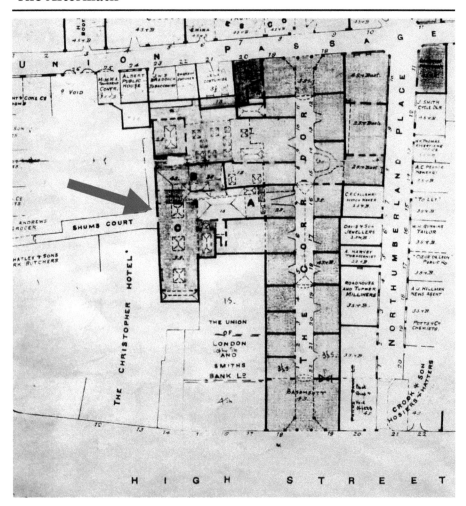

Plan of the Corridor Arcade c1840
The arrow indicates the location of Freemasons' Hall. *Bath in Time*

This Lodge was never involved in any way with tenancy at the Hall in York Street. They remained at the York House Hotel until 1829, when they moved to the White Lion to share accommodation with Royal Cumberland Lodge.

However, they would ultimately join forces with the other surviving Lodges and Orders in finding a joint home five years later, when they all signed a 21-year lease to meet at rooms created for them by the architect Henry Goodridge above the new Corridor Rooms behind his Corridor shopping arcade opposite the Guildhall. Once again, the main driver in that new arrangement was Charles Maddison, newly-appointed Deputy Provincial Grand Master by Col. Kemeys-Tynte.

It was Maddison who made the announcements to the other Lodges regarding the content of the lease, how the rent and costs were to be apportioned, and the organisation of the committee responsible for obtaining new furniture. He was also one of three Masons who stood personal surety for the Lodges' undertakings, his being the largest exposure as the Lodge of Honour was responsible for half of the total rent of forty pounds per annum, a position echoing that of Royal Cumberland, and Charles Geary, relative to the York Street Hall some fifteen years earlier.

Above: The Corridor Temple today now part of a furniture showroom. *By kind permission of sofa.com*
Top: Goodridge's 1833 sectional drawing of the Corridor Hall. *Bath Record Office*

Within weeks of opening, the new rooms hosted a Provincial Grand Lodge meeting, after which: *In the evening, about 70 of the brethren, in full clothing, sat down for a most elegant dinner, provided in the Hall by Brother G Temple, in the first style of taste and comfort, with an assortment of wines allowed to be, in flavour and quality, never surpassed.*

New furniture was acquired for this Hall at a total cost of £101-9s, of which Lodge of Honour contributed just over half. The Lodges also received a very generous donation from Col. Kemeys-Tynte in the form of a new Masters' Chair. However, this chair was not as ornate as the one, at that time, still gathering dust in the lower room at York

223

Street, but it was certainly sturdy, and moved with the Bath Lodges when they eventually acquired their current home in 1865. It is today on display in the Bath Masonic Museum, and was actually able to be pressed into action again during 2016 while the replica of the chair at Barnstaple was being refurbished.

A number of the 2016 Lodge Masters remarked that it was probably the most uncomfortable chair they had ever had to use. This echoed an

Master's Chair and Pedestal from the Corridor Hall on display in Bath Masonic Museum. *Bath Masonic Hall Trust*

anecdote that has come down through the years regarding a Lodge Master at the Corridor Hall, who was chatting with the PGM at the Festive Board after a meeting and made a similar remark, not being aware who had presented the Chair to them some years earlier. The reply he received, apparently, was that it was designed that way because no Lodge Master should ever feel fully-comfortable when in the Chair.

Two years after the Corridor Hall was opened, another Provincial Grand Lodge meeting was held there for a special purpose that was reported in the Bath Chronicle:

A Grand Provincial Meeting of the County of Somerset was held at the Masonic Hall in the Corridor in this City for the purpose of the Brethren of the Province presenting their Grand Master, Colonel Tynte MP, with a piece of plate as a testimony of the esteem in which he is held as a Brother by the whole Craft of the County. At half-past eleven, the Grand Master, Officers, and Brethren entered and were received with the customary honours. Shortly afterwards, the Provincial

Grand Lodges of Bristol, Leicester, Dorset and Wiltshire were severally received with the usual honours. Brother Maddison, DPGM, then proceeded in the name of the Brethren to present the PGM with the superb token. The speech of Brother Maddison on the occasion,, we are informed, was remarkable for its elegance and was delivered with a fervency which gave proof that it was that sort of eloquence which is spoken from the heart. The worthy PGM, in return, expressed his acknowledgement at receiving such a gratifying mark of esteem, and in a highly complimentary speech recommended the Brethren to ever cherish those principles of Fraternal benevolence towards all which they evinced towards each other. The Tribute of Plate consists of a vase designed from the Warwick Vase with a cover and pedestal, the two figure-handles representing Faith and Hope

Vase presented to Col. Kemeys-Tynte which stands more than two feet high, and is now on display in the Museum at Grand Lodge in London. *Bath Masonic Hall Trust*

surmounted on top of the cover by the mythical representation of Charity with her three children. The body of the vase is chased in bold relief with pomegranate fruit and flowers. The pedestal is square enriched with borders of acacia leaves and bears the inscription: "Presented to C.K.K. Tynte Esq, MP Right Worshipful PGM of Free and Accepted Masons for the Province of Somerset by his faithful and devoted Brethren of the Province as a token of their sincere and Fraternal attachment, and in gratitude for his undeviating and successful exertions in the cause of Masonry generally, and more particularly in his own Province. 21st October 1836."

Sussex Arrives

Although the intimation from history was that the Hall was empty from the time that Geary locked-out the Lodges until he eventually sold it nearly twenty years later, the reality was considerably different, with Lodge of Virtue meeting regularly in the lower Lodge Room. But were Lodge of Virtue alone in using the Hall after 1824?

It's time to look more closely at the fourth Lodge that existed in Bath, and for ease of reading this section, all references to Royal Sussex Lodge No.69 will be simplified to 'the Lodge' and those to Royal Sussex Chapter No.69 to 'the Chapter'. Any other Lodges or Orders will be referred to by their full name.

Although this Lodge participated in the early arrangements to build the Hall, they had withdrawn from the project by the time the lower lodge room was opened in 1818. But that doesn't mean that they remained opposed to Freemasons' Hall. In fact, on 4th September 1826, they became the second Lodge at that time to use it for meetings, where they were subsequently joined by their attached Chapter.

This came about after they became unhappy with their long-standing accommodation at the Greyhound Inn, having suffered what were described as *a series of insults*. They decided unanimously to move to Freemasons' Hall at an agreed rent of £14 per annum, and stayed there for nearly five years, with no apparent problems. However, by 1830 they were clearly struggling financially because they decided to suspend their summer meetings that year. In response to their situation, Charles Geary reduced their rent to a nominal £2 a year, a further indication of his willingness to assist the Fraternity where he could.

However, in March 1831 just months after Lodge of Virtue had held what would be their last meeting, the Brethren of this Lodge: *unanimously resolved that the Lodge should be removed in consequence of the Hall being advertised for sale and that Notice be given to Mr Geary on or before the 25th instant of the intention of the Brethren to quit the Hall on the 24th June next.* Despite exhaustive searches of archives, I have been unable to find any advertisements for the sale of the Hall in 1831. So it can only be assumed that, following his retirement from his wine business at the end of 1829, Geary may have decided that there was little future for him with the building after Lodge of Virtue finally folded. Because of that news, Royal Sussex moved again, this time to the White Lion where Royal Cumberland had been since 1823. It wasn't the last time that they would occupy York Street, however.

Assuming that it was Geary's desire to sell the Hall in 1831, he presumably found it difficult to find a buyer, making it attractive to take a long-term tenancy for a Chapel the following year. Regardless, Geary did not rent out the lower lodge room at all, where the Lodge furniture remained for the whole of that period. Maybe he still envisaged the possibility that the Fraternity would return there in some form, but that possibility became more remote when, in 1834, all Bath Lodges and their associated Chapters signed the lease for the Freemasons' Hall in The Corridor.

The cohabiting of the new hall caused occasional petty disputes between the Lodges, but there was one more major flourish to come when, in 1840, this Lodge's new Master made a series of proposals. William Gover-Gray was a young solicitor who was obviously keen to move things forward, and his Mastership was a turning point for the Lodge. The membership had dwindled after they moved to the Corridor, with a number of long-standing members resigning. It is interesting to note that virtually all of them reapplied to be joining members during Gover-Gray's time in the chair.

His first proposal was that the Lodge be renamed the Royal Sussex Lodge of Perfect Friendship and Virtue. He was obviously attempting to reconcile some history, and although the response from a vote was not unanimous, he received a majority in favour, following which an application was made to Grand Lodge. No reply is recorded in the Lodge minutes, but as the name remained unchanged it can only be deduced that the application was unsuccessful. He then made another proposal, which was to move the Lodge back to York Street. He could not have imagined the hot water this would land him in.

A few weeks later, a resignation occurred of one of the Lodge Officers who had *behaved in a most unseemly and unmasonic manner at the late dinner of the Lodge at Bro. Parker's Hotel.* The resignation was accepted unanimously and in response Gover-Gray called an emergency meeting to elect a replacement, but could not proceed because no member would take the empty position, even temporarily, in order to allow the election to take place - another echo of past problems in the defunct Lodges. So in June 1840 another emergency meeting was called, this time by Col. Kemeys-Tynte, who attended along with his deputy Charles Maddison. The Colonel advised the members that he *met the Lodge in his official capacity owing to certain allegations of irregularities which had occurred during the Mastership of Bro. W. G. Gray, but with the view of settling the business in a satisfactory manner.*

This ostensibly referred to the Officer's resignation, but it quickly became apparent that there was another, unannounced, agenda operating. The minutes of the meeting continue: *Capt. Maddison then stated that W.Bro. Gray contemplated moving the Lodge to the old Masonic Hall in York Street. This he believed would be attended with serious consequences to the Craft generally, more specially destroying the unanimity of feeling and purpose that had, until these unhappy circumstances, characterized the Brethren in Bath.* Then, referring to the York Street Hall, he said: *It was a place rendered particularly obnoxious to the Craft by recollections which he hoped from this time would be buried in oblivion. He asked for a distinct pledge from the Worshipful Master, that he would not countenance the removal.*

Gover-Gray agreed to make such an undertaking provided the other charges were dropped. Col. Kemeys-Tynte then stated that: *The charges had not been officially made to him, consequently there were none to withdraw. He had heard of the irregularities of the proceedings of the Worshipful Master* [Gover-Gray] *and had come to Bath with the view of restoring order. As the Worshipful Master had acquiesced to the proposition of the Deputy Provincial Grand Master* [Maddison], *he would not at any time take notice of the irregularities alluded to if the Worshipful Master remained true to the pledge given that day.*

This was really quite astonishing, particularly in a Fraternity that shuns political machinations of any kind, a fact obviously not lost on the membership present who in response to the Colonel's next action, which was to appeal to them to grant the re-instatement of the Officer who had resigned, unanimously refused to do so! Arrangements were then agreed on how to resolve the future election of a replacement, after which: *the meeting ended with the congratulations of the Provincial Grand Master on the pleasant termination of the business.* Clearly political spin was already alive and well in early Victorian times.

What makes even less sense, however, is why this occurred some ten years after the Lodge had vacated the York Street building, having spent five uneventful years there. Surely, if the building was still *particularly obnoxious to the craft* in 1840, then it must have been even more so in 1826, less than three years after the original issues associated with it had arisen? However, it should not be forgotten that, in 1840, Maddison was still the main personal guarantor on the Corridor lease. So was this somewhat of a déjà vu moment, similar to that suffered by Whitney and Geary almost twenty years earlier, when their personal financial status was threatened by Earl Manvers' action? If so, it cannot be ignored that Maddison may simply have been using his position to avert any similar fragmentary developments in the Corridor and, of course, at the same time protect his own financial position.

But that was not the end of the matter, either for Gover-Gray or the Lodge. Following his re-election as Master for a second year, in May 1841 Gover-Gray received an invitation from the Master of Royal Cumberland Lodge, William Fraser, to visit them together with his senior officers, one of whom was William Underwood Whitney, who had returned to the Bath Fraternity as a member of this Lodge.

Even though both Lodges met in the same rooms, on their arrival, as was customary for all visitors at the time, they were asked to wait outside of the Lodge while permission was obtained for them to be admitted. More than half an hour elapsed, during which time Whitney decided to leave; the remaining officers were eventually advised that Gover-Gray *would not be admitted as he had made himself obnoxious to a member of the Royal Cumberland Lodge.* Gover-Gray protested that he had attended by invitation and requested the Brother concerned to withdraw to settle any misunderstanding, as was the normal manner, only to be told that the Lodge had passed a resolution excluding him unless he consented to pay an admission fee of five guineas. Gover-Gray refused to do so, and left.

Royal Cumberland Lodge minutes show that it was their Treasurer James Wodderspoon who was the Brother concerned; apparently he had been the subject of an insulting remark made by Gover-Gray, although no mention is made of when and where the incident took place. Gover-Gray subsequently denied this, and there followed a good deal of correspondence between the Lodges until the matter came before Provincial Grand Lodge in the following October.

How deep the rift had been allowed to develop is illustrated by the contrast in the minutes each Lodge were provided by their own representatives at the same meeting. According to the minutes of this Lodge, Royal Cumberland simply made a full apology. According to Royal Cumberland, Wodderspoon's accusation was corroborated, but

Gover-Gray refused to withdraw the offending remark. However, Royal Cumberland's minutes also record that Gover-Gray was not in attendance but do not explain how his refusal was received. Their minute writer could not resist adding a barbed additional comment regarding the apparent lack of stewards provided by the other Lodge.

The reality was that, after the Provincial Grand Secretary had declared that reconciliation was hopeless, representatives had brokered a private compromise that neither party wished to disclose within their own Lodge. As Royal Cumberland issued the invitation in the first place, this may suggest that there was some mischief afoot, in which case it would be difficult to rule out the possibility that Matthew Patton was involved somewhere, as he was in attendance at the meeting where the incident occurred, and James Wodderspoon had been proposed by him for membership of Royal Cumberland Lodge some ten years earlier.

Nevertheless, Royal Sussex were not covering themselves in glory during this period and, as their Master, Gover-Gray has to take a deal of the blame for this. Factions were clearly forming within his membership, and he was not helping by his continued desire to take the Lodge back to York Street, despite his previous undertaking to the Provincial Grand Master. In November 1841, he once again proposed this and received unanimous support; as a result, their first few meetings of 1842 were held at York Street. What makes this continued desire to move more difficult to understand is that the Corridor was owned by Gover-Gray's brother-in-law, Henry Goodridge; so his apparent need to remove his Lodge must have caused some consternation in family circles as well.

Jacob Seale was installed as the new Master of the Lodge on 10th January 1842 at York Street, the Freemasons Quarterly reporting: *The Public were admitted gratis to Freemasons' Hall, York Street, preparatory to the installation of the Worshipful Master of the Royal Sussex Lodge No. 61. The room was brilliantly illuminated with gas and wax-lights, and was magnificently adorned with the varied and striking paraphernalia of the Order. The Furniture, we understand was that used on the occasion of the consecration of the building by HRH the Duke of Sussex, and is of the most gorgeous description the Master's Chair alone being valued at fifty guineas. The jewels and emblems were exceedingly brilliant. Nearly 800 persons were gratified with the sight of these curious ornaments.* This suggests that they may have been using the main room for this display, which had become available after the Chapel had stopped meeting there late in 1841.

Within weeks, Seale called for a special meeting to be held back at the Corridor Rooms to further discuss the matter of which venue they would use. He was the Lodge's representative that had brokered the deal with Province and Royal Cumberland Lodge a few months earlier. Gray and nine other members opposed this meeting, but it went ahead in their absence, attended by just eight members including Seale. A letter was read out from the ten opponents, plus another from a third faction that had also met separately outside of the Lodge. From the minutes of this meeting, Gover-Gray's situation becomes clearer.

Seale explained that the reason for calling the meeting at the Corridor was that *the present occupier of the old Masonic Hall, refused to allow Bro. Bennett to have the keys of the lower Lodge room, accusing the said Bro. Bennett with the intent to steal the Knights Templar warrant if allowed possession of the keys, which he would not allow the keys out of his possession (without being himself present) to the said Bro. Bennett.* This would sound all too familiar if the occupier referred to was Charles Geary, but the minutes record William Gover-Gray as that occupier. They also record that Gover-Gray was offering *the use of the room in the Masonic Hall, York Street for the nominal sum of one shilling per quarter.* So from this, do we deduce that Gover-Gray had already entered into some form of arrangement with Geary, either to purchase the Hall from him or to lease the Lodge room? Or was he acting professionally, as a solicitor on behalf of Geary, in one final effort by the owner to have the, once again empty, Hall used for its original purpose?

There is a clue in the advertisement for the auction of the hall four months later, which mentions that: *On the Basement is a Spacious Room, now used as a Masonic Lodge, at an annual rent of 12 guineas.* That is a substantial sum for the Lodge to afford alone, and taking into consideration Gover-Gray's almost desperate gesture of reducing the rent, it would suggest that Gover-Gray may have taken the lease on the Lodge room himself, and sub-let it to the Lodge. In which case, had he done so on behalf of more than one tenant?

There is a clue that others were using the Lodge Room, in the reference to the potential removal of the Knights Templar warrant, another throwback to previous times. Unfortunately, there is a huge gap in the minutes of Antiquity Encampment for this time, so it is unknown where they were meeting, or if they were meeting at all, although there had been a reference in the Minutes of Royal Sussex in 1827, during their previous residence, where the Master explained that he had postponed from their original date: *the reason of his putting off the meeting of the Brethren for this night instead of the preceding one was that he wished to accommodate the Knight Templars on the previous night under a strong case of Emergency*. So the presence of the warrant within the York Street building would suggest that Antiquity Encampment still maintained some presence there in 1842 and, therefore, may have been another sub-tenant.

Either way, the game was up; Gover-Gray's objections were overruled, and subsequently the Lodge returned to The Corridor. One has to wonder why the ten boycotted that meeting, as they easily outnumbered the members that did attend. It is probably fitting that, once again, the stubborn nature of individuals involved in this ill-starred building should result in the loss of what would be its final chance of survival in its intended form.

Gover-Gray was brought before the Lodge and severely censured. His response was to express *his regret for the past and his full determination for the future to act differently*. There was one final attempt in July 1842 to remove the Lodge back to York Street, proposed by one of the oldest members of the Lodge, but this also failed, although only on Seale's casting vote as Worshipful Master. Gover-Gray never attended another Lodge meeting thereafter, although after all of this was reconciled, the Lodge did acquire a regular visitor in the form of a certain member of Royal Cumberland - Matthew Patton.

This set of incidents in the 1840s were referred to by Peach in one of his histories, although he dated them to 1826; so how could such an error have occurred? Well, he may have been unaware of either occupation, as he maintained that this Lodge had no interest at all in the Hall. Having the story related to him at a later time, perhaps he could only connect it to the earlier period, especially as the names Gray and Geary are easily confused if hand-written. The clincher would have been the reference to the proprietor of the Hall being the cause of the problems, there only having been one actual proprietor in those times.

If there did exist any business arrangement between Gover-Gray and Geary, this was quickly dissolved, as Charles Geary had decided that the time had finally come to end his ownership.

AL5817

FREEMASONS' HALL

PART SIX
LETTINGS,
SALES &
LOTTERIES

Lettings

The Financial Committee had always intended to subsidise their activities by attracting external lettings, which is why regular Masonic meetings all took place in the lower Lodge room. That room was self-contained, with its own external entrance linked to a separate staircase, leaving the upper room available for these lettings. As was related earlier, such income was sporadic at best, a situation that was inherited by Charles Geary after the building was assigned to him.

As an experienced businessman, Geary no doubt recognised that this failure within what purported to be a business plan would have to be corrected if there was to be any chance of him seeing a return on his investment. So he quickly set about finding users for the upper room, exampled in mid-October 1823 whilst all the ructions surrounding the lockout were evolving, by a Mr Bullock exhibiting: *for a few days only, a pair of those majestic and interesting quadrupeds, The Wapeti.*

To take commercial advantage of the opportunities provided by visitors to the City for the winter season, an exhibition was staged for the three month period from December 1823 to February 1824, featuring a Panorama of the Algerines Campaign. These touring attractions, known as Peristrephic Panoramas, were extremely popular during the first half of the nineteenth century, and consisted of large

---

Masonic Hall, York-Street

Mr BULLOCK, of the Egyptian Hall, Piccadilly, London, respectfully acquaints the Inhabitants and Visitors of Bath, that he has engaged, for a few days only, the above spacious and convenient Hall for the EXHIBITION of

A PAIR OF THOSE MAJESTIC AND INTERESTING QUADRUPEDS

The WAPETI

Or Newly Discovered Elk of the Missouri

WITH THEIR YOUNG

And the pleasing Appendage of the LAPLANDERS' DRESSES,

DOMESTIC IMPLEMENTS, SLEDGES, &c, &c

These beautiful Animals are now in the *full pride of their growth*, and have become so docile, as to be *rode* and *driven in a carriage*, by their *visitors*.

Open from ten till dusk. Admission 1s each

Advertisement in the Bath Chronicle, 16th October 1823

painted canvasses on rolls featuring scenes up to forty feet wide. A narrator described the scenes depicted within a large cut-out screen, resembling a theatre proscenium, which concealed the mechanism. In the early productions, at the end of each scene the curtains closed so that the rolls could be slowly hand cranked to the next scene; the whole performance was conducted with musical accompaniment, to provide a spectacle not dissimilar to that of early theatrical tableaux.

A typical Peristrephic Panorama performance
Private Collection

The advertised panorama was provided by the Marshall Brothers; these gentlemen were among the first, and the most famous, to stage these types of exhibition, and their productions were in high demand. They had staged a similar event at the Hall for a short period prior to Christmas 1822, which shows that display must have achieved some commercial success for the Marshalls to renew their booking after Geary took over the building. The Algerines Panorama was, by 1823, quite an old exhibition, but the response must have been positive, because the Brothers extended their stay for another month during March.

But instead of continuing the existing exhibition, it was replaced by a Panorama of King George IV's Coronation, their very latest production. That particular panorama was renowned as one of their finest efforts, incorporating continuous moving scenes that were cranked across the watchers' view as the commentary progressed; it had been exhibited for the first time just weeks after the Coronation itself.

The sensation it had caused in London during the second half of 1823 is portrayed by a caricature print published at the time, showing crowds trying to cram into the building where it was on display, and featuring various speech bubbles including one man asking his wife: *Do you think it is worth half a Crown to see it my Dear?* She replies: *Half a Crown! I assure you it's worth a Sovereign, it beats all the panoramas I ever saw.*

The Moving Panorama or Spring Garden Rout by C Williams
Courtesy of Bill Douglas Cinema Museum University of Exeter

The appearance in Bath was the first it had made outside of the capital, so must have been a major attraction in the City during the latter part of that season. It was a major coup for the Hall to host it, although it had to compete with another popular touring attraction of the time, Madame Tussaud's famous waxworks, on display in Quiet Street.

The Marshall Brothers Panorama of King George IV's Coronation was so popular that miniatures were produced for sale to the public. *South Australia State Library b1560288*

During April 1824, a Mr Rogers gave Astronomical lectures, then in late May and June, another Panorama, this time of the last years of Napoleon Bonaparte by W. Barker and Co, was on show. In July a banquet was held when: *upwards of 90 sat down to dinner at the Masonic Hall, to congratulate Mr Prout, on his taking the Christopher Inn in this City.* Considering that, less than three years previously, a Lodge had not considered it possible to accommodate two-thirds that number for a dinner, Geary must have made improvements in the catering facilities.

But there were no exhibitions for the season in 1825, and only one letting that year, in March, when Mr Lloyd returned with his Astronomical Lectures. In fact there were few entertainments in Bath at that time, probably because another financial crisis had occurred culminating in a run on the Banks, known as 'The Panic of 1825'. The causes, the bursting of yet another investment bubble, were not dissimilar to what we experienced in the first decade of this century with the sub-prime mortgage fiasco, but the consequences were much greater. Several large London banks went to the wall, taking with them ten per cent of all country banks in England, including some in Bath.

But it wasn't just the economic situation that was effecting the season in Bath; in November 1823, the city suffered severe flooding just at the time that the season was starting, making much of the lower part of the city inaccessible. During preceding years when the water did not reach street level, buildings like Freemasons' Hall would flood at the basement levels; even if the stench from these waters could be overcome, during flood seasons furniture from lower rooms had to be stored at higher levels making those areas unlettable.

Although these annual floods had became commonplace, after the one in 1823 the famous engineer Thomas Telford was called-in to provide a report on the causes, which turned-out to be due to excessive development around the river basin. The solution, mainly engineering works to the river downstream of the city, cost in excess of £50,000 at a time of severe financial stringency; but without them the city would have suffered a further hammer-blow to its attractiveness to visitors.

FINE ARTS

The BARKER GALLERY, Masonic Hall,

YORK STREET

THE Nobility, Gentry and the Public are respectfully informed that an exhibition of the united WORKS of Mr. BARKER and Mr. BENJAMIN BARKER *will OPEN for Public Inspection at the above Hall, on SATURDAY the 15th;.*

Consisting of Entirely ORIGINAL PICTURES

Many of which have been recently painted and never before exhibited to public view; amongst which,

The celebrated Charge of the Life Guards, in
The Battle of Waterloo,

Will form a conspicuous feature. - The Hall is fitted up in a style suitable for the occasion, and is kept well aired by constant fires.

Admittance, 1s. - Subscription Tickets for the Season are issued (not transferable) at 5s. Each. - Open from 11 till 4.

☞It being the particular wish of the Proprietors that the Juvenile Mind should feel gratification from this display of Art, in the department of Painting, they have decided on admitting all such, under the age of Twelve Years, at *Sixpence* each.

Advertisement in the Bath Chronicle, 13th December 1827

There then appear to have been no external lettings at all for over two years until 1827, when the upper room was let as a gallery to: *exhibit the united works of Mr Barker and Mr Benjamin Barker.* The Barkers were a dynasty of Bath artists that would eventually extend to three generations; the *Mr Barker* mentioned here was Thomas Barker, a portrait painter and probably the most successful, and famous, of them all; Benjamin was his younger brother, a landscape painter.

Their father, also Benjamin, developed a keen interest in horses as a boy living on the estate of his wealthy father. When that passion extended to horse racing, he lost a considerable amount of money gambling and was disowned by his father. He decided to become an artist and moved to Pontypool in South Wales, where he worked decorating Japanned Ware. In 1783 he moved to Bath to work as a portrait painter, but found that he could not make sufficient money and supplemented his earnings by working for a local coachbuilder, Charles Spackman, painting coats of arms on carriages.

Thomas, the eldest son, was fourteen when the family moved to Bath. The boy's talent was noted by Spackman, who provided training for the young artist in return for an interest in his output. In 1790, Spackman arranged for Thomas to go to Rome where he became friends with the sculptor Flaxman and set up a Society of English Art Students. Thomas then lived in London for a while before returning to Bath in 1800. He commissioned the architect Gandy to build him a large house in Sion Hill with a 30-foot picture gallery to exhibit his works. This was named Doric House, after the large columns that adorned the outside. In the picture gallery, he painted a fresco entitled *"The Massacre of the Sciotes"* that covers one entire wall.

Both brothers were exhibited regularly at the Royal Academy between 1800 and 1830, but it is fair to say that by the time they opened this exhibition in Bath, when Thomas was 57 and his brother 51, their better years were probably behind them.

Left: Thomas Barker Self Portrait
Holburne Museum Bath
Below:
Season Ticket to the Barker Gallery
Bath in Time

Regardless, the first exhibition ran until the end of March 1828, then closed for a week whilst it was refreshed with new and additional works before reopening for a second run through to mid-June. This would be the first of three consecutive exhibitions, occupying the upper room for at least six months of each year until the autumn of 1829.

For the Christmas season of 1829/30, the Marshall Brothers returned with a new Panorama of the Battle of Navarino, and continued with an additional show featuring the Battle of Trafalgar until early April.

MASONIC HALL, YORK-STREET, BATH

GRAND ADDITION

MESSRS. MARSHALLS most respectfully inform the Nobility, Gentry and the Public of Bath, that they have just added, prior to the final close of their

PERISTREPHIC PANORAMA

OF THE BATTLE OF

NAVARIN

City of Constantinople, &c.

Their Splendid Panorama (never before exhibited in Bath) of the ever-memorable

BATTLE OF TRAFALGAR

And DEATH of NELSON

The Figures being as large as life, the Ships of War on the largest scale, and accompanied by a FULL MILITARY BAND, give a complete sensation of reality.

Day Exhibitions from 12 to 4. Evening ditto 7 and half past eight o'clock

Boxes, 2s, Gallery, 1s, Children, half price. Descriptive Books, 6d.

Advertisement in the Bath Chronicle, 28th January 1830

Following that, in May 1830, one of the more bizarre exhibitions at the Hall occurred when an advertisement appeared in the Bath Chronicle: *Siamese Youths - These extraordinary double boys, respectfully inform the Ladies and Gentlemen of Bath, that they will be happy to receive their visits daily, at the Masonic Hall, York Street, from 12 to 5 in the day, and 8 to 10 in the evening. - Admission, One Shilling. They will remain in this place for four days only, being engaged to exhibit in Bristol on Monday next.*

These were undoubtedly Chang and Eng, the pair of conjoined twins from Thailand. The term 'Siamese Twins' derived from the title of a later short story by Mark Twain based upon the brothers. They were discovered in 1829 by an American merchant named Captain Abel Coffin, who took them on a world tour, of which this appearance would have been part; at the time they appeared in Bath, they would have been just nineteen years of age. They eventually took the name Bunker and settled in America where they lived into their sixties, unseparated, with their wives and a total of twenty one children.

The Siamese Twins This lithograph from 1830 showing Chang & Eng aged 18 was the image on sale at York Street. *Wellcome Collection*

In September 1830, there was a lecture from a Mr Fitzgerald, billed as: *Author of a Popular Political Pamphlet and formerly Classical Lecturer at the Feinaiglian Institution, near Dublin, principally intended to disprove the infidel doctrines lately promulgated by Carlile and the Rev. Robert Taylor.* It is interesting that Freemasons' Hall was chosen for this lecture, as Richard Carlile was known as 'The Devil's Freemason' due to his publishing to the general public, in 1825, a small red-covered book called 'The Manual of Freemasonry', a publication wherein: *all the secrets of masonry are there fully and completely exposed, and that anybody purchasing may know the whole secret for 2s 9d.*

Left: Richard Carlile by an unknown artist
National Portrait Gallery
Right: The Manual of Freemasonry
Bath Masonic Hall Trust

Nearly two-hundred years on, Carlile is now considered by historians as an important reforming free-thinker, whose dedication to a cause that often landed him in jail was to be admired. Back then, he was a dangerous radical, particularly after he linked-up with Taylor who became known as 'The Devil's Chaplain', and their regular meetings at the Rotunda in London's Blackfriars Road, the building that became the focus of the movement that led to the passing of the Reform Act, were considered infidel missions against Christianity.

Shortly after Fitzgerald's visit, there were two fundraising events at the Hall. The first was: *A Concert of Sacred Music for the benefit of a late Member of the Abbey Choir, where several of our most respectable professional gentlemen were present.* A month later there was a concert in support of the Bath Park Improvements - Charles Geary was a major supporter of the Royal Victoria Park.

BATH PARK CONCERT

Messrs. FIELD, VINER, PITMAN and C.MILSOM

RESPECTFULLY inform the Public of Bath and its vicinity, that they intend, on THURSDAY Evening, the 28th October, giving a

CHORAL AND MISCELLANEOUS

CONCERT

At the MASONIC HALL, York Street

The profits of which will be appropriated to the Funds of the

BATH PARK IMPROVEMENTS

The whole of the Professional Aid on that occasion will be rendered gratuitously

The Organ, which will be erected for the performance, is the property of Mr. JAMES NOBLE, who has allowed the use of it on this occasion

The Choruses will be ably supported by the BATH CHORAL SOCIETY, and the different Choirs.

Single Tickets, 4s; or, for the accommodation of families, six tickets, One Guinea; to be had at Messrs. Packer's, White's, Patton's, Milsom's, Robbins's and Pitman's Music Warehouses; and at Mrs. Meyler's Library, Abbey Church-yard.

Doors to be opened at half-past six, and the performance to commence at 7 o'clock - Tea will be provided at the end of the first Act. Price 6d each.

Advertisement in the Bath Chronicle, 28th October 1830

For the 1830 Christmas Season, W. Smith & Co exhibited a working model of a copper mine. The Chronicle reported shortly after it opened: *We are ourselves well acquainted with the mine of which the model is a copy, and we are surprised at the extreme faithfulness of the imitation. All the operations incidental to mining are represented with a correctness which is truly astonishing. The machinery of the model, like that of the original, is worked by water, and the whole has a remarkably pleasing effect.* The Model was exhibited from December through to March 1831.

In May 1831, a large meeting was held at the Hall to rally support for the re-election of Edward Sanford, MP for Somerset, a leading reformer in the Whig Party. In those days there was no party selection process, so as well as being in competition with representatives of opposing parties, several gentlemen from the same political party would stand in opposition to each other; one of Sanford's Whig opponents that year was Charles Kemeys-Tynte, Colonel Kemeys-Tynte's son, who was standing for parliament for the first time. The Hall was used as the headquarters of Sanford's campaign, and the committee formed for the purpose contained a number of local Freemasons, including Joseph Spry and Charles Geary.

Political meetings at the time were rowdy affairs, often attended by opponents as well as supporters, with plenty of banter, all faithfully reported in the press (together with the reactions of the crowd). During this meeting, a Mr Henry Godwin had a few words for the young Mister Tynte:

If the opponents of reform can boast of spending their sixty thousand pounds to secure their object, surely we shall be enabled to show them that the good cause has also ample means at its command (Cheers). What pretensions, I will ask, have Mr Tynte and Mr Gordon for coming forward? Mr Tynte lately said at the Quarter Sessions dinner that he had just returned from his travels; I can only say that his case is similar to that of many other gentlemen - he does not seem much the better for his travels (cheers and laughter); he must have left his patriotism behind him at the Custom House as this virtue is highly taxed - at all events not a particle of it appears in his advertisements, and I fear that he is deeply **Tynted** *with Anti-Reform principles (Laughter). Gentlemen, we will send back Mr Tynte on his travels; we will know what he is before we give him the prize he seeks. He is, I understand, a very good young man, and has gained some prizes at college; let him come back to us with more openness of conduct and we will then think of rewarding him!*

One cannot help but wonder, as the Hall's proprietor was undoubtedly in attendance, whether he would have allowed himself a slight smile on hearing these remarks. Sanford was successful in gaining re-election; the Colonel's son would have to wait until the next election before he could join his father at Westminster.

The Exhibition for the Christmas Season that opened on 14th November 1831 was the return of Madame Tussaud's waxworks to the City for the first time since they had competed with the Coronation Panorama nearly eight years earlier. Their exhibits stayed in the Hall through to February 1832.

In May 1832, a large public meeting was held in the Hall by the parish of St James with regard to the Reform Bill, which had been defeated by the House of Lords, despite wide-ranging support in the country. This forced the resignation of the Government, and a great deal of public unrest; the period became known as 'The Days of May'.

SOMERSET ELECTION

MR. SANFORD's COMMITTEE sit daily at the MASONIC HALL, to receive Subscriptions, and to co-operate with the Freeholders for securing the Election of this FIRM SUPPORTER OF REFORM.

Freeholders! Such Men as Mr SANFORD and Colonel GORE LANGTON being returned for Parliament for this great County, and without expense, will confer immortal honour on you, and

Set a glorious Example to all England!

FREEHOLDERS! Be in your places at WELLS on FRIDAY next, not later than Ten o'clock at the furthest, or your Adversaries will be before hand with you.

LANGTON and SANFORD

GIVE your votes to Langton and Sanford, the tried and proved friends of Reform! They are your proved friends, they are friends of your country, the supporters of your King!

Reject with scorn the base idea that the Representation of Somerset is to fall sacrifice to the wealth of Mr. GORDON, and tell the man who dares to brandish his purse in the face of the Freeholders that he mistakes your character when he thus dares to insult you.

Reject with equal decision the insidious pretensions of Mr. TYNTE, who conceals his principles, whilst calling for your support!

REMEMBER! The man who splits his vote in favour either of TYNTE or GORDON, is an enemy to Reform.

LANGTON and SANFORD for Ever!!!

Advertisement in the Bath Chronicle, 5th May 1831

M ADAME TUSSAUD and SONS have the honour to announce to the liberal public of Bath and its Vicinity that their SPLENDID EXHIBITION (now containing a number of NEW FIGURES of CELEBRATED CHARACTERS) which in 1822 was honoured with the most liberal patronage, will be OPENED for inspection, for a SHORT SEASON, on MONDAY morning next, Nov. 14th, in the MASONIC HALL, York-Street, which will be fitted up for the purpose.

Admittance One Shilling

Open from Eleven till Four, and from half-past Six till Ten.

A Band will attend the PROMENADE in the Evening.

Advertisement in the Bath Chronicle, 10th November 1831

In July, another meeting was held where Mr H.B. Hobhouse put forward his candidacy to become MP for Bath in the forthcoming election, the first after the Reform Act had finally been passed by Parliament; he was a director of the largest bank in Bath, but ultimately unsuccessful in his parliamentary ambitions. In September, another political meeting heard the views of a different candidate, Mr. John Roebuck, who was ultimately successful in becoming one of the two MPs that the City returned at that election.

That was the last time that the hall was used for such events, because towards the end of 1832, Geary agreed a long-term lease with the Reverend Morstead who opened a Dissenter's Chapel in the main room. Under the arrangement, that room was fitted-out with benches for services held on Wednesday and Friday evenings, and twice on Sundays, with additional prayer meetings on Thursday and Saturday evenings, an arrangement that continued throughout the remaining part of the 1830s.

So it can be seen from all of these events that, far from the building becoming a millstone around his neck, Charles Geary was able to gain income from it by renting the upper room for public events, in addition to letting the lower room to at least three Masonic organisations.

End Game

After the last withdrawal by Royal Sussex Lodge, the final part of the story began to take shape. Charles Geary, by then well into his seventies, retired and living in relatively comfortable circumstances between his Bath home in Prior Park Buildings, and his London home off Grosvenor Square, decided to dispose of the Hall, unsurprisingly as he had lost both tenants in the space of a few months.

The first intimations of this were the appearance of an advertisement in the local newspapers during March 1842, offering the building for sale by Private Contract. Particulars were advised as being by application to the Bath Herald Office, the newspaper owned by his sister, Mary Meyler. When this proved of no effect, he decided to offer it by public auction.

The public notices appeared during late June stating that Messrs English and Son would offer the property; this was the same Edmund English who helped produce the revealing report in 1824.

On 18th July 1842 the auctioneer's hammer fell at a price of just £1300, less than a third of what Geary had outlaid nearly twenty years earlier. The buyer was Reverend Wallinger, on behalf of the Bethesda Chapel which at the time occupied the old Catholic Chapel in Corn Street.

Messrs ENGLISH and SON

Beg respectfully to notify that they

WILL SELL BY AUCTION,

At their ROOMS, MILSOM STREET

On MONDAY, July 18th, at Eleven for Twelve o'clock

THE MASONIC HALL

THIS noble Building, which was erected at a cost of nearly £3000 by the present proprietor, is one of the most elegant and substantial fabrics in the city of Bath, and stands prominently forth among its highest architectural ornaments; having a frontage of classic and chaste design in York Street - closely approximating the Literary Institution, in the centre of the city, on the south of the Abbey Church, in a neighbourhood of the highest respectability, and within three minutes' walk of the Guildhall

This beautiful structure was erected originally for Masonic purposes, to which one of its rooms is still devoted; but is admirably adapted, as to situation and accommodation, for a place of Religious Worship, for Lectures, or for Public Exhibitions.

Its contents, on the ground floor, are a Noble Room, with cove ceiling 50 feet long by 30 feet wide, and 20 feet 8 inches in height, lighted by two spacious dome windows, so constructed as to keep the apartment perfectly free from the direct solar rays; a small room adjoining, patent Water Closet, and two Spacious Entrances, by flights of pennant steps, to massive doors. This floor is present used as a place of worship, at a rental of £80 per annum.

On the Basement is a Spacious Room, now used as a Masonic Lodge, at an annual rent of 12 guineas; two Ante-rooms, and a very large Kitchen, unusually well fitted up, Scullery, excellent Cellars, and all necessary Offices

1842 Auction Advertisement in Bath Chronicle

The Freemason's Quarterly included a piece on the final demise pointedly recording, amidst the history of the various pecuniary problems, that the Hall had not found favour with the Provincial Chief of Somerset. They continued: *Our object is to rescue from oblivion the material fact that Bath, the queen of the west, did once possess a Masonic Hall; but while expressing our regret that, as such, the building has ceased to be, it is no small gratification to know that it will resume its holy character by a rededication to the Almighty as an Episcopal chapel. The Earl Manvers was mainly instrumental in accomplishing this great Masonic object, aided by the zeal and exertions of various Brethren, among whom Bro. Thomas Whitney was most prominent.*

Previous histories suggest that the furniture, still in the basement of the building, was also offered at the same auction, but failed to reach the reserve price of 300 guineas; this was the total sum that Geary had calculated as owing to him back in 1823. However, the newspaper notices of the time do not bear this out, the only other lot being offered at that July auction being a house in Pulteney Street previously the residence of the late Lord Carrington. There is a resolution in Royal Cumberland Lodge's minutes in June of that year that *the Treasurer with Bros. Barrett and Fraser be empowered to purchase any Lodge Furniture expected to be sold by Auction*, but no later mention of why they did not do so. Similarly Royal Cumberland Chapter's minutes of the same time record it was *agreed that the Three Principals do form a committee for the purpose of procuring the necessary furniture for the use of the Chapter*. Nothing further was recorded in either minute book regarding the auction.

Somewhat bizarrely, there is a reference in the Royal Sussex minutes of 19th September 1842, two months after the sale, that: *the Lodge then adjourned to the Old Masonic Hall York Street for the purpose of more effectively raising Bros. Baldwin, Parker & Newton who were raised accordingly.* This would suggest that use was still being made of certain items held there, presumably not available at the Corridor Rooms, even though the York Street building itself had been sold. This could suggest that Geary was unable to secure full vacant possession in order to complete the sale until the furniture was removed; the phrase in the auction notice: *early possession may be had,* rather than vacant possession as is usual, would seem to back-up that possibility.

The only other mention of the furniture at this time comes in Royal Cumberland Lodge's minutes of November 1842, referring to a letter received from Geary which was *put on the pedestal*; however no mention is made of any discussion about it. It was most likely the document, dated October 4th 1842 and circulated to all Masonic Lodges throughout the country, which advertised that: *as 300 Guineas is the Sum required for the Purchase of the Property, and being well aware of the difficulty of any Lodge to appropriate such a sum from its Funds for that purpose, I have been strongly advised, and do intend, to dispose of the Whole in One Lot, by way of Chance.*

BATH; OCTOBER 4th, 1842.

To the W. MASTER, OFFICERS, and MEMBERS of the Lodge No.____

WORSHIPFUL SIR AND BRETHREN,

IN *consequence of the BATH MASONIC HALL having recently been SOLD for a PLACE of RELIGIOUS WORSHIP, it has now become necessary to DISPOSE OF THE MASONIC FURNITURE which has hitherto been attached to the Premises. It appears that the Sum of* **£645 15s. 0d.** *has been expended in the production of this Superb Collection, and as 300 Guineas is the Sum required for the Purchase of the Property, and being well aware of the difficulty of any Lodge to appropriate such a Sum from its Fund for that purpose, I have been strongly advised to, and do intend, to Dispose of the* **Whole in One Lot,** *by way of Chance.*

This Celebrated Furniture was prepared for, and used at, the Dedication of the Hall, by His Royal Highness the Duke of Sussex, is in the highest preservation, and—without exception—is allowed by every Brother who has seen it to be the most Unique, Complete, and Splendid, to be seen in any Lodge throughout the United Kingdom.

There will be 300 Receipts issued, from No. 1 to 300 inclusive, at **£1 1s. 0d.** *each, or 5 Tickets, taken together,* **£5 ;** *and the DRAWING will irrevocably take place at Bath, on MONDAY, JANUARY 16th, 1843.*

Receipts *are now ready for delivery ; and may be obtained by a remittance, or Post Office Order, pre-paid, addressed to Mr. GEARY, No. 2, Prior Park Buildings, Bath ; and, should any PARTICULAR NUMBER be required, an early application is necessary to prevent disappointment.*

I remain,

Worshipful Sir and Brethren,

Very Fraternally yours,

CHARLES GEARY,

P.M. & P.P.S.G.W. PROVINCE OF SOMERSET.

N.B. The Furniture will be on View, in the present Lodge Room, until Saturday, the 15th Instant.

The Circular of 1842 from Charles Geary
describing the furniture to be offered in the lottery
Bath Masonic Hall Trust

The draw was to be conducted on Monday 16th January 1843 at Meyler's Library in the Abbey Churchyard, which was also owned by Geary's sister Mary and her son Charles Geary Meyler. There was an anonymous letter published in the Freemasons Quarterly Review, presumed at the time to have been sent by a member of a Bath Lodge, which asked about the legality of the lottery. However, this extract from the minutes of Loyal Lodge No.312 in Barnstaple, for October 1842 shows that it wasn't only Bath who were interested in the subject: *Proposed by Brother Cutcliffe, and seconded by Brother Chanter: that the Worshipful Master do make inquiry as he is going to London, if the Lodges in general do intend to participate in the chance of obtaining the Furniture in the Masonic Lodge, Bath, if so that any Number of Shares, not exceeding Ten Pounds be invested, for the purpose according to the discretion of the Worshipful Master - carried by seven to four.*

The reply printed in the magazine was that *we see no impropriety in the proposed method of disposal of the elegant Masonic furniture at Bath.* The official green light having been shown, some two hundred tickets were sold, sufficient for Geary to allow the draw to go ahead. However, none of the Bath Lodges attended the event, thereby abandoning any chance of reacquiring what certain of their number still considered their lost property. Among the crowd that did gather to witness the proceedings were Brothers Harris and Whitefield who had travelled from Loyal Lodge in Barnstaple as their nominated representatives, the Lodge having purchased several tickets.

History suggested that Geary also purchased a number of tickets, thereby loading the lottery to his favour. In fact, he was entitled by the lottery laws at that time to leave in the draw any unpurchased tickets which could then be drawn in his favour. However, it was announced at the sale that he had withdrawn fifty of those unsold tickets to reduce the chances of that occurring. Nevertheless the winning ticket, number 212, was one of the remaining unsold ones, leaving Geary 200 guineas better off, but still with a load of furniture to dispose of.

The final act was the circulation by Geary of an offer to dispose of it all for the sum of 100 guineas. That was the balance of the debt owing, suggesting that Geary saw the recovery of the whole debt as paramount to the sale, but not the need to make any profit above that figure. There is no mention of this circular in Royal Cumberland's minutes, so it may be that Geary only sent it to those that had purchased tickets, hence the historical impression that the furniture was sold without the knowledge of anyone in Bath. This time, however, he did find a buyer, the representatives of Loyal Lodge making their second, and this time successful, visit to Bath during March 1843 to collect their new acquisitions. Having received the circular, they had quickly organised a subscription among their members and raised the necessary funds.

Their delight at finally achieving their goal was tempered slightly by the need to pay for some renovation, presumably due to storage damage, but more so by the realisation after delivery that their existing lodge room was a touch on the small side to accommodate it. Both were quickly overcome, as recorded by the Freemasons' Quarterly Review in 1843: *the Brethren becoming the purchasers of the splendid and celebrated Bath Masonic furniture and paraphernalia, have found it necessary to remove to a larger and more commodious Hall, and they have consequently met during the last Autumn, in the Assembly Rooms, which have been taken for the purpose. It is a cause of congratulation to the Craft in general, that this splendid furniture, which was collected and arranged at Bath, regardless of expense, is again restored to its legitimate purpose.*

The formal opening of their new Lodge room occurred on May 6th 1844 with the holding of a Devon Provincial Grand Lodge there. The local newspaper reported: *The Assembly Room was magnificently decorated with the paraphernalia of the Lodge which is of the most costly description. The respectable part of the public were admitted to view it on the previous day, and hundreds, we believe, were gratified with the sight. There would have been a procession to the Church intended to have been arranged with great splendour but this part of the usual proceedings on such occasions was prevented by the refusal of the vicar to allow a sermon to be preached.*

The Loyal Lodge accounts show the subsequent sale of pieces of furniture and regalia to the newly-formed Lodge Benevolence at Bideford contemporary with the acquisition of the Bath Furniture. Although this may have included some of the items from Bath, Bruce Oliver's opinion was that, due to the low prices recorded, it was more likely the old Lodge furniture that had been replaced. This makes far more sense, and was probably pre-agreed as six of the founder members of the new Bideford Lodge were from Barnstaple.

Loyal Lodge's attached Chapter paid for all of the Royal Arch items, and some of the general items were purchased by members, presumably for their own use; these included drawers, cupboards and benches. A chandelier and a breast plate were recorded as *purchased by a Bro. Chanter for £5*; he also proved to be a major benefactor when he loaned the Lodge an additional £21 to make-up the shortfall between the subscriptions and the final outlay.

Once again, the Bath Furniture was indebting its owners, and the interest soon began to accumulate in addition to the amount of the debt. However, John Chanter played a big part in Devon's public life; being a well-respected local attorney and antiquarian who was instrumental in the preservation of Barnstaple's ancient municipal records. For several years he waived any demand for repayment, and as there is no record of the debt ever having been discharged, it must be assumed that he eventually converted it into a permanent donation.

In reality, what was known as 'The Bath Furniture' might now be renamed 'The Barnstaple Furniture', as it has resided in that town's principal Lodge many-times longer than it was in Bath.

After the Sale

Before considering any conclusions that can be drawn from this re-examination of the evidence, it is worthwhile taking a look at what happened to all of the people and places after their individual final acts of the drama played-out.

It is fair to say that, after 1843, Freemasonry in Bath settled-down to a far-less dramatic history. Although the three surviving Lodges had agreed in 1834 to share the accommodation at The Corridor shopping arcade, where the owner, architect Edmund Goodridge, had provided the set of rooms specifically laid-out for the purpose, they did not do so exclusively over the next twenty years, during which some moved around the various familiar hostelries as well. Eventually, in 1865, a committee was formed to examine, once again, the possibility of jointly-purchasing premises. This time, under the chairmanship of John Lum Stothert, Worshipful Master of Royal Sussex Lodge and the chairman of one of the City's main employers, crane-makers Stothert & Pitt, the quest was successful.

The building acquired was the disused Catholic Chapel in Old Orchard Street, previously the original Theatre Royal, and it was dedicated as a Masonic Hall on 3rd December 1866. Not only do those three Lodges, Royal Cumberland, Royal Sussex and Lodge of Honour, still meet there to this day, over the ensuing, and less-eventful, 150 years a further four Lodges have also grown from them. Royal Cumberland Lodge celebrated its 275th anniversary in 2007 and, five years later on 11th February 2012, Royal Sussex Lodge became the second Lodge in the city to celebrate a bicentenary.

John Lum Stothert Chairman of the Committee that purchased the current Bath Masonic Hall. *Museum of Bath at Work*

Interior of the current Bath Masonic Hall
showing the replica Master's Chair. *Bath Masonic Hall Trust*

In 1930, an accurate replica of the Master's Chair was presented to the current Bath Masonic Hall by W. Bro A Leonard Fuller, the Provincial Senior Grand Warden for Somerset, since when it has seen hundreds of Worshipful Masters pass through it.

The building is also shared by the Royal Arch Chapters attached to Royal Cumberland and Royal Sussex Lodges, plus Antiquity Encampment of Knights Templar; to these have also been added a further twelve Masonic Orders and Degrees meeting regularly in the building. It is owned in Trust by the seven Lodges, and guided public tours covering the history of the building and the associated Masonic Museum in the vaults are now provided throughout the year.

After the original Freemasons' Hall in York Street was purchased at auction in 1842 by Baptist Minister Reverend I A Wallinger, it became the Bethesda Chapel. In 1866, it was sold again to the Quaker Society of Friends, and became the Friends Meeting House. One of the main drivers among their membership behind the purchase was Isaac Sewell, who lived at the time at Moorlands, a large house in Englishcombe Lane; his daughter Anna would later become famous as the author of

252

'Black Beauty'. At the time of writing, the building is still in Quaker ownership, although it is no longer used solely for religious meetings. In the mid-1980s it was converted to provide rentable accommodation in the basement area that was originally the lower lodge room, which has been used since then by various local charities. The building has been on the market for most of the current century, and plans were submitted in 2005 to convert it into a restaurant, but this failed to materialise; instead the main hall is once again being occasionally used for occasional exhibitions including, in 2011, one featuring panoramic photographs of views from all parts of the world.

Most of the furniture remains in the Loyal Lodge in Barnstaple, where it is still used for regular Lodge meetings, the portrait of Thomas Dunckerley presiding over their Festive Boards much as it did 230 years earlier in the Royal Cumberland Lodge Room.

The 2nd Earl Manvers soon tired of his holdings in Bath, and was rarely seen in the City after the early 1830s, splitting his time between his two major estates in Nottinghamshire at Thoresby Hall, and the family's main seat at Holme-Pierrepont. He died in 1860, and his son disposed of the entire Bath estate in 1874.

As a personal friend of the Duke of Sussex, Grand Master of the United Grand Lodge of England, Col. Kemeys-Tynte had the duty of being one of three executors to the estate after the Duke's death in 1843. As well as being Provincial Grand Master and Provincial Grand Superintendent for Somerset, the Colonel was appointed Junior Grand Warden of England in 1830, and rose to the position of Supreme Grand Commandant of the Masonic Knights Templar in 1846. He continued to carry out his Masonic duties in all of these positions despite being almost totally blind from around 1850, right through to 1859 when failing health restricted his attendances just a few months prior to his death in 1860 at the age of 82.

In 1851 he sold the estates he inherited from his father, including Burhill which eventually became the property of the Guinness family, who turned it into a Golf Club in 1907. It was commandeered by the War Ministry during World War 2 and would become famous as the location, along with the nearby Silvermere Lake, where Barnes-Wallis and his team developed the bouncing bomb used in the Dambuster Raids.

Col. Kemeys-Tynte served as Member of Parliament for Bridgwater from 1820 to 1837; after a gap of ten years, his son Charles John Kemeys-Tynte won the seat back for the family in 1847 and held it himself for nearly twenty years thereafter; Charles John was also a high-ranking Freemason, holding the post of Provincial Grand Master for Monmouthshire for many years.

In 1844 Col. Kemeys-Tynte tried to reclaim the Wharton Barony for his family, to which he held a distant connection via his mother's Kemeys descendancy back to 1613. Wharton was a famous name in Freemasonry, the first Duke, Philip Wharton, having been Grand Master in 1723. He was a Jacobite who was eventually outlawed for high treason, following which his titles, which were assumed to have been made by letters patent, were declared extinct. It later transpired that the barony was created by writ and could therefore be passed down through the female line. As a consequence the Committee for Privileges in the House of Lords ruled that at the death of the Duke of Wharton, the barony should have fallen into abeyance between the Duke's sisters who would have been entitled to the barony in turn, before it once again fell into abeyance on their deaths, where it remained in the nineteenth century with three equal claimants, the senior of whom was Col. Kemeys-Tynte. The Committee for Privileges, however, also ruled that it did not have the authority to terminate the abeyance because of the existence of the judgment of treason. Seventy-two years later the matter was finally resolved in favour of Col. Kemeys-Tynte's great-great-grandson, who became the 8th Baron Wharton in 1916.

Capt. Charles Maddison, having been a founder member of Lodge of Honour, was its Master in three two-year spells: 1827/8, 1833/4 and 1840/1. He fulfilled several minor Provincial appointments before becoming Deputy Provincial Grand Master to Col. Kemeys-Tynte in 1833, a post he held until his death in 1843, aged 73.

John Ashley was a member of Lodge of Perpetual Friendship in Bridgwater for just one year. Unlike some of his fellow members of Royal York Lodge, he did not join Lodge of Honour when it formed in 1825; in fact there is no record of him maintaining Lodge membership after 1824. In 1827 he published a leaflet on the National Anthem entitled *Reminiscences and Observations respecting the Origin of God Save the King* adding supplementary observations the following year; both are still considered of high merit today. He died in 1830, aged 70.

William Gover-Gray moved away from Bath with his family in 1850, and set-up a new law business in Liverpool. It was, by all accounts, very successful, with a number of individual offices in various parts of the City as well as in Manchester; from this he became fairly prosperous. However, some of the investments he made would not prove as judicious, and in 1865 he was declared bankrupt having lost his fortune when the Life Association of England (Limited), of which he was a major shareholder, went into liquidation. He died in West Derby, Liverpool in 1874.

As for Thomas Pitter, whose activities were the original source of all the financial losses, he re-emerged briefly in May 1826 as a Draper in Warwickshire, before having all of his assets seized by his creditors in recovery of debts accumulated on a Lease for the premises he occupied. He then simply disappeared into the mists of time, except for a brief reappearance in 1842 as a 65-year-old working, along with his 70-year-old wife, as Silk Weavers in Coley Street, the sweat-shop centre of the Victorian textile industry in Reading.

Matthew Patton maintained his business in Milsom Street, while his wife gave harp and guitar lessons from their original premises in St Andrew's Terrace. He acted as musical director at local concerts and balls, as well as being an occasional soloist on the violincello; his daughter Louisa became an accomplished vocalist. The family were also involved with performances of sacred music, particularly in their home parish of Walcot. In 1832 he moved his music warehouse from Milsom Street to 8 Fountain Buildings, just a few doors from where Geary ran his wine and brandy merchants from 1798 to 1829. Patton took a ten year lease, at the end of which he moved again, reuniting the businesses once more at St Andrew's Terrace.

His business contracted substantially after he was involved in a series of court cases that became a cause célèbre locally. They centred around a young apprentice named Charles Osmond, who was indentured to Patton in 1834, and a book of Glees that disappeared from his shop. Glees were short songs sung 'a capella' by small groups of singers at parties and dinners. It was reported in the local newspapers that, when Osmond attained his majority at the age of 21, he *refused to serve any longer, and accordingly left Mr Patton's service, this, together with other circumstances, gave rise to a great deal of angry feeling on both sides; his father took proceedings against Mr Patton in the Court of Requests, for 16s-6d, and succeeded. After that a series of unpleasantnesses occurred.*

Patton then discovered that a copy of 'Whetestone's Collection of Glees' had gone missing from his shop several years earlier and was being offered for sale by a rival seller, having become inscribed with his ex-apprentice's name. He attempted to prefer charges against the boy before the local Magistrates, but they *recommended him not to pursue the case any further.* However, he persisted in obtaining a warrant for Osmond's arrest, but when the case was heard: *the Magistrates unanimously dismissed it, adding at the time that Osmond left their presence without the slightest blemish on his character.* Osmond was from a respectable family, and their lawyers immediately issued civil proceedings against Patton for False Imprisonment.

Patton's reaction was to have the lad arrested again, this time bringing him before the Bath Quarter Sessions on a charge of larceny, despite the advice of the Court's Clerk of Indictments not to do so. Osmond's defence had always been that he had purchased the book from Patton, and when this second case was heard in January 1841 *the Jury after a momentary consultation acquitted the prisoner.*

The civil action then proceeded to the Somerset Assizes at Taunton in April 1841, with Patton as the defendant. During the case which had *caused considerable excitement,* many witnesses appeared for Osmond, including the Clerks of both Bath Courts and the Chief Officer to the Quarter Sessions, all confirming in person their advice to Patton against taking any of his actions. Several acquaintances were called as witnesses, one stating that *upon one occasion, when there was a party at the plaintiff's father's house, both Mr and Mrs Patton were there, and actually sang out of the very book which the plaintiff was charged with having stolen.*

Patton's defence was that he *was not influenced by material motives; that he only acted on a sincere wish that justice should be done, and that he had just and reasonable grounds for making the charge that he had made.* In his address to the jury, Osmond's Counsel stressed that *Character was of the highest importance to every man, but it was more especially so in this case, where a young man of such respectability stood in so precarious a position through the perverseness and obstinacy of his prosecutor. He did not call upon them for vindictive damages, but he did call upon them to give such damages as would show to Mr Patton, and to the world, their sense of conduct like that which had been pursued towards Charles Osmond.*

In his summing-up, the Judge advised the Jury *that if they were satisfied that there was no malice on the part of the defendant, and that he had fair and reasonable grounds for the course he had taken, it would be their duty to give him their verdict. But if, on the other hand, they were of the opinion that the prosecution was a malicious one, instituted more for the purpose of annoying the plaintiff than for promoting the ends of public justice; and that there were not fair and reasonable grounds for the assumption made by the defendant, then their verdict must be for the plaintiff, with such damages as they thought would meet the amount of injury sustained by the plaintiff.* This time, Patton could not escape the penalty of his vindictiveness: *The Jury, after a few minutes' deliberation, returned a verdict for the plaintiff - damages £50.*

In 1851, Patton's business once again moved, this time to Hay Hill just around the corner from Fountain House. The advertisement of the removal announced that *Mr Patton most respectfully acquaints his friends and the public in general that he purposes selling off his extensive stock of Ancient and Modern Music, Piano Fortes, Harps, &c, &c at one quarter of their original cost.* By 1854, the business had moved to smaller premises at 10 Miles Buildings, and the family had fallen on hard times, probably as a result of the *long and severe illness* that Matthew Patton suffered during 1853, as recorded in the minutes of Royal Cumberland Lodge of November that year. In February 1854, the Lodge made a motion to the Province for a grant of fifty pounds be made to afford him relief, and the minutes recorded that *a sum of Five Pounds be granted as a loan to Bro. Patton to be repaid from the expected grant from PGL.* However, there is no record of any success in the motion prior to his death, at the age of 75, in September that year. The only other mention was of one pound being granted to his surviving relatives the following year. Although he was First Principal for Royal Cumberland Chapter many times, the final time being in 1846, and he was honoured on many occasions by his Chapter, when he died in 1854 no valediction was recorded.

Thomas Whitney moved to York Street in 1835, taking premises at No.11 directly opposite Freemasons' Hall. One has to wonder why he would do that, as his first view of the world when he opened his shutters every morning would have been the building that had subjected him to such pain. After resigning from what was essentially the rump of Lodge of Virtue in 1830, there are sporadic references to his becoming a member elsewhere, but these only last for short periods, and dwindle after the early 1850s. He died in 1861 at the age of 84.

His brother, William Underwood Whitney, the Worshipful Master of Lodge of Virtue when the Hall was erected, appears to have set-up his own business at Worcester Villas, on the outskirts of Bath, from around the time that Thomas set-up in York Street, indicating that the previous partnership had dissolved. He eventually became a joining member of Royal Sussex Lodge in December 1839; his joining fee was waived *in consideration of services already rendered to the Lodge.* He became Worshipful Master of Royal Sussex in 1843 and held the Chair for three years. In the years after his Mastership ended, membership of Royal Sussex appears to have dwindled considerably, and a gap of some eight years appears in the Lodge minutes after 1846 apparently caused by an unnamed Secretary absconding with the books; from the small amount of correspondence that has survived, we find the name T. Whitney appearing as a member for a short period during that time.

In 1852, a letter was received from the Grand Secretary which illustrates the state that the Lodge must have reached by that point, because it threatens the Worshipful Master with being summoned to Grand Lodge to explain why the Lodge should not be erased. This appears to have been ignored, as the following year notice of erasure was issued due to no returns having been filed since 1848, and no payments made to the Benevolent Fund for thirteen years. This fate was avoided at the eleventh hour by an appeal by the new Worshipful Master-elect, one William Underwood Whitney, who took the chair for the final time in 1854, after which the Lodge made a quite remarkable recovery. He died in 1862 aged 74.

And what of Charles Geary himself? There are no records of his attending any Masonic meetings in Bath after 1831, when Lodge of Virtue finally surrendered its Warrant. He had become a member of Enoch Lodge No.11 that met just around the corner from his London home, and he appears to have conducted the remainder of his Masonic career in that Lodge without taking any office.

He did, however, maintain his interest in public benevolence, in Bath becoming a member of the Park Committee in 1830. In the October of that year he provided the use of the Hall gratis for a Grand Concert in aid of the Park Improvements; this concert took place just days after the Princess Victoria and her mother, The Duchess of Kent, had made an official visit to the City, during which they granted permission for the completed project to be named 'The Royal Victoria Park'.

He sold the wine business at the end of 1829 to a Mr Robert Hulbert, one of two brothers who owned the Brewery at Pickwick, near Corsham, along with several public houses in the area. Following this, he had a close involvement with the Bath Employment Society from its creation in 1830 as a means for identifying and creating meaningful work for the many unemployed labourers in the city. He took a great interest in public committees, particularly those tasked with improving the highways around the city, and appears to have been a prime mover in the provision of an additional central river crossing by the creation of North Parade Bridge. Reports in the local papers show that he would often be called upon to chair public meetings on important matters, such as the repeal of the unpopular Window Tax, and although he never sought public office after his retirement, he eventually became an active member of the local Conservative Association.

In 1830, Geary moved his Bath home to Grosvenor Place, a stylish new terrace of regency houses on the London Road near to St Saviours Church, the building of which was another project that he was closely involved with as Churchwarden for Walcot Parish from 1827 to 1832. He does not appear to have relaxed his busy lifestyle in retirement, because he was also elected Church Commissioner for Walcot Parish for three successive five-year terms from 1827.

Despite the manner in which he was treated over Freemasons' Hall, it did not deter him from maintaining his generosity in financially assisting organisations he was involved with. Although the amount involved was much smaller, there was another occasion when he personally lost-out because of this, but in such a manner that the editor of the Bath Chronicle at the time was moved to composing, in his leader editorial, a public-admonishment of those responsible, spread over two columns.

The first part of the story appeared in a report of a Walcot parish vestry meeting during August 1834, the nineteenth-century equivalent of what we now call a Parochial Church Council meeting. As this was a public meeting where the accounts were being presented, it was probably an AGM; during the proceedings the then churchwarden was called to account for why a debt of more than seven hundred pounds, for expenditure that Geary had undertaken some years earlier when he held the same post, had not been settled.

The Parish had not held sufficient funds at the time, so Geary had dipped into his own pocket to cover them in the short term. It would also appear that Geary was not chasing the repayment, but that the indebtedness had come to the attention of parishioners from it showing

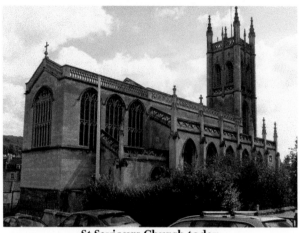

St Saviours Church today
As can be seen, this is a substantial building

in the accounts when there was, by then, sufficient funds available to clear it. The report showed that:

The vestry was unanimous as to the justice of Mr. Geary's claim; the thanks of the meeting were given to him for his disinterested conduct in not requiring interest for the sum (above £700) which had been voted to him at a former vestry. The vestry also acknowledged the justice of another claim of £232, for apparatus for heating St. Saviour's Church; for which another vestry will be called this day.

Once again, Geary had waived personal gain in favour of an organisation that he supported; but he was still owed a substantial sum, that particular bill for £232 coming from a situation described by the Chronicle Editor: *On the completion of St Saviour's Church, it was found that it would not be fit for the reception of a congregation without the erection of an apparatus for duly airing it. The want of such an apparatus was so great that the Bishop declined consecrating the Church until it was supplied. This being the case, Mr. Geary, in order that no time might be lost, gave instructions for the construction of the apparatus, not doubting that the parish would readily sanction a proceeding which was necessary for the more speedy opening of a Church containing more than 700 free sittings, and which might, therefore, be regarded as offering a great public benefit.*

However, when the second vestry meeting was convened to approve the additional claim, Geary became the victim of some mischief. An anonymous parishioner had circulated a leaflet in advance of the meeting suggesting that it had been called to raise additional rate payments from all parishioners, instead of simply rubber-stamping the settling of a bill from existing funds. The result was an unusually-large attendance and, apparently, some shenanigans during the conduct of the vote, the result of which was that the payment was voted down by a narrow majority, and Geary was once again out of pocket.

The generosity of Geary's original action, ensuring the successful completion of a large project when the parish itself was financially-embarrassed, had not gone unnoticed in the Bath Chronicle. The proprietor of the newspaper at that time was Henry Carrington, the son of a famous poet, who had moved to Bath when he married a local girl, subsequently acquiring the newspaper which he also edited. When he was made aware of this later injustice, he pulled no punches:

Looking at the case in an equitable point of view, we think it most cruel and unjust to refuse him payment of the money which he has disbursed for the benefit of the parish. The most serious accusation which can be brought against him is that he has acted in error; Mr. Geary is acknowledged to have been an upright, persevering and attentive parish officer; a moderately-expressed vote, therefore, disapproving of his conduct in this particular instance, but ordering the payment of the £232 would have amply met the justice of the case.

That would normally have been the limit of such editorial comment in those less-sensationalised times of journalism; but Carrington was young, enthusiastic in regard to any of the causes that he supported, and ecclesiastical matters were one of his passions. Being already well-involved with local churches, he obviously had someone known to him in the crosshairs, and he wasn't going to hold his fire on this occasion:

For those who act from conscientious motives we can entertain no disrespect, however wrong we may deem their conclusions, but we have sound reason for knowing that the greater proportion of those who attended were not influenced by motives so creditable. One of the leading oppositionist (whose name we would publish if we knew it) had, previous to the meeting, issued the following lying handbill: "Parishioners of Walcot! A Vestry Meeting is called for Thursday next, the 14th instant, for the purpose of taking into consideration the propriety of **Figuring a Church Rate.** *Be therefore on the alert! Be punctual in your attendance at the Vestry-room, and see that you are not unnecessarily taxed. Signed A RATE-PAYER"*

As persons who write patriotic handbills and print them at their own expense are not likely to be ignorant of the subject in which they take so great an interest, it is manifest that this "Rate-Payer" knew he was fibbing when he sent out his placard; he could not but have been aware that the meeting was not held for the purpose of figuring a Church-Rate. Care should be taken that they who, like our "Rate-Payer," take mean and unfair methods to obtain their object, should be known, in order that their exertions may be neutralized.

In 1840 Geary moved his Bath home away from Walcot Parish, to Prior Park Buildings where he purchased a slightly smaller, but similar style, house to the one he owned in Grosvenor. He lived there for the remainder of his life together with a housekeeper and maid, not more than a few yards from where his sister Mary Meyler lived with her family. He died in 1851 at the age of 80.

In Conclusion

It is fair to say that, having inspected all of the evidence now available, there was not one single person responsible for this debacle, but a number of individuals at the centre of the events. There were sufficient opportunities throughout for all of them to recover the difficult situation; that those were all either ignored or aggravated is particularly disappointing because, of all people, Freemasons by their very oaths are bound to maintain peace and harmony wherever possible. Unfortunately there was very little evidence of that in what has been examined in these pages, and nobody comes out of this saga with any great credit, some with little or no credit at all.

Nevertheless, the previously-accepted account evolved by history was somewhat unfair in singling Charles Geary out to take sole responsibility for this sad story, and I hope that his involvement is now able to be viewed in a less derogatory light. It was Geary that made the selfless move in 1823 to avoid what would have been quite a scandal for the Fraternity, not only in Bath but in the wider community, had it become public knowledge at the time. There may have been other members in Bath who possessed enough personal wealth early in 1823 to be able to dig into their pockets to the tune of nearly four thousand pounds, but they didn't; not even to a assist to a small degree. It was Geary who was the only one both able and willing to do so.

However, this is not intended to be a whitewash; it could also be interpreted that he was doing so because he had caused the original problem, and was therefore responsible for sorting it out. But there is no evidence to show that he took any decisions that could have caused the losses incurred; in fact entirely the opposite, considering that it was his voice back in 1816 that expressed the greatest concern as to the organisation's ability to carry the project through. What exactly it was that caused Geary to take the lock-out action in October 1823, and whether or not it was fully-justified, we shall probably never know.

Because of that action, he has subsequently been identified with certain other occurrences, some of which are now shown to have been attributable to Thomas Whitney instead. It was Whitney who was the main driver behind the original proposal; he was the person selected to receive all of the subscriptions prior to building work commencing, and may even have been the author of the original sketch of the building's frontage. After completion, he was the first chairman of the Financial

Committee and he organised the pageantry around the dedication ceremony. He later became the subject of actions by others in the local Fraternity that may have been influential on the decision to close the Hall to the Lodges, following which he was the subject of official hearings before the Board of General Purposes which resulted in his suspension. That summary is not a million miles away from the original story appended to Charles Geary's name.

From some accounts, Whitney may have been an abrasive individual, but there are no clues in his first fifteen years of membership to show that he was anything other than a willing and able member of the Fraternity. It was only when things started to go badly wrong that this other side of his character emerged, resulting ultimately in his losing all rationality and conducting a personal campaign against the higher echelons of the organisation .

The trigger-point for that change appears to have occurred at the beginning of 1820, just months after the building he had championed had been officially dedicated in a grand ceremony that he had been central in organising. That was the point at which his Lodge discovered that their secretary, Thomas Pitter, had absconded taking the majority of the Lodge's funds with him and leaving behind virtually no record of membership payments received over several years. This was potentially ruinous for what was, at that time, the largest Lodge in the City, and it was Whitney who immediately volunteered to take on the administrative task of bringing those records up to date.

Pitter was also the secretary to the Hall Financial Committee and, as the details of his fraudulent activities emerged, it became clear that committee had been seriously effected as well. This resulted in Whitney not only losing his position as Chairman, but also his place on the committee. He was still a shareholder in the building but, more importantly, he was also one of only two personal guarantors on the finance underpinning it. All he could do was watch from the sidelines as his project lurched from one crisis to another, until in 1822 the knock came on the door from the landlord's bailiff, exposing him to potential personal financial ruin and, possibly, the loss of his livelihood.

The rescue scheme put off the inevitable for less than a year, until in March 1823 Charles Geary came to not only the Fraternity's rescue, but to Thomas Whitney's as well. The result was Whitney's personal financial situation was secure, but all of his investment in the building was lost, financially as well as in the vast amount of effort he had put into the project. Plus matters in his Lodge were not improving, with the finances still under intense pressure through the membership halving, and the Installation of a new Master whose main focus appeared to be on the social status of that membership.

It was at this point that another financial matter, miniscule by comparison, arose. When Whitney's part in it came under the microscope, he simply snapped. The consequences were some months in arriving, but when they did they put him fully on a collision course with both his Lodge Master and the Provincial Grand Master. Although the matter appeared at first to be resolved, the wider fall-out put the skids finally under not only the Hall, but also his Lodge. The actions Whitney then took may have been with the best intentions of saving his Lodge, but they gave the impression of increasing desperation and resulted in the suspension of his Lodge, at which point another personal issue hit him through the bankruptcy of his brother.

The stress associated with all of this must have been immense - his brother, who was also his close business associate, in debtor's prison; the building project he had been the leader in creating closed to its intended users; and the Lodge that he had been a leading member of for twenty years destroyed. Worse still, he had not only been found guilty in his necessary absence by the highest authority in the Fraternity of being the author of the Lodge's downfall, but also of disgraceful personal behaviour unbecoming his status as a Freemason.

None of that is meant as an excuse for what he then went on to do, many bear greater burdens without sinking to such depths, but it does provide an indication as to why, ultimately, Grand Lodge were somewhat more lenient with him than he may have otherwise deserved. Even so, it is doubtful that this all happened without there being some catalyst to cause such reactions and, from the evidence available, that catalyst can only have been Matthew Patton.

The professions of these central characters provide some insight into the potential tensions at the time. At the local level, we have Geary, a self-made gentleman trader in high-class goods, with instincts based on refined taste and experience with the higher grades of society; Whitney was an Apothecary, well used to dealing with scenarios where quick and accurate diagnosis and decisions were necessary for the well-being of his customers; Patton was a musician and teacher, a calling where time and practice bring improvement and refinement, but only where basic talent exists in the first place.

On the surface, Patton appears well-respected within the Fraternity, and the general impression of him was that he was extremely diligent and considered in all of his actions. Such attributes are highly-important in an organisation that exists on stability and, in normal times, such characters can be a useful asset. But when matters become somewhat less-stable, or fast moving, such traits can become a handicap. Committees tend to handle crises less well than individuals, and rarely reach consensus easily; in such circumstances, majority votes can marginalise those on the losing side, causing them to react undemocratically. Unfortunately, Patton's actions also show that he could be a pedantic character, and ultimately this developed into vindictiveness, and not only within the Fraternity.

On the authority side, Colonel Kemeys-Tynte was a gentleman-soldier from the landed gentry. Looking through his eyes from the distance of his HQ and on high in the Fraternity, he would have taken a dim view of the rabble skirmishing in his remote north-eastern outpost, particularly if the dispatches he was receiving were being written from a personally-biased viewpoint. Stir into that equation a relative from a military family with high standards and ideals, but with a skeleton in his career cupboard, and a high-ranking Royal friend who, it may have been perceived, needed to be protected personally from any potential organisational scandal, and there exists a fairly-volatile scenario.

The Hall finances were already in some difficulty when the building was dedicated, but because the greater focus at the time was on the visit of the Grand Master, nobody noticed what was happening in the background. This was the point that Geary and Patton became more closely-involved. All three men were shareholders, and over the next two years neither Geary nor Patton missed more than one meeting of the Finance Committee. So if Geary was bankrolling the Hall, which undoubtedly he was, then Patton cannot have been unaware of that assistance unless, of course, he was utilising the proverbial Nelson's telescope, a technique he demonstrated on more than one occasion as a senior officer of both his Lodge and Chapter.

It was the tontine that caused the first disagreements between the three, with Patton withdrawing from the committee while Geary remained. It was from this point also that Geary stopped attending his Lodge, where Patton was the current Master. Thereafter Patton took the standpoint that his Lodge and Chapter were not in debt to the Hall, a posture he doggedly retained thereafter despite it being a clear case of self-delusion. Maybe he was genuinely ignorant of business matters, the only possible explanation for his believing that he was still a shareholder in the Hall even after he had appended his signature to the release document transferring sole ownership of the building to Geary. But that was no excuse for his subsequent actions, particularly after Geary essentially baled-out all of the Lodges and Orders following the failure of the tontine, an action that we know, from his own letters, Patton believed to be nothing short of speculation.

There is evidence that both Whitney in particular, and Geary to a lesser extent, believed that Patton took action to undermine the tontine process; he certainly seems to have attempted to undermine the development of other Chapters in the City, and the latter agenda was at the centre of his action against Whitney regarding the sale of the Pedestal. Had that action been contained by Col. Kemeys-Tynte, as he obviously believed that he had, then the Hall may well have survived.

But it is now obvious that the actions taken in Bath between 6th and 17th October 1823 were the real cause of the final downfall, not only of the Hall itself, but also of Royal York Lodge of Perfect Friendship. Those actions were commenced by Maddison's ill-conceived and unauthorised suspension of Whitney for behaviour unrelated to his Lodge, an action he appears to have taken without consulting anyone else. That action may have been prompted by Patton, probably through frustration at receiving no response from Grand Chapter for some three months with regard to his charges against Whitney.

That the Colonel rushed immediately to Bath to put a stop to Maddison's action, followed within a week by his appointment by Grand Lodge as Grand Superintendant in order to examine the charges, showed that the higher-echelons finally recognised the urgency required to put out a fire that they had left smouldering for too long. But even their belated action proved insufficient to stop it from becoming an all-engulfing conflagration because, from this point forward, they were always one step behind the game, and never regained any control over the individuals at the heart of the problems.

Geary's action in slamming the Hall doors shut in Patton's face could not be interpreted as an action in support of Whitney, neither, as was nefariously suggested by Maddison at one point, would Whitney have colluded by persuading Geary to take such action. By the time of the closure, the hearing had been scheduled and Geary had agreed to appear in support of Whitney and, being the most rational of the three men, Geary would have seen the dangers in creating additional turbulence in advance of the hearing. In fact, he plainly states his reasons for the closure in his letters prior to taking action, in that he required the Lodges to enter into legal agreements for their tenancies, a request they had ignored for more than six months.

But he also wished to prevent any more of his property being removed from the building. That second reason shows that something had already been removed before October 17th, and that could only have been the Royal Cumberland Lodge Warrant and Minute Book, an action that enabled them to meet officially in another venue, and that could only have been authorised by Patton as the Master of the Lodge.

I believe that Patton was frustrated following the intervention of the Colonel in diffusing the action initially instigated by Maddison and, as a result, decided to remove both his Lodge and Chapter from the Hall. Having forced the reaction from Geary, Patton purported to hold the moral high ground due to that action having been taken against his Lodge; he then stage-managed an identical set of affairs for his Chapter, before attending the Whitney hearing the week after, but not before he had further roped-in Maddison and his officers by inviting them to two of his own Lodge meetings. Patton expected to defeat everybody at that Provincial Grand Chapter hearing, first Whitney because of his previous behaviour, then Geary for his action in supporting a dishonoured Companion, which would then have opened the door for him to bring forward the subsequent action of Geary in closing the Hall to complete the rout. But it didn't work out that way.

Whitney apologised before the Provincial Grand Chapter and paid the money demanded by Patton on behalf of his Chapter, thus fully-satisfying the first two charges in favour of the Chapter. Patton was then persuaded to drop his final charge against Whitney of slander, although in reality the Colonel probably told him to withdraw it, being not prepared to support it in any way. A Provincial Grand Master would certainly not have allowed any further business to be introduced into an emergency meeting that had not been convened to examine it. Any path Patton may have hoped to manufacture to bring-forward the recent events surrounding Geary and the Hall was thus eliminated.

There can have been no doubt that Whitney had made accusations against Patton of his being at the root of all the trouble in Bath, because he had repeated them in print just weeks prior to the hearing, and circulated them to all members of Royal York Lodge, including the Colonel who had been made an honorary member earlier that year. But it needs to be remembered that, at this stage, the various Grand Lodge processes were still in the future, so the behaviour he was accused of must have appeared out-of-character at that point in time.

Then there was the status within the Province of these three men. All were long-serving, and experienced, Freemasons with high Provincial rank but, of the three, Whitney's reputation was by far the highest. He had organised two major and highly-successful festivals, filled the high rank of Provincial Grand Senior Warden twice, and been instrumental in the presentation of a gift to a former DPGM. But for the minor matter of the cost of a banner, he had never previously been in contention with either Province or Grand Lodge.

But there is another, more-likely, reason in that the Colonel knew the accusation to have been correct to some degree, which he would have gleaned from talking to his cousin, Maddison, who he must have confronted after having had to rush to Bath. In response to the PGM's demand for an explanation for his actions, Maddison may have confessed to those actions being encouraged by Patton, the only way he could have avoided his having to answer charges for unconstitutional behaviour himself. The Colonel's highly-conciliatory action at the subsequent Provincial Grand Chapter hearing should have been the end of the matter; he would certainly have expected that from his military experience where the decision of a commanding officer is final. That it was not put to bed suggests that he didn't detect the frustration smouldering in Patton, possibly because it was being concealed.

Regardless, what occurred after the Royal York Lodge meeting on November 7th was all a consequence of what had gone before. Having moved membership to the Colonel's Lodge fifty miles away prior to convening it, Maddison watched his Lodge implode in front of him, then walked away from the wreckage. Despite the efforts of the Colonel to revive it, they were doomed by the factionalised nature of the membership, and the external influences being applied. In the end, the Loder/Jarratt affair was the most convenient excuse to bring the matter to a close, and could only have been brought to the Colonel's attention by an insider - and that insider was probably the Immediate Past Master John Ashley, who had also moved his membership to Bridgwater.

What part Ashley played back in 1817/18 was more than he admitted to, but it is indisputable that he embellished that situation to move the focus of any enquiries away from himself. His subsequent actions, detailed in the appendices, make his whole involvement, and his potential allegiance to Patton, far clearer than is obvious in the main story. However, that is somewhat incidental as Whitney brought matters on himself by his own efforts to save the unsaveable, followed by a stubborn refusal to accept inevitability.

Whatever anybody may have thought could be reconciled at the time, there were three unrecognised, and insurmountable, hurdles:

Firstly, Patton was never going to take his Lodge or Chapter back to the Hall, and his continued pursuit of revenge for whatever wrongdoing he perceived to have taken place was a demonstration of that;

Secondly, in the mental state that he had evolved to, Whitney was never going to take what had happened lying down, and

Finally, Maddison, like many before him, was intent on Bath possessing a Lodge whose membership was 'of the first rank in society'.

In the end, none of these three men had any real care for what effect their personal desires or emotions had on those about them, a situation that the early 20th century American Supreme Court Justice, Louis D Brandeis summed-up in his famous quote:

The greatest dangers to liberty lurk in insidious encroachment by men of zeal, well-meaning but without understanding.

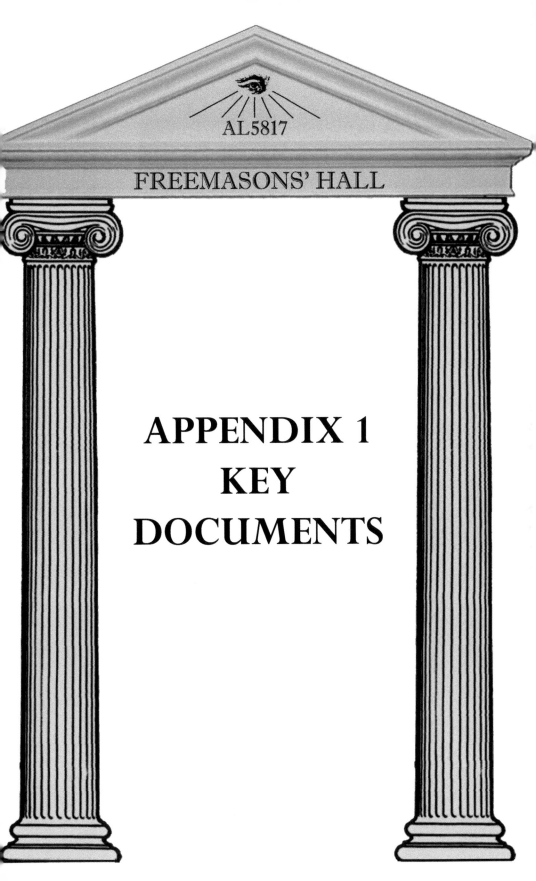

AL5817

FREEMASONS' HALL

APPENDIX 1
KEY
DOCUMENTS

Key Documents

There are three key documents mentioned throughout the text of this book - the 1822 Tontine, the 1823 Assignment and the 1824 English & Spry Report. This appendix provides the full unabridged contents of those three documents.

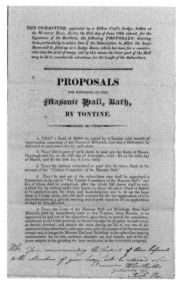

The Tontine was the first attempt at rescuing Freemasons' Hall, and was issued on 28th June 1822. There is an original copy of this document in the Bath Masonic Museum, and the contents printed here are transcribed from that copy.

The Deed of Assignment was the document that transferred full ownership to Charles Geary, and was issued on 25th March 1823. No original copy now remains in the Bath records, but the contents here are as transcribed in full by George Norman into a history he produced that was published in the Transactions of the Somerset Masters' Lodge in 1917. It is probable that an original may have been kept in the Masonic Museum at Bath, but was part of the records destroyed when that building was bombed in 1942, the Museum sustaining the main hit from that damage

The English & Spry report was the final attempt at bringing some order to the chaos of Freemasons' Hall as well as that of Royal York Lodge of Perfect Friendship. It was issued on 13th January 1824, but no original copy appears to have survived in Bath, and it was never mentioned in any of the previous histories produced on this subject. The contents here have been transcribed from a copy held in the Museum & Library of Freemasonry at Grand Lodge in London.

The Tontine

THE COMMITTEE appointed by a Fellow Crafts Lodge holden at the MASONIC HALL BATH, the 28th day of June 1822 submit, for the Signature of the Brethren, the following PROPOSALS: desiring them particularly to notice, that if the Subscription be filled, the large Room will be fitted up as a Lodge Room, which has been for a considerable time the wish of many, and by this means the lower part of the Hall may be let to considerable advantage for the benefit of the Subscribers.

PROPOSALS

FOR DISPOSING OF

Masonic Hall, Bath,

BY TONTINE

1. THAT a Fund of £4000 be raised by Tontine with benefit of survivorship, consisting of 200 Shares of £20 each; and that a Debenture be delivered to each subscriber for each share.

2. THAT £10 in part of each share be paid into the Bank of Messrs Cavanagh and Co on the 25th day of December, 1822; £5 on the 25th day of March, and £5 the 24th day of June 1823.

3. THAT the amount subscribed be paid into the above Bank to the account of "Tontine Committee of the Masonic Hall."

4. THAT by and out of the subscribers nine shall be appointed a Committee, to be called "The Tontine Committee of the Masonic Hall;" any five of whom shall be competent, after the whole 200 shares shall be subscribed for, by writing under their hands, to direct the above Fund of £4000 to be applied to pay the debts and incumbrances, and to fit up the large room as a lodge room, and who shall account for the due application of it to the subscribers at a general meeting, and deposit vouchers for its application as shall be then directed.

5. THAT the Lease of the Masonic Hall and Buildings, from Earl Manvers, shall immediately made to five Trustees, being Masons, to be appointed by and out of the subscribers upon trust, to permit the committee, mentioned in the tenth proposal, to let and manage the

property in such a way as therein directed, and receive the rents during the life of any two of the nominees of the subscribers, and upon trust, after the decease of all the nominees except one, to assign the Masonic Hall and Buildings to the subscriber naming such nominee, for his own exclusive absolute use and benefit, and at his expense subject to his granting of the lease mentioned in the fourteenth proposal.

6. THAT the subscribers respectively shall, on paying the last instalment on the 24th day of June, 1823, or within fourteen days after, leave at the office of the Solicitor for the Tontine the name in writing of the lives on which they respectively will risk their chance of becoming owners of the Masonic Hall and Buildings; such lives to be resident in England, Scotland, Ireland, or Wales.

7. THAT one subscriber of any two or more shares may (if he think fit) name one life for the whole: but if any two subscribers name the same life, the subscriber whose name stands first on the subscription -list shall be entitled to have the election of the continuing life.

8. THAT, in order to bring the Tontine to a speedy conclusion, no life shall be named whose age shall be under 60 on the 24th day of June, 1823.

9. THAT, at the time of naming the life, evidence of the age of each life to be named (not being a Peer or Baronet of whose age the Red Book shall be deemed to afford sufficient evidence) shall be given by a certificate of baptism, and an affidavit shewing the identity of the person; or an undertaking shall be signed by each subscriber to prove the age of the life at any future period, or in default thereof to forfeit all his interest in the Tontine.

10. THAT once in each three years, by and out of subscribers, shall be appointed a committee, consisting of seven members, any four of whom shall be competent to act, and to fill up any vacancy occasioned by death or otherwise, who shall hold a meeting once in each quarter of a year at least, at the Masonic Hall, and shall then and there decide on the mode of letting, repairing, and managing the Masonic Hall most conducive to the interests of Freemasonry, and (subject to such interests) most beneficial to the subscribers; and

that the duties of such committee shall continue during the lives of any two nominees of the subscribers.

11. THAT out of such committee shall be annually appointed by themselves a treasurer, who shall receive the rents or other profits of the Masonic Hall and Buildings, and pay the expenses of repairs, taxes, outgoings, and other incidental expenses; and from the net balance, by order of the committee, make an equal annual dividend to the subscribers whose nominees shall be living on the last day of each year, if claimed in twenty-one days after the end of each year.

12. THAT (if required by the committee) such evidence of the existence of the lives respectively shall be given to the committee as shall be satisfactory to them, within seven days after the end of each year, by leaving the necessary documents at the Masonic Hall; and that all subscribers who (if required) do not leave such documents, shall not be entitled to the last dividend, unless their respective nominees shall by them be proved to be living at the end of the next or some subsequent year, within five years inclusive.

13. THAT if the subscribers respectively do not (if required) produce evidence of the existence of life of their respective nominees during five successive years, such lives shall be deemed extinct.

14. THAT, on any one subscriber becoming entitled to the whole of the Masonic Hall and Buildings, he shall immediately grant a lease of the whole to the Masters of the Three Lodges for the time being, for all of the residue of the original term of ninety-nine years, at a net annual rent of £100, the Lodges doing all repairs, and paying all rates, taxes, and outgoings whatsoever.

15. THAT if the Lodges will not then accept a Lease on such terms, the subscriber naming the surviving nominee shall be at liberty to enter into and take possession of the Masonic Hall and Buildings, but not of the jewels, paraphernalia, and furniture of the Lodges and Chapters, which shall be deemed and declared to be the property of the Lodges and Chapters respectively.

16. THAT each subscriber shall be entitled to one vote at all meetings in respect of each share; and where they shall be an equal number of votes, that the chairman for the time being shall have a casting vote.

17. THAT the subscription be opened to the public, but that no person who is not a Mason shall be eligible to the committees

18. THAT the necessary deeds and writings for carrying this Tontine into effect shall be prepared by Mr. Redman, solicitor, and perused and settled by Mr. Preston, of Lincoln's Inn, London, barrister-at-law.

19. THAT a Book for Subscriptions be immediately opened at the office of Mr. Else, No.1, Northumberland-Buildings, Queen-Square, Bath.

Subscriber's Names	Residence	No	Subscriber's Names	Residence	No
Mr Meyler		1	Mr Abraham	Milsom Street	1
Alex Erskine Esq	Sydney Place	2	C. Maddison Esq	Belmont	1
Dr Barlow	Sydney Place	1	Mr C. Geary	Fountain Hse	2
J.S. Soden Esq.	Gay Street	1	Mr Whitney	Cheap Street	2
Col. Brown	Cavendish Place	2	Mr Stillman	Corn Street	1
Admiral Bullen	Seymour Street	1	Mr R.M. Payne	Union Street	1
WM. Redman	St. James Pde	2	Mr Govey	Belvedere	1
G. E. Hay, Esq	Park Street	2	Mr W. Harris	Bathwick	2
Mr H Perry	Westgate Street	1	J. & W. Stothert	Northgate Street	1
Mr R Shew	Bladud's Bdgs	1	Mr. Bird	Cornwell Bdgs	1
G. Alcock Esq	Park Street	1	Mr Withers	Swindon	1
Mr G P Manners	Rivers Street	1	Mr Walters	Kingsmead Terrace	2
Richard Else Esq	Northumberlnd Bdgs	1	S.A. Hogg Esq	Bathwick Street	2
Dr Muttlebury	Edgar Buildings	5	Earl Manvers		5
Rev J. Portis		2	J. Davies Esq		2
J.H. Spry Esq	Gay Street	2	Mr Pinker		1

The Assignment

To all to whom these presents shall come: We whose names are hereunto subscribed and seals affixed send Greeting, Whereas some time in or about the year one thousand eight hundred and twenty Proposals were distributed in order to the collecting by Subscription Monies for erecting a certain Building in the City of Bath to be called "The Masonic Hall" and to be used for the purposes of Freemasonry and in compliance with such proposals the several persons whose names and seals are hereunto subscribed and affixed Did subscribe several sums of money And Whereas the sums of money so subscribed were paid into the hands of Messieurs Cavenagh, Brown and Company Bankers of Bath and of certain other persons thereunto authorized and were afterwards applied in erecting the said building   And Whereas the sums of money so subscribed and expended were insufficient to cover the expenses of the said building and by reason thereof many large sums of money are now due and owing in respect of the said building and on security thereof   And Whereas Charles Geary of the City of Bath Wine Merchant hath proposed to the several persons parties hereto That if all the Subscribers to the said building will execute such Release and Discharge as hereinafter contained and permit him the said Charles Geary to obtain a lease of the said Building from Earl Manvers (the ground landlord thereof) to and for the absolute use and benefit of him the said Charles Geary He the said Charles Geary will obtain such lease and pay off all the debts and incumbrances affecting the said building Save and except the sums of money subscribed by the Subscribers towards the erection of the said Building And Whereas the said parties thereto in consideration of such proposal of the said Charles Geary and being satisfied that the value of the said Building does not exceed the amount of the said debts and Incumbrances Have consented to execute such Release and discharge and give such authority as hereinafter contained Now Know Ye and these presents Witness That in consideration of the premises and of the sum of five shillings of lawful money of the United Kingdom of Great Britain and Ireland current in England to each of us the several parties hereto in hand well and truly paid by the said Charles Geary at or before the sealing and delivery of these presents (the receipts whereof are hereby acknowledged)

We the said several parties hereto Have and each and every of us Hath remised released exconerated and discharged and by these presents Do and each and every of us Doth remise release exconerate and for ever discharge the said Charles Geary his heirs executors administrators and assigns and all and every other persons and person whomsoever and his their and every of their Lands tenements goods chattels estate and effects whatsoever and wheresoever And also the said Building called the Masonic Hall situate and being in York Street in the City of Bath And also all its rights members and appurtenances whatsoever of and from the several sums of money so subscribed by us the said parties hereto as aforesaid. And all benefit interest and advantage to be had or derived from the said sums of money or any of them And of and from all actions suits claims and demands whatsoever for or in respect of the same sums of money or any of them

And further Know Ye That we the said parties hereto and each and every of us Do hereby assign release and quit claim unto the said Charles Geary his executors administrators and assigns All Estate right Title Interest Claim and Demand whatsoever both at Law and in Equity or otherwise howsoever of us and each and every of us of into or out of the said Building and premises called the Masonic Hall and all their right members and appurtenances To the end intent and purpose That the said Charles Geary may obtain a Lease of the same Building and premises to and for his own absolute and exclusive use and benefit And further Know Ye and we do hereby authorize empower and direct the said Earl Manvers and all and every other persons compellable thereto (so far as we lawfully may or can) to grant and execute unto the said Charles Geary his executors administrators and assigns a Lease of the said Building and premises to and for his own exclusive use benefit and disposal As Witness our hands this twenty-fifth day of March One thousand eight hundred and twenty three.

Schedule of Signatories and Amounts Surrendered

Baron Browne Mill	£20-0-0	John Cole	£7-10-0
Jn. Morris	5-0-0	Fras. H. Falkner and	
Ed. Brown	20-0-0	H. Godwine (Exors	
Thos. Whitney	10-0-0	of the late G. Stothert	
Robt. Shew	7-10-0	deceased	50-0-0
Geo. Edm. Hay	15-0-0	Isaac Wilson	7-10-0
Joseph Sigmond	11-5-0	William Waters	5-0-0
John Ashley	1-5-0	Tho. M. Cruttwell	5-0-0
John Corney	7-10-0	Mw. Patton	2-10-0
Wm. Clanrod	5-0-0	Geo. F. Whale	5-0-0
P. Michel	5-0-0	W. D. Fellowes	10-0-0
G. Alcock	10-0-0	Stephen Allen Hogg	37-10-0
Henry Smith	2-10-0	Walter Harris	50-0-0
George Fuller	18-15-0	Henry Dixon Tylee	10-0-0
Geo. Fowell Watts	15-0-0	John Pinch, Architect	12-10-0
Fred. Bannatyne	20-0-0	R. M. Payne	2-10-0
Thomas Clavey	2-10-0	Joseph Parker	20-0-0
Thomas Field	7-10-0	John Thorman	50-0-0
J. Portis	15-0-0	J. A. Sanders	5-0-0
J. M. Bullen	5-0-0	Geo. Manners	14-14-0
J. Sadler Gale	2-10-0	Isaac Jaques	5-0-0

English & Spry Report

To the W. Master And Brethren of the Royal York Lodge of Perfect Friendship.

BROTHERS ENGLISH and SPRY having been deputed by the Members of the Royal York Lodge to hold a Meeting with Brother GEARY, for the purpose of investigating his claims, and endeavouring to accommodate the differences which have unhappily subsisted between him and the Members of the Royal York Lodge, beg to lay the result of their communications before the Brethren, assuring them, that in the spirit of conciliation, they candidly and fairly examined the statement of Brother G., without prejudice on the one part, or favour on the other part. That they have examined the accounts from the earliest period of the erection of the Masonic-Hall to the present time, and likewise every entry of expense which has occurred, by whom paid, and by what authority directed to be paid.

It will be necessary before a just estimate is found of the claims held forth by Brother Geary, for rent due to him, by the different Lodges, for the occupation of the said Building, to trace from the beginning the authority which directed the Building, the Finance Committee which directed the payments, and the way in which it ultimately fell into the hands of Brother Geary. It appears that in the year 1816, a proposition was made to build a Masonic-Hall by Shares of £5 value, which was encouraged by many Brothers who were very sanguine of its success, and a Committee was formed from each Lodge for the purpose of directing the building and superintending the payments. In the Cumberland Lodge Brother Geary opposed the measure, not thinking it likely to succeed; he afterwards acceded to the plan, and was named one of the Trustees on the part of the Cumberland Lodge; Baron Brown Mill on the part of the Royal York Lodge; and Brother Withers, of Stratton, near Swindon, on the part of the Lodge of Virtue.

To enable the building to commence before the receipt of the Shareholders' payments, Earl Manvers, in the year 1817, was solicited to advance £1000, for which security was given by Brothers Geary and Whitney. For the purpose of arranging the receipts and expenditure – a general Financial Committee was formed, composed of three

Members from each of the three Lodges. This Committee managed the internal concerns of the Lodges, and from a reference to the minutes and transactions of the Committee - it will be perceived that when there happened a vacancy in the Committee, either by death or resignation, that vacancy was filled up by the general voice of the Lodge. The examination of the Financial Committee Book, contrary to the expectation of Brothers English and Spry was sufficiently conclusive to shew that every expenditure had been made with the concurrence of the different Lodges; as of course the act of a delegated Committee must be considered the act of the Lodge. It appears that at the Meeting of the last Committee, held March, 1823, at the Masonic-Hall, Brothers Geary, Maddison, Manners, Tarratt, Govey, and Hayes jun., were present - Brother Geary in the Chair - the regularity of which proceedings are certainly not in unison with the generally received opinion. Having thus shewn the origins and proceedings of the Financial Committee, it now only remains to state the situation in which Brother Geary stands with regard to the Masonic-Hall, and the nature of the claims he has submitted to the Lodges and Chapters.

Brothers Geary and Whitney having become security for the £1000, neither principal or interest of which had been paid from the period of its advancement, Earl Manvers came to the resolution of legally proceeding against the above Brethren, the fear of which induced Brother Geary to take the premises on his own shoulders, most probably with the ultimate loss of more than £1000. Although Brothers English and Spry cannot in any way justify the conduct of Brother Geary in detaining the Paraphernalia of the Lodge, yet they do consider that if Brother Geary had openly stated the above circumstances to the various Brethren of which the majority were ignorant, they would have come forward in the most honourable way as Masons and as men, to have assisted a Brother, who, in reality, had only acted on behalf of the Lodges, and whose zeal for Masonry had led him into those embarrassments, which, to many other Individuals, not so independent, must have ended in total ruin.

Some conversation having formerly taken place on the subject of rent, and it having been asserted that so much from the makings, and so much from the quarterages, were appropriated for that purpose, Brothers English and Spry, have with the greatest attention, investigated the accounts, and find that every sixpence has been appropriated to the payment of various debts, salaries, furniture, and ornaments of the Lodges, but that nothing has ever been paid in the shape of rent, neither is there any mention made of rent. Messrs. English and Spry suppose that the rent was never taken into consideration, from an idea that the arrears of the Masonic-Hall would be paid off by the Tontine formerly projected. Whatever may have been the cause, from the evidence of the books before the Lodge, no rent or any thing in lieu of it, was ever paid or suggested. Every benefit arising from the letting of the Hall, was likewise paid in to the Financial Committee, which has been also paid away by their direction. It appears that the demand made by Brother Geary on the various Lodges, is £300, at £60 the year for five years. Whether or no this is a legal demand is not the question, Is it a just one? Though Brothers English and Spry are not aware how this demand is to be paid, yet upon looking over the whole circumstances, seeing the debt Brother Geary has entailed upon himself, and the relief he has afforded his Masonic Brethren, by such a step – considering also that this sum is near £180 less that the interest now due, and which Brother Geary will have to pay on the £1000 due to Earl Manvers – they consider the sum very moderate; they however leave this question for the further consideration of the United Lodges, conceiving that this measure can only be regularly discussed with regard to its final accommodation, by a Meeting of all the Lodges concerned, when from a knowledge of the whole circumstances they will no doubt act as becomes Brethren and Masons.

As a great deal of misrepresentation has gone abroad on this subject, the above Brothers suggest the propriety of printing the above statement, that every Member may be furnished with a copy, and that the Provincial G.M. be requested to convene a Meeting of the three Lodges, that this matter may be finally settled, that no altercation may again be heard, and that Peace, brotherly Love and Harmony, may again be restored within the precincts of the various Lodges in Bath.

EDMUND ENGLISH

JOSEPH HUME SPRY

Bath, January 13, 1824

AL5817

FREEMASONS' HALL

APPENDIX 2
THE MISSING
FURNITURE

Missing Furniture

O ver the intervening 175 years, some items of furniture have been disposed of, either through their no longer being of use to Loyal Lodge, or simply succumbing to the passage of time.

Some of the disposals occurred during or after the move of Loyal Lodge in 1966 from their previous premises in Queen Anne Street to the current Masonic Hall at Trafalgar Lawns. It may not have been possible to see those items, other than seventy-five years ago a member of Loyal Lodge, Bruce Oliver, conducted substantial research with accompanying photographs.

Other disposals had occurred much earlier around the time of purchase, either to the Brethren themselves, or to the new Lodge of Benevolence No. 719 at Bideford. That Lodge was warranted on 5th May 1843, just weeks after the furniture had arrived in Barnstaple, and a number of Barnstaple Brethren were among its founder members.

When the furniture was purchased, the money was raised by issuing a number of £1-10s shares, and Lodge of Benevolence is recorded in the detailed Furniture accounts as purchasing nine of those shares. So it is logical to assume that the needs of this new Lodge were part of the original plan to buy the Bath Furniture, and the accounts show a number of entries for disposals to Lodge of Benevolence in exchange for the value of their shares. Bruce Oliver believed the majority of these disposals were regarding the old Loyal Lodge furniture, which makes perfect economical sense in the circumstances.

As a consequence of all of this, it has been possible to identify most of the items listed in that original 1842 document published for the Lottery and entitled the *Catalogue of the Magnificent Masonic Jewels &c &c lately attached to the Freemasons Hall, Bath.* Those contents were itemised under 29 headings, and I will now go through those items one by one, indicating where details are already contained in Part 4 of this book, providing information on items no longer available but detailed by Bruce Oliver in his research, or simply indicating that they were sold or there is no record of them any longer.

Item 1. An elegant Pedestal' Cushion of rich Genoa Crimson Velvet, trimmed with Gold Lace and Tassells to correspond, with a handsome Mahogany Stand, mounted on Brass Legs, in the best preservation. The Mahogany stand is still in use as a kneeling stool, although the cushion has long since been replaced.

Item 2. A complete and superb Set of Silver Jewels (16 in number), for the W. M. and Officers of a Lodge, massive, of the best workmanship, and ordered at an unlimited expence; they are enclosed in a Morocco Leather Box, lined with Velvet. These are still in use, and shown in Part 4.

Item 3. Nine sundry Silver Jewels. There is a record of sundry jewels being sold to the Lodge of Benevolence as part of the settlement for the shares they had purchased, but as those were almost certainly the old Loyal Lodge Jewels, they would not have included this item. There is, however, a possibility that these nine 'jewels' were in fact the Working Tools for the various degrees, in which case some still survive at Barnstaple, including those shown below.

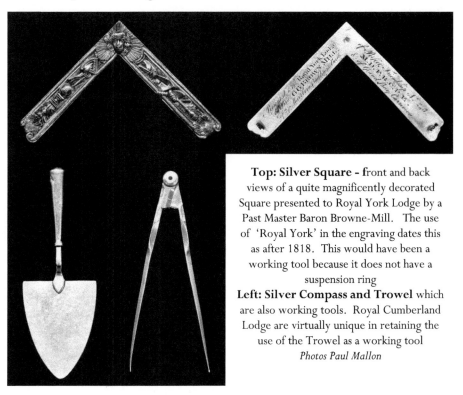

Top: Silver Square - front and back views of a quite magnificently decorated Square presented to Royal York Lodge by a Past Master Baron Browne-Mill. The use of 'Royal York' in the engraving dates this as after 1818. This would have been a working tool because it does not have a suspension ring

Left: Silver Compass and Trowel which are also working tools. Royal Cumberland Lodge are virtually unique in retaining the use of the Trowel as a working tool
Photos Paul Mallon

Item 4. A handsome and costly black Silk Gown, for Chaplain, of the best material. This item no longer exists

Item 5. Three magnificent Brass Candlesticks, only 3 sets cast; one for the King of Prussia's Lodge, one for the Grand Lodge of England; and the above. These Candlesticks were purchased at a cost of Forty-two Guineas. Still in use, and shown in Part 4.

Item 6. A full and fine-toned Organ, 11 feet high, 3 feet deep, and 5 feet wide, with *Swell,* and 6 Stops; viz Open Diapason, Stop Diapason, Dulciana, Principal, Flute, and Fifteenth. Built by *Lincoln,* of London, and is in perfect condition. This item remained in use until 1995, when it was replaced with a modern instrument. It was last surveyed by the British Organ Society at Barnstaple Masonic Hall on 27th November 1992, and their records both confirm the above description and

The Organ can just be seen behind the left hand pillar in this photo from Queen Anne Street. *Bath in Time*

show that it was made by Johannes Lincoln in 1801 in London. So it would have been a second-hand instrument when acquired for the York Street Hall. He made a number of organs around that period, but not too many survive today. I do not know whether it was sold to a collector or scrapped.

Item 7. Fine three-quarter-length Portrait of P. G. M. the late Thomas Dunckerley, Esq., painted by *Beach,* in his best style; and is the *original* Portrait from which the well known Masonic Engraving of the above W. Brother was made, 4 ft. 3 by 3 ft 3½, in a handsome Gilt Frame. Still hanging in the Dining Room at Barnstaple, and shown in Part 4.

Item 8. A most elegant and richly-chased Brass Chandelier, with four Gas Branch Lights; of very recent construction, & has been universally admired for the elaborate and splendid workmanship. Sold in 1845 for four guineas to Bro Chanter.

Item 9. A superb Chair for the W.M., elevated on an appropriate Platform, and was greatly admired by H. R. H. the Duke of Sussex, at the Dedication of the Hall. This is still in use, and shown in Part 4.

Item 10. An elegant Canopy of Crimson Figured Merino Damask, trimmed with Bullion Lace, and Tassels to correspond for the Chair of the W. M. This item no longer exists.

Item 11. Two elegant Chairs, for the S. and J. Wardens, beautifully painted in Oak and Gold, With carved Masonic Emblems, to correspond with the Chair of the W. M. and with elevated Platforms. The Senior Warden chair is still in use, and shown in Part 4. However, there is some doubt around whether the Junior Warden's chair now at Barnstaple came from Bath, being more probably their old Master's Chair having been modified. There is a record of a Warden's chair being sold to Bideford in 1843, but that was most probably the old Barnstaple chair for the Senior Warden which would have been replaced. There is no record of the specific disposal of a Junior Warden's chair, so maybe the Bath one was irreparably damaged, either in transit or later when in use.

Item 12. A very handsome and highly ornamented Partition, with sham Organ, painted in Oak and Gold, to correspond with the Organ, 15 feet 8 wide, by 13 feet high, in the centre of which is a recess to receive the Chair of the S. W. This item no longer exists. Because of its size, it was quite likely broken-up and used for other purposes; for example, the frame of the table supporting the original tracing board, as shown in Part 4, incorporates the same decoration as was used on the organ. As this screen was originally made to mimic the organ at the other end of the York Street Hall, then it is possible that table frame was made from parts of it

Item 13. Two handsome and Ornamented Chairs, for the Chaplain and Past Master. There are two different pairs of chairs still in use that could match this description - see Part 4. Bruce Oliver identified them as two Hepplewhite-style chairs, pictures of which are overleaf. The chairs shown are no longer at Barnstaple, and it is thought they went to auction some time ago.

IPM & Chaplain Chairs disposed of in the 1990s. *Bath Masonic Hall Trust*

Item 14. Two splendid and matchless *Brass Pillars*, J and B., 9 feet high, and correctly formed and ornamented, according to Masonic authority. Still in use, and shown in Part 4

Item 15. A Carpet for Lodge room floor, 32 feet by 18. This would have been the chequered carpet known as the Masonic pavement. There is a record of a Masonic Pavement being sold to Bideford for 10s in 1843, but that would have been the old Barnstaple carpet. One this size, with low usage, would have been worth far more. However, as these carpets normally wear out in sixty to seventy years, the original Bath one will have gone probably 100 years ago.

Item 16. A complete Set of Silver Chased *Gauntlet Jewels* for the several officers. These items no longer exist.

Item 17. A large Masonic Dial to stand opposite the J. W. This is still in use, and shown in Part 4.

Item 18. Two handsome carved Pillars, with Arch 14 feet high, for the Royal Arch degree. Minutes show these were sold in 1845 for £1 to Bro Chanter, so they were probably too large to accommodate in the Barnstaple Lodge Room

Item 19. Seats and Benches for the accommodation of the Brethren. These were sold in 1845 for £1-12s-6d to Bro Chanter.

Item 20. 1st Degree - A most complete and handsome set of Furniture in every particular. Still in use, and shown in Part 4.

Item 21. 2nd Degree - consists of a splendid Set of furniture, which is unanimously allowed to be unrivalled in any Lodge; it includes a superb Temple to receive the Candidate, and is entered by ascending a handsome Mahogany winding Staircase of Seven scientific Steps. Some of these are still in use, but the two main items listed here were not used regularly, and by the 1980s had fallen into some disrepair. There is correspondence in Bath records of these items being offered to them during 1994, hence the picture below taken during a visit by Bath Brethren, but nothing came of this. I understand that these items were sold later to a collector, and are now possibly in the USA.

Inner Chamber & Winding Staircase for the Second Degree
pictured during a visit from Bath. *Bath Masonic Hall Trust*

Item 22. 3rd Degree - The Furniture peculiar to this Degree is also of the most complete and unique description, in which are included Transparencies of great beauty and magnitude. The H.A is of full size, and dressed in the acknowledged costume of the country. The Coffin, highly ornamented, and covered with Black Velvet, has attached to its Plate. These are still in use

Item 23. Royal Arch - The Furniture required for this Degree has been got up with correct attention to the Order in every part, and includes Standards, Surplices, Jewels, Robes, and Dresses for the Principals, Sojourners, &c., with a complete set of Arches, Vault, Pedestal, Brass Plate, &e. &c.; so that nothing is left to the imagination, but every approach is *realized*, and all in excellent condition. This was all sold to the Chapter of Loyalty & Virtue No.312, and is still in use at Barnstaple.

Item 24. A White Satin Covering for the Lodge in the centre This item no longer exists.

Item 25. Secretary's Pedestal, with Branch Lights. This is still in use, and shown in Part 4, although it no longer has the lights.

Item 26. Seven dozen Masonic Wine Glasses, all perfect. These were in fact Firing Glasses. Three dozen were sold in 1843 to Bro Chanter for 18s. The balance of the remainder are still in use.

Item 27. Two handsome Masonic Banners for Public Processions. These items no longer exist, and there is no record of their disposal. It is probable they were used in the 1819 dedication ceremony, and would therefore have been of little use to Barnstaple.

Item 28. Two elegant Stands, 6 feet high, Black and Gold, richly Carved, and placed on each side of the W. Master's Pedestal to support lights, if required. These are still in use, and shown in Part 4.

Item 29. A set of 15 large Drawers, with 3 Cupboards, painted in Oak, and locks to each. A most convenient piece of furniture, and made for the Tyler's use to hold the more portable Paraphernalia of the Lodge. Minutes show these were sold in 1843 for £5 to Bro Knox, so were never used by Loyal Lodge.

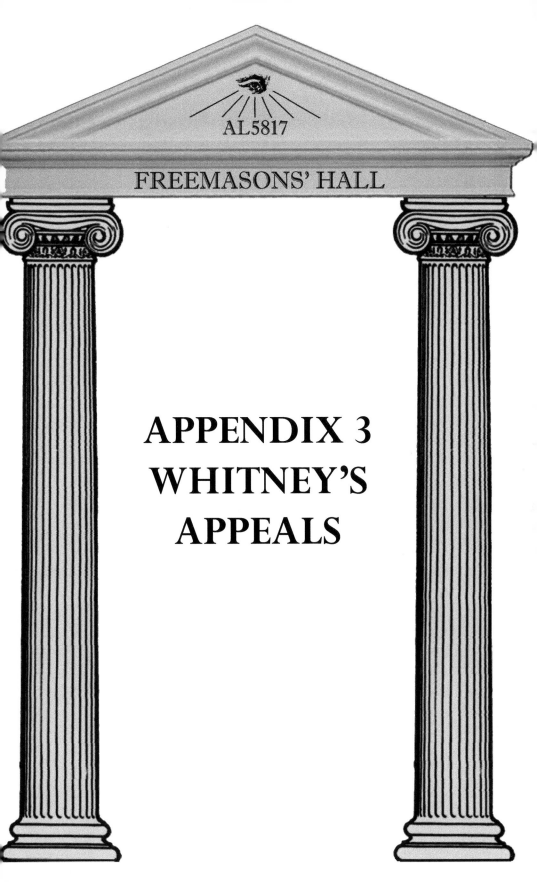

AL5817

FREEMASONS' HALL

APPENDIX 3
WHITNEY'S
APPEALS

First Appeal

Peach's history virtually ignored the story of Royal York Lodge of Perfect Friendship, although in a footnote he referred to Thomas Whitney as *a Brother possessed of great ability and no little Masonic zeal, but like many others he allowed his love of power to lead him into irregular courses in the attainment and retention of it. Brother T Whitney had caused much scandal by a persistent disregard of several indispensible rules, and notwithstanding repeated remonstrances and resignations, he persisted in his remorse course and, there can be no doubt, for selfish ends.* That may sound familiar, as it is not dissimilar to his judgement of someone else he had never met - Charles Geary. However, in the case of Thomas Whitney, Peach's judgement was probably closer to the mark.

I have traced the spark that started the fire in his Lodge back to Thomas Whitney's behaviour at a meeting of Royal Cumberland Chapter on July 22nd 1823, which was described as being *most Unmasonic and Outrageous, using the most Violent, Insolent and degrading language and Epithets possible, Clenching, Raising and Wielding his fist* concluding his abuse by several times calling the Most Excellent First Principal *'Scoundrel and Liar'*.

That subsequent to this meeting, those flames were continuously fanned by Matthew Patton, the First Principal in the passage above, has already been shown, and I do not intend to return to that part of the narrative. However, Patton was not alone in adding fuel to the inferno that would eventually consume the Lodge, and this Appendix will go into more details of the contributions of two Past Masters of the Royal York Lodge, Charles Maddison and John Ashley, during the various hearings that were formed at Grand Lodge during the following year.

It will also examine how the PGM, Colonel Kemeys-Tynte, became embroiled in these matters to the point that his own reputation became singed by those proceedings. But first, here is a quick summary of what transpired to bring about the first hearing before the Board of General Purposes in April 1824.

Following Whitney's outburst, Patton made several attempts to bring him to book during July, being primarily thwarted by there being no Provincial Head of Royal Arch in Somerset. After Whitney was unilaterally suspended from his Lodge on 6th October by its Ruling Master Charles Maddison, for his alleged behaviour in the unassociated

Chapter, Col. Kemeys-Tynte travelled to Bath to have that decision reversed, then was quickly appointed as Royal Arch Grand Superintendent for Somerset. He immediately set about bringing these matters to an end on 7th November 1823, when Whitney was brought before a Provincial Chapter disciplinary hearing in Bridgwater and, as a result, made a full apology for the incident.

On that same day, however, Maddison had called an emergency meeting of Royal York Lodge back in Bath while Whitney, officially the Lodge Secretary at that point, was in Bridgwater. Whether Maddison was anticipating some greater form of punishment than occurred, something happened either during or just after that meeting that caused him to submit his resignation on 15th November by letter to the Lodge. A Lodge meeting convened on November 27th appears to have resulted in the resignations of both Wardens as well, but conciliatory work by the Colonel brought about some stabilisation of the situation by Christmas 1823, with the Junior Warden Dr Muttlebury holding the Chair pro-tem until a replacement was available.

Following several abortive attempts, Thomas Whitney was elected Master on 12th February 1824, but within days Col. Kemeys-Tynte wrote from London to Past Master John Ashley that *Having learnt, on my way through Bath, that great irregularity has taken place at Royal York Lodge in respect to nominating and balloting for a WM for the ensuing year, I think it necessary to direct you to defer the Installation of any Brother as WM.*

There is something curious about the start of that letter that I discovered, purely by chance, when consulting local newspaper archives of the times. It concerns the Colonel's comment *Having learnt, on my way through Bath.* Although there could have been a perfectly-valid reason for the Colonel having to visit Bath, he had no obvious interests in the City other than Freemasonry. His estates were in West Somerset, Monmouthshire, London, Surrey and Yorkshire but, in 1824, Bath was not on a direct coaching route between any of those.

The closest direct route between his home and London was the south-western route through Devizes via Wells and Frome, and even if he was using his own carriage, he would still have to use coaching routes to be able to change horses en-route. If he used public coaches, passing through Bath would incur the minimum of an overnight stay as the arrival of the slow local coach from Bridgwater to Bath did not coincide with the departure of the London Mail coming from Bristol.

During the winter, coaches averaged barely five miles per hour. The distance from Bridgwater to London is around 150 miles, meaning that actual travelling time would have been around 30 hours. However, at that time coaches generally only travelled during the day, and with daylight in February being less than ten hours, the entire journey would have taken around three days. So an unnecessary detour on a lengthy journey was something to be particularly avoided.

From examination of the local newspapers in February 1824, I found the following report in the Bath Chronicle: *A prodigious fall of snow on the night of the 13th inst accumulated so rapidly that the coaches to and from the West of England were greatly impeded in their progress, and many of them stopped. At Hindon the roads were nearly impassable, the snow being drifted to 12 and 14 feet in height.* The final Lodge election took place the evening before this happened, the 12th, and Hindon is just 20 miles south of Bath on that south western route. Winters at that time were intensely cold, so it is doubtful that such a fall of snow would have cleared rapidly, or that anyone might have commenced a coach journey while it persisted, let alone elect to pass through anywhere unnecessarily.

As the PGM he could, of course, do as he wished; nevertheless, it is curious that a man of his standing should find need to apparently disguise such an action, unless intelligence from Bath was reaching Halswell independently, and from a connection he might not wish to reveal. This may also explain the Colonel's comment in his reply to Patton in the previous July that he had received his letters regarding *T Whitney's conduct which I was not at all surprised at, when first I heard of it from a prior communication.*

The Colonel exchanged correspondence with Ashley throughout February and March in an attempt to find a way forward, but made little progress. This was brought to a sudden end when Thomas Whitney decided to make an appeal direct to the Board of General Purposes at Grand Lodge. In that document, Whitney outlined all of the reasons he believed had been used by the Colonel to unjustly, in his opinion, suspend the Lodge; in so doing, he exposed all of the irregularities, including those that Col. Kemeys-Tynte had chosen, at least temporarily, to turn a blind eye to, defending them essentially by citing a similar irregular lack of observation in previous years. On top of that Whitney peppered the appeal with accusations against the Colonel, the final paragraph running as follows (all punctuation and emphasis as the original):

294

If his visit to Bath had been with the kind and fraternal intention of endeavouring to pour balm into the wounds the R.Y. Lodge has received during the last 12 months: - If he had come in the spirit of peace to promote harmony and good fellowship amongst the existing members (37 IN NUMBER) which I conceive to be the bounden duty of every head of a Province: - At his suggestion, the members would have instantly rescinded the proceedings of 12th February (if they are irregular) and have as readily gone to another Election - Instead of this, what is the harsh treatment we have received? He has given us no opportunity to comply with his directions in his letter of Feb. 20th, however unnecessary we conceive it! The Lodge is declared suspended and deprived of its Masonic privileges - THE WARRANT and Minute Book taken possession of by the PGM and removed 107 miles from the Province! We are held up as disgraced in the eyes of the Craft, in this City, and are already stigmatized as such, in the mouth of every Mason we meet!!!! And for what? - Why for the venial offence of having permitted two Brethren to exercise a privilege never before questioned upon the election of a Master, or any other occasion for the last five years!

Even if there had been a scintilla of truth in any of the personal accusations, it was so buried in the plethora of invective that the Board would have had to take a great deal of time to try to find it. When the Board met the following month to deliberate on the appeal, the Colonel, Maddison and Ashley all travelled to London to provide their evidence. That the Board took four hours to deliberate is testament to their admirable patience, especially as Whitney chose not to attend, submitting several documents by post instead. In the circumstances the conclusions were no real surprise, the report concluding:

It appears to this Board that the appeal of Brother Thomas Whitney is frivolous, vexatious, and disrespectful to the Provincial Grand Master. That the conduct of the R.W. Prov. Grand Master appears to have been throughout actuated by a laudable anxiety of reconciling the differences and extinguishing the spirit of discord which he found in the Royal York Lodge of Perfect Friendship at Bath No.243 and that for that purpose he adopted measures that appear to this Board not only to be warranted by the very disorganized state of the Lodge but in our opinion the best which existing circumstances could have been adopted to extinguish the Discord that prevailed and to restore Harmony to his Province.

It is worth clarifying at this point that the originals of all of the documents referred to in the Board's various judgements do exist, but are contained in their records, which are not open for general inspection. However, copies of various documents were circulated at the time, whether with Grand Lodge permission or not, some of which may not have contained the full transcript of the original, especially if they were part of a circulation intended to support a particular party-view. However, the proceedings in open Grand Lodge were copiously minuted and those minutes are available, so it is their contents that form the primary basis of the information provided in this appendix.

The Board's conclusions centred on the membership status of two members, Stephen Jarratt and George Loder, and whether that status made them eligible to vote in an election for the Master of the Lodge. They added several pages of explanation of how they came to their conclusions, including an interesting note on the warrant and minute book: *The warrant and Minute Book which are said to have been taken by the PGM and by him removed from the Province, had not been in the possession of the Lodge for some time previously, they having been seized by Brother Charles Geary under a claim for arrears of Rent due to him from the Lodge and they were by that Brother entrusted into the keeping of the Prov Grand Master - The Furniture of the Lodge is still detained by Brother Geary.*

Leaving aside the references to rent and furniture, which had no bearing on the matters under consideration, this contains a strange anomaly, as Whitney was making his assertions in March 1824; Geary had indeed transferred the documents to the safekeeping of Col. Kemeys-Tynte as stated, but three months previously, as had been advised by the PGM himself to the Grand Secretaries in a letter dated 9th December 1823: *the W. Master and both the Wardens of the Royal York Lodge have struck work having resigned their Offices without having appointed any successors. The Warrant of the Lodge is now in my possession.* That was less than a fortnight after the officers had resigned, and two weeks prior to the Colonel returning the warrant to the Lodge personally, on 23rd December 1823. The Lodge could not have met to conduct the first election in January 1824, under Dr Muttlebury, without it, so it follows that Col. Kemeys-Tynte must have removed it a second time when he ordered the suspension in February 1824. What this also shows is that any Royal York Lodge meetings convened by Maddison during the previous November could not have gone ahead legally without some form of dispensation from the PGM, as the Lodge was not then in possession of its Warrant. If any such dispensation was given, which is doubtful, there is no surviving record of it.

Neither should we lose sight of this being a Lodge that had been established for well over sixty years making it the second most senior in

Bath. Numbered among its members were professionals, high-ranking military men and successful businessmen, some of whom had been Freemasons in the city for more than twenty years. This was not a bunch of country bumpkins capable of naive mistakes; neither were Thomas Whitney or John Ashley inexperienced senior Freemasons.

It would not have been unprecedented for the PGM to nominate an external Past Master to conduct a ceremony, allowing the Lodge to continue, but the question of the validity of the election would have had to be resolved before he could authorise such a step. Therefore, regardless of how any of his actions were subsequently viewed, by Whitney in particular, the Colonel was simply doing his job in suspending proceedings until it was.

The matters of timing of summonses, etc, would have been relatively easy to overcome by reissuing them correctly and proceeding with a new election, but if that were also sparsely-attended, then the memberships of Brothers Jarratt and Loder would be the main stumbling block; if they were not eligible to vote, then the Lodge had potentially reached the point that it could not assemble the necessary quorum for such an election. But what had been the real status of those two members who had been at the centre of this illegal election?

Trumpeters

Stephen Jarratt and George Loder were both professional musicians. George played the flute, and at the time of his initiation was a member of the Theatre Royal Orchestra along with Jarratt who played trumpet and John Ashley, a bassoonist.

George Loder was part of Bath's most famous musical family. His daughter, Fanny, was probably the most accomplished member of the dynasty, a pianist whose portrait still adorns the boardroom of the Royal Academy of Music to this day. George's son, also named George, was later a founding member of the New York Philharmonic Orchestra and also become a Freemason, both here and in the USA.

Several others from the extended family were members of other local Lodges, and Royal York Lodge minutes show that they often visited that Lodge. So, it is fair to assume that at least one relative would have been in attendance at George Loder's Initiation, Passing and Raising ceremonies and quite capable of making sure that, had any irregularities occurred, the appropriate action was taken to correct this.

George's brother John David, probably the most successful person in the family, was already a member of Royal Sussex Lodge in Bristol, from where he became a joining member of Royal York Lodge after George's Raising - again, something an experienced Mason would not do if there was any hint of irregularity in a Lodge. The story of Loder and Jarratt's initiation is summarised in the evidence given by Ashley to the Board of General Purposes:

Shortly previous to the meeting holden by Brother Williams, Brother Whitney who was then Master of the Royal York Lodge and had taken the chief, almost entire arrangement and management for the meeting, observed to him (Brother Ashley) that it would be desirable and proper to have two Trumpeters upon this occasion, but as he Whitney was not acquainted with any, he requested Bro Ashley to speak to some of the Trumpeters belonging to the Orchestra at the Theatre and to ask them to become Masons. Brother Ashley at first objected on the ground that it was not proper to solicit anyone, but upon Bro Whitney urging the Business he said he would convey to them any Message Brother Whitney might desire. Whitney then asked him to communicate his wishes as Master of the Lodge that they would be made and if they consented he as Master would initiate them gratuitously. He made the communication accordingly to Messrs Loder and Jarratt and they gave their Assent, whereupon he brought them to the Lodge, and introduced them to Bro Whitney by whom they were initiated - consequently he was no further concerned in their introduction than being the bearer of Bro Whitney's Request and upon their complying introducing them to that Brother as Master of the Lodge. Bro Ashley added that independent of his dislike upon Masonic Principle to solicit any Man to become a Mason, he would not on his own account have made the application to Messrs Loder and Jarratt because belonging to the same profession and engaged at the same Theatre he would not have chosen to lay himself under a personal obligation to them by soliciting their Services as professional Men without any remuneration.

Which all sounds straightforward; the two Brethren were initiated into the Lodge in the year of Brother Williams' meeting, of which more below, but remained at the status of serving members. The Board's conclusion on 26th April 1824 was *that it appears by the evidence of Brother J Ashley, given before the Board that they were introduced and initiated by Brother Whitney, in the year 1818 as Musical Brethren, without payment of the customary initiation Fees, that no dispensation was produced in the Lodge, to authorise such a Proceeding and these Brethren paid nothing more than the registering Fee. Under these circumstances that these Brothers are not legal Members of the Lodge, and could not be entitled to vote on any occasion.*

On the above evidence, Whitney should have been aware of this and, therefore, not gone ahead with any election where their inclusion would cause an irregularity. However, there is also a letter to the Grand Secretaries from Whitney, dated 10th March 1824, asking: *Will you be kind enough to inform me officially whether Brothers G Loder & S Jarratt are intitled to the privilege of a vote in the election of a WM?* This was written two weeks after Ashley had answered the Colonel's questions, but two days before the Colonel gave his final confirmation of the Lodge suspension. Whether this was a genuine enquiry, or simply sent with the purpose of belatedly shutting a stable door, we cannot know.

There is no record of any reply, but it is doubtful one was received as, in his appeal dated 19th March, Whitney asserts that *as they pay their annual contributions with the other Members to the Funds of the Grand Lodge, and Provincial Grand Lodge, this has ever been considered by the Lodge, a sufficient title to vote when necessary; and this is the question to be determined:- Whether these Brethren registered Masons, and paying the above quarterages, had or had not a right to vote on the night of my Election?*

There is one glaring error in the Board's verdict - the date of the Initiations, which the Board surmised as 1818 from the returns of the

Lodge. However, the reason given by Ashley for their Initiation, Brother Williams' meeting, took place over a year earlier, on 24th March 1817. So why the discrepancy? More to the point, why did the Board not notice this, as Williams' meeting was important enough to be reported at length in the April 1817 edition of 'The European Magazine and London Review' as *a General Meeting of the Lodges in Bath, for the purpose of making certain communications from the Grand Lodge.* It consisted of separate morning and afternoon sessions at the Guildhall, between which was a service in Bath Abbey preceded by a procession through the streets of the city. The report states: *that upwards of 60,000 persons were assembled to witness the highly interesting scene; and the windows of the streets through which the procession passed were literally thronged with all the beauty and fashion of the City and neighbourhood, who seemed enthusiastically enraptured with the impressive scene.*

The proceedings had commenced at the Guildhall at 10 am, then: *At half-past twelve the Brethren proceeded in Masonic form up the Market-Place, through Broad-Street, York-Buildings, Milsom-Street, Burton-Street, and Union Street, to the Abbey Church, where divine service was performed.* Bearing in mind that the front doors of the Guildhall and Abbey in Bath are physically less than a hundred yards apart, to take a processional route of nearly a mile in length confirms that this was quite an occasion.

It was also a precursor for the dedication of the Hall two and a half years later, the various lists of participants showing that the procession contained representatives of all fourteen of the Somerset Lodges that existed at the time, plus fifteen more from other Provinces, as well as the full Provincial Grand Lodges of Somerset, Dorset and Bristol. They were preceded by a Troop of the North Somerset Yeomanry, accompanied by side escorts of the Rifle Corps and *cavalry extending the whole length of the procession,* two full military bands, one at the front and one in the middle, and concluded by another Troop of Cavalry.

After the afternoon session *at five o'clock the Brethren retired from the Guildhall, and assembled at the Kingston Assembly Rooms where a most sumptuous dinner was provided by Tully in his best style and upwards of 330 sat down.* Among many toasts and testimonials *unanimous thanks were voted to Brothers Whitney, Ashley, Cottell, Hayes, Brooke, Edwards, Redman and Howe, the Stewards and Conductors of the meeting, for their great skill and care in the management and arrangement of the proceedings* as well as to *William Williams Esq. The Provincial Grand Master for the County of Dorset, appointed by special commission from His Royal Highness the Duke of Sussex to preside.*

So this was obviously the meeting referred to in letters to the Grand Secretary, first from Samuel Browne in 1817, previous to his attempted takeover of Royal Cumberland Lodge, viz: *Since I had the pleasure of seeing you here, at the late Grand Provincial Meeting, Masonry has taken a very lively turn,* and by Thomas Pitter in his letter of 1818 inviting the Duke of Sussex to conduct the Hall Dedication, viz: *the Somerset Cavalry about 200, exclusive of Infantry will line the Streets through which the procession will move - the same facility that was afforded to our last meeting in passing along.*

From further investigation, it emerges that the intended main business was the Installation of Arthur Chichester to fill the vacant PGM post in Somerset, that ceremony to be performed by the Duke of Sussex. However, shortly beforehand Chichester had been taken ill, and there was insufficient notice to cancel the event, so it went ahead with different business and without the Duke. At the dinner, amongst numerous other toasts to various officers and their responses, *The health of Brother A. Chichester was drunk with applause,* but there was no response to it - there couldn't be, because he wasn't there. This would also explain why he did not meet the local Brethren for the first time in his official capacity until two months later, the meeting that Samuel Browne attended as stand-in Master of Royal Cumberland Lodge.

The magazine report is more than five pages in length and, in keeping with the times, contains the most minute detail down to the names of every proposer of a toast and singer of a song, even that of the wine supplier; but there is no mention of any trumpeters, not in the Guildhall, the Procession, the Abbey or the Kingston Rooms. Indeed, why would two professional trumpeters, one of whom was actually a flautist, be needed in addition to two full marching bands, from which any of the trumpeters could be seconded to provide such services as were needed?

The Board also observed that *it was stated by Brothers Maddison and Ashley that they never knew Brothers Loder and Jarratt to vote on any Ballot. However this point does not appear to the Board to be of much importance as it is evident that the Initiations of those Brethren having been illegal they could not possess the right.* So in the view of the Board, Jarratt and Loder were not simply unqualified to vote as members of the Lodge, they were not even Freemasons! So, leaving the membership issue to one side, do the surviving minutes and correspondence of Royal York Lodge give any clues as to whether these two gentlemen were actually initiated?

Unfortunately not; there are four minute books in the archives in London, but there appears to be another that is missing. The third book runs up to 30th July 1817, the fourth commences at October 8th 1818, the date of the Lodge's first meeting at Freemasons' Hall. So there is a gap of just over a year in those minutes. As for the returns, the nearest surviving to this period is dated 29th February 1820, and lists Loder and Jarratt as having been proposed on May 14th 1818, initiated May 28th 1818, passed June 30th 1818 and raised 31st July 1818. Unfortunately, minutes for these dates are in the missing book, so cannot be cross-checked. However, there is no indication that the dates were queried by the Grand Secretaries at the time the return was submitted, or subsequently.

That same return shows Ashley as having been a member since 1802, but does not show Maddison; this is because he did not join the Lodge until July 11th 1820. His first attendance as a member was on 26th October 1820, which means that Maddison could give no evidence as to the validity of the membership of the two Trumpeters, whose Initiation, whichever date was applicable, pre-dated his joining. Ashley, on the other hand, had been a member long-enough not only to know their status, but also would have taken part in their various ceremonies, as an Officer of the Lodge at the time.

Examination of the first few meetings in the fourth minute book shows that George Loder attended on 22nd October 1818, and both he and Jarratt on 5th November, but there is no indication of their holding any different status from the other members listed as present. Looking back at the third minute book, there is no mention of either of them at all in any minutes contained in there, which go up to 30th June 1817. Bearing in mind that Brother Williams' Grand Meeting took place in March 1817, had they been enlisted for that meeting, as was suggested in Ashley's evidence, one might have expected to see their names mentioned in the third minute book at some point prior to July 1817. Ashley's evidence also included a reference to Brother Williams' Meeting, that *Brother Whitney who was then Master of the Royal York Lodge had taken the Chief, almost entire arrangement and management for the meeting.* Yet the magazine report clearly showed that Ashley was also one of the stewards of the meeting; in fact his is the second-mentioned name in the list, suggesting he was actually Whitney's deputy on the stewards' committee.

As will be covered later in this Appendix, there was a second Board hearing in December 1824, which also examined the proceedings around Jarratt and Loder, and where Whitney had to answer further charges on these matters. For continuity, it is easier to also examine the evidence from that hearing at this point.

The December hearing re-examined all of the information from April's, with additional evidence extracted from Col. Kemeys-Tynte, Ashley and Maddison. In concluding their judgement on one charge pertaining to Whitney allowing himself to be illegally elected Master in February 1824, the Board decided: *That Brothers Loder and Jarratt had been illegally initiated and therefore were not entitled to the privileges of Masonry must have been known to Brother Whitney because he was Master at the time they were initiated being just prior to the meeting held in Bath by the R.W. Brother William Williams which took place in March 1817.* So once again, reference to the two trumpeters having been initiated illegally, although the date of the grand meeting had, at least, been established correctly.

The next charge related to the actual matter of their initiation: *That the above named Thos. Whitney as the Master of the Royal York Lodge, in the year 1817 or 1818 did introduce and initiate into the Mysteries and Privileges of Free Masonry Mr George Loder and Mr Stephen Jarratt improperly for unworthy considerations and without any Dispensation having been granted for their purpose, either from the W.M. Grand Master or Prov. Grand Master.* Again, it is curious that the Board, having just delivered a verdict that Loder and Jarratt were illegally initiated in 1817, should allow the very next charge for their consideration to be worded so loosely, referring to the same initiation having occurred *in the year 1817 or 1818.* Worse still, the wording intimates that Whitney was Master in both years, whereas Ashley had succeeded him in 1818, and would have been in the chair as Master on all of the pertinent dates shown against the trumpeters on the annual returns.

There appears to be even more confusion in the actual wording of the Board's appraisal of the evidence: *Brother Whitney in the Grand Lodge stated in contradiction to the Evidence given by Bro Ashley before the Board on the 13th April that Brothers Loder and Jarratt were proposed and introduced to the Lodge by the said Bro Ashley and that they were utter strangers to him, Brother Whitney, until so introduced in the Lodge and Brothers Loder and Jarratt have each made a similar statement.* The decision made by the Board was that: *it appears Brother Whitney during his Mastership endeavoured* to suppress the fact of their Initiations by not making any entry in the Books of the Lodge either as to the Propositions, Initiations or otherwise and this in violation of the Laws of the Grand Lodge and that he afterwards inserted them in a return as having been initiated during the Period of Brother Ashley's Mastership. *From this Evidence the Board are unanimously of opinion that the Charge is fully proved.* Even though Loder and Jarratt had confirmed that they were proposed by Ashley, not Whitney.

A few months after the second hearing, Ashley was involved in wrapping-up the affairs of the Royal York Lodge. That duty should have fallen to the final Master, but as Whitney had not been elected, and Maddison had walked away from what should have been his responsibility in order to set-up a new Lodge in Bath, it was Ashley who was left holding the baby. He wrote to the Grand Secretaries on 7th March 1825 regarding Loder and Jarratt, who were seeking to continue their membership in Bath, with support from Ashley:

The moment I received yours [a letter] *dated February the 27th, I communicated it to Brothers George Loder and Stephen Jarratt and at their request drew up a brief petition for them according to the instructions you sent, which they copied, and transmitted to London. I have heard indirectly that the petition was granted by the Grand Lodge and shall esteem it a favour if you will have the goodness to drop me a line when convenient. I beg to signify that Brothers Loder and Jarratt wish to know (supposing their petition granted) how they may obtain their Grand Lodge Certificates.* So does this mean their original certificates had been taken from them after the hearings, or that they never had one in the first place?

The Grand Secretaries obviously had some misgivings, as they requested further information, in reply to which Ashley wrote on March 20th: *They are positive that they were made in order to attend the grand festival headed by Brother Williams which was held in the year 1817. What the motive of the person could be, who returned them as made in 1818, I know not, unless it was to make it appear that they were initiated when I was W.M. instead of Brother Thomas Whitney, who left the Chair at the end of 1817. As the minutes and transactions of the making, passing and raising of Loder and Jarratt have been torn from the Lodge book, and they gave no document that can accurately prove the precise days, I am ready to vouch for them that they were initiated into the three degrees of Craft masonry in the late Royal York Lodge No.243 and I hope, under the existing circumstances of the case, you will grant them certificates in the form you think the most Masonic and the moment I receive your answer the money will be remitted.*

So another conundrum: a Past Master with years of experience, gives evidence before the Board of General Purposes on his oath (twice) that two gentlemen that he worked with, and therefore knew well, had not been properly Initiated into his Lodge, that he had not seen the ceremony performed and that no evidence existed to show that it had. Three months later, he is stating that he knows they were properly Initiated, Passed and Raised, but that the evidence had been *torn from the book* by persons unknown, for reasons unknown, and that the Secretaries should take his word, under his same oath, that both men were entitled to their certificates.

It is difficult to resolve this because documentation that could give the full story is not available for examination; but sometimes what you don't have can be just as revealing as what you do. I have examined the return showing the dates of Initiation, Passing and Raising of these two Brethren during 1818, along with the third minute book covering the period prior to and after Brother Williams' Grand Meeting in March 1817. That third book is the one where their Initiations would have been recorded if, as per Ashley's evidence, they were illegally Initiated by Whitney. Yet it shows no evidence of having any pages torn from it.

What is not available is the minute book covering the dates shown on the return which, if we believe the returns and Ashley's later letter to the Secretaries, can be the only book from which any evidence of these two gentlemen being Initiated can have been eradicated. But if that is the case, why would anyone feel it necessary to tear out pages that backed-up the dates on the return, pages that would show that these gentlemen were not Initiated until the dates shown on an official return, and more than a year after it had been suggested at the hearings that they were?

In his appeal, Whitney himself had made it clear that the point around which the survival of the Lodge pivoted was *Whether these Brethren registered Masons, and paying the above quarterages, had or had not a right to vote on the night of my Election?* So it would follow that Whitney would benefit by those pages being removed, provided they showed the trumpeters had joined as serving Brethren. But equally, if they showed otherwise not only would that have made his election legal, but also have proved that Ashley's evidence was not correct. So I think the answer to that conundrum comes down to when it became necessary that those pages should disappear, and who had control of the minute book at the point they did.

In April 1824, the Board of General Purposes had decided not only that Loder & Jarratt were not members possessing sufficient status to vote, but they were not even Freemasons. In December 1824, the Board essentially rubber-stamped that earlier view. Yet by March 1825, Loder and Jarratt had been issued Grand Lodge Certificates confirming their status as Masons, and allowing them to join the new Lodge that had been created in Bath.

There is one further piece of evidence that, presumably, was not available to the Board, as the Order it would have come from is not overseen by Grand Lodge. This concerns the acceptance into Antiquity Encampment of Knights Templar of one Stephen Jarratt in May 1821, a situation he could never have achieved unless he was properly Initiated, Passed and Raised. This occurred on the same night that Capt. Maddison was also accepted as a member, and at a time when John Ashley was the second in command of the Encampment. More details on this aspect are contained in Appendix 4.

All of this further begs the question, was the real target of all of this not Whitney himself, but the Lodge he appears to have been so desperate to save? After all, it was Ashley who was summoned to the December quarterly meeting of Grand Lodge to explain why the Lodge should not be erased, but instead of doing that he gave reasons why it could not survive, even though non-attendance would have produced the same result - the erasure of the Lodge.

The coup-de-gras he delivered was not only sufficient to secure that erasure, but to ensure there was no possible way back. By doing so, he cleared the path for that new Lodge to be created in the City within weeks.

Further Appeals

The April decision of the Board of General Purposes was circulated to all Lodges in the Province of Somerset. The Colonel then instructed the members of Royal York Lodge to meet him on 29th May 1824, with Thomas Whitney present. Both the appeal and the report from the Board were read out, following which the PGM requested an apology from Whitney, which was not forthcoming. That meeting in Bath was the last involving members of the Lodge, but it was not the end of Thomas Whitney's protestations - not by a long chalk.

He circulated a letter, dated 18th June, to all Bath Lodges stating his intention to appeal to Grand Lodge at their September meeting. That letter prompted Col. Kemeys-Tynte to write to William White in exasperated tones on 23rd June, concluding: *I therefore now send you a set of charges against him* [Whitney] *which I request you lay before HRH the Duke of Sussex officially from me as Provincial Grand Master of Somerset. I am ready to prove my allegations at any time, & I sincerely hope that an early one may be appointed for I would readily shorten my stay in Wales & sacrifice my own Private Interests when necessary to meet a case like this.*

Whitney received a copy of the charges and on 25th June submitted his appeal, including a request for the Grand Master to stay the new charges until after this latest appeal was heard. It contained eight rambling points, the essence of the most pertinent being:

That he was unable to attend the Board hearing due to *a family affliction of an imperative and painful nature.*

That during his attendance at the subsequent meeting in Bath on May 29th he heard *for the first time the particulars of the Report of the Board as laid before the Grand Master but* omitted *in the Communication sent to him by Bro. White Grand Secretary.*

That he did *most seriously consider himself* aggrieved *by their decision and avails himself of his privilege to appeal to the Grand Lodge against it.*

Taking these points one by one, there was evidence of a family occurrence that caused Whitney's inability to attend. The clue is in the entry in the London Gazette, mentioned earlier in the book, indicating that his brother William was facing a Petition as an Insolvent Debtor to be heard in the Old Bailey during July 1824. At that time, it took around two months for a bankruptcy petition to be scheduled for court time, so it is highly likely that his brother's dire personal financial situation had come to notice during April 1824, in which case this would almost definitely be the *family affliction of an imperative and painful nature* referred to. However, although it is possible that a Grand Secretary may have omitted to include a copy of a Board judgement when communicating with the appellant, it is not likely. It is also difficult to believe that Whitney could have remained unaware of the decisions during the four weeks between the publication of the Provincial circular and the Bath meeting.

Nevertheless, his second appeal was heard at the quarterly Grand Lodge on September 1st 1824, and following the reading of his original appeal, the full report of Board in response to it, and this, his latest appeal, Grand Lodge minutes record the following:

Brother Whitney then addressed the Grand Lodge at considerable length stating that at the Board of General Purposes on 13th April a great deal of evidence was produced which he could not anticipate and which by reason of his absence he had not the opportunity then to answer and the Board by such evidence had been misled. He was free to admit that had he been a Member of the Board he should upon the same evidence have come to a similar decision, and if he could not now shew that such Evidence was erroneous he would certainly merit the censure the Board had passed upon him. He declared in the most solemn manner, as a Man and a Mason, and appealed to the Almighty as his Witness that he entertained the highest possible respect for the R.W. Prov. Grand Master, Brother Tynte, and that any expression he had used, or any Conduct he had pursued that might bear a contrary appearance had been produced by a feeling that the Prov. Grand Master in his letter to Brother J Ashley dated 24th February last had intended to imply that any statement made by him (Bro. Whitney) was not to be relied on and he naturally felt hurt that his veracity should thus be doubted: - the Prov. Grand Master however having now explained that such was not his intention or meaning, he regretted that he had said or done any thing which bore the appearance of disrespect towards an Individual he so much respected. That he had before offered to make an apology and was still willing to do so as it was farthest from his intention to do any thing to wound the feelings of that R.W. Brother.

In regard to the irregular initiation of Brothers Loder and Jarratt he stated that they had been introduced into the Lodge by Brother J Ashley PM and not by him, Brother Whitney, that it is true they were initiated without any payment beyond the Registering fees to the Grand Lodge (which fees were accordingly paid over in their next Return) that no dispensation was obtained to initiate them as Serving Brethren, because at the time there was not any Prov. Grand Master for the County and there was no time to apply for dispensation from the Grand Master as the Lodge was desirous of having their Services in the Capacity of Trumpeters upon the occasion of R.W. Brother Williams Prov. Grand Master for Dorset holding by direction of the M W Grand Master a general meeting of the Brethren in Bath.

That the reason for Brother Maddison having been elected without a Ballot was that that Brother had expressed a dislike to such a mode of proceeding although he was willing to take the Chair should his election be unanimous.

That he had allowed Brothers Loder and Jarratt to vote at the Meeting on the 12th February last, because they had always been permitted to exercise that privilege.

Brother Whitney then read several Papers in Evidence of the occurrences he had alluded to and also one from Brother Charles Geary in which that Brother stated that Prov. Grand Master had expressed to him his dissatisfaction at the Lodge having elected Brother Whitney to be the Master. Upon the reading of this Paper the R.W. Brother Tynte immediately declared the greater part of it to be untrue.

Brother Whitney further stated that he had sent in his resignation and consequently was no longer a Member of the Lodge No.243 but he was notwithstanding anxious to exculpate the Lodge (as far as he was able) from the censure under which it was placed.

Brother Whitney having retired (as also the Prov. Grand Master at his own suggestion) it was moved "That this Grand Lodge fully concurs with the Resolutions and Opinions of the Board of General Purposes as contained in their Report to the M.W. Grand Master dated 26th April 1824 on the subject of Brother Thomas Whitney's Appeal against the suspension of the Lodge No.243 at Bath by the R.W. Prov. Grand Master for the county of Somerset and the Grand Lodge hereby confirms the said report."

It was then moved as an Amendment "To omit the 1st Resolution" The Question being put on this Amendment, the numbers appeared for the amendment - 49, Against it - 32, Majority - 17. The Question was then put on the Original Motion so amended and it passed unanimously in the affirmative, viz: "That this Grand Lodge fully concurs in the Resolutions and Opinions of the Board of General Purposes as contained in their Report to the M.W. Grand Master dated 26th April 1824 on the subject of Brother Thomas Whitney's Appeal against the suspension of the Lodge No.243 at Bath by the R.W. Prov. Grand Master for the county of Somerset and the Grand Lodge hereby confirms the said report omitting the first resolution of the Board set forth in their Report."

For clarity here, that first resolution in the Board's original report read: *It appears to this Board that the appeal of Brother Thomas Whitney is frivolous, vexatious, and disrespectful to the Provincial Grand Master.*

This was also the point at which Grand Lodge issued the final summons for the Lodge IPM to attend the next Quarterly Meeting to prevent the Lodge being erased. So although Royal York Lodge was clearly confirmed as a lost cause, the members of Grand Lodge must have heard something from Whitney that the Board did not know in April, significant-enough to reverse the Board's conclusions as to Whitney's personal motives. This must have been particularly important, as a lot of Whitney's evidence appears to be an admission of at least some culpability in the matter of Loder and Jarratt.

According to many historians, The Duke of Sussex was not the most flexible individual to occupy the position at the head of the Fraternity; indeed, the very circumstances prevailing at the time required someone at the helm who was prepared to stand firm against any opposition to the Union, and this the Duke did with unstinting resolve. Nevertheless, this matter must have caused personal embarrassment to the Duke, as not only was the word of a Provincial Grand Master being challenged in open Lodge, but also that of a close friend whom he had personally-selected for the post. His displeasure is confirmed in P R James' 1962 Prestonian Lecture by a personal direction to the Board of General Purposes that in future *they were not to receive any affidavits during the course of their investigations.*

Col. Kemeys-Tynte once again sent out a communication to all Lodges in the Province, the contents of which were recorded at an emergency meeting of Royal Cumberland Lodge on 7th September 1824: *The WM directed the attention of the Lodge to the present Official Communication accompanied by a letter from the RWPG Master setting forth that "as many misrepresentations and false statements are Industriously circulated on the subject that the Official report of the Grand Lodge be legibly inserted on the minute book of this Lodge".*

Once again, this matter should have reached a logical conclusion, because all Somerset Lodges had been advised of the amendment showing the omission of the first resolution against Whitney personally. The decision to give further time for the Royal York Lodge to get its act together should not have caused any issues, should they have desired to do so, because Whitney was no longer part of it, having resigned.

Plus he had personally once again dodged punishment and could continue membership of the Fraternity although, presumably, the locals may have preferred in a different Province. So now would have been a good time for him to retire gracefully from the field - wouldn't it?

Unfortunately, what he may have perceived as his latest 'victory' merely spurred him on to further indiscretions. He seems to have taken offence to the PGM's circular, as on 16th September he sent out another letter, this time not just to the Fraternity in Bath but copied to all Somerset Lodges plus high-ranking officials in other Provinces.

In the letter, Whitney first asserted that *The Grand Lodge were of Opinion and did declare in the usual way that my Appeal "Was **not** Frivolous vexatious and disrespectful to the Prov G Master"* and claimed that the reversal of the decision of the Board of General Purposes had been an *honourable acquittal by the Grand Lodge, as far as regards myself.* There was good foundation for Whitney to state that, and had he stopped there, matters may have evolved differently. But he didn't.

The letter continues: *in recent communication to the Lodges relative to the Quarterly meeting, the RW having thought proper broadly and unjustly to assert that "Many misrepresentations and false statements are industriously circulated on the subject" and which as usual he desired each Lodge to record upon its minute, I am absolutely compelled, deeply as I regret the necessity, to lay the following additional & painful fact before you.* He then referred to the Geary affidavit, adding that *although the Provincial Grand Master "first pledged himself on the word of a Mason and the Honor of a Gentleman that his statement should be in strict accordance with truth" yet in his Evidence (see the report) he did deliberately deceive the Board of General Purposes by a statement as far from truth as the East is from the West.*

Whitney may have been treading a very fine line up to that point, but he had now crossed it. A full Provincial meeting was called on October 15th 1824, attended also by Grand Secretary William White from London, but from Bath only by Royal Sussex Lodge, where it was recorded that a copy of Whitney's letter of 16th September had been received by Lodge of Unanimity & Sincerity in Taunton, and was laid before them. Having examined it, together with confirmation that a similar letter had been received by the PGM's own Lodge, the members unanimously resolved:

That the conduct of Bro. Thomas Whitney has been influenced by motives disgraceful to him as a Mason; that the measures adopted by him are subversive of the fundamental principles of the Order, intended to alienate all confidence in the PGM, undermine his authority and to produce discord and confusion in the Craft of this Province. Under this conviction, founded on the knowledge of the character and conduct of the said Thomas Whitney, this Provincial Grand Lodge will be pleased to lay their sentiments before the MW Grand Master The Duke of Sussex, with a prayer on behalf of this Provincial Grand Lodge, that he may be expelled the Craft, as a measure essential to the general interests of the order and the Peace, Harmony and Credit of the Craft in the Province of Somerset.

Col. Kemeys-Tynte had no option but to take action in such circumstances and, having received the full backing of the October Provincial meeting, he launched a full official assault on the turbulent Whitney, laying six charges before the Board. Five were those originally sent to Grand Lodge in June that had prompted Whitney's second appeal; to those were added the contents of this new letter. In addition, Charles Maddison suddenly popped-up to lay his own charge against Whitney regarding the conduct of the Lodge prior to Maddison's resignation as Master.

All were laid before the Board of General Purposes on November 22nd 1824. Grand Lodge minutes record that *a letter from Brother Whitney was received urging the adjournment of proceeding till the monthly meeting in December. The R.W. Prov. Grand Master and Brother being in attendance they were informed of the contents upon which the Prov. Grand Master stated that he had travelled 150 miles for the sole purpose of attending the Board, that he had twice before been brought to London on account of the Appeal by Brother Whitney and had brought witnesses from Bath that he had two Brothers now in attendance who had come from that City for the purpose of giving evidence on the charges both of whom were Professional Men who had declared their utter inability to remain in London beyond Wednesday the 24th that he the Prov. Grand Master in consequence of the Proceedings of Brother Whitney had been compelled to travel from 1200 to 1500 miles within a few months at a very considerable personal inconvenience to himself to the neglect of his own private concerns. He could not consent to have his time consumed, his domestic concerns and comfort destroyed and his mind kept in a state of constant anxiety merely to suit the caprice of Brother Whitney who had assailed him by the most scurrilous abuse and defamatory language, not only by circular letters addressed to the Lodges in his Province but also in the Public Daily Newspapers. He therefore required it as an act of justice to himself and for the Peace and Justice of the Craft that the Board not delay beyond the 24th. The Board after mature deliberation felt it their duty to proceed with the least delay and accordingly adjourned to Wednesday the 24th November and dispatched a peremptory summons to Brother Whitney to attend on that day and that should he neglect to attend the Board would notwithstanding proceed on the Charges.*

They reassembled on the 24th when a letter was read from Whitney asking for another adjournment and enclosing a certificate signed by Dr Long (a member of Royal York Lodge) confirming that he was too ill to travel. The Board then decided to hear the evidence from the Colonel, which *occupied a space of time exceeding 6 hours* then adjourned to the 1st December, sending a further summons to Whitney to appear on that day. However, all they received was another letter from Whitney advising *his inability to attend in consequence of his continued indisposition* and enclosing another certificate signed by Dr Long.

The Board reported to the Grand Lodge meeting later that same day that *Brother Charles Maddison attended and produced a variety of evidence in support of his several charges, but for the reasons before stated (Bro Whitney not being in attendance) the Board could not proceed further.* Grand Lodge then resolved: *That Brother Thomas Whitney be summoned to attend the Board of General Purposes on the 4th Instant at 11 o'clock in the forenoon precisely and that the Board do then proceed finally on the Charges preferred whether the said Brother Whitney attend or not.* Grand Lodge then dealt with the matter regarding the erasure of Royal York Lodge, after which a special Grand Lodge meeting was called for 11th December to hear the Board's final report on the charges against Whitney.

The report of the Board meeting on 4th December records that their final summons had been served on Whitney personally at 8.45pm on 2nd December. As had happened on the previous occasions, he chose not to attend, the Board recording that *a Letter from Brother Whitney received by Post on that morning was read, wherein he stated his inability to attend, partly by reason of his own Health and partly in consequence of Mrs Whitney's indisposition. He however added that as his Letters of the 13th and 19th November contained all he had to say on Paper he should reserve his intended observations on the Charges of the Prov. Grand Master and Mr Maddison, till he should be before the Grand Lodge to make his defence.* This suggests that Whitney was arrogantly snubbing the Board in order to make a further appeal should their decision prove not to his satisfaction.

The Board report extends to more than 30 pages in the Grand Lodge minutes, and covers a lot of what had gone before, ultimately reaching the same conclusions on those matters. The Colonel's new sixth charge was *That Thomas Whitney has in various instances (subsequent to the meeting of Grand Lodge on 1st September last) improperly interfered with the Lodges of this Province by sending them various false statements of the Resolution of the Grand Lodge of 1st September last accompanied by grossly indecent, disrespectful & malicious insinuations & reflections on the Honour & Character of the PGM as well as evident falsehoods, tending to create a want of confidence between the Lodges of the Province & the PGM & a general dissatisfaction & disunion amongst the Craft at large.* The Board annexed a copy of Whitney's September letter and concluded succinctly that they *will not make any comment upon its contents as the Grand Lodge will best be able to form a judgement of its tendancy by hearing it read. But confine themselves to their Unanimous Opinion that the charge is fully proved.*

They then turned to Maddison's charge against Whitney *For having in his Appeal to the Grand Lodge dated March 19th 1824 inserted the following unfounded accusation against my Conduct when WM of the Royal York Lodge No.243. "The Immediate PM Brother Ashley, when applied to, positively refused the Chair in consequence of the discord, and confusion, existing in the Lodge, and occasioned by the Proceedings of the late WM." And again, "Hopes were now entertained, that Brother Muttlebury would assume the Chair, but on the above night of Election, for reasons similar to those expressed by Brother Ashley he also positively declined it". These calumnious assertions I am prepared to prove, are positive and wilful falsehoods and that instead of the "discord and confusion" being occasioned by my "Proceedings" they are wholly attributable to his own unmasonic and highly reprehensible Conduct.*

It is difficult to understand why Maddison had waited until October to officially complain about statements in the March appeal, having had the opportunity to raise these when he provided his evidence in April. His submission is full of confirmation of his own exemplary conduct as Master, backed-up by documents which purported to be historical testimony from others to support those assertions, including *a Paper signed by 106 Masons in Bath praying for Whitney's Expulsion from the Craft as necessary to restore the Peace and Credit of the Institution.* This paper, later referred to as a petition, was dated 3rd July, two months prior to Whitney's September appearance before Grand Lodge, which would surely have been a more relevant point for it to be presented?

In his verbal evidence Maddison observed *that until he was appointed one of the Masonic Financial Committee at Bath and in that Capacity had occasion to notice the disrespectable neglect of their pecuniary arrangements he appeared to possess the esteem of Brother Whitney who repeatedly honor'd him by*

Compliments rather more than flattering, but from the moment he presumed to investigate those arrangements he became the object of Brother Whitney's inveterate opposition, he alluded to this for the purpose of showing the Board that all the disgrace which has been brought upon the Craft in the Province of Somerset originated in the unworthy cause of Finance and pecuniary difficulties arising principally if not entirely from the measures pursued by Brother Whitney. In addition: Brother J Ashley and C Maddison both stated that the discord and dissatisfaction which prevailed in the Lodge were occasioned in the first instance by the deranged and confused state of their Finances and Accounts which were solely managed by Brother Whitney who gave directions for the expenditure, and in most cases without even consulting the Lodge,

So here is an implication that Whitney had been mismanaging the Lodge's funds, in fact that he was the sole cause of their parlous financial state. Yet we know the real cause was the fraudulent action of Thomas Pitter, all of which had occurred under Ashley's Mastership, and before Maddison joined the Lodge. Lodge correspondence shows that Whitney had done a lot of work to identify and resolve some of the issues, but this appears to have rankled with Ashley and Maddison, as they complained *That Bro Whitney was constantly introducing the Subject of raising the means for defraying the Debts which disgusted the Brethren, and they could not obtain any satisfactory statement of the Accounts from him.*

Yet this would suggest that Whitney had more interest in sorting-out their problems than the Master and Immediate Past Master, who were only concerned that such activities *disgusted the Brethren* being concerned with *the unworthy cause of Finance.* Furthermore, Whitney was not the Treasurer of the Lodge, that post was held by Colonel Browne who had taken over after Pitter absconded, and was subsequently responsible for producing accounts.

The six charges laid by the Colonel were all found proven by the Board. Some of the documents presented by Maddison, including a copy of a letter published in the *Public Ledger* Newspaper, were disallowed as they *did not appear to be embraced in, or to have any immediate bearing upon the Charge exhibited.* Regardless, the Board found *decidedly and unanimously that the Charge of Brother Maddison against Brother Thomas Whitney is fully substantiated and proved.* The Board concluded the report succinctly with their decision to *submit to the Grand Lodge the Justice and propriety of expelling the said Thomas Whitney from our Order.*

On the weight of the evidence, this was the overwhelmingly correct conclusion. Whatever perceived-injustice had started Whitney on his deluded crusade against the authorities, he had gone well-beyond any limits of good judgement and behaviour. The Grand Lodge of 11th December resolved and ordered *That the said Thomas Whitney be peremptorily summoned to an Especial Grand Lodge to be holden on Wednesday the 22nd December instant at 8 o'clock in the Evening punctually to shew cause why he should not be expelled from the Fraternity.* Whitney did attend on that date, when he was conducted into the room and the various reports were read. The minutes continue:

Brother Whitney then entered upon his defence and replied to the several charges at great length and produced such evidence as he deemed necessary. Throughout his address he declared that he had no intention to offend against the laws of the Craft although he now admitted that many acts of irregularity had been committed, that he did not intend any thing personally offensive to the R.W. Prov. Grand Master and that he was prompted to send the circular of 16th September to several Lodges in the Province because he felt he had been accused of making false representations that he was not the inventor of the denial which had been given to the Prov. Grand Master's statement that denial having been contained in Brother Geary's affidavit, he had merely repeated it not having any means to know that it was not correct.

So, in a last desperate attempt to avoid personal disgrace, and having based most of his campaign against the PGM on evidence from the only person to have shown any inclination to provide support for him, he decided to throw that person under the bus as well.

The minutes continue: *The Prov. Grand Master replied at some length and particularly denied the correctness of the Statement made by Brother Geary in his affidavit when after a great deal of discussion it was moved and seconded "That Brother Thomas Whitney be expelled from the Fraternity." It was moved as an amendment "That under all the circumstances of the Case, the Motion for expelling Brother Whitney go no further." The question being put on that amendment, it was negatived. Whereupon a second amendment was moved. Viz "That Brother Whitney for the offences proved against him be suspended from all Masonic Functions and Privileges for the space of 12 Months and do then attend the Grand Lodge to be admonished." The question being put on the said amendment, it passed in the affirmative.*

It is puzzling why, despite all of the evidence provided in the various reports from the Board of General Purposes, there was still sufficient doubt left in the minds of the assembled members of Grand Lodge about this matter for at least some of them to not want to pass any sentence on Whitney at all and, in the end, this must have swayed the meeting to commute the final sentence to a suspension. Whatever that doubt was, it may explain why Whitney appeared to be uncomfortable with facing a tribunal behind closed doors, but had no problem with addressing an open Grand Lodge meeting.

I don't believe the final decision had anything to do with Geary's affidavit which was, in the end, just one person's word against another and where both parties so genuinely believed what they were saying that they were both prepared to swear so on their individual honour. Whitney's cardinal error was not recognising a genuine misunderstanding until it was too late to undo the widespread damage he had caused by attempting to use one side of it to disadvantage the other. Even so, such lack of consideration for either party is so far from that expected of any Mason that it should have warranted his expulsion. So are there any clues beyond Grand Lodge minutes as to what else he may have mentioned while he had *entered upon his defence and replied to the several charges at great length and produced such evidence as he deemed necessary* in order to secure such leniency for the second time in three months?

Looking again at Maddison's evidence on finance, part of it specifically mentioned the Hall Financial Committee. Maddison's experience of the Finance Committee spanned 1822 and 1823, when the tontine was in play, after Earl Manvers had called-in his loan but before Geary took-over the Hall. During that time any discussion on *raising the means for defraying the Debts* could have just as easily referred to the Hall as the Lodge; indeed, with Whitney exposed at that time to personal financial ruin, it would be understandable if his thoughts were concentrated on ways of improving his own position. So did he challenge that evidence?

If he did, he may have introduced that it was Thomas Pitter who had embezzled large sums of money, that the Lodge had not received the expected support of the Board in recovering them, and so on. In doing so, it would have become apparent that both Maddison and Ashley had, at the very least, been economical with the facts in asserting that the only reason for the *deranged and confused state of their Finances and Accounts* was that they *were solely managed by Brother Whitney*.

More to the point, some members of Grand Lodge may have recognised Pitter's name, plus the close connection it held to the Grand Master with regard to his mother and sister's patronage of the lacemaker. Quite probably this may have been the first that even the Duke was aware of the problems surrounding Pitter; maybe it became apparent only at that point that certain individuals had been active, for obvious reasons, in keeping the matter away from his family at the time it occurred. Or maybe Whitney simply expressed the extent of his knowledge of the facts, and the potential that held. Like a lot of this story, without the missing documentation we will never know but, regardless, Whitney was suspended instead of expelled.

This result was reported back to a Somerset Provincial Lodge Meeting held at the Guildhall in Bath on February 1st 1825, and chaired by Col. Kemeys-Tynte. That was the meeting at which, it was alleged by Patton, Geary made his remarks regarding Patton's involvement at the centre of this whole sorry affair. Following that meeting it was instructed that the minutes be circulated to all Lodges in the Province, where they were, once again, to be copied longhand into every minute book. Royal Cumberland Lodge chose to record the salient facts only; presumably their Secretary had, by then, developed writer's cramp on this subject!

Three weeks later, on February 21st, a petition was sent to Grand Lodge for the founding of a new Lodge in Bath signed, among others, by Charles Maddison. As he had played a central role in the demise of Royal York Lodge and in the Board hearings, it is pertinent to look at the evidence he presented, and his personal history, in greater detail.

Cashiered

One of the primary differences between the April and December Board hearings was the additional charge levied by Charles Maddison, the final Master of Royal York Lodge. His actions in attempting to suspend Whitney were contributory towards escalating the, already difficult, situation within the Lodge, and by walking-out of the chair on November 15th he only exacerbated them. So, as his evidence stressed his own exemplary conduct, it is worth examining Maddison's short term of office to see how the contemporary minutes and correspondence support that.

Maddison joined Royal York Lodge on July 11th 1820; the minute book reads: *Bro C Maddison late of Tyrian Lodge No.475 Derby was this evening balloted to become a member of this Lodge and unanimously approved of.* He was installed as Master on 9th January 1823 by his predecessor, John Ashley, who had held the post for the previous five years. However, we now know from his own evidence that Maddison considered *he had never been regularly installed as Master and consequently had never been obligated.* Other evidence suggested that his election may have been irregular as well.

The very next day, 10th January 1823, Maddison sent a letter to the Grand Secretaries which commenced: *Being elected Master of the Royal York Lodge of Perfect Friendship No.243 my first and anxious care will be to correct any irregularities which may have occurred from want of information, or which may inadvertently have crept into use.* He went on to highlight a particular financial problem:

One most essential to the credit and prosperity of the Lodge immediately presents itself. It is the mode in which returns of the Members have been made, including all the names whether present or abroad. In consequence the funds of our Lodge are considerably embarrassed, and must continue so while the principle is adhered to. We are in advance at this moment to the Grand Lodge, Provincial Grand Lodge and Financial Committee a very large sum, much of which in all probability may never be repaid. Many of the Brethren for whom these advances have been made are abroad, others dispersed where we know not how to address them. This has been the case for a series of years, and of course it is not possible, the funds of any Lodge, however economical its internal arrangements can support such a charge, amounting to 14s/6d for each member. He then gave details of how other Lodges dealt with the situation, asking if Royal York could adopt such methods.

The reply, written in a somewhat exasperated tone, was received within days from Grand Secretary Edwards Harper: *I beg to observe that according to the Law of the Society it is required of all Lodges, once within a year, <u>at least</u> to make a regular return of all <u>contributing</u> Members, absent as well as present, provided they have been called upon <u>and paid</u> the regular & accustomed dues to the Grand fund but <u>not otherwise</u> because it is intended that this be a personal and individual contribution of <u>subscribing</u> Members to the Lodge; but not by any means that Lodges should be called upon to pay for those who do not themselves contribute to the funds. If any other line of procuring has been adopted, it is contrary to the meaning and extent of the Law and should in future be rectified.*

This exchange suggests that the Lodge had been voluntarily making contributions out of its funds that it had no reason to make; there being no further correspondence on the issue, if Maddison's only motive was to recover the lost funds, it had simply not worked. For the rest of his term in the Chair, only Maddison's name appears on correspondence from Royal York Lodge to Grand Lodge, suggesting that either he had decided to by-pass his Secretary, or he no longer had one. The secretary at the time of his installation was Thomas Whitney.

There are several interesting aspects of this correspondence. First, Maddison's declared intent to put right what he perceived as *irregularities* within a Lodge of which he had been a member barely three years; crusading spirit rarely falls well with long-term members. Next, that there had been excess payments to various bodies; we already know that Pitter's activities had left the Lodge not only well in arrears of their contributions to Grand Lodge, but also lacking in copies of the necessary paperwork. As this had been brought in line during the years after Pitter absconded, that must have been achieved during Whitney's time as Secretary; so which Secretary is the subject of this veiled criticism - Pitter or Whitney?

Finally, one of those fee-receivers that he perceived the Lodge to be *in advance at this moment* was the Hall Financial Committee, of which he was by then a member, having joined it in March 1822, the same time that Patton had left. He served alongside Whitney and Geary until its demise; he also subscribed for one share to the tontine, so he must have had some grasp of the events surrounding that action. Was that the main source where it was perceived *much of which in all probability may never be repaid?* Worse still, did he also consider that payments made by the Lodge to the Financial Committee had been demanded unjustly, or remitted too readily by someone with more interest in the Hall than the Lodge? However, if that had been the case, one has to query why the minutes of the final meeting of the Hall Financial Committee on March 10th 1823 record: *Bro Maddison paid into the hands of the Treasurer £19-7s -5d for fees up to Christmas last on account of the Royal York Lodge.*

There is also that strange letter that he wrote to the Grand Secretaries on 10th June 1823, which he concluded: *It is true there was one disturbed spirit among us, and only one, but that is, I hope, subdued.* It would be easy to interpret that disturbed spirit as Thomas Whitney, except that this letter was written six weeks prior to his outburst in Royal Cumberland Chapter, and a fortnight before Whitney had attempted to obtain payment from Provincial Grand Lodge for the disputed banner. So if it was Whitney he was referring to there is no obvious indication as to what may have *disturbed* him at that point, and nothing further is recorded after that last meeting at Freemasons' Hall in July until the action to suspend Whitney at the beginning of October.

Maddison was called before the Board of General Purposes during the April 1824 proceedings, but does not appear to have given much evidence, other than confirming the number of members as being considerably lower than the official returns show at the time he resigned. His evidence regarding occurrences in the Lodge would have been far more valuable in April, so his tagging-on to the later hearing in December 1824, after the Lodge had been erased, could suggest some degree of revenge being enacted. This may have revolved around Whitney's letter to the Board on 13th November when, among other things, he asserted that Captain Maddison had *deserted his Post in defiance of his obligations as Worshipful Master.* That is a statement that would doubtless hit a nerve with any retired Army Officer especially when, according to Maddison, they were the deranged utterances of a person whose *personal Hostility against me was inveterate.*

Maybe such animosity was the cause of Maddison resigning the Chair by letter, rather than in person. However, one might expect a 19th-century military man to be perfectly-able to face any enemy who was armed merely with words and an attitude. Even less-convincing was his verbal evidence to the second hearing in answer to Whitney's accusation of desertion, when Maddison insisted that *he had only been invested with the Jewel of his Office and without further ceremony placed in the Chair which fact being fully known to Brother Whitney his accusation is most unjust and calumnious. Had he been regularly installed it would certainly have been imperative upon him to have continued in the Office till the end of the year.* Whitney's later submission to Grand Lodge stated that *Maddison had not been elected because he wanted to be selected unanimously.*

It is difficult to understand quite what Maddison intended by providing this evidence. Was he, by declaring he had not been correctly installed as Master, attempting to illustrate how irregular the proceedings were within his own Lodge at a time that he was responsible for it? If so, why did he not point this out in his evidence to the first hearing, the one that was actually investigating Lodge irregularities and why had it taken him ten months as Master to discover the errors? Or was he attempting, some time after the event, to justify in some way his peremptory action of walking-out and taking his officers with him - hardly the actions of a Freemason, even in such extreme circumstances.

In January 1823, as a new Master and one who had never held the post in any Lodge previously, Maddison would have accepted the installation ceremony as correct by the simple fact that his predecessor performed it, assisted by members holding the same rank, and observed by members from other Lodges. If anyone had seen a discrepancy, they would have suspended the ceremony there and then and started again, not waited ten months before mentioning it. Even if some minor aspect had been overlooked, the Master could later be re-installed using the correct methodology - an embarrassing situation, but not unprecedented or insurmountable. But in this case, according to Maddison, when he eventually discovered the discrepancy he not only immediately resigned the office, but also his membership of the Lodge.

There was also an earlier reference in the Royal York Lodge minutes of 27th February 1821, where *Bro Maddison as Senior Warden took the chair and opened the Lodge in the first degree when he initiated his son, J G Maddison esq in the first degree of Masonry.* At that time, Maddison had never been an installed Master, which precluded him from conducting any ceremony. So if all of this was meant to be a further indication of quite how far conduct of the Royal York Lodge had strayed from the rulebook over the period under examination, it was not Whitney who should have been accused of such irregularities, but the person who was Master during all of Maddison's membership - John Ashley.

Even outside of the context of everything else that was occurring, this is very strange, as is the Board's apparent acceptance of it. It would not have been difficult for them to examine these aspects, as Ashley was in attendance at both hearings. Yet both he and Maddison escaped any detailed examination of their part in such matters.

In the correspondence files, there are two further letters sent by Maddison to the Grand Secretaries in February 1824, nearly three months after he resigned. The first dated 11th February, the day prior to Whitney's irregular election, states: *I returned Bath only last night and am extremely sorry my unexpected detention from home has prevented my making the proper return of the RY Lodge with that punctuality at the close of the year which it was always my intention to have done. Enclosed is a draft on my Bankers for the fees remaining due to the Grand Lodge.* The attached return showed the names and fee payments for a total of 47 members, considerably more than he and Ashley gave in evidence to the Board a couple of months later. This also demonstrates that he was personally holding Lodge funds long after he had resigned, as well as acting as the Secretary, whose job it was to compile and submit the returns.

The Grand Secretaries must have had some queries regarding that return, because just over a week later, on February 19th, there is another letter from Maddison, commencing with some specific explanations that allude to the lack of contributions from absent brethren, the matter he had raised a year earlier at the commencement of his Mastership. He concluded that part of the letter with: *I am sure you will hold in mind that I am not responsible for any fees previous to my taking the chair and being no longer a member of the RYL the books &c have all been delivered to our worthy Brother Manners Secretary to the Lodge who will give you every information which may require a reference to them.* There is no record of Manners taking that office.

The second part of the February 19th letter is in reply to a specific question regarding his own status, and reads: *I am at a loss to account for my name being returned as a joining member of the Tyrian Lodge. I was made many years ago in that Lodge I cannot exactly recollect the date. I was on a visit at Lord Scarsdale's from where a large party went for the purpose, and among the rest the Duke of Devonshire, which will perhaps enable you to ascertain the period. All the fees were paid at that time, and I ought to have been register'd and receiv'd a Certificate. I have occasionally visited the Lodge since, but was never a member of it.* This was a strange statement to make. Surely he was not suggesting that he had never received a Grand Lodge certificate, as he could not have become a joining member of Royal York Lodge without one.

Furthermore, someone by then so familiar with returns, certificates and the like, having ostensibly taken that responsibility during his time as Master, should have recognised the Lodge where he was raised would normally obtain that document for him, and that was Royal Cumberland Lodge back in July 1810.

In Grand Lodge records, there is just a marginal note in the Tyrian Lodge register that appears to show he was initiated on 25th September 1809. I contacted Tyrian Lodge, but they could find no record of him at all. A further trawl of Grand Lodge membership records did not show him as a member anywhere else between his final attendance of Royal Cumberland Lodge on 14th December 1810, and his joining Royal York Lodge in July 1820 quoting current membership of Tyrian. So, Masonically, where had he been during those ten years?

Up to this point Maddison had appeared more of a victim of the circumstances than a main player, but this curious twist in his involvement caused me to investigate him more closely, which revealed a very pertinent part of his earlier personal history.

After he retired from the 19th Light Dragoons in 1797, Captain Charles Maddison returned from India to his family's new home at Dunstable in Bedfordshire. In January 1804, he took a new commission as a Captain in the Bedfordshire Militia, following which he was stationed in Bristol. This would not have been unusual, as international tensions were very high at that time resulting in many people joining their local defence and volunteer units; for example, early in 1805 Charles Geary became Quartermaster of the Bath Regiment of Volunteer Infantry, joining fellow Lodge members Robert Shew (his brother-in-law) and William Redman, who were Lieutenants, and Rev Charles Phillott who was the Chaplain.

Maddison's service in the Militia did not last long, however, because he was Court-Martialled in August 1804 along with five other officers. In total, they faced twelve charges, of which six involved Maddison, four in joint action with other defendants and two specifically applicable to him. They were:

1st Charge. That the defendants have, within these last eight months, combined and confederated together, to prejudice and traduce their Colonel in the eyes of the Officers and soldiers of the regiment, in various ways; and particularly by convening, and holding meetings or committees in an overt, unauthorized and unlawful manner.

2nd. For propagating, in the Garrison of Bristol, scandalous and ill-founded reports, to the prejudice of and injurious to the character and reputation of their Colonel.

3rd. That they also did on the 24th day of April, 1804, or thereabouts, sign a letter or paper containing a statement of imaginary grievances, exaggerated, erroneous, and unfounded; which paper was written without the privity, knowledge, or consent of the Non-commissioned Officers mentioned therein.

5th. That Capt Charles Maddison did, on Sunday 11th March, 1804, when the regiment paraded for church at Bristol; in the presence of many spectators, behave in a cruel manner, unbecoming the character of an Officer and a Gentleman, by having repeatedly and violently stricken William Goddard, a private in his own company, with a stick, so as to disable him to carry his firelock and perform his military duties for several days.

10th. The said Captain Charles Maddison did absent himself from his duty, when on Stapleton Prison Guard, on the night of the 14th of June, 1804.

Among the various verdicts returned, Maddison was found guilty on all charges against him. In addition, he had previously pleaded guilty to a twelfth charge: *Against Captains Maddison and Smith, for breaking their arrests during the trial.* He was sentenced to be cashiered.

Reading the trial summary it became clear that the officers concerned were attempting to collect evidence against their commanding officer, a Colonel Moore, who they suspected of withholding moneys from the non-commissioned officers and ranks. Subsequent to their objects being revealed, Col. Moore brought the charges against them. In his overview, the Judge Advocate General, Charles Morgan, having laid the results before King George III, reported to the commander-in-chief, HRH Duke of York, the following: *His Majesty noticed with surprise the uncommon bulk of the minutes, and expressed much concern that the extreme protraction of the trial has in great measure been occasioned by the contentions and hostile disposition of the parties towards each other, which manifested itself almost throughout the proceeding in a degree very disgraceful to both; and I have it in command to acquaint your Royal Highness, that His Majesty has determined, as a measure essentially necessary for the upholding of discipline, good order, and harmony in the corps, that, as well the prosecutor Colonel Moore, the several defendants be displaced from their respective situations as Officers of the Bedfordshire Regiment of Militia*

The faint echoes that this document was beginning to emit became louder as the individual judgements were read. With regard to the first two charges, the Court found that the meetings were not illegal or unauthorised, as they had been formed under the main defendant, Major Monoux, who at that time was in temporary command and who subsequently obtained permission from a more senior officer to continue to prepare evidence to substantiate charging Col. Moore. However, they found that parts of the charges were proven because *it appears that some men who had made no complaint were examined at such meetings, and among other things respecting claims which they were told were due to them, which the prisoners have not proved to have been due, and which conduct had a tendency to excite discontent in the regiment.*

With regard to the third charge they found that Maddison had sent the letter to Col. Moore, accompanied by another sealed letter to the General which *had been evidently wafered and sealed.* All defendants were acquitted on that charge, except for Maddison because the court found: *that among several charges made in those statements against Colonel Moore two were erroneous and unfounded.* This was because: *the letter, accompanying the said statements, was written and signed only by Captain Maddison without any reference to the other prisoners.*

The fifth charge was found proved in part, viz: *that Captain Maddison did strike William Goddard on the parade as a mode of correction, in the opinion of the Court, highly reprehensible; but it appears that he was immediately reproved for it by Lieutenant Colonel Gilpin, on the parade, when he expressed his regret for what he had done, stating his inexperience of the army in Great Britain, having lately returned from foreign service in India, with which explanation Lieutenant Colonel Gilpin expressed himself satisfied.*

Charge Ten, the one of being absent from duty, was also proven and related to Maddison being two hours late in inspecting the garrison guard; this may seem less important than the charge suggests, but when coupled with the breaking of his arrest, which he admitted to, shows some lack of discipline. Could it also have been the cause for such an over-reaction to the accusation by Whitney of *deserting his post?*

What comes through loud and clear from this old case is that the conspirators, as they were viewed, appear to have had good reason to assemble evidence against Col. Moore; the fact that Moore was also dismissed from the Regiment at the end of the trial tends to back this up. Nevertheless, there was subterfuge at work in their actions, and Maddison was at the centre of it. Who knows, they may have succeeded but for Maddison's action of gilding-the-lily by adding erroneous evidence to the letter to the General, evidence that seems to have been obtained by persuading lower ranks to submit opinions that they may not have held without his assistance.

On top of that, there is the striking incident on parade. We will leave -aside any 21st-century reaction to the suggestion that striking a subordinate on parade would have been considered more acceptable in the colonies than at home, it is the suggestion given by Maddison that his inexperience of home service was the cause of this indiscretion that I found so resonant with the evidence he gave to the Board of General Purposes twenty years later - the evidence that he was not in a position to deal with matters due to his not having been initiated properly.

In 1804, Maddison and his confederates amassed evidence against another officer who was guilty of wrongdoing, and who ultimately suffered the consequences. However, due to Maddison's overzealous approach in, amongst other things, the inclusion of false evidence against their quarry, the accusers suffered the same ultimate fate of losing their positions in the regiment. Twenty years later, there are hints of a similar approach towards the Board of General Purposes hearing, but not perhaps the same result.

Regardless, in 1823 Maddison took two unilateral actions - his suspension of Thomas Whitney and his resignation of the Master's chair - that were pivotal in the loss of The Lodge of Perfect Friendship. To that can be added his attendance at the Royal Cumberland Lodge at the meetings where Patton was formulating action against Geary, his calling of a Lodge Meeting on 7th November while Whitney was at the Provincial Chapter hearing, his later, supposedly unsolicited, letter to Royal Cumberland where he denied discussing anything with Patton that was used in evidence against Geary, and so on.

This all suggests an agenda was in play, one that was neither conducive to the future prospects of Freemasons' Hall, the Royal York Lodge of Perfect Friendship, or certain of the individuals associated with them. Whether it was an agenda solely of Maddison's design, or in conspiracy with other forces, we shall never know.

Letters to the Editor

On 4th October 1824, an article appeared in one of the major London newspapers of that time, *The Public Ledger and Daily Advertiser* under their heading of *Masonic Intelligence*. It commenced:

About three weeks ago, was held in their Hall at the Freemasons' Tavern, the Quarterly Meeting of the Grand Lodge of England: the Duke of Sussex in the Chair. An important and unprecedented question was brought before the meeting, namely an appeal against the decision of the Council for General Purposes; and its result has thrown many distinguished Freemasons - as well as the Duke of Sussex - into considerable consternation. The article then went on to explain that *the power of appeal to the Grand Lodge against any decision of the council exists, but it is a power which there is no previous instance of a Freemason having called into action.* There followed an outline of the conduct of the meeting, which bears little similarity to the Grand Lodge minutes, other than the correct statement of the voting numbers. The article concluded:

The result carried consternation to the platform, and the parties there immediately proceeded to another room to consult on what steps should be adopted in so extraordinary and unexpected a crisis. As may be imagined, this curious affair has excited no common sensation in the "Masonic world" and the Duke of Sussex and Colonel Tynte's friends are not a little puzzled to know what will be done, and whether Colonel T. will continue the office of Provincial Grand Master, and the further suspension of the Bath Lodge, after the reversal of the judgement and censure pronounced on Mr W. The Duke of Sussex was greatly surprised at the result.

As we know, the only 'reversal' was of the first charge, not of any other aspects of the Board's judgement. So as this was a somewhat inaccurate relation of events, was it simply a journalistic fishing mission of the type that have littered the pages of newspapers over hundreds of years? Had nobody responded to it, as would have been normal in Masonic circles, it may simply have disappeared into the ether. However, two weeks later on October 18th a long explanation, under the Editor's imprint, was published in the same newspaper regarding how the original came to be inserted, including:

When we read the statement, it appeared to us to contain a complaint made by an individual of certain injuries which he had sustained at the hands of a powerful body of whom the greatest jealousy ought to be entertained, inasmuch as their proceedings are in a great measure enveloped in a veil of secrecy. Acting under this impression, and having the fullest reliance of the accuracy and honour of the individual from whom we received the information, we felt it our duty, as public Journalists, to submit the statement to our Readers and the Public; and unbiased by any feeling of partiality towards any of parties concerned, who are all alike strangers to us - unshackled as regards the Society, not having honour of possessing any of the advantages attached to being a Mason, we laid the statement before the Public without adding a single comment of our own Since doing so, we have been informed that the statement is in many respects erroneous. If such is the case, it becomes our duty, and it is equally our inclination, to correct those errors.

What is of interest here is their statement that they had *the fullest reliance of the accuracy and honour of the individual from whom we received the information.* They also state that the people named in their article *are all alike strangers to us,* which confirms that none of those named (Col. Kemeys-Tynte and Whitney) supplied the information. As the newspaper was published in London, this would suggest the source as being somebody who would be recognised by the newspaper as holding fairly high status in the Fraternity there. Which immediately begs the question, to what end did that person do this, because the original article showed neither Grand Lodge, nor the PGM, in a positive light?

What was, effectively, intended to be a retraction by the Editor then went on to quote verbatim an article that had appeared in the *Taunton Courier* on 13th October 1824. This lengthy article incorporated a more accurate account of the meeting, along with criticism of the *Public Ledger* for allowing itself to be misled. Within the article, the full Grand Lodge Resolution was reproduced (a faithful copy of the original), followed by a new interpretation of it:

This Resolution, it will be seen, fully concurs in the Resolutions and Opinions of the Board of General Purposes; confirms the said Report, omitting the first Resolution, but concurs in the opinions and confirms the same words at the conclusion of the Report; which words were: "that the appeal of Brother Whitney is frivolous, vexatious and disrespectful to the Provincial Grand Master."

The second part of this interpretation, commencing *but concurs in the opinions...* is entirely missing from any Grand Lodge minutes or documents; I have read them several times, and fail to see how this interpretation can have been arrived at, let alone been published as a matter of fact in a public newspaper.

There is no doubting the information in the Taunton newspaper originated from Provincial Grand Lodge, as it preceded their Emergency Meeting convened in Taunton on the 15th October which was attended by Grand Secretary William White, where they discussed what to do about Whitney's circular letter of 16th September.

This meeting, which was poorly-attended, was also reported in full in the *Taunton Courier* of 20th October, including a statement made by White at the Festive Board, that he had taken *an opportunity of stating that, having heard of the of the unbecoming proceedings of one of the Brethren of the Province, he was desirous of personally ascertaining the general state of the Craft within it, and was most happy to find that with one exception on the part of an individual, whose base conduct merited the severest reprehension, he found a due zeal for the honour of their venerable and benevolent Institution everywhere prevailing in the highest and most satisfactory degree.*

Once again, there is some degree of gilding-the-lily here. White can not have merely heard *of the unbecoming proceedings of one of the Brethren* because he was in attendance as Grand Secretary at the Grand Lodge meeting on 1st September, meaning he wrote the minutes. It is also doubtful he went elsewhere in the county during his visit, let alone Bath, so his glowing appraisal would have been based on limited personal contact with local Provincial Officers. So I still fail to understand why, with Whitney essentially self-destructing before them, it was necessary to keep hammering away at his character, particularly in public, unless there was another agenda in play.

A summarised version of the first Taunton article also managed to find its way into the *Bristol Mirror*, where the writer appended his own commentary that *when or how these brotherly contentions are to terminate we know not. It is reported that Brother Whitney threatens to expose all the secrets of the craft. - What! - ALL!* This was quickly countered in the following issue, after their receipt of a letter from Whitney condemning the *silly report at the conclusion of your paragraph.*

Whitney also wrote to the *Public Ledger*, who published his letter in full on 21st October, under the following statement from the Editor: *As we have already stated, we are wholly impartial in this question and acting up to that declaration of impartiality we delay not a moment to give insertion to Mr Whitney's letter. We have also to inform that Gentleman that we are in possession of a copy of his Appeal to the Board of General Purposes and also a copy of the Report of the Board to his Royal Highness the MW Grand Master upon it; but in compliance with the request of Mr Whitney we shall refrain from publishing any part of those documents for a few days.*

So here we have an apparent scenario where somebody high enough within the Fraternity to have access to confidential Grand Lodge documents, was passing them to newspapers for publication. On the other hand, the person who is branded as guilty of *unbecoming proceedings* is stopping their publication. Once again, had Whitney left it there, he may have regained some ground but, unfortunately, he couldn't help but have a public swipe at Grand Secretary William White: *If the Brethren of the Province are misled by the ambiguous and contradictory minute issued by the Grand Secretary, it is the bounden duty of that individual to undeceive them - to speak out and make himself intelligible, as far as regards the real meaning of the above decision.*

That should have ended this short flurry of media activity in London, Taunton and Bristol and, indeed, nothing more was published for a couple of weeks. Then, on 4th November, a letter appeared in the *Public Ledger* signed under the nom-de-plume *Cultor Veritatis* (the truth):

Sir, It is much to be regretted that any subject should gain publicity tending to lessen the character for harmony and brotherly love, which Masonry has so justly obtained: such, however, I fear, is likely to be the consequence of the statements which have lately appeared in your columns relative to certain proceedings within the Province of Somerset. It is an old adage that "one tainted sheep will affect a whole flock" but happily it does not apply in the present instance, for the conduct of the individual who has given rise to the late proceedings, has been reprehended throughout the Craft. He then appended a full copy of the resolution agreed at the Provincial meeting of 15th October, the one requesting Whitney's expulsion, and the comment: *In addition to the foregoing, a Petition has been signed by 106 members of Lodges within the City of Bath, and presented to the Provincial Grand Master requesting the expulsion of the individual in question from the Fraternity.*

The only reason for this letter being sent would have been to stoke a fire that was perceived as going out. And it worked, because on 13th November a long, indignant letter was published from Thomas Whitney, which included remarks such as: *Sir, I will tell you and leave you to say whether I merit the scurrilous epithets and libellous language sent forth, under the sanction of Col Tynte, his Provl. Lodge and a Writer, who, ashamed of his name (and well he may, for I know him well), shield himself under the Jesuitical signature of CULTOR VERITATIS. A worm will turn when*

331

trod upon, and however grating it may sound in the ears of the P.G. Master, he shall not attempt to drag me forth - to hold me up to public Masonic reprehension - unanswered on my part.

Whitney then went on for a column and a half repeating much of what he had circulated previously in his letters to the Lodges, naming names, and adding fresh accusations, such as: *until the whole of my case is laid before the Craft, it is utterly impossible for any individual to form an adequate idea of the persecution with which I have been pursued, under the name of Masonry, by Col. Tynte's usual Aid-de-Camp, Mr Charles Maddison; and for what? Because I have resisted a barefaced attempt to wrest the warrant from the present Members of the York Lodge.* Plus, regarding Maddison: *The Grand Lodge shall have a fair opportunity of knowing something more of the genuine character of this gentleman and his Anti-Masonic proceedings both before and after he quitted the Lodge, as well as the manoeuvres adopted by him the frighten the Members into a resignation for the obvious purpose of getting the Warrant transferred to him.* And: *Col. Tynte has openly declared that he will put an extinguisher upon the Lodge, for no earthly purpose but that of placing the warrant in the hands of his confidant and secret advisor, Mr Maddison.*

These, and others in the letter, are potentially-libellous comments. One might expect, therefore, that they would be challenged, if necessary in a court; that they weren't at any time is worth noting. More to the point, when Maddison tried to introduce this letter into evidence in support of his charge at the second Board hearing, it was minuted that *as these matters do not appear to be embraced in, or to have any immediate bearing upon the Charge exhibited by Brother Maddison the Board have refrained from making any comment or report thereon.*

As might be expected, it did not take long for *Cultor Veritatis* to respond at length, including lecturing upon the use of an affidavit in Whitney's appeal *made by an individual who, I can prove, was upon a former occasion the tool of Mr W. and whose improper conduct on that occasion is at the moment the subject of complaint and investigation.* Probably the most interesting assertions were that *he does not know me well* and, regarding the original article contents, that *supposing he (Mr W.) had not any communication with the individual who conveyed it for insertion, is it not possible that it might have emanated from himself?*

On the 25th November, another letter appeared signed by *A Subscriber of One of the Bath Lodges* which essentially criticised most of *Cultor Veritatis'* assertions without ostensibly supporting Whitney in any way.

The most interesting point made here was regarding the Provincial Meeting of 15th October not being representative of the whole Province, as *instead of assembling to the number of 100 to 120 as on former occasions, their muster consisted of about 30 individuals, including Provincial Officers! Now, if all the Officers were present (13 in number) this leaves a maximum of about 17 Members, including Visitors!!*

On 1st December, *Cultor Veritatis* responded to this that the small attendance was due to *there being on the same day a Fair at one place, and several Local Public Meetings at others.* He concluded by observing *I know from whence it emanates, and the motives that actuate the writer.* The final letter appeared on 6th December from someone terming themselves *Lector Constans* (constant reader) who ridiculed some of *Cultor Veritatis'* assertions as *vastly amusing*, including *how interesting the proceedings of the meeting must have been to those who would have left them for the childish amusement of attending a Fair!!!* He concludes that *Cultor Veritatis, having been the principle Agent in the bickering correspondence that has taken place, amicably declines any further controversy on the subject. Like a snarling cur, who having evinced nobler animals in quarrels originating in his ill temper, sneaks away and leaves them to settle the matter between them.*

Thus another unedifying episode in this saga came to a close, at around the same time that Grand Lodge put a full stop on the Masonic proceedings. But who was *Cultor Veritatis*? For me it boils down to two candidates, Maddison or Patton. Despite the assertion that *he does not know me well*, which was potentially just a device to throw others off the scent, there was simply too much insider information in his letters for it to be anyone else.

That Whitney thought he knew the identity but failed to mention a name, whilst being happy to continually name Maddison, plus the veiled references to Geary *whose improper conduct is at the moment the subject of complaint and investigation* coupled with the date of the very first letter being contemporary with the start of Patton's pursuit of Geary, would all tend to suggest Whitney thought it was Patton. The only thing that goes against that assumption is that these letters were somewhat shorter than one might have come to expect from him!

If it was Patton, it won't have been the first time that he pursued Masonic disagreements through newspaper columns, as will be seen in Appendix 4.

AL5817

FREEMASONS' HALL

APPENDIX 4
ANTIQUITY
ENCAMPMENT

The Antiquity Warrant

Antiquity Encampment of Knights Templar had elected not to move to the Hall until 1820, remaining at the Greyhound Inn which they shared with Royal Sussex Lodge and its own new Royal Arch Chapter, formed in 1818. This may have been due to influence from John Dixon, the Eminent Commander from 1811 to 1813. Dixon had been the prime mover in reviving the Encampment in 1811, following a period when the Warrant had remained dormant. In 1812, he had also been the first Master of Antients Lodge No. 49b, later renamed Royal Sussex Lodge. This was founded by long-standing Atholl Masons, so the Encampment's revival may well have been achieved under the same auspices.

Templar Historians have related that in May 1819, the members defeated a motion proposed by Dixon to change the name of the Encampment and attach it to Royal Sussex Lodge, following which they replaced Dixon with Matthew Patton. Subsequently, Dixon attempted to hold meetings of the Encampment at the Greyhound and install new members. It eventually took an instruction from the Grand Chancellor and Registrar in London to put a halt to his activities, although there is no indication of his returning the Warrant.

A committee was appointed by Samuel Croker, then Provincial Grand Commandant for Somerset, and chaired by Frederick Husenbeth, his equivalent in Bristol, to uncover the differences existing in the Bath Encampment. Husenbeth became frustrated at being unable to resolve matters due to Dixon's continued refusal to attend, issuing a warning of dire consequences if matters were not amicably settled. Subsequently, Dixon was expelled from the Order, and the Encampment removed from the Greyhound Inn at that time.

At their first meeting at Freemasons' Hall, the eminent commander was Matthew Patton and his deputy John Ashley, Master of Royal York Lodge. The attendance roll, which included new applicants, read like a who's-who of local Freemasonry at the time. At that meeting the by-laws and charges were agreed, including an installation fee for new members of one hundred guineas. Some historians believed that this money was used to finance the Hall project, meetings continuing there until April 1823, after which there is a gap of 33 years because the Encampment once again went into a period of dormancy.

This all sounds plausible, until it is examined against the actual minutes. Probably the most glaring error here is the massive Installation fee - the equivalent of a king's ransom at the time. A quick glance at the account book shows that total income for 1820 was £42-6s, and it didn't take long to find the minute recording that *the Installation fee for the first year should be __two__ guineas, to be raised to __three__ guineas for the benefit of the Permanent Fund.* The underlining is in the handwritten minutes, and the word "two" is a bit obscurely written to the point that it could be interpreted as £100. However, this proves that Antiquity Encampment was not a mysterious source of funding for the Hall Project.

The "100 guinea" entry in the Minutes
Bath Masonic Hall Trust

The minutes do, however, reveal much of the fairly turbulent course of events over the two years preceding Antiquity taking-up residence at the Hall in July 1820, events that will doubtless produce echoes in the mind of the readers. The book commences with a declaration:

BLADUD HEAD INN, LADYMEAD, BATH
Friday 7th June AL.1815, AD.1811, AO.693, AC.497
Present Sir Ben'n Plummer, Past Grand Expert of the Grand Conclave of Knights Templars, Palestine, Rhodes, &c, &c, Sir Abra'm Nonmus of the Baldwin Encampment, Bristol, Sir Matt'w Patton, Do, Sir Henry Dixon Tylee, Do, Sir George Godby of True Friendship, Bristol
When a communication was read from Sir Rob't Gill, Grand Chancellor & Registrar, Authorising Sir B Plummer to revive the Warrant of Antiquity of Time Immemorial formerly held in this CITY having laid dormant many years.

It then lists the officers for that first meeting as follows:

> John Dixon - Grand Commander
>
> Matthew Patton - 1st Captain
>
> John Pearson - 2nd Captain
>
> Henry Dixon Tylee - Chancellor of Registrations
>
> Abraham Nonmus - Treasurer
>
> John Ashley - Master of Ceremonies
>
> Joseph Pinker - Senior Standard Bearer
>
> George Godby - Equerry

The minutes are sparse before stopping in 1814. After a gap of five years, they recommence with a meeting on May 18th 1819 where the members, apparently answering a normal summons, discover that their Warrant is missing, along with their Commander; they therefore adjourn until May 24th. These minutes are signed by Matthew Patton (as 1st Captain), John Ashley, Henry Dixon Tylee and Joseph Pinker, but no list of other attendees is provided.

The May 24th minutes detail that Patton, proposed by Ashley seconded by Tylee, was elected Commander, who then proposed Ashley as 1st Captain and Tylee as 2nd Captain, both seconded by Pinker and elected accordingly. It was then unanimously approved, that Past Commander Dixon fill the *Honourable Post of Master of Ceremonies*. Then the following: *Sir Kt Dixon then proposed that this Encampment be attached to the Royal Sussex Lodge and take its name, which was negatived. Sir Kt Dixon then proposed to install two persons in waiting without ballot - or even the Warrant being present, which was negatived without a division.*

This suggests that Dixon was present for all of this; however there is no list of attendees and the minutes are unsigned. They conclude with a blank page headed: *Copy of Mr Dixon's Circular as within alluded to....* Needless to say there is no such document included, nor any allusion to it within the minutes. However, the wording suggests that Dixon's proposals were actually made by post.

Even though the reader has doubtless become all too familiar with such conundrums during this story, it is difficult to imagine that Dixon would have been present, in which case this has all the hallmarks of the order being usurped, particularly as these elections should have taken place under the Warrant, which is admitted as missing. The next minutes a week later, June 2nd, list the same four members attending.

They note that the minutes of the previous two meetings were unanimously approved, then proceed as follows: *The undersigned Companions unanimously agree to refer the legal measures for the recovery of the Encampment Warrant which has been purloined from the Society Chest, to Brother Turner, Solicitor and that he be fully-empowered to obtain a Barrister's opinion and to follow-up proceedings as Mr Turner in his wisdom may think proper. Sir Kt Ashley proposed that Sir Kt Dixon having purloined the Encampment Warrant from the Society Chest, and his still persisting to withhold the same from the regular members thereof and also the said Dixon not appearing at this meeting to a regular summons sent to him for the purpose to answer the same and for his having called a meeting and Installed ten persons illegally without having given the least notice to the regular members - such conduct being Unmasonic and contrary all rule or order and in defiance of common honesty, truth or justice - that the said Dixon be forever expelled from this Encampment unless he Immediately returns the said warrant to the proper place in the Society's Chest and makes a free and proper apology to this Encampment for his infamous and unmasonic conduct - which proposition was duly seconded by Sir Kt Patton and unanimously approved.*

This was signed by all four individuals, Pinker signing as Equerry. Below this, a list of all members was provided, which consisted of the four attendees, plus honorary members - Husenbeth and Boyce - and the following note: *The above names with Sir Kt Dixon, the late Sir Kt Ling - all for the last five years belonging to this Encampment.*

William Boyce was the person who featured in minutes during the 1790s, where various unusual degrees were taken by him, under the auspices of Thomas Dunckerley, and Frederick Husenbeth was Provincial Grand Commandant for Bristol, and high ranking in the Camp of Baldwyn. So, are we to believe that, in 1819, this very old order had just seven members remaining, two of whom were honorary? Yet the proposal suggests there were plenty around who wished to join, as Dixon had recruited ten, although whether this was according to the rules is unknown at this point.

Although the proposal is attributed to Ashley, anyone having read all of the preceding pages will recognise that verbose charge as being pure Patton in content. So here we have yet another pursuit of a fellow Mason who had, apparently contravened all Masonic rules - at least according to Matthew Patton. However, I cannot but wonder why this should be occurring so soon after the creation of a second Chapter in Bath, Royal Sussex Chapter receiving its Charter on 29th October

1818, and removing the absolute monopoly on Royal Arch Masonry in Bath previously held by the Royal Cumberland Chapter, run for many years by Matthew Patton.

What is also interesting is this puts Ashley in very close association with Patton, something that wasn't wholly obvious previously. Remember, this is the same John Ashley who would deliver the final coup de gras to Royal York Lodge of Perfect Friendship four years later whilst simultaneously providing dubious evidence against Thomas Whitney revolving around the trumpeters Jarratt and Loder. The next piece in the minute book is a letter dated 28th June 1819 from Husenbeth to Patton:

I have this moment, 8 o'clock, seen Mr Plummer who handed me a letter from Bridgwater stating that Mr Dixon had written to Mr Croker saying that he would on no account accept of the mediation of anyone from Bristol & should hold the Warrant and furniture as his own property. The registrar of Bridgwater complains likewise in his letter to Mr Plummer of not receiving any answer from you. The business standing thus, I consider it useless to come to Bath tomorrow, and assure you that whenever there is a brighter prospect of doing good you shall find me at your command.

'Mr Croker' was Samuel Croker, Provincial Grand Commandant for Somerset, and 'Mr Plummer' was Benjamin Plummer, former Senior Grand Warden of the Antients Grand Lodge prior to 1813, who assisted Dixon in founding what became Royal Sussex Lodge in Bath. He also officiated at the revival of this Encampment in 1811, as Grand Expert of the Grand Conclave of Knights Templars. So, together with Husenbeth, this is obviously the high-level 'committee' referred to by previous historians, but it is clearly being ignored by both sides. To an extent, the letter shows some frustration from Husenbeth - but with both parties, not just Dixon. It doesn't, however, contain any 'dire warnings', just a statement that when they both decide to resolve the issue, then he will be happy to help.

There is nothing further until January 26th 1820, when there is another, much longer, letter from Husenbeth to Patton:

I was in hope I should not receive reply more a letter from you so full of obloquy and defamy of the characters of Mr Dixon and his Knights. You are well aware that the law of the land is sufficient tribunal to prevent any delinquency against society and you are, I am confident, equally aware that a society which holds charity for its basis from its first to its last obligation can only form resolutions for inflicting Masonic censure upon individuals or a body of true Masons, when current reports are establishing in truth the facts. How far Mr Dixon or any of his members merit your relentless censure is not known to me, and in fact will not present one single obstacle against the basis upon which both parties are at variance. I am requested by the officers of Grand Encampment in former communications, but more recently by 2 communications received last week, to use my utmost exertion to restore Harmony among you. But my dear friend how shall I proceed in my endeavours to effect it if you lay such obstacles in the way? You wish only to have the Warrant out of Dixon's hands that you may oust him and his newly elected Knights out of the camp, in order to make it more respectable. This kind of proceeding cannot be sanctioned in Masonry. However it be by birth, situation in life, and debt to fortune we may be, must be owed to chance, and if our behaviour while assembled in Lodge is courteous and Masonic, we there call one another by the amiable title of Brothers, which out of Lodge we are at libitum to substitute by a different appellation. I mean by this not to infer that you are to sit and assemble with every character, and must have no course to my former observations, that such characters ought to face the ordeal of the common law, and when there proclaimed unworthy members of society, then be proclaimed very unworthy to sit in a Lodge. As long as this cannot be substantiated, and the objects of your blame behave well in Lodge, you will have a hard matter to find a law in any of the Masonic codes whereby you have a right to exclude them. Dixon's Knights are regularly Installed, which I have proved by such Authority as cannot deceive me, and why you should still persist in refusing an accommodation upon terms proposed, and to meet all together in Camp is to me a profound mystery. If the Grand Conclave should meet under present circumstances, then I shall go to London, and assure you shall use my utmost endeavours to bring about a reconciliation. I trust that when thus freely and honestly expressing my sentiments to you upon this affair, you will not consider anything personal, no my friend! I value you and your friends too much to even harbour a sinister thought against any of you. I have now corresponded with Dixon and his party, and do only act upon the desired basis of the wish of the Grand Encampment who having placed confidence in me, and request me to use my endeavours to reconcile you. I think as a true Mason I should still want that excellent cardinal virtue Justice were I to accede to any proposal in any party that does not tend to a reconciliation any official instructions you may be desirous to send to London I will faithfully deliver, and remain truly and sincerely, Dear Patton,

your friend &c, &c L C Husenbeth

Without the sight of the previous correspondence, it would not normally be right to make a judgement based upon just one side of a discussion. However, there are some interesting clues within the text, not least of which is the assertion that Dixon's newly-elected Knights had been properly installed, and were at least entitled to be admitted to Antiquity Encampment.

Seeing the manner in which the opening of Husenbeth's letter is written, and knowing how Patton subsequently behaved in other similar circumstances, it is not difficult to perceive that Patton had embarked on one of his ill-considered crusades. Nevertheless, one might hope that such well-meaning and sincere intervention by a long-standing and true friend, as well as a highly-experienced Mason, would bring some sanity to proceedings. Unfortunately, this is Matthew Patton we are talking about and, although it caused him to take some pause, the next minute book entry shows that the intervening months had not dimmed his perceived need for justice. On 14th July 1820 Patton and his three cronies assembled the first meeting of Antiquity Encampment to be held at Freemasons' Hall. The minutes read:

Sir Kt Dixon not having attended to a summons sent him to produce the Warrant which he purloined from the Society's Chest in the year 1819 the resolution proposed at the last meeting [on June 2nd 1819] is thus fully carried into effect and he, the said Sir Kt Dixon late Commander of this Encampment, is hereby forever expelled from this said Camp of Antiquity accordingly. It was also resolved to send a letter to the Grand Registrar Sir Kt Gill in London, stating that this Encampment intends holding its regular meetings as heretofore for the dispatch of business by virtue and under the legal authority of the purloined warrant. According to the advice of the D G Master of the Order Sir Kt Burhardt and the subjoined opinion of Sir Kt Husenbeth Sir Kt D C of the Baldwin Camp Bristol, viz: 'The Warrant of your Encampment being removed by the unmasonic conduct of the said Dixon does not Invalidate meetings. A robbery or forcible removal of any warrant without the concurrence of the majority of regular members does not authorise Dixon to hold an Encampment, nor will it on the other hand prevent your assembling as usual.'

This Encampment having thus regularly convened by & with the foregoing advice & under Authority of the Powers delegated to the before named the majority of the Regular Members, of our said Warrant of 'Antiquity' &c, the undernamed gentleman Companions of a R.A.C. were regularly proposed for Installation & duly seconded by Sir Kt Patton & Sir Kt Ashley:

Companions Ralph & Stillman as Sentinels

Comp Dr Baron Brown Mill	Comp. H Spry*
Comp. Capt Barton*	Lt Wm Bagshawe*
Mr Thos Whitney	Mr Dorset Fellowes
Mr Wm Whitney*	Mr Turner*
Mr Jno Cole*	Mr Ellis*
Mr Jno Morris*	Mr Alcock
Mr Ch Geary*	Mr Seine*
Mr Jn Physick	Mr A Loder *
Mr Wm Redman*	R Withers)
Mr Erskine*	Osbourne) Swindon
Mr Hay*	John Sheppard)
Mr Shew*	T Field*
Col Browne*	Revd Mr Portis*
Barry	Parsons
Comp Jones*	Comp Prescott
Comp Whatley	Howd Burrell
Comp Holbrook	Capt Fellowes*
Comp Davis*	Saunders*
Adml Bullen	Hansford
Dr Muttlebury	Col Cooper
Manners	Revd F Smith
Richardson	Jno Stroud*
Watt*	Capt Hatchet
Clutterbuck	Capt Marshall
Maj Shawe	F Loder
Mouse Crowdy	Revd Partridge
Jno Loder	Lassiter
Capt Amey*	Revd Thos Hale*
Ruddle Browne*)	Jarratt*
Jno Sheppard) Swindon	

This impressive list of sixty names augured well for the future success of the Encampment. The reader will already be familiar with quite a few of them, as they feature in other parts of the story, but it is worth re-iterating here that this was all taking place at Freemasons Hall in 1820, the year after the building was officially dedicated, three years prior to the assignment to Geary, and four years prior to the collapse of Royal York Lodge of Perfect Friendship. It is also worth noting the name of Jarratt on this list, which I will return to later. But first, let's analyse what has happened in this Encampment between May 1819 and July 1820.

Of the eight named members when the Warrant was revived in 1811, only five are mentioned in May 1819 - John Dixon, Matthew Patton, Henry Dixon Tylee, John Ashley and Joseph Pinker. Of the eleven further members shown in the account books as being Installed between 1811 and 1814, none are mentioned at all, so it would appear that of the 19 names shown as members previous to May 1819, 14 have left and Dixon is 'persona non grata' having *purloined the Warrant*.

Looking into those missing names, four - Richard Tucker, John Millington, William Box and Charles Guyat - were members of Lodge of Temperance & Morality in West Lavington, south of Devizes in Wiltshire. This was a good half-day's travel by coach from Bath, so it is feasible that the creation of a new Encampment closer to their Lodge may have been responsible for them leaving. However, the early Knights Templar Encampments in Wiltshire had all disbanded by 1810, and none were revived until more than twenty years later, so such explanation does not hold water.

A similar assumption may initially be made regarding John Roake who was a member of Lodge of Unanimity in Wells, a similar distance south of Bath. However, no other Encampments existed in Somerset at that time. That leaves five who were still members of Lodges in Bath - John Pearson and James Ames of Royal Sussex Lodge, Benjamin Botch and Abraham Nonmus of Lodge of Virtue, and John Beaumont Jr of Royal York Lodge. Pearson and Nonmus were also at the revival of Antiquity in 1811, the latter being listed as a member of the Camp of Baldwyn in Bristol, of which Husenbeth was also a member. Baldwyn continued to meet throughout what was a turbulent period for Knights Templar after the union of the Grand Lodges, so it is more likely these Knights all returned to that organisation.

The four surviving names are: Matthew Patton - the main instigator of procedures against Geary and Thomas Whitney from 1823 onwards; John Ashley - the main provider of evidence against Thomas Whitney in 1824; Henry Dixon Tylee - the professional organist who joined Royal Cumberland Lodge with Geary in 1804 to help revive the ailing Lodge; and Joseph Pinker - who features little in the story, except significantly as the person sent by Patton from Royal Cumberland Lodge to obtain the keys to the Hall from Geary in October 1823, at the lock-out. In addition to these four, Boyce and Husenbeth were both honorary members, and Ralph & Stillman were the two Tylers employed by the Hall, and therefore filled the equivalent roles for the Encampment

Then suddenly, once Dixon is ousted, there are sixty potential new members. The minutes and account books show, of those, 28 were Installed over the next three years (shown in the list above with an asterisk*) plus seven more who were not on that original list; those seven included Captain Maddison.

There are, however, some interesting names on the list who did not carry their intention forward into membership leading up to 1823. The most obvious is Thomas Whitney, but in addition Baron Browne Mill, Dr Muttlebury, Admiral Bullen and George Manners also declined to take Encampment membership. All five took part in financing schemes for the Hall, were members of Royal York Lodge of Perfect Friendship and were later involved with the attempts to save that Lodge in 1824.

So by 1823, the Encampment had a healthy membership of more than forty, after which all records simply cease. The last minutes and accounts-received records are dated April 30th 1822, just weeks prior to the issue of the Tontine. The last accounts-paid records are dated April 1823, just weeks after the assignment of the Hall to Charles Geary. Neither do the, admittedly skimpy, accounts records show any payment to the Hall Finance Committee between the Encampment taking residence in 1820 and the assignment in 1823.

The next instalment in the Warrant saga emerged with another letter to Patton from Husenbeth dated September 9th 1820:

I was duly honoured with yours of this morning, and am sorry that after the very handsome manner in which Col Tynte, your R.W.P.G. Master has acted in your affairs, Mr Dixon should still obstinately refuse to accept the friendly terms proposed by that Gentleman. The charge you appear to make against our admitting Mr Dixon and others into our assemblies of Knighthood is founded upon a principle that cannot be defended in Masonry, from the EA to the highest degree. We have nothing to do with the differences existing in another Province between 2 parties who I must beg to be allowed to assure you, we shall at any time admit upon proof of their being legally obligated, and able to give satisfaction according to Rule. That both requisites were found in those brothers & Companions I will myself attest that charge cannot stand. I have ever but once had any private conference with Mr Dixon and I must confess the man was reasonable in what he said, I am confident he will do me the justice to say that instead of giving him the least encouragement to act hostile, and particularly in the manner stated in yours of this morning, he will tell you that my advice was constantly for a friendly arrangement. I am sorry to find that even the public are called upon to become your judges and especially in matters that should be locked up in your breast as Masonic. It is impossible to describe the impressions your Paper War is making on public opinion against Masons and Masonry in this City as well as in Bath and firmly believe that the injury will be very great. I have ever valued you as a friend & assure you my good opinion of you is not in the least lessened, but as a Mason I must decline interfering further in this affair and wish most sincerely Peace might be established amongst you such as it happily is at present in Bristol. Indeed my dear Sir! I am at present out of all Office, having at the last Rosae Crusis meeting resigned my office as G. Master in favour of Mr R Smith. I am collecting all my Masonic documents which I shall deposit in the archives of our Hall and shall only attend Masonry in future as leisure may permit.

Although there is no copy of the letter from Patton that prompted this response, again it is not difficult to read between the lines, especially in conjunction with Husenbeth's previous letter from nine months earlier. Whereas previously he was entreating Patton to reach a compromise, here he is expressing some disbelief as to how he cannot countenance that. This is, without doubt, a very strong, but polite, rebuke of Patton's continued animosity, particularly as Husenbeth obviously found Dixon more reasonable than he had been led to believe. The reference to *the impressions your Paper War is making on public opinion against Masons and Masonry in this City* also cannot be ignored.

Dixon was a Miniature Painter, with a studio in Northumberland Place. His specialism was full-colour paintings on ivory at seven guineas, but when this work was in short supply, he produced silhouettes for five shillings. This was a profession that required great diligence, concentration and patience, so not exactly a profile that one might associate with someone possessing aggressive inclinations. Of course, he may have been a very different personality, but equally it is difficult to avoid wondering whether this is yet another individual that began acting entirely out of character once Patton got under his skin.

Husenbeth clearly had known Patton some time, and it is difficult to avoid the conclusion that, certainly in his eyes, Patton has changed - and not for the better. At the end he washes his hands of the matter, extremely politely, and whether his final comments as to his having decided to leave all offices was due to this saga, we can only speculate.

Again, this is all happening three years before the problems with Thomas Whitney emerged so, bearing in mind Col Tynte's obvious involvement in the early days after his becoming PGM, shouldn't this earlier behaviour by Patton have acted as some form of clue as to why matters at the hall began to unravel in 1823?

This letter is pasted between the minutes of 7th and 14th September, but there is no mention with regard to any discussion of its contents. At the regular meeting on November 21st 1820, the minutes show that Patton was still Grand Commander, Ashley 1st Captain and William Underwood Whitney 2nd Captain, the three Worshipful Masters of Royal Cumberland Lodge, Royal York Lodge of Perfect Friendship and Lodge of Virtue respectively, all three originally Moderns Lodges. Dixon was still very prominent in Royal Sussex Lodge, originally an Antients Lodge, so it is difficult to ignore the obvious philosophical differences, especially as not one member of Royal Sussex Lodge was also a member of Antiquity Encampment at that time.

A Miniature by John Dixon c1817
Alex Cooper Auctioneers

The minutes show that new Bye Laws were approved at this meeting, then: *By which it is resolved that Sir Kt Dixon - not having been able to justify his conduct in sending an insolent circular letter (herewith copied) to each of the members of the Encampment - he was severely and deservedly reprimanded for such conduct being Ungentlemanly, Unmasonic, Unjust and contrary to the rule of good order - and stands reprimanded accordingly.*

It is worth noting that Dixon is not shown on the attendees list, so there is no evidence that he was present to receive this so-called reprimand. The minutes conclude with another lengthy and repetitive condemnation of Dixon that is, again, pure Patton. So nothing that Husenbeth said in either of those very sincere letters had any impact on Patton. Indeed, we mustn't lose sight here that Patton's immediate junior, Ashley, appears to be making no attempt to reign him in either.

This throws a completely different light on what happened in 1824 when Ashley was challenged by the Colonel as to the legality of Whitney's attempted Installation into the Chair of Royal York Lodge, especially when both Maddison's and Ashley's evidence to the Board of General Purposes during 1824 is examined in conjunction with a minute of the Encampment dated May 29th 1821: *This evening Companion Capt Maddison & Gislot of the R York Chapter, Comp Ruddle Brown of the R Cumberland Chapter, Comps Pallin, Jarratt and Bennett, having been unanimously approved of by ballot were duly Installed as Sir Kt Companions of this Most Holy Grand Christian Encampment.*

Comp Jarratt is no other than one of the trumpeters whose status as Freemasons was called into question in that evidence by both Ashley and Maddison, and who the Board found had been irregularly initiated in 1817 - and thus not only unqualified to vote in a Lodge, but also to take up membership of any Order. Yet here we have that same Jarratt shown as a Companion of the Royal Arch, which in turn proves he must have been previously raised as a Master Mason - both status needing to have been confirmed by the Encampment prior to his being balloted to become a Knight Templar.

So, how on earth could Maddison not have known Jarratt was bona fide, when he was Installed as a Knight on the very same evening just three years prior to giving evidence that Jarratt was not even a Freemason? More to the point Ashley, as 1st Captain of the Encampment, would have been involved in conducting that very ceremony!

At the next round of officer changes, Jarratt became Herald for the Encampment. And what were the duties of the Herald at that time within Antiquity? Why, to announce arrivals by the playing of a trumpet.

Bibliography

Ashley, Thomas P	*An Abridged History of the Royal Cumberland Lodge, No.41* (Bath 1873)
Bath Masonic Museum & Library	*Records of Royal Cumberland Lodge No.41* (1732 -1845)
	Records of Royal Cumberland Chapter No.41 (1782-1845)
	Records of Royal Sussex Lodge No.53 (1812 -1845)
	Records of Royal Sussex Chapter No.53 (1782-1845)
	Records of Lodge of Honour No.379 (1825-1845)
	Records of Antiquity Encampment No.1 (1811-1823)
	Ars Quatuor Coronatorum - various issues (London 1932-2009)
	Freemasons Quarterly (London 1842)
	Transactions of Somerset Masters' Lodge - various issues (Somerset 1917-1967)
Barbeau, A	*Life & Letters at Bath in the 18th Century* (Stroud 2009)
Berman, Rick	*Schism, the Battle that Forged Freemasonry* (Brighton 2013)
Borsay, Peter	*The Image of Georgian Bath,1700-2000* (Oxford 2000)
British Library	*Bath Chronicle* various issues (Bath 1750-1845)
	Bath Herald various issues (Bath 1750-1845)
	Bristol Mercury various issues (Bristol 1815-1845)
	The European Magazine & London Review Vol 71 (London 1817)
	London Gazette various issues (London 1790-1845)

349

Bibliography

Buchanan, Brenda J	*Bath History Vol.6* (Bath 1996)
	Bath History Vol.7 (Bath 1998)
	Bath History Vol.8 (Bath 2000)
	Bath History Vol.9 (Bath 2002)
Carlile, Richard	*Manual of Freemasonry* (London 1825)
Chancellor, E B	*Life in Regency & Early Victorian Times* (London 1926)
Cresswell, Paul	*Bath in Quotes* (Bath 2006)
Davis, Graham	*Bath exposed!: essays on the social history of Bath, 1775-1945* (Bath 2007)
	Bath History Vol.12 (Bath 2011)
	Bath History Vol.13 (Bath 2013)
Egan, P	*Walks Through Bath* (Bath 1819)
Fawcett, Trevor	*Voices of Eighteenth Century Bath* (Bath 1995)
Green, Mowbray A	*The Eighteenth Century Architecture of Bath* (Bath 1904)
Gould, Robert F	*The four old lodges, founders of modern freemasonry, and their descendants* (London 1879)
Harper, Charles G	*The Bath Road: history, fashion, & frivolity on an old highway* (London 1899)
Ison, Walter	*The Georgian Buildings of Bath* (Reading 2004)
Jones, Bernard E	*Freemasons' Guide & Compendium* (London 1950)
Kenning, George	*Masonic Encyclopedia and Handbook of Masonic Archeology, History and Biography* (London 1878)
Library & Museum Freemasonry	*Records of Royal York Lodge of Perfect Friendship No.243* (1757-1823)
	Records of Lodge of Virtue No.311 (1767-1831)
	Minutes of Grand Lodge (1820-1829)
	Correspondence with Bath Lodges - various folios (1815-1845)
	Correspondence with Province of Somerset - various folios (1815-1845)
	Annual Returns for Bath Lodges - various folios (1732-1845)
	Freemason Membership Registers (1751-1921)
Lowndes, William	*The Royal Crescent in Bath* (Bristol 1981)
	They Came to Bath (Bristol 1987)

Murch, Jerom   *Biographical Sketches of Bath Personalities* (Bath 1843)

Mainwaring, Rowland   *Annals of Bath, 1800 to 1838* (Bath 1838)

Neale, R. S   *Bath, A Social History 1680-1850* (London 1981)

Oliver, Bruce W   *The Bath Furniture* (AQC Vol 61, 1944)

Oliver, Rev. George   *Revelations of a Square* (London 1855)

Priestland, Pamela   *From Domesday to Dukedom and beyond - The History of the Pierrepont family* (Nottingham 2010)

Peach, R.E.M   *Historic Houses in Bath and their Associations Vol 1 & 2* (London 1883)
Bath Old & New (Bath 1891)
Street Lore of Bath (London 1893)
Craft Masonry in the City of Bath (Bath 1894)

Preston, William   *Illustrations in Masonry* (London 1781)

Swift, A & Elliott, K   *The Lost Pubs of Bath* (Akeman Press 2005)

Tyte, William   *Bath in the Eighteenth Century* (Bath 1903)

Wade, John S   *Go and Do Thou Likewise: English Masonic Processions from the 18th to the 20th Centuries* (AQC Vol.122, 2009)

Walker, R G   *Freemasonry in the Province of Somerset 1725-1987* (Wells 1987)

Wood, John   *A Description of Bath* (Kingsmead Reprint 1969)

Yarker, John   *The High Grades in Bristol & Bath* (AQC Vol 17, 1904)

Yates, Martin   *Freemasonry in the Province of Somerset from 1733* (Somerset 2010)